Praise for

TWILIGHT MAN

"In *Twilight Man*, Liz Brown uncovers a noir fairy tale, a new glimpse into the opulent Gilded Age empire of the Clark family."

—Bill Dedman, coauthor of the *New York Times* bestseller *Empty Mansions: The Mysterious Life of Huguette Clark and the Spending of a Great American Fortune*

"Some years ago, Liz Brown opened a drawer at her grandmother's house and found a photograph that led her into a head-spinning real-life film noir: a tale of wealth, greed, corruption, fraud, lies, lust, and every other variation of the seven deadly sins, embodied in a gloriously grotesque cast of characters. Amid the mayhem, the shadowy figure of Harrison Post emerges as a phantom hero—charmed at the start, doomed by the end, and, now, resurrected by Brown's spectacular, empathetic feat of storytelling. A thoroughly astounding book."

—Alex Ross, author of *Wagnerism: Art and Politics in the Shadow of Music*

"With a vividness that borders on the uncanny and an insightfulness that's frankly dazzling, *Twilight Man* offers a striking tale of self-invention, dissolution, empire, and grief. Echoes of Chandler, of Fitzgerald, and of Wilde abound, but in the end Liz Brown's utter assurance and her relentless intelligence make this story entirely her own. An essential work of queer, and of California, history."

—Matthew Specktor, author of *Always Crashing in the Same Car*

"*Twilight Man* is a page-turning tale of love, honor, secrets, and deceit. Fortified by meticulous research, with prose both efficient and elegant, Liz Brown takes us on a journey of discovery into family, language, class, and culture. Brown's revelations about gay life before Stonewall are enhanced by her keen understanding of the shifting social constructions of identity. *Twilight Man* is reclaimed history—and a delightfully good read."

—William J. Mann, author of *Tinseltown: Murder, Morphine, and Madness at the Dawn of Hollywood*

"Liz Brown reclaims a beguiling lost world of fake countesses, dilettantes, and fantastically wealthy eccentrics who populate this secret history of the love that dare not speak its name set in a Los Angeles you never knew existed. It's a portrait of a covert high society that determinedly erased itself over the decades, and a stunning, poignant personal account of a Lotusland heretofore unexplored."

—Matt Tyrnauer, director of *Scotty and the Secret History of Hollywood*

"Liz Brown has done extraordinary work of untangling a family mystery that has as much to show us about one family as about the making of the American West. On one level, *Twilight Man* tells the story of Gilded Age power, wealth, and corruption, and their destructive legacies. On another level, it's an intimate portrait of queer life lived in the shadows of family reputation and moral crusades of the early twentieth century. Brown gives us a compelling and beautifully written book about the difficulties of writing queer lives, and the importance of such work in reshaping our sense of the past."

—James Polchin, author of *Indecent Advances: A Hidden History of True Crime and Prejudice before Stonewall*

"Drawing on more than a decade and a half of research, Brown tells a riveting, heartbreaking tale of intimate betrayal and unlooked-for generosity, as well as of the unexpected fortitude, capable of surviving even Nazi prisons, of a delicate-looking man with excellent taste. This is a lovely, powerful book, woven together with great narrative skill and told with deep humanity."

—Caleb Crain, author of *Overthrow*

"*Twilight Man* is a peek through the keyhole of history into a scintillating, secretive demimonde filled with gilded mansions, bibliophilic lovers, hush-hush dealings, and tragic twists of fate. Liz Brown probes the previously invisible dark matter of California mythology with a painterly eye for detail and an uncanny ability to read between the lines. This is the queer noir you didn't know you needed."

—Claire L. Evans, author of *Broad Band: The Untold Story of the Women Who Made the Internet*

"A darkly glittering story, brilliantly told, *Twilight Man* is riveting, wise, and superbly researched. Brown weaves together big American lies and forgotten lives, Hollywood self-invention and extractive capitalism, vulnerability and violence—to show that the way we tell history always matters."

—Lisa Cohen, author of *All We Know: Three Lives*

"*Twilight Man* is a richly captivating true-life gay love story, plunging from the intoxicating heights of the Jazz Age into a shady, gripping tale of betrayal and blackmail. It's the history of one of the greatest fortunes ever made and lost, revealing for the first time through queer eyes the seductive links among the worlds of Frank Harris, Edith Wharton, F. Scott Fitzgerald, Raymond Chandler and the mythical origins of Los Angeles."

—Thomas Adès, composer of *Powder Her Face* and *The Exterminating Angel*

"[An] absorbing debut . . . A history of power, corruption, greed, and betrayal."

—*Kirkus Reviews*

PENGUIN BOOKS

TWILIGHT MAN

Liz Brown has written for *Bookforum*, *Elle Decor*, the *London Review of Books*, the *Los Angeles Times*, and *The New York Times Book Review*. She lives in Los Angeles.

TWILIGHT MAN

LOVE AND RUIN IN THE SHADOWS OF HOLLYWOOD AND THE CLARK EMPIRE

LIZ BROWN

PENGUIN BOOKS

PENGUIN BOOKS

An imprint of Penguin Random House LLC
penguinrandomhouse.com

Page 385 constitutes an extension of this copyright page.

LIBRARY OF CONGRESS CATALOGING-IN-PUBLICATION DATA
Names: Brown, Liz, 1971 May 20– author.
Title: Twilight man : love and ruin in the shadows of Hollywood and the Clark empire / Liz Brown.
Description: [New York, New York] : Penguin Books, [2021] | Includes bibliographical references.
Identifiers: LCCN 2020055014 (print) | LCCN 2020055015 (ebook) | ISBN 9780143132905 (paperback) | ISBN 9780698184732 (ebook)
Subjects: LCSH: Post, Harrison. | Clark, William Andrews, 1877–1934—Family. | Gay men—United States—Biography. | Gay couples—California—Los Angeles—Biography. | Inheritance and succession—California—Los Angeles—History—20th century. | Americans—Foreign countries—Biography. | Los Angeles (Calif.)—History—20th century.
Classification: LCC HQ75.8.P673 B76 2021 (print) | LCC HQ75.8.P673 (ebook) | DDC 306.76/62092 [B]—dc23
LC record available at https://lccn.loc.gov/2020055014
LC ebook record available at https://lccn.loc.gov/2020055015

Printed in the United States of America
1st Printing

Set in Birka LT Pro
Designed by Sabrina Bowers

For
Clark George Palé
1942–1965

I have been a stranger here in my own land:
All my life.

—Sophocles, *Antigone*

CONTENTS

PART THREE
1934–1938

PART FOUR
1938–1945

PART FIVE
1945–1946

TWILIGHT MAN

INTRODUCTION

Harrison Post, 1922.

I wasn't looking for Harrison Post when I opened the drawer, but I found him. There he was in a framed studio portrait, glowering, arms crossed, dark hair slicked back, shades of Rudolph Valentino. I assumed he was a forgotten movie star.

He'd inscribed the photograph with a flourish:

For: Alice McManus
With the sincere good wishes of
—Harrison Post, 1922

That was my grandmother's name.

She had died several days earlier in her home in San Francisco. This was the summer of 2003. I hadn't seen her much in the recent years. At the time, I lived in New York. The rest of my family—my parents, my two brothers, and my sister—lived in California. That was where I was born and raised, but I rarely went back.

I'd lived on the East Coast for more than a decade, and my parents and I didn't speak often. In the mid-'90s, I told them I was gay and they stopped calling the apartment where I lived in Brooklyn with my girlfriend. I didn't go back for Thanksgiving or Christmas. I didn't go back when my sister graduated from college or when my father had heart surgery, but I did go back after my grandmother died that July.

One of my brothers picked me up at the airport and we drove to suburban Walnut Creek, where a cousin was hosting a party in his backyard, an informal gathering to celebrate my grandmother and her legendary sweet tooth. At first, I felt stilted, out of practice being with family, but then came the pints of coffee ice cream, boxes of See's molasses chips, and the lemon meringue and pecan pies. Dessert is our first language, and my wariness melted away. Afterward, my uncle drove me to San Francisco, where I was going to stay at my grandmother's house with my parents and sister.

Uncle Rich had been a dentist. He'd overseen my childhood teeth cleanings and X-rays. He was in his sixties and retired now. Divorced, a father of five, grandfather of more, he was fiercely committed to his family and to bachelorhood, driving a convertible with a license plate that read DLITEFUL. It was a word he used often—for food, wine, music, his children, and everything else in the world that brought him joy. There'd been a period when we both lived at my grandmother's house, unlikely but happy roommates.

Now, in the car, he asked about life in New York. I was cautious. I said I lived with a woman and that things were hard with my parents. I didn't say much more because back then even the smallest glimmer of light exposed more pain than I could manage.

My uncle put his hand on my knee or maybe he took my hand and squeezed it. And then he told me about a friend of his whose son was gay. I knew this friend and I knew he came from the same Irish Catholic world as my mother and uncle, and my uncle was telling me how his friend had said that it was simple: he loved his son and wanted him to be happy. It was a kind moment, tentative but generous.

And then it shifted. "You know," he said, "there's this book . . ."

I knew instantly what he was talking about. I hadn't read the book, but I'd heard my mom talk about it, sometimes on the long rides from San Francisco to our home in Chico. It was a scandalous biography written decades ago about my grandmother's Uncle Will and his family.

This much I remembered: Uncle Will was the son of a wealthy copper baron, and he'd been married to my grandmother's Aunt Alice. There were rumors in the book about Uncle Will having male lovers, rumors about boys. Supposedly the family had tried to buy all the copies and destroy them. It was, like many of my mother's stories on those car rides, something I'd only half listened to.

To others, my uncle's segue might've seemed strange, but within my family it wasn't unusual to swerve from a moment of tenderness to whispered scandal about strangers from the past. I understood Uncle Rich to be telling me that I wasn't alone, that the family had other secrets. He may have even used the phrase "skeletons in the closet" as we sped across the Bay Bridge to San Francisco, rising white and chalky in the distance.

Now the moment was changing again, the giddy gossip dissolving into something else, a feeling both heavy and empty. We drove down the streets I'd always known, down Broadway, past the Convent of the Sacred Heart, the big gray mansion with the marble hallways where I'd gone to high school in Pacific Heights, and then we were turning down Steiner, left on Vallejo, and pulling up alongside my grandmother's house, the first time I would know it without her.

My grandmother was born in 1905 in Virginia City, Nevada. She was named after her father's sister, Alice McManus. Aunt Alice, my great-grand-aunt, married William Andrews Clark Jr. in 1907.

"Have you heard of Huguette Clark?" I often begin. Sometimes that's all it takes when I'm trying to explain the family that my grandmother's uncle came from. If there's a flicker of recognition, I add a few details: The copper heiress who lived to be 104. Three-hundred-million-dollar estate. Spent the last twenty years of her life in a hospital room even

Will Clark, Alice McManus Clark,
and Alice McManus, circa 1911.

though she had homes in Santa Barbara and Connecticut and a penthouse on Fifth Avenue in Manhattan. Collected dolls.

Today the Clarks have come to be known, or re-known, through the strange story of an elderly recluse, the last member of a once-famous Gilded Age dynasty. When Huguette Clark died in 2011, she left behind an estate of $300 million, competing wills, a sprawling legal dispute in Manhattan Surrogate's Court, and a public suddenly hungry for her odd story. She'd lived in a kind of chosen obscurity for much of her long life, but after her death, that private world spilled open. Within five years, two biographies were published—*Empty Mansions* by Bill Dedman and Paul Clark Newell Jr. and *The Phantom of Fifth Avenue* by Meryl Gordon—and countless articles have been headlined with the phrase "reclusive heiress."

By most accounts, Huguette had been healthy enough to live in her Fifth Avenue penthouse, the sixty-acre estate in Santa Barbara, or her twenty-two-room mansion in New Canaan, Connecticut, but in 1991, she arrived wrapped in sheets at the Beth Israel Medical Center for treatment for skin cancer and never left. She was highly knowledgeable of Japanese architecture. She owned hundreds of antique French dolls and had hired Christian Dior to design couture wear for some of her most prized pieces. She liked to watch *The Smurfs*. These were some of the details that emerged about Huguette's years in seclusion—or captivity, depending on whom you believe.

There were plenty of accounts to indicate she maintained connections to people outside the hospital and showed a curiosity, albeit idiosyncratic, about the world. But the gothic strains of her story were too compelling to give up. Palatial estates lying empty. Housekeepers dusting furniture that's never used. Echoes of Miss Havisham and Norma Desmond. All that money, all those dolls.

So when I ask if someone knows who Huguette Clark is and they do, the next part is simple: "Uncle Will," I say, "was her half brother. It's *that* Clark family," and that's all it takes to conjure up an aura of wealth and intrigue.

But if the listener never noticed the headlines about Huguette, I offer broad strokes. I say that Uncle Will came from a wealthy Montana mining family, that his father was William Andrews Clark Sr., Gilded Age tycoon and US senator.

My great-great-grandfather Andrew McManus came to America as a ten-year-old from Ireland in 1848 at the height of the Great Famine. He eventually migrated west to the arid mountain town of Virginia City, home to the Comstock Lode. In the nineteenth century, there were many men like him flooding west to seek their fortune.

One of those men might arrive in a boomtown, as Andrew McManus had in Virginia City, or, say, the man settled in Butte, Montana. That man might buy a newspaper. William Andrews Clark Sr. owned the paper. The man might buy a stamp to mail a letter. Clark owned the postal service. The man might pay to take a streetcar. Clark owned the streetcar. The man might put what money he'd managed to scrape together in a bank. Clark owned the bank. The man might take out a loan from the bank to buy a stake in a claim. Clark owned the loan. And if the man defaulted on that loan, Clark owned the claim. Clark owned not just mines, but towns and people. There were many men like Andrew McManus, but there was only one William Andrews Clark Sr. And Uncle Will was his son.

In 1919, Uncle Will single-handedly founded the Los Angeles Philharmonic. He also helped establish the Hollywood Bowl. He built the Clark Library, which holds the largest collection of Oscar Wilde's work and is devoted to the study of English literature from the Tudor period through the eighteenth century. The building and its five-acre compound in Los Angeles's West Adams neighborhood are now part of UCLA.

Uncle Will had been married before. His first wife, Mabel Duffield Foster, died in 1903, a month after giving birth to their only child, William Andrews Clark III. Several years later, Will married Aunt Alice.

The couple never had children, and their niece Little Alice, as they called my grandmother, became a kind of surrogate daughter. She traveled with them, spent time at their extravagant Los Angeles estate, and summered at their lakeside compound in Montana. Uncle Will and Aunt Alice asked my grandmother's parents if they could adopt her. For Will, who'd been raised with an American version of royal entitlement, it may not have seemed a strange request, but to my grandmother's parents this was unthinkable and they declined.

My grandmother was thirteen when Aunt Alice died in 1918. Uncle Will remained close to her, as well as to her siblings. He was generous, paying for her to attend Marlborough, an elite private school for girls in Los Angeles's Hancock Park, as well as a finishing school on the East Coast. She and her sister and brother continued to spend summers at Mowitza Lodge, his vacation home on Salmon Lake. Photos show a rustic sanctuary with archery contests and speedboats, a Boston terrier named Snooks, and Uncle Will in a velvet jacket, playing the violin among the trees. He attended my grandmother's first wedding in 1927. The ceremony was officiated by Monsignor Tonello, a sort of celebrity priest, who was a close friend of Enrico Caruso and a member of Uncle Will's traveling entourage. The marriage was short-lived, and after her divorce in 1932, she came to Los Angeles and stayed with him for several months, attending the Olympic Games in the midst of the Great Depression.

Uncle Will did not live long enough to go to my grandmother's second wedding in 1935. He died the year before, leaving her $10,000, which she used toward the down payment for the house on Vallejo Street, where she and her new husband, my grandfather, raised their family.

My grandmother adored her uncle. As a child, she loved to listen to him sing Christmas carols in French, and so she decided to name her first child Noël. That is my mother. My grandmother lived more than sixty years in the house she bought with her inheritance from Uncle Will. He wasn't her father, not even a blood relative, but whether we realized it or not, we all lived in his legacy.

The house was big and it was expensive to heat. At night my grandmother would turn the thermostat down. In the mornings it was always cold, and often, when I was little, I would climb into her bed, and we would lie on our sides, back to back, the soles of our feet pressed together, keeping each other warm.

We called the house "Vallejo Street," even though it was one among many on the block. It was four stories, painted white, and there were usually red geraniums in the window boxes. There were two staircases. The main one was right there when you opened the front door and stepped into the foyer. The other was tucked out of sight, narrow and winding behind the kitchen. Those stairs were for maids and butlers, but my grandmother didn't have maids and butlers. There was a woman who came to vacuum and dust every couple weeks; otherwise my grandmother was alone in the big house.

By the time I was born, the years of traveling with her glamorous aunt and uncle were long behind her. She was no longer a young woman riding beside handsome young men in speedboats on Salmon Lake, but a gray-haired grandmother, teased for her love of ice cream and pecan pie.

She dressed simply, usually in plain slacks with a flowered shirt, and she kept her hair in a short bob parted on one side, held in place with a bobby pin. When we took the 22 Fillmore bus down to the Marina to go shopping at the Safeway, she always wore a hat—usually a simple blue canvas one—and always gloves.

She had rules and systems only she understood. She burned her toast, then scraped the charred bits into the sink. She warmed her orange juice in the microwave. Every week or so she poured a bucket of water into the toilet bowl, though, as my father pointed out, she could achieve the same effect by flushing.

There were rules about how we always had to hang the bath mat up to dry after taking a shower and were never to go in the kitchen in our bare feet. But she didn't care if my siblings and I watched TV, and so we did, as much as we could, since we didn't have a television set in our home in Chico. Even when she went to bed, my grandmother would say it was fine if we stayed up and kept watching.

The freezer was stocked with pints of ice cream. In the kitchen, in one cupboard was a jar of jelly beans, the fat kind. In the dining room cupboard, there was always a carton of Whoppers and a box of See's molasses chips or peanut brittle, and sometimes Sunkist Fruit Gems. She must have known I stalked her candy stashes, because they often moved.

I loved Vallejo Street for its warrens and pockets and passageways. Under the main stairway was a closet where the ceiling sloped down to the floor. That was where the umbrellas were kept, along with the vacuum, an old canister model with a fabric hose.

I loved the back staircase, which wasn't actually in the back of the house but in the middle, walled off from the rest of the rooms, so it seemed like the back. You could sneak away and yet still be inside.

There were two closets off the master bedroom. One had been my grandfather's. It was large enough to walk inside and spin around, arms out, and it had a window. I remember once finding a bag of mints, the chalky kind with green centers. He was still alive at the time, so I couldn't have been more than five.

The other closet in the bedroom was my grandmother's and it was actually a hallway to the bathroom. There was a vanity with a mirror and a dresser. You could've played a tight game of hopscotch in there. There was a window and a door to another closet with my grandmother's clothes. The shelves were lined with hatboxes. I don't remember her wearing any of those hats preserved in tissue. They were from a time long before she had grandchildren skulking through her home looking for candy.

I knew the house's corners and byways. I knew the drawer with the stubby pencils, the wallet calendars free from the bank, and the stockpile of batteries for when the ones in the remote control went dead. I knew the one pane of chicken-wire glass on the back staircase. I knew the mucilage bottles, the clumps of rosaries, the rubber bands gone dry and brittle in a box that had once held checkbooks.

I knew when the heat came on, deep in the heart of the house. As a child, I'd crouch down on the orange-carpeted floor of the dinette, a small room with cantaloupes on the wallpaper. I'd wait next to the large square vent at the base of the wall, listening for the click, when the warm air would come rushing out, the house finally breathing.

I'd like to think I knew where everything was in the house, but it was too big. There were too many rooms, too many closets, too many boxes, too many drawers. That was part of its magic, always promising a new hiding place, a new secret.

When I was fourteen, I moved into the home on Vallejo Street so I could attend the Convent of the Sacred Heart, on Broadway, a couple blocks away. It hadn't always been a school. It had been built by James Leary Flood, son of one of the "Bonanza Kings" from the Comstock Lode. After the earthquake in 1906 destroyed Flood's home on Nob Hill, he promised his wife, Maud, that he'd build her an unbreakable "house of marble on a hill of granite." When he died in 1926, she gave the mansion to the Religious of the Sacred Heart.

My English classes were in the front parlor. Euro Civ was in Maud's bedroom, US History was in James's, and there was a secret panel between the two. Traditions like the Christmas Noëls or the Senior Tea continued as they had when my mother had been a student there. She may have wanted me to grow up in her past, but I got a different education.

This was the late 1980s in San Francisco. In the silver heir's mansion, a man came to talk to us about AIDS. His name was Christian Haren. He'd been an actor and a model, the Marlboro Man in the early 1960s. Now he was an activist, and in the room that had been the Floods' grand ballroom, now our chapel, he talked about sex and desire and the pain of shame with an openness I'd never experienced and wouldn't again until I was out of college. He was handsome, irreverent, and kind, and he talked about fear and death and told us to take care of one another.

When I lived with my grandmother during high school, it was just the two of us in that big house. My grandfather had died ten years before. My parents stayed in Chico with my younger sister; my brothers were both in college. In all the time my grandmother and I spent together, I never heard her mention Harrison Post.

I left California for college on the East Coast, and after I graduated I kept thinking I'd return. First, though, I followed a woman to New York.

After I told my parents I was gay, they stopped calling me at home. When I think about estrangement, I think of a river cutting into the soil, a little bit more each year. I think of something slow and gradual, of nearly imperceptible corrosive elements, like those grade-school science experiments of soaking teeth in Diet Coke.

My mother did call me at my job and she did send mail. The envelopes that arrived with her slanted cursive were often filled with photos from family gatherings, which may have been meant with kindness, but to me they seemed to say, "Look at what you are not a part of." Sometimes, though, the photos didn't have anyone in them—just the dining table set with silver, china, the enamel salt cellar, and candlesticks that had belonged to a great-aunt, maybe Aunt Alice. And sometimes she sent photocopies from the newspaper: a wedding notice of someone I'd known in grammar school. It gave me a hollow feeling, thinking of her at the local copy store, at the machine with her dimes and nickels, pressing the newspaper to the glass, waiting for the green band of light to flare and fade, wanting to reach me, and yet the contact left a bruise.

It's a strange thing to feel yourself disappearing from the place you come from. Did I long for a phantom limb, or did I become a phantom limb? Weeks of not calling, then months. Me not calling. Them not calling. One way to fight is to relinquish, to simply not advance. You retreat and you wait for them to come to you, but then they don't, so there you are, there you stay.

It all receded—the back staircase on Vallejo Street, the attic window where I could glimpse the bay, the click and rush in the vents when the heat came on. I didn't know if it was being taken from me or if I was letting it go.

My grandmother was ninety-seven when she died. I have no memory of the last time I saw her. Likely she was in her bed, the one I'd crawled into as a child so we could warm each other's feet.

My memories of the funeral are sparse. The service was at St. Dominic's on the corner of Bush and Steiner in the small side chapel. At the grave site in Colma, there were two or three blue canvas chairs, but no one wanted to sit in them and they were taken away. And then, back at the house, the flurry of dishes and drinks and hors d'oeuvres, and that "after" feeling—a sense of depletion I've only ever felt at funerals.

What has stayed with me all these years, more than the funeral or the reception, is a stretch of time when the commotion was over, or perhaps it hadn't yet begun, and I was rummaging through drawers, searching not for candy but for something that would bring my grandmother back to me. I would've been happy to find an ancient mucilage bottle or a collection of string, but they were gone.

In a chest of drawers in the living room I found a rolled-up panoramic photo of her class from Marlborough. Her hair, as always, is parted on one side, dark brown and dramatic in its wavy fullness. She wears a dark dress. She's taller than the girls on either side of her and looks as if she has just finished smiling or is about to start. I can see both my mother and me in the tall, watchful girl.

Upstairs, I continued my search. I looked in her bedroom, where I'd watched Johnny Carson tear open envelopes and Benny Hill ogle and chase. It's where I'd stared, hungry for something I couldn't name, as David Bowie told his China Girl she shouldn't mess with him. His face was sharp—lips like blades, mouth a slit, eyes bits of glass. He pumped his hips, sang into the skinny microphone. *I'll give you television*, David Bowie told me. *I'll give you eyes of blue.*

I opened a drawer, and I saw him.

I picked up the framed photo. I didn't know there'd ever been anyone named Harrison Post. He wasn't sneering, but he wasn't smiling either. He wore a dark jacket, white collared shirt, open at the throat. His handwriting, with swoops and flourishes, came from another time. The *P* in *Post* billowed like a flag. His hair was dark and glossy, his gaze defiant, like he might challenge you to a duel—or to bed. I wanted him as soon as I saw him.

My mother knew nothing about him. I searched for his name on the internet and found only post offices in the many towns named Harrison.

In 1922, the date of the photo's inscription, my grandmother would've been sixteen, perhaps still at Marlborough. This was a year after Paramount Pictures released *The Sheik* with Rudolph Valentino, and Harrison Post bore a distinct likeness to the "Latin Lover." I figured he was a second- or third-tier silent film actor, and that Alice McManus, then a starstruck teenager, had sent away to a celebrity magazine like *Photoplay* for his autographed headshot. I liked thinking of my grandmother, whom I'd only known as an elderly woman with idiosyncratic routines, as a young fan, and I took the photo back to Brooklyn.

Six years passed before I got my hands on the book that Uncle Rich mentioned. *The Clarks: An American Phenomenon*, written by William Daniel Mangam, was first published in 1939 by Silver Bow Press. The Clark family may have tried to destroy all the copies of the notorious book, but they didn't succeed.

I'd been slow to seek it out. I had other quests. I was writing a novel. I was teaching. A relationship had ended. Another had started. And I was an ambivalent detective, apprehensive about opening other drawers. By then the estrangement with my family had softened into a new and fragile peace, one I didn't want to test.

And yet I was curious about Uncle Will. If there really were male lovers, if these rumors were true, I would have a new kind of kinship. Every so often, during my office-job boredom I'd search for Mangam's book on the internet. I found it on rare-book websites, priced in the hundreds of dollars, more than I was willing to spend. Eventually it occurred to me that I could simply look in a library, and so I did.

Within weeks of requesting a copy of *The Clarks* through New York University's interlibrary loan system, I was checking it out from the Bobst Library on Washington Square. On the train back to Brooklyn, I skipped past the frontispiece photo of an unsmiling white-haired William Andrews Clark Sr. and thumbed through the stiff pages, looking for mentions of my grandmother.

There's one, but it doesn't use her name. The passage is about the division of William Andrews Clark Jr.'s estate after his death on June 14, 1934:

> With the exception of two nieces and one nephew by marriage (relatives of the second Mrs. Clark)—each of whom was left ten thousand dollars—all the other individuals who received cash bequests under the will were servants.

This was the money that became the down payment for the house on Vallejo Street, but what I read next made me forget about that:

> The three individuals taking the most under the last will and testament of W. A. Clark, Jr., are George John Pale [*sic*], Raymond Lemire and Harrison Post, all perverted disciples of Clark.

How many silent revelations have unfolded in a New York City subway car jammed with strangers? What did I take in first? That Harrison Post had been Uncle Will's lover? That an expression like "perverted disciples" existed? That each time I'd gone looking for my grandmother I found Harrison Post instead?

For the past six years I'd passed his portrait in my hallway without knowing anything beyond his name and his face, and suddenly here he was in the scandalous book, as if he'd been waiting.

The author had more to say about the man in the photo on my wall:

> Harrison Post, born in Brooklyn, of Russian parents, met W. A. Clark, Jr., in a San Francisco store where Post was employed. Small, dark, and with Semitic cast, Post, then in his middle teens, was of the type known as "twilight men."

This was a new term to me.

In 1931, André Tellier published a novel called *Twilight Men*, billed as the story of a young man and "his first awareness of his own sexual longings," as well as "his own, queer world of jealousies and courtship, gaiety and sadness." *The Encyclopedia of Homosexuality* includes an entry for the expression but casts doubt on whether it was actually used much, while noting that "images of shadows and of darkness were common in the fiction of the period—and, given the obligatory tragic ending, all too appropriate."

I also learned, thanks to William D. Mangam, that, through Will

Clark, Harrison entered an enchanted world of privilege and luxury—mansions, horses, jewelry, a Rolls-Royce, a private loge at the Los Angeles Philharmonic.

My grandmother had saved the portrait of her uncle's lover for eighty years. She was gone and I couldn't ask her what she understood about who he was, or even what had happened to him. All I knew is that she'd kept his photo in a drawer, that it had been necessary to save Harrison Post and also to hide him, and that I, knowing nothing, had the impulse to bring him into my home and put him on display.

By the time I was checking out Mangam's book from the library, the Clarks had mostly faded into the shadows of American history. I knew, though, that one member of the family was still alive.

Huguette Clark was a year younger than my grandmother. As girls they'd played together at Salmon Lake. Over the years they'd exchanged Christmas cards. Huguette had sent a condolence note after my grandfather died, and then, it seems, the two women who'd been children together once upon a time in the Clark empire let the thread between them drop.

Occasional news stories about the reclusive heiress and her various properties had surfaced in the recent years. I'd saved these and at times thought about writing to my grandmother's one-time playmate, imagining that she might connect me to my grandmother and that I might be a conduit to her own childhood, but I never did. The Clarks weren't my blood relatives. It felt presumptuous, even intrusive or predatory, circling a wealthy elderly woman. I never found out what I might've learned if I had written. Huguette died on May 24, 2011.

As it happened, a few weeks after her death, I found a new path into the world of the Clarks. That summer I made my way back to California. It was just for a few months. My girlfriend and I were house-sitting for friends who lived in Los Angeles and looking after their dog—a sweet, aging golden retriever named Alice.

Soon after we got to LA, I looked up William Andrews Clark Jr. on Facebook. His photo, one I hadn't seen before, showed him standing, arms crossed, glancing over one shoulder, dapper in a handsome suit and brimmed hat. I sent a request for his friendship, he accepted, and so we became friends, and soon he—or the person managing the account—invited me to the opening reception at the Clark Library in

West Adams for the exhibition *Oscar Wilde and the Visual Art(ist)s of the Fin-de-Siecle.*

A century had passed since the railroad and real estate tycoon Henry Huntington first developed the exclusive enclave of Victorian mansions where Will Clark had made his home. Back then, he'd had neighbors like Edward Doheny, Ramon Novarro, and director Busby Berkeley. In the following years, as the wealthy white residents moved to newer luxury developments like Hancock Park and Beverly Hills, Hattie McDaniel, Joe Louis, Ray Charles, and other prominent African Americans moved in. The luster faded, though, in the 1950s when the Santa Monica Freeway was built, slashing through the thriving Black neighborhood. Neglect followed in the 1960s and '70s, though much of West Adams remained a middle-class neighborhood, visited by waves of gentrification.

Through all those decades, the high brick wall encircling the library and its grounds on the north side of West Adams Boulevard had endured. The gates were open that day. We turned onto Cimarron Street and pulled into the parking lot, which I learned was where Will Clark's imposing mansion had once stood. He'd also built an observatory on the property, but that was long gone as well.

The library was still there—a redbrick jewel box with white frosted edges. The lawn stretched out before it like a bright green lap pool. After the bleached-out LA streets, it was luxurious to be in a world so abundantly verdant, as if we'd happened upon a secret door to an open pasture—highly manicured, but still a lush idyll in a parched town. It's a curious trick about the Clark Library that the space feels so open, so expansive, and yet also contained and private.

We followed the brick walkway around the long sunken lawn to the ornate building. The doors were open and we walked inside. Sunlight glared off the marble. A handful of people drifted by, gazing down at the letters and papers in the hallway vitrines. I looked for someone with a sign-in sheet, ready to give my name and get checked in before we were mistaken for interlopers, but no one was policing the crowd.

The ceiling was covered in a trompe l'oeil painting with naked muscular men in torquing poses, as well as symbols of Will's artistic and scientific interests, such as a horn and a violin, pen and paper, and an armillary sphere. At the end of the hallway stood a bronze bust of the bearded Clark Sr. Will had named the building after his father, who'd died in 1925.

I felt timid and illegitimate, an impostor among scholars, more kin to Harrison, the movie star manqué of dubious heritage, than the scion of an American copper fortune.

I got a plate of food and a glass of wine. I glanced down at a sketch of Max Beerbohm's famous portrait of Oscar Wilde—elephantine, small eyes, plump lips, gaping mouth, the man made into a grotesque.

A dark-haired woman in a green-and-white sundress was giving the history of the building to a small group of people. I hovered and then spotted another woman with a name tag and drifted her way.

Often when I try to unspool this strange snarl of Harrison Post and the Clarks, I refer to "my grandmother's uncle." Sometimes I unleash a laborious sequence of connections, saying "my grandmother's aunt was married to William Andrews Clark Jr.," and then go from there. I never referred to him, though it would be accurate, as "my great-granduncle," and instead I'd interpose my grandmother between the two of us, because to collapse the distance between Will Clark and me seemed an overreach. The connection is too circuitous, too tangential. It's not blood. I could never make any claim to his legacy or imagine myself part of his rarefied world. And yet there I was eating cheese with my girlfriend on his lawn.

I introduced myself to the woman with the name tag and said that I was related to Clark's wife Alice. This, I thought, would be of interest and would assert my right to mingle among the academics and archivists. I wanted to ask about Harrison, but even now in the twenty-first century, I wondered if it would be unseemly in such a decorous setting to inquire about Clark's "perverted disciple." It was not.

"You should talk to Becky," the woman said after I finished my spiel, gesturing to the woman in the green dress.

Becky was Rebecca Fenning Marschall, a librarian with a friendly, wide smile and immediate warmth. Again, I unraveled my connection to William Andrews Clark Jr., and she listened attentively. As I talked about Uncle Will and Aunt Alice, my anxiety evaporated, and I plunged ahead: "Do you know anything about someone named Harrison Post?"

Becky's eyes glittered. She pointed across the lawn where, through the open gateway, we could glimpse a high white wall across the street.

Mr. Clark, as she called him, built a home for Harrison there. She also said that some time ago a relative of Harrison's had contacted the library, curious to know more about him, but there was little they could tell her. All of Will Clark's personal letters had been destroyed after his death.

"Harrison has a really strange story," Becky said, and then she looked up at the naked men gazing down from the ceiling. "They're all different bodies," she said, "but they all have his face."

It was always 'whisper, whisper' whenever Harrison's name came up," Sue Lombardi told me over the phone. Sue is the niece of Madeleine Post Starrett, Harrison's foster sister. Becky had given me Sue's email, and after trading messages, I'd called. This was the first time we spoke.

"I think it was because of the gay thing," she said.

I was in an actual closet when Sue said this. I was back in New York working at an office job in Midtown where everyone sat at cubicles, and this thin-walled closet was the only sanctuary for a private conversation.

My ambivalence about pursuing the mystery of Harrison Post had vanished. Until then, I'd been circling his story, picking up a thread, letting it go, drifting away, but after that summer in Los Angeles, I didn't wait for him to come to me anymore. Now I was on his trail.

Incredibly, Sue, a retired art history professor who lived in the Oakland hills, was telling me that she had a box with Harrison's journals. Her voice was crackly with excitement. "If you're ever out here, you should come by and take a look."

Weeks later, in Sue's living room, I thumbed through Harrison Post's address book. The first name I recognized was Greta Garbo, listed under the *A*s with the movie star's lover, Mercedes de Acosta, a poet and playwright perhaps better known for her flamboyance—black capes, tricorne hats, ferocious love affairs—than her writing.

But this was only the beginning. After hours looking through the hard-backed journals, filled with Harrison's dizzying scrawl, and his scrapbooks, filled with more movie stars, came yet another revelation. Sue and I discovered we weren't the strangers we thought we were. In fact, Sue and her husband were good friends with one of my father's oldest friends. She also knew an uncle of mine, and she'd once met my parents. The world was shrinking and expanding at the same time. A couple glasses of wine followed. When I finally got ready to leave, Sue pointed to the notebooks. "You can take them," she said. "I know you."

I packed up Harrison's small address book and his journals and got on BART back to San Francisco. I'd booked a surprisingly cheap room at the Huntington Hotel on Nob Hill. The house on Vallejo Street, a couple miles away, had been sold several years before, and yet here I was still slipping through secret passageways, its mysteries continuing on even as it was now gone from the family.

That evening, I went down to the hotel restaurant—the Big 4, named for the tycoons who'd founded the Central Pacific Railroad—and I sat alone at my little table with its flickering battery-operated candle, dazed and happy, in the wood-paneled saloon, oblivious to the fact that I was right then retracing Harrison's steps.

Weeks later I would read his diary entry from May 4, 1946:

> Reading and reading—wrote letters—at 9:30 p.m. Jordan Phelps came for me—we went to the Zebra Room—Eugene Fritz, owner of the Huntington and many other places—The uniformed door man—greeted us—we were invited but crowds were not invited—Fritz said that he didn't want to have all those "fairies" around his houses—that the police are on to them—which is the truth—after all the Huntington is one of the smartest places of the world—and it was amusing to find—just a handful of people—I enjoyed it ever so much better—good looking women and men. I was very drunk—Jordan and Wally drove me home.

Back in New York, I started transcribing his journals. The labor of deciphering Harrison's tiny, spidery writing was tedious and sublime. I wouldn't permit myself to read beyond what I transcribed. I wanted to keep pace with his days. It was exhilarating and vertiginous to step into another person's life, but it was also excruciating. By then I'd clicked through records on Ancestry.com and I'd seen the news clippings. I knew what Harrison could not—how and when he would die.

Harrison Post, 1946.

Becky was right. Harrison Post's story was stranger than I could've imagined when I opened that drawer in my grandmother's room and first saw his face. In the albums that Sue gave me, I'd found a much different photo. This one wasn't taken in a studio with soft lighting but by a photographer covering a sensational story about a man who'd been swindled out of his fortune and taken captive in Nazi-occupied Europe. This shot was taken in 1946, the same year Harrison was getting drunk at the Huntington Hotel. In it, he's still meticulously styled, his gaze still arresting, but he's a markedly different person from the brooding young man with "Vaselino" hair.

More than two decades have passed between the two images. The silver-screen gaze is gone, and the camera, or the person behind the camera, is no longer the focus of his stare. Harrison's face is gaunt, eyes sunken, cheekbones sharp. He seems almost waxen—an effect of age, illness, or something else that isn't easily defined. He's seated, twisting to one side, jacket wrinkling at the shoulders. It's possible to read many things in his expression: expectation, distress, defiance. In one hand he holds a ring, and in the other a pocket watch and a cigarette lighter. These, the caption explains, were what remained of the vast wealth he'd inherited from Will Clark.

The article beneath that picture recounted a tangled, bewildering conspiracy about a man who'd been swept into one of the greatest fortunes in America only to be cast to the margins, a man taken captive in bizarre and gothic circumstances by his own family only to be released into darker, larger, historical forces. An invented Hollywood millionaire, he swanned among movie stars and glided through the glamorous, reckless, dizzying 1920s, his life bracketed by the fading Gilded Age and the barbaric rise of twentieth-century fascism.

What had begun as a story of coincidence and charmed encounters had taken a sharp turn into something that was at times bizarrely disjointed and deeply sinister. I'd been adrift from my family, looking to hold on to my grandmother, when I first saw Harrison Post's face. Now I was back in the family and deeper in a past than the one I'd imagined, lost in corners and passages none of us had known.

I won't pretend I didn't have an agenda when I started to track Harrison Post's life with Will Clark. I wanted to recuperate a lost gay history as a way to assert my own queer lineage, salve my sense of injury by illuminating a love story that had been wrongfully erased. It would mean vindication for Will and Harrison—and for me. If only it were that simple.

I have said my ties to Will Clark are too circuitous to claim heritage. They are, but that's also a hedge, because I've had a sense that there might be aspects of this legacy I didn't want, other drawers I'd rather not open. I was right. This isn't the story I set out to tell but the one I found: a tale of greed, corruption, myth, and sometimes grace.

This is a story about America, which means it is a story about money and power. Taking metals and minerals out of the ground is one of the most poisonous ways there is to accumulate a fortune, and the Clark empire was, without question, a poisonous one—when it came to the earth, air, and water; when it came to democracy; and even when it came to those who benefited from its wealth, who lived far from the

Charlie Chaplin and unidentified friends, 1922.

open roasting pits and smog-spewing smelters, cushioned in ease and glamour, like Harrison Post.

One more photo. A candid from one of Harrison's scrapbooks. In it, a group of people stand, arms linked, everyone squinting. At first glance, you see four figures. On the left is a matronly woman dressed in a coat and hat, her hand up to steady the brim. And then next to her is Charlie Chaplin. He's in costume—tuxedoed, mustached—but posing as the actor, not a character. Next to him stand two men—one with a smooth owlish face, the other balding with a full white mustache. Then, with a closer look, you realize there's a fifth person—or presence.

The four people are squinting at the camera because the photographer is standing with his back to the sun, and you can see his shadow—head, torso, elbows out—dark against the ground. I have no way of knowing that that shadow belongs to Harrison Post, but given the strange ways he's come to haunt history, I choose to believe that it does.

A NOTE ABOUT A SOURCE

In the introduction to William Daniel Mangam's *The Clarks: An American Phenomenon*, Edward Ross, a sociology professor from the University of Wisconsin, calls the book a "priceless social document," insisting that it was "not just another piece of muck-raking, for it manifests no eagerness to tear aside a shimmering veil or pillory a character much in the public eye." According to Ross, the book is instead "a new kind of biography," one that tells the story of "how the senior Clark by the free use of money thoroughly corrupted and debased the public life of the virile young commonwealth." The professor ventures more: "In his portrayal of personality the author gives no sign of being swayed by any kind of feeling for the subject—either love or loathing; the only emotion apparent is loyalty to the truth."

This last statement, if one has read the work in question, is an astonishing thing to believe. *The Clarks* seethes with emotion—resentment, indignation, rage. It may have seemed a new kind of biography, but it was not without feeling for its subjects, and its author could hardly be considered an objective party.

William D. Mangam and William Andrews Clark Jr. first met in 1898 at the University of Virginia, where they were both students, and they soon became good friends who knew each other by their nicknames—"Buck" and "Junior." After college, Buck moved to Butte, Montana, where for the next thirty years he was employed by the Clarks, chiefly as an accountant and secretary for Will's various business interests. Then, in 1939, he published *The Clarks* with the Silver Bow Press, a company whose only other publication was the second edition in 1941.

Originally titled *The Biography of Copper King W.A. Clark and His Tarnished Family*, the book appears to have been Buck's only work in the genre (or any other, for that matter), and it is a remarkable specimen, engorged with bile, grievance, and character assassination. The book is divided into chapters devoted to each family member and his or her moral turpitude. The vices were various—corruption, bribery, adultery, extortion, venality—but Buck reserved his greatest outrage for Will, and he questioned the motives behind his old friend's much-lauded philanthropy. As Buck saw it, Will's identity as a public benefactor was a sham, "a character behind which he could screen his private life," which included "unnatural relations," "aberrant practices," and, somewhat more neutrally, a "mode of living."

Buck's book presents a conundrum. *The Clarks* abounds with mistakes and misspellings—"Strubetzkov" instead of Troubetzkoy, for instance. Harrison Post was in his early twenties when he met Will, not his "middle teens," though this may not be Buck's error, since Harrison frequently adjusted his age. For all the prefatory assertions of objectivity, the book is clearly driven by the author's urge to settle a score. Many of the claims seem suspect because they are so impassioned, so coated with emotion, and yet because Buck was one of Will's closest advisers and he had the actual receipts for thirty years, many of his claims are also grained with truth.

Until the recent interest in the life of Huguette Clark, the titillating and strident biography was a prominent text in the history of the family. Contemporary writers tend to approach it like a wadded tissue of unknown origin—if it has to be touched, make it fast and don't look closely. Citations and footnotes may qualify its inclusion as source material, but it is still included.

If a fact is presented to a reader covered in emotion, namely spite, is it still a fact? At some point, does subjective bile corrode objective material beyond recognition? If a fact is no longer reliable as a fact, meaning it's not a fact at all but hearsay, speculation, or fantasy, can it still be used—a negative space into which we pour our own conjecture? Without substantiating evidence, it seems that very little of Buck Mangam's book could stand up in a court of law, but this isn't a trial, and according to Ambrose Bierce, the historian is "a broad-gauge gossip," as was Buck Mangam—as am I.

While many of Buck's claims are clearly prejudiced, it would also be impossible to tell the story of Will Clark and Harrison Post as deeply without his angry book. Some of the details, like those regarding travel, for instance, can be substantiated by passenger lists and other archival sources, and I have corroborated what I can and made judgments based on my own knowledge of this history about what can be rightfully included.

In his portrait of a family ruled by greed and dissipation, Buck produced a second image—that of a man scorned. A legacy of corruption trails the Clarks. They make easy targets for demonization, and Buck soared to the occasion, but for as much as he was willing to expose, he never answered the obvious questions. Why, if they were so vile, did Buck work for them for thirty years? And what accounted for his dramatic turnabout?

An eighty-five-year-old defamation lawsuit archived in the basement of the Los Angeles County Hall of Records offers some clues. Because of course there's another story behind the story that Buck Mangam sought to tell, and however much he might protest, the author was no neutral presence in his own book. Nor is he in this one. He is both a vexing source and a key player whose quest for revenge would change the lives of Will Clark and Harrison Post.

HOUSE OF DREAMS

I knew nothing but shadows, and I thought them real.

—OSCAR WILDE, *THE PICTURE OF DORIAN GRAY*

That summer, Porto Marina Way was still a new road. Construction crews had cut switchbacks into the coastal slope a few years before, and now the motorway snaked around the Italianate mansions down the hillside to Harrison Post's house at the edge of the ocean. From there, he could watch the waves crash against the shore.

Three miles out, America stopped. That's where the gambling boats dropped anchor. At night their lights glittered in the dark Pacific. It was 1929, and the shadow world existed in plain sight.

The twisting streets and terraced developments of Castellammare, the latest luxury subdivision in Los Angeles's Pacific Palisades, had been modeled after the Amalfi Coast, and the new residents—film directors, movie stars, a wool magnate—were required to build their houses in a suitably Mediterranean style. Harrison Post complied. He filled his seaside home with ornate tapestries and dark, heavy furniture and called it Villa dei Sogni—House of Dreams.

A small, dark-haired man, he had elegant hands that were usually engaged with a cigarette. He owned a set of dominoes made of ivory and gold and when he played he always won—one tile clicking against another, mind and fingers in harmony until he slid the last ivory in place and smiled: "Domino." Then on to the next cigarette.

He was not a movie star or an industry tycoon, though he counted those people among his friends. He was fine-boned and he had dark, deep-set eyes. His gaze was watchful and appraising. He longed for his surroundings to be beautiful yet objected to charges of snobbery. "It is not so," he once wrote when so accused, though he did concede, "I do dislike vulgarians." It was a subtle distinction, and he was a man who cherished subtlety.

True, the Rolls-Royce wasn't subtle. It was one of five that had been manufactured that year. He'd had it specially painted with yellow pinstripes.

The average person in America probably knew of Harrison's good friend Bebe Daniels. All they had to do was pick up *Photoplay* or any other fan magazine to learn about the starlet's arrest for speeding, her extravagant wedding to leading man Ben Lyon, or her day playing ping-pong with Charlie Chaplin. But the average person wouldn't know Harrison Post.

When his name did end up in the papers, he was usually identified as a "clubman" or an "art collector," words that meant wealth. Some labels were more blunt: "Hollywood millionaire." There were other words that people used for him, but those were whispered, or written in unsigned letters sealed inside envelopes with no return address.

"I do evade many things," he once wrote. He had good reason to evade and good reason not to say what it was that he evaded.

On Sundays, Harrison took his Rolls-Royce to the polo field at the Riviera Country Club and watched the horses thunder across the green turf as their riders lunged low, mallets swinging. It was called the sport of kings, but here it belonged to LA's version of royalty, movie stars like Spencer Tracy and Will Rogers. In the stands, Clark Gable peered through binoculars. Beyond the grass lay a spread of orchards, and, farther still, the high ridge of the Santa Monica Mountains sheltered them all.

Harrison wasn't merely a man who knew famous people. He was a man who famous people knew. They knew him to be a lavish host, opening his homes—he had another closer to the heart of LA in West Adams—for a production of *Macbeth* or a luncheon for riders from the club. That summer he welcomed Robert Ehrmann, the tennis ace from Cincinnati, to Porto Marina Way.

The young man had come west with his parents a few months earlier to hone his game at the Miramar Beach Club. By June, Robert's parents had left, while he, seduced by the company and the sunshine, remained. Tall with brown hair, the tennis player made friends easily on the club circuit. Champion May Sutton Bundy, who years before had shocked British spectators by baring her elbows and ankles on court, had invited Robert to join her at Wimbledon that season, but England's grass courts had none of the allure of the Villa dei Sogni.

Harrison lived there with his sister, the Countess Barbieri. A small woman, about five foot four, she had the same deep-set eyes as her brother, though hers were pale blue. She was passionate about her Brussels griffon, Sidlaw Trotsky, and happy for an audience. Together she and Harrison shared their history with Robert, who in turn shared it with a hometown reporter. The tale published in a Cincinnati paper was a sad one but thrilling too. It went like this:

The two siblings had grown up in Montana. Their father, an early pioneer of the state, made his "vast fortune" in copper and silver. They were young when their mother died. Soon after, Mr. Post died too, and they became orphans—though, as it turned out, the fortunate kind.

Their late father had been good friends with another Montana pioneer, Senator William Andrews Clark Sr., and while they didn't say it in these words, everyone knew Clark was a man of phenomenal wealth, far beyond their father. Along with sprawling mines of copper, zinc, and silver, Clark owned streetcars, postal services, banks, forests, water rights, and newspapers. He'd spent $20 million to build a railroad from San Pedro, California, to Salt Lake City. People called it the Clark Road. A sleepy depot along the route would one day become Las Vegas. Clarkdale, Arizona. Clark County, Nevada. He made his fortune in the Gilded Age and left his mark well into the twentieth century.

To the general public, the man who had accumulated and presided over this immense fortune was a peculiar figure—short, dandified, birdlike with small bright eyes, a bristly goatee, and a whorl of white hair that he sculpted into theatrical tufts. He was considered prickly and aloof; "there are icicles in his handshake," wrote historian C. B. Glasscock.

But that wasn't how he'd appeared to the Post siblings. As they explained, the senator had adopted the two children and raised them as his own, sending his young wards abroad to be educated, where, the newspaper reporter observed, they were "brought into close contact with that polished mondanity [*sic*] which is the acme of the gifted ages handed down to succeeding generations from time immemorial."

The senator had been dead four years when Robert Ehrmann arrived at Villa dei Sogni, but the late tycoon's legacy was there in the "handsome house filled with treasures acquired from many palaces in Italy." Harrison had also amassed an impressive library, full of "rare books and countless first editions" that the columnist likened to a miniature Huntington Library, the sprawling property established by railroad magnate Henry Huntington. And yet the more astute observer of LA's high society would have drawn a comparison to the holdings of a different nobleman: the Clark Library.

Harrison's book collection was small compared to the one that belonged to the senator's son, William Andrews Clark Jr. Will—as Harrison called him—had a library of ten thousand rare books on his estate in West Adams, which he had deeded a few years earlier along with the building, a beaux arts curio of brick and marble, to the University of California.

The column doesn't say much about Will, but it needn't have. Most readers would've known his name was synonymous with unimaginable wealth. Smooth-faced, unlike his father, Will kept his chestnut hair neatly parted and combed to one side. Also unlike his father, he wasn't known for accumulating money, but for giving it away. In 1919, Will had spent $200,000 to found the Los Angeles Philharmonic and since then had spent even more to keep it afloat. He was also one of the major donors behind the creation of the Hollywood Bowl and helped underwrite the orchestra's concerts in the amphitheater. Along with the library, he built an observatory on his palatial grounds, where he sponsored lectures and welcomed visitors to gaze at the night sky through his telescopes.

Will was twenty years older than Harrison, but the two men were clearly close. Robert Ehrmann reported to the Cincinnati journalist that Will had invited Harrison, his sister, and Robert to his vacation home—"a veritable palace"—in Montana for the summer. He also mentioned that Will and Harrison were planning to buy the Palais Rose in Paris. The opulent mansion on Avenue Foch belonged to Anna

Gould, the socialite daughter of robber baron Jay Gould. The building, modeled after the Grand Trianon of Versailles, would pass from one American heir to another.

Robert Ehrmann came from a well-to-do family and moved in moneyed circles, but that still hadn't prepared him for the brother and sister who lived by the sea among antiques and jewels, who glided between America and Europe as if boarding a streetcar, if a streetcar came with champagne, servants, and an endless supply of cigarettes. The tennis ace was plainly enthralled by the siblings' rarefied world and the article concluded with the reporter musing that the young man might be well fitted, as Harrison Post clearly was, to the "life of the dilettante."

And yet there were others who weren't so readily beguiled, and there were other details about Harrison Post that didn't make it into the *Cincinnati Enquirer*'s account. If the story that he and his sister spun for Robert Ehrmann seemed too charmed to be true, that's because it was.

Countess Barbieri was not a countess. Her name was Gladys, and her ex-husband, whose name she still used, wasn't a European nobleman. He was from Chicago. Their father, Mr. Post, hadn't been a mining magnate. He hadn't even been Mr. Post. His name was Mark Harrison. He'd lived in many states in America, but Montana hadn't been one of them. Who, then, was Harrison Post?

There were those who thought they knew. They found him suspiciously dark, suspiciously effete, suspiciously Jewish, or, in the words of one detractor, "with Semitic cast." There were other words that trailed the man with the Rolls-Royce and the famous friends and the villa on the coast: "vice," "perverted practices," "unnatural relations," "degenerate." Few believed that he was a foster brother to Will Clark or that the two men were even friends—not exactly. Their relationship was far more intimate than that, and in 1929 it was criminal.

So much was criminal then. Just down the way from Villa dei Sogni was Doc Law's Drugstore. Everyone knew the pharmacy was a front for booze, just as everyone knew what the twinkling lights signaled three miles off the coast. Everyone living in this idyll by the ocean had a hidden cache—false bookcases, secret tunnels—and a bootlegger's phone number. Nearly everyone led a double life. The mayor of Los Angeles had been handpicked by underworld bosses. The head of the vice squad ran his own brothel. Most of the cops in Los Angeles were on the take, and out in the Palisades they all were.

Harrison Post's life wasn't doubled. It was refracted, one medium moving through another. Like a beam of light warped by water, he passed through society, his truth bending into something new.

For a decade now, the country had been living in low-light conditions, in the gloaming between legality and criminality, between aspiration to wealth and actual capital, between a fantasy of America and its reality, between the bait and the switch. Two years earlier, forty thousand people in California had lost their savings during the collapse of the Julian Petroleum Corporation, a speculative oil company that turned out to be a Ponzi scheme. Had it been a sign of darker days to come? Not according to the popular new president. That March, as the stock market continued its giddy climb, Herbert Hoover gazed out from the dais to the crowd gathered at the Capitol for his inauguration and proclaimed, "I have no fears for the future of our country."

In the Villa dei Sogni, a small, secure outpost of the Clark empire, fear was inconceivable. If there were whispers, what of them? What if the neighbors in West Adams complained about Harrison's parties? Not the luncheons—the other gatherings, the ones that happened late at night. What if the district attorney's office paid an unwelcome visit? Such matters could be troublesome but also swiftly managed, for instance, with the purchase of a new home far from provincial minds, or a sudden trip to Paris. Harrison wasn't oblivious to the rumors, but they were of little concern. Whatever his past had been, it didn't matter in 1929, because in that moment Harrison Post was, in fact, who he appeared to be, who he was meant to be—a man of wealth and refinement. With money, power, and status, he knew he was safe, not just from detractors and gossip but also from the swerves of fortune that sent others scrambling.

That summer everything was still possible. The Dow had climbed more than three hundred points and could go higher. A bootlegger could become a man of class, the way James Gatz became Jay Gatsby. Like Harrison Post, F. Scott Fitzgerald's Jazz Age creation was known for his beautiful clothes, ritzy parties, and whispered crimes. Of course, Gatsby was a character in a book and Harrison a man in real life, but they were both part fiction, author and invention alike.

In a state named for a mythical island, in a town named for angels, in a house named for dreams, Harrison Post fashioned a glittering and protected world. The house, the furniture, the books, the car, the money—all of that was real. So was the sky above, same as the ground below, and the surf crashing against the sand.

Another cigarette. The waves were always louder at night, but then we listen better in the dark.

PART ONE

1882–1919

Will Clark, circa 1882.

1

A TRAIN TO LOS ANGELES

"Nothing is fixed," Stella Adler once said.

The acting teacher was talking about a central truth in American theater, specifically in the work of Will and Harrison's friend Eugene O'Neill, whose plays explore the dark undercurrents of family life, but Adler applied her thesis to the country as well: "No religion is fixed, no family is fixed, no property is fixed—nothing gets rooted long enough for it to hold on."

America was named and built by people who arrived in speculation, flight, and bondage. Some fled persecution, some famine. Others came seeking fortune, for themselves and for the empires they served. These newcomers spoke of the land as if it were a new world, as if it had sprung into existence upon their arrival, as if the past were the interloper and those who'd made their home on the continent for centuries were the ones with strange tongues and customs.

No one in the place they called America was rooted, but they wanted to be, and by the dawn of the electrical age, it seemed possible—at least it was for Cornelius Vanderbilt, Andrew Carnegie, John D. Rockefeller, and the four dry goods merchants from Sacramento who were building the western stretch of the First Transcontinental Railroad. And certainly it was for William Andrews Clark Sr., who at the time owned nearly half the country's copper. Every lumen in every light bulb, every click in every telegraph message depended on that red metal clawed from the earth. With his extraordinary fortune, Clark had good reason to believe that he could be fixed, that his property could be, and so could the boy who bore his name.

A portrait of the copper king's son made around 1882 shows a dark-eyed, milk-pale child standing beside a pedestal, clutching a book. William Andrews Clark Jr. wears a jacket, breeches, and stockings, each ornamented by a thin arrow rising up the calf—an American dauphin. Though born in Deer Lodge, Montana—copper country—on March 29, 1877, the namesake son was raised in France and Germany. He was about six when the portrait was made, around the time he was brought back across the Atlantic Ocean to be acquainted with his country and his language.

It was for this reason that one Gilded Age morning in Manhattan, his mother brought him to Vanderbilt's Grand Central Depot, deposited him on a train, and sent the six-year-old off alone to Los Angeles, where his grandmother lived and his aunt ran a school. To ensure he didn't get lost on the cross-country journey, Will's mother wrote his name and destination on a sign, and then hung it around his neck before she said goodbye.

In the early 1880s, such a trip would've begun with the boy boarding a steam locomotive at New York's Grand Central Depot. In Chicago, he would've switched to the Union Pacific railroad line all the way to Omaha, where he'd transfer and take the Central Pacific over the original transcontinental route to San Francisco and then travel the final leg on the Southern Pacific down to Los Angeles.

Despite the abundant comforts of a luxury sleeper car—walnut paneling, damask curtains, attentive porters—the trek would've been a complicated and exhausting one for a grown traveler. A six-year-old boy with little command of English, navigating multiple transfers, alone among countless strangers, made for an extremely vulnerable passenger, all of which makes the account either more implausible or astonishing.

As an adult, the copper heir enjoyed this story and told it often, though it may have been as much an invention as Harrison Post's pioneer father. Still, whether or not it had actually happened, the tale of the boy crossing America by himself revealed something true, which is that Will Clark was born into a family that believed he could travel the world alone because his name and the vast fortune it represented would always keep him safe.

His father wasn't born into wealth but driven relentlessly toward it. Once, when Clark Sr. was discovered by a local journalist poring over files and reports in his office after midnight, the mining magnate explained his dogged ambition:

> "You probably think that I am plodding along here because of a desire to make money. If you think so you are wrong. I have more money than I could by any possibility spend. I have more than will be good for my children, perhaps. So it is not for money that I do these things." Pointing to the piles of reports he continued. "This is a game to me. If I were to stop it I would die."

Most people knew the little millionaire simply as "W.A."—fittingly efficient for the terse, seemingly aloof man. He didn't always inspire affection, but no one disputed his tenacity or his love for the game and the fact that he so frequently won at it. The scale of his empire was so massive that in hindsight it seems a foregone conclusion that he would become a titan of the Gilded Age, and yet his early years don't suggest it was inevitable.

He was born on January 8, 1839, in Connellsville, Pennsylvania. His parents, both of Scotch Irish descent, were farmers, and he was raised in a log cabin, one of eleven children, four of whom died in childhood. W.A. was ten when a carpenter building a sawmill just north of Sacramento spied gleaming flakes in a riverbed, prompting thousands to race to the Sierra foothills, a gold rush that collapsed seven years later. He missed out, too, on the rush for silver ore in the Comstock Lode at the western edge of the Utah Territory.

At seventeen, he moved with his family to Iowa and briefly studied law at Iowa Wesleyan University, but he never finished his degree. Instead, he took a job as a schoolteacher in Missouri. His teaching career didn't last long either, due in part to the outbreak of the Civil War in 1861, but more likely because of news of mineral rushes in the Rocky Mountains. He claimed to have fought for the South, but no records account for his service.

Contained and wiry, young Clark had a jutting chin, small eyes, a shock of red hair, and a restless energy. In the fall of 1862, he set out with a team of oxen to Gregory Lode, a craggy outpost forty miles west of Denver. He brought three books: Edward Hitchcock's *Elementary Geology*, Theophilus Parsons's *The Law of Contracts*, and a volume of poems by Robert Burns. The last suggests a man who sought relief from the business of accumulating and protecting wealth, but it's doubtful "the little red-headed man," as he was known in his prospecting days, ever did.

He was too late for the windfall at Gregory Lode, but there was news of gold farther northwest in Bannack, so he trekked up to what was then the Montana Territory. At the Jeff Davis Gulch, he set to work sluicing and netted around $2,000 (roughly $50,000 today), but he made another discovery that would yield far more profit.

In America, a frontier isn't simply a line between two regions or between what is known and unknown as much as it is a boundary between a resource that hasn't been monetized and one that has. In W.A.'s era, the obvious resource was the mineral wealth beneath the earth's surface. Thousands of men were flocking west to do the body-breaking work required to extract it.

But W.A. soon realized there was another resource, one far more accessible than the gold and silver buried underground: the miners themselves. The men dreaming of future fortunes were a vein waiting to be tapped, and W.A. quickly relinquished the fantasy of striking it rich in a riverbed for the realities of buying low, selling high, and cornering markets. Soon, the little red-headed man was traveling from camp to camp, selling pickaxes, tents, and food to the exhausted, hungry, and ever-dreaming miners.

It wasn't physically easier or safer to haul freight through the Rocky Mountains than it was to dredge and claw the earth, but the profit was better and more certain, and W.A.'s mind was made for profit, selling a pair of elk antlers to a saloon owner for ten dollars and marking eggs up to three dollars a dozen. He had a keen sense for commodity shortages yet remained savvy enough never to be accused of price gouging, unlike, for instance, merchants in Montana's Virginia City, who quadrupled the price of flour within a two-month period. After a visit from a man on horseback waving an empty flour sack and leading nearly five hundred armed men, the merchants readjusted their pricing.

That instinct for self-preservation served W.A. well. The war he'd avoided had claimed hundreds of thousands of lives. With the surrender of the Confederate forces in 1865, more people—customers—began flooding west to the territories, and W.A. expanded his operations to the Pacific Northwest. He established a store in the flourishing gold camp of Helena and another in Idaho Territory's Elk Grove. He branched out into mail delivery, securing a postal route from Missoula to Walla Walla, and into banking, making loans to local merchants at 2 percent interest. By 1869, he'd started a wholesale mercantile and banking business fifty miles west of Helena in the town of Deer Lodge. Now nearly thirty, he was an established businessman in the exploding frontier, ready to start a family.

In most accounts, W.A. leaves a chill in his wake, vanity and a desire for admiration being his most human qualities. C. B. Glasscock notes that he was "too formal, too cold and calculating, too neat and polished to be a popular hero in a mining camp." He strove to elevate himself above his customers, preferring adulation to camaraderie. "Few loved him," Glasscock observed, "but many courted him."

Kate Stauffer appeared to be one of the few. A pretty, dark-haired daughter of a prominent businessman in Connellsville, she and W.A. had known each other as children. The banker returned to his childhood home, set about courting her, and they were soon married. After a honeymoon in Chicago and St. Louis, they settled in Helena, where Kate gave birth in 1870 to their first child, Mary, or Maizie. Soon after, the Clarks left the roiling boomtown for the leafier Deer Lodge, and a year later a son, Charlie, was born. If her husband was considered touchy and remote, Kate offered a benevolent, humanizing presence. The *Butte Miner* described her as "unassuming in manner, domestic in her habits, and a model wife and mother in all that the term implies."

Now the leading financier in the Montana Territory, W.A. had expanded his business from lending credit to buying gold dust from miners and reselling it to banks on the East Coast. But as sales began to wane, he cast about for new business opportunities, setting his sights on the sparse mining camp of Butte.

High up in the Rockies, forty miles west of the Continental Divide, the dry, seemingly unremarkable hill sloped down into a small valley. A series of gold strikes there in the 1860s had since sputtered into nothing, though a few dozen miners remained tenaciously working a handful of quartz mines. They insisted veins of silver ran deep below. But even if they could extract the ore, the men told W.A., they had no means to build the smelters necessary to refract it nor could they afford to transport it to Utah, the closest place where it could be processed. Other men's aspirations had proven lucrative before. It cost W.A. little to purchase a stake. He bought into four claims, a marginal investment that would yield an extraordinary American fortune.

The teacher-turned-banker trusted his own expertise foremost, but he was also smart enough to know he wasn't an expert in mining—yet. Instead of rushing to sink shafts into his new properties, he went back to school. He and Kate deposited Maizie and Charlie with his parents in Iowa, and then, ore samples in tow, the couple traveled to New York City, where Clark spent two years at Columbia University's School of Mines. Then he reassembled his family and returned to Montana to capitalize on his investment.

Some 150 million years before W.A. bought his claims on that barren mound of earth, two tectonic plates collided. The oceanic one—the one we call the Farallon Plate—crashed into the western edge of the North American plate, what is today Utah. Because it was the denser of the two, the Farallon Plate slid downward, subducting, shoving molten rock, or magma, up through the crust, which then bulged and hardened into the Sierra Nevada mountain range. Another eighty million years later, the Farallon Plate surged back up against the continent, scraping eastward beneath the overlying plate and thrusting up another more massive formation, the Rockies.

While the magma that made it to the earth's surface exploded, heaving rocks and ash into the air, the molten rock beneath the crust cooled into masses of granite—batholiths—that cracked as they crystallized. Hot water coursed through those new crevices and eventually evaporated, leaving behind hunks and streaks of metal.

The miners working the lonely hill weren't mistaken. They were perched near the southeastern edge of the Boulder Batholith, a minor remnant of the Farallon Plate's ancient journey that stretched one hundred miles north to Helena and a mere twenty-five miles east to west.

The silver was close to the surface and that was what the miners dug up first. Zinc and manganese came next. Finally, the real treasure: the veins of copper, some fifty feet wide. In the beginning, W.A. had sold men pickaxes. Now he sold money, advancing funds with high interest so they could buy into claims, and then he foreclosed and took the claims for himself.

Before long, mine shafts—some as deep as 6,000 feet—pierced the hill. Towering iron head frames loomed like gallows. With drills, dynamite, and shovels, men crammed into steel cages and plummeted down the narrow chutes, dropping at a speed of 800 feet per minute. In cramped tunnels they blasted through hard rock, shoveling waste and ore into carts to be dragged by mules to the shaft stations, piled into the cages, and then hauled up to the surface. The once-sleepy hill vibrated and shuddered from the explosions below and the constant heave of steam-powered hoist engines. Miners, loggers, swampers, carpenters, blacksmiths—they were all part of the thrumming Clark operation.

Life aboveground had its own boisterous rhythm too. The handful of shacks soon morphed into a gridded town with streets named Granite, Quartz, Silver, Porphyry, and of course Copper. Butte boasted hurdy-gurdy dance joints, pool halls, parlor houses for upmarket prostitution, and Pleasant Alley, a row of half-exposed stalls known as "cribs." From saloons to sex to gambling—faro, poker, craps, roulette—men could lose money as quickly as they could make it.

But for W.A., there was no question of merely making or losing money; it was a matter of making the most. That was the game, and his primary opponent was an Irish immigrant named Marcus Daly, who'd first arrived in Butte as a representative for the Walker Brothers, a mining and banking concern in Salt Lake City. Daly was coming to get a firsthand look at the ores the firm had been receiving from Butte's Alice Mine. Impressed, he bought into the operation on behalf of the company and for himself, but it was his purchase of the nearby Anaconda Mine, financed by George Hearst and others, that established him as W.A.'s enduring rival.

Fifteen when he'd emigrated to America, Daly had sold newspapers and worked the docks in New York City before heading west to the Comstock Lode, where he rose through the ranks to mine foreman. He had no formal education and, unlike W.A., never appeared to crave one or the social cachet it offered. Where Daly was earthy and unpretentious, ready to share tobacco and liquor with any man, W.A. was fastidious and standoffish, a dandy in a dirty town. By now he'd developed his signature coiffure; along with ornate tufts of hair, a springy goatee and bushy mustache erupted from W.A.'s face, a fortification through which one might glimpse but never fully see him. Somewhere behind those whiskers was a man. Certainly behind those small, bright eyes was a mind churning and calculating. Daly was no less driven, but the Irish immigrant didn't shrink from his scrappy origins nor did he incline, as W.A. did, to giving speeches. Daly liked money, but he liked people too. W.A. liked money, and he seemed to like people most when they were in an audience.

Their battle began when Montana was a territory and it continued into statehood. When Daly launched the Anaconda Mine, W.A. bought the neighboring water rights, essential for his rival's eventual smelting operations. After W.A. started the *Butte Miner*, Daly countered with the *Anaconda Standard*, both newspapers unabashed mouthpieces for the two magnates. When W.A. had $400,000 in gold coin shipped from London in kegs to underwrite checks for his banking customers, Daly parried with kegs that boasted $700,000. The dueling operations included not just the thousands of men toiling underground, but also the lawyers who argued their property claims, the judges who ruled in their favor, and the legislators who passed laws advantageous to their interests.

There was no shortage of spoils. Along with the Gambetta, Colusa, Travona, Original, and other mines, W.A. owned the largest bank in the region. Soon the railroads had reached Butte. More men poured in. More metal poured out. With the arrival of the arc lamp, the first commercial use of electricity, demand for copper surged.

As W.A.'s business empire grew, so did his family. In 1874, Kate gave birth to a son, who lived only a week. A year later she had twin girls, Jessie and Katherine, or Katie—and then in the spring of 1877, a boy.

William Andrews Clark didn't give his name to his firstborn son. Only after he'd amassed a Gilded Age fortune did the former schoolteacher bestow it on one of his children. Charlie had been born to an enterprising banker, Will to a copper king.

Few people in America have been born into such riches, and yet Will's first year was marked by sorrow. He was only a few months old when his two-year-old sister Jessie contracted pneumonia. She died in April 1878, weeks after his first birthday. Montana may have been the origin of the Clarks' phenomenal fortune, but it was also where the family buried two children. That fall, they sailed for France.

Paris was in the midst of its own boom, having emerged from the battle of the Commune. In the Tuileries, gardeners tended the once-scorched, now-blooming gardens. Up on Montmartre, workmen toiled on the white dome of the Sacré-Coeur basilica rising against the skyline. Hot air balloons floated above the Seine. Will and his family arrived in a city newly illuminated with arc lamps.

Far from belching smokestacks and pits of roasting ore, thirteen million people flocked to the Exposition Universelle where they heard Alexander Graham Bell's telephone ring and Thomas Edison's phonograph warble. In the Trocadero Gardens, visitors walked inside the colossal copper head of the Statue of Liberty, the new republic's gift to commemorate America's abolition of slavery and its embrace of independence.

Just a few months later, in January, Edison patented the incandescent light bulb. The electrification of the world had already begun, and now the pace accelerated. Telegraph wires, telephone lines, light sockets—all needed the red, ductile metal that Will's father was pulling from the earth, or rather, his legions of miners were extracting, doing the dangerous, poisonous work of scraping and plunging and smelting, while acrid green smog filled the air in Butte and sulfuric soot settled on the grass and coated the windowsills and the Clark fortune continued to swell.

For thirteen centuries—from the coronation of Clovis I until Louis XVI was stripped of his title in 1792—France had had a king. Since then, the country had roiled between revolution and backlash, republic and empire, until finally after the disastrous Franco-Prussian War, Napoleon III was deposed in 1870. The French monarchy might be over, and yet the imperial impulse still lived on. It wasn't driven by the divine right of kings but of capital. America called itself a republic, but as W.A. proved, if a man owned enough of its resources, along with its banks, postal services, and utilities, he might as well consider himself sovereign.

In Europe, W.A. had discovered a new game: collecting art. Among the vestiges of faded empires, he could imbue his New World wealth with Old World prestige. He gathered up the remnants of the bygone dynasties to decorate his palace back in Butte—tapestries, rugs, vases, ceramics, stained glass—though he also embraced contemporary art, especially the landscapes of Jean-Baptiste-Camille Corot and the Barbizon School. While Kate remained with their children, cosseted by nannies and governesses and tutored in French and German, as befitting royal issue, W.A. began a ritual of seasonal migration. He spent most of the year in America, presiding over his growing kingdom, returning each winter to his family. In 1880, a son, Paul, was born in Paris.

Six years passed and it was deemed time for the Clark children to come back to America, to learn their own language, to discover how much they possessed. Twenty years before, Will's father had driven a team of oxen from Missouri to Colorado, when the nation had consisted of twenty-five states wrenched apart by war. Now it had been knit back together and stretched from one end of the continent to the other. The railroads hurtled people and goods across the land, prosperity bloomed, and much of it belonged to Will's family. And so the day came when his mother took him to Grand Central and sent him off alone across the country.

At the end of the journey, when the boy finally arrived in Los Angeles, he alighted at a two-story wooden depot surrounded by freight yards, pastureland, and mountains. It was quieter than Paris, quieter than New York, quieter than Butte, not that Will would've had much memory of the raucous mining town. Los Angeles had grown at a different pace from the rest of the country. No waterway or harbor had designated it a strategic spot for trade. No mineral rushes had swept through. No smokestacks fumed.

Adjacent to the frontier but apart from the boom, Los Angeles had idled. It was a ranching town. The mining years had been good ones—the demand for beef in the foothills had been constant—but these pastures weren't a destination for fortune seekers. A small housing boom had spurted and fizzled a decade earlier. The former pueblo's rhythms belonged not to the incessant, propulsive churn of industry but to seasons, to grazing schedules and harvests.

That was about to change. There would be men, like W.A. surveying the arid hill of Butte, who intuited the riches to come. They understood even better than the copper baron how people and their desires were raw material to be turned into commodities. Harrison Gray Otis, a farmer's son from Ohio, had just been made editor of the *Los Angeles Daily Times*. Within a few years he'd blanket his Midwestern homeland with pamphlets advertising the orange groves and mountains that now greeted young Will Clark. The town had to pay a $600,000 "subsidy" to persuade Southern Pacific to build a depot, since Los Angeles wasn't already a center for trade or industry, but Otis had foresight. Eventually they'd tear down the modest depot and build the Arcade Station in its place, all the better for a picturesque welcome among William Wolfskill's orange groves. Staging was essential.

None of this meant anything to Will. For the boy, Los Angeles was simply where his grandma lived. The carriage wheels clacked over the road. Water trickled through the zanjas, the ditches irrigating the town. Three mountain ranges ringed the Los Angeles Basin, like a cup tipping into the Pacific Ocean. It wasn't granite and quartz and streaks of metal beneath the earth's crust, but a cretaceous slurry of sand and oil. Here, land was as unfixed as land could be and yet the boy was secure, safe within his father's extraordinary realm.

They trundled past Los Angeles Park, once a camp on the western outskirts of the old pueblo. Now a white picket fence kept out stray cows and sheep. A church steeple rose high above Second Street. A new grid had been laid down over the one the Spaniards had built a century earlier, as if no one had been there first.

His grandmother lived on Olive Street, named for the trees that lined the road. Their silvery leaves glinted in the sun. Olive was the same word in French and English. Will was there to learn his native language, just as Los Angeles was about to learn its most enduring lesson, to sell itself.

2

THE BOND

In 1946, Harrison Post rolled a tissue-thin piece of airmail paper into a typewriter and began to write:

> N ow, I will tell you something of my lifeso that rumour will have nothing but the truth, should this come up later on, otherwise/ forget it. My name was (isnt it orrible) Albert Weis Harriosn.

By then the Rolls-Royce was gone. So were the horses, the furniture, and the silver. So was Robert Ehrmann. As the young tennis ace had drifted into the Villa dei Sogni that summer, so he drifted out, back to Cincinnati and eventually Miami, where he settled into playing the club circuit.

By 1946, the house of dreams was gone. Will was gone. Gladys, too, and with her, the books, antiques, art, and the money. The sale of alcohol was again legal in America, and most nights that year were filled with alcohol. It seems likely that the author of the letter—the man who called himself Harrison Post—composed it toward the end of a liquor-soaked evening, and this may be one of the reasons it makes for a confusing read.

Another reason is that the letter, as it survives today, has been cut into three pieces. Like so much that remains of Harrison Post, it's tantalizing, confounding, and riddled with gaps.

It was in this short, disjointed autobiography that Harrison admitted he evaded many things—"for the reason it is no one's business." Another reason he evaded many things was to protect the name of Will

Clark, and still another was that although alcohol wasn't criminal anymore, it was still illegal to be Harrison Post.

Nevertheless, he was willing to put into words what he hadn't told Robert Ehrmann: the truth. It was full of misspellings and uncertainty. "My own mother was very pretty as I remember her." Even to Harrison, his background was hazy. "My father was not too bad, a brilliant man, but a drunkard."

He was born in 1897, though he admitted he'd been flexible on the matter, insisting this wasn't due to his vanity but his sister's. "Gladys was several years my senior, personally I wouldn't care if I was eighty, but it was important to her. She wanted to be married, etc. so I was ostensibly 1904, April 19."

The siblings' claim that their family had a connection to Senator Clark wasn't entirely off the mark. However, it wasn't their father who'd known the mining magnate. It was their grandfather: "General Albert Weis, the Confederate Army originally from Galveston Texas, his family from Alsace-Lorraine, he was a very rich man, he was a friend of Senator Clark, he controlled 388 theatres of the south, The American Theatrical Agency." This, at least, history confirms, to a certain extent. With Harrison—as with his sister—there was truth and there was flourish, the latter so often trailing the former. Albert Weis was a successful impresario, but he hadn't owned such a suspiciously precise number of theaters, more like 250, and he hadn't been a general but a colonel in the Confederate Army.

Gladys was fond of flourish too, but she took it further than Harrison ever dared. "She possesses that priceless of all gifts," he once wrote of his sister, the fake countess. "She believes her own lies."

William Andrews Clark Sr.'s history is still with us, partly because of his well-documented penchant for corruption, but mostly because he accumulated astounding sums of money. Although his holdings were less extensive, Albert Weis also left a trail through his theatrical empire and other business interests. However, most people who lived through the Gilded Age did not leave such marks. Their tracks are harder to locate. If the Clark family history is a solid road of wealth and more wealth, the Harrisons' is a haze in the air that clears as soon as you look at it. To tell their story is to try to draw a line around vanished mist.

"Mark Harrison from Syracuse" sounds like a real person who comes from a real place. That's who the salesman said he was, but he was not from Syracuse. He came from the town of Kishinev in what is now the Republic of Moldova. And whatever name was given to him when he was born in the Russian Empire in the 1860s, it wasn't Mark Harrison.

It could've been a customs agent who renamed the Russian immigrant without a second thought, or perhaps Mark gave himself a name that bore no trace of his past. This will become such a pattern with the Harrisons that it might be called a family trait, if Harrison is the name for them, and if it can be a family trait to cast off one's personal history. In any case, his birth date, his given name, the year he arrived in America—all of this remains part of the mist, though it's reasonable enough to assume that at some point before 1892 he might have lived in Syracuse.

In any case, when he arrived in Galveston that year, Mark Harrison was real enough that he got a job selling clothes at E.S. Levy, a local outfitter for men and boys. Real enough that he attended a dance party that spring with a group of the city's popular young set, which included an eighteen-year-old Jennie Weis, daughter of a prominent Galveston businessman.

An extension of the barrier islands that border the edge of the United States from Maine down the Eastern Seaboard around the tip of Florida, Galveston wasn't formed by subterranean changes in heat and pressure, but by the tides and the wind coming off the Gulf Coast. The thirty-mile sandy ridge, separated from the rest of the state by Galveston Bay, was home to the largest city in Gilded Age Texas, with a population of twenty thousand. A thriving port and cultural center, it included a vibrant and prosperous Jewish community of which Albert Weis was a leading figure.

Born in Strasbourg in 1842, Weis was three when his family arrived in New York City and settled on the Lower East Side. Like Clark, Weis was soon drawn west, though he did in fact enlist with the Confederate forces, fighting at one point under the command of General Nathan Bedford Forrest, later the first Grand Wizard of the Ku Klux Klan.

After the war, Weis settled in the bustling port city, where he started a dry goods firm that specialized in clothing and "gentlemen's furnishing goods," which grew to include an office and factory in Manhattan. By the early 1890s, Weis had branched out considerably. With Henry Greenwall, he founded the American Theatrical Exchange, a syndicate that controlled theaters and opera houses throughout the South. They also built Galveston's Grand Opera House, at the time one of the most impressive stages in the country and still standing today despite more than a century of hurricanes.

Weis was president of the Galveston Water Commission, the Island City Savings Bank, a director of the First National Bank, of the Texas Land and Loan Company, and the Galveston Packing and Canning Company. He served as an alderman and founded the Harmony Club, a community center for the city's Jewish elite.

Like Clark, Weis rose steadily from merchant to business executive to capitalist aristocrat, though never to the level of industrialist tycoon. And like Clark, Albert Weis returned to an earlier home to marry. His bride, Rebecca, was the daughter of a horse dealer and grain merchant in New York City. The couple had four girls and four boys, all raised in a stately Victorian mansion in one of the city's most exclusive neighborhoods.

In the photogravure that accompanies his entry in *American Biography: A New Cyclopedia*, Albert Weis gazes off in the distance. The ends of his full mustache are waxed and turned up. He wears a waistcoat, tie, and jacket. The immigrant from Strasbourg had become an American man of means in the Gilded Age.

It remained to be seen if the same future awaited Mark Harrison. In his late twenties, he was older than the others at the small social gathering that spring—enough to seem more traveled or worldly than the young men who were part of Jennie's usual set. Likely Mark asked Weis's daughter to dance with him that night. They at least spoke, because six months later the two traveled across the bay to the county clerk's office in Houston.

There, they signed their names to a marriage license. The justice of the peace signed his name next, and then a second form to be kept on file at the courthouse was brought out and all three parties signed that as well. On this record, someone—a clerk perhaps—has written in slanting cursive: "Reporters: please do not publish—you will confer a favor upon me."

From the beginning: Do not tell.

The *Galveston Daily News* had been attentive to Jennie Weis from her earliest years. The fourth child in the prominent family, she was born in 1874, and the paper had assiduously reported on her poetry recitations, maypole dances, Purim balls, and the time she held the *B* in the acrostic that spelled out *George Ball High School*.

Jennie wasn't the first Weis daughter to be married. A year earlier, Bella, the eldest girl, had wed. Like so many Weis family functions, this event was closely watched by the local paper and its readers. No one warned off the reporters. In fact, the *Galveston Daily News* gushed out two columns under the front-page headline BRILLIANT NUPTIALS, describing the throngs of well-wishers who packed the B'nai Israel Temple despite heavy rains, as well as the palms, ferns, calla lilies, and chrysanthemums covering the bimah. The bride, "the cynosure of all eyes," wore "Venetian white pompadour silk, with duchess lace and a royal bridal veil looped with orange and apple blossoms."

The reception for Bella and her new husband, held at the Weises' home, was "a most sumptuous and recherche affair." The couple's "beautiful and costly" gifts included a trunk of silver, a tapestry parlor set, a diamond-studded gold watch, a jeweled writing set, "a handsome piano lamp," a bisque swan, a Dresden candelabra, and a $1,000 check. There were silver carvers, tea sets, ice cream spoons, dessert knives, fruit plates, and pickle dishes.

When it was time for Jennie's nuptials, they were hardly deemed "brilliant" or given a front-page send-off. Instead, they were the subject of an attempted cover-up.

The Weises were apparently happy enough about the men whom Bella and, later, another daughter, Frances, married—one a prominent retail merchant, the other a manager in the theatrical circuit—to throw lavish weddings for them, but they didn't do this for Jennie. Albert Weis, like William Andrews Clark Sr., excelled at appearing fixed. This was not the case with the man who said he was Mark Harrison from Syracuse. Suspicion trailed the salesman. An angry business partner once claimed Mark had served time in prison, though no crime was ever specified.

There are people whose edges quiver. The lines around their race, their class, their origin, or whom they desire are not clear or obvious. They make us nervous. We do not want them marrying our daughters, not after all the work we've done to fix ourselves.

The clerk's plea went unheeded. A journalist from the *Galveston Daily News* felt no obligation to whoever had scrawled out the request for silence. However, the editors did bury the item at the bottom of the fifth page on September 4, 1892:

Quiet Wedding

> Yesterday afternoon a quiet marriage ceremony was performed by Justice Schwander of this city. The contracting parties were Mark J. Harrison and Miss Jennie Weis, both of Galveston.

Absence is a tell. Omissions are evidence. No eager throngs, no flower girls, no satin, no silk, no trimmings, no bridal veil looped with orange and apple blossoms, no prevailing colors, and no family.

One of the first lessons in drawing an object is to begin with the negative space. It reveals not just the object—the bowl of fruit, the chair, the house, the bride—but also what's not there.

The void was all the more notable, a month later, when Frances was married. Though this event didn't command the swell of attention that Bella's wedding had, a reporter did enthuse that "the bride was attired in a blue directoire suit and standing before the minister, beside the handsome groom, made a striking picture of modest maidenhood merging into happy wifehood." And yet Jennie, another society daughter, whose childhood dances and recitations had been fondly reported, didn't even get to be a bride in her hometown paper. Instead, she was a "contracting party."

Shame lives in the quiet shrouding that courthouse wedding. It lives in the clerk's scribbled plea. In silence, invention blooms. A shotgun marriage is one rationale for the hushed nuptials, except for the fact that the couple's first child, a daughter, was born more than a year after they were married. If Jennie was pregnant on her wedding day, she didn't carry to term.

Mark Harrison was clever and enterprising enough to master English and he was skilled at sales, but he didn't have wealth or property. Nor was he fixed by Anglo-Saxon heritage. Neither was Albert Weis, but the older Jewish immigrant, who'd arrived in America during waves of global dislocation brought on by famine, war, and revolution, had managed to root himself. He'd built a sprawling theatrical syndicate. He'd established his own Jewish aristocratic class. He'd done all this and kept his own name. Jennie took it for her first child.

On December 17, 1893, after the newlyweds had left Galveston for New York, Jennie gave birth to a girl and named her Albertha. A year later, another girl was born. This was Gladys. Then, in 1897, Jennie gave birth to a son.

Now that there was a boy to carry the patriarch's name, Jennie took it from her daughter and gave it to her son, as if that would make him heir to her father, the wealthy impresario, instead of the child's own, a rootless salesman—as if a name is enough to fix a person.

Albertha became Claire Leicester Harrison. The boy became Albert Weis Harrison, a theft he didn't commit. Gladys remained Gladys.

Albert wasn't born into wealth but into its memory.

Pack and move, and then pack again and move again, and then do it again and again. That much is clear about his earliest years. It's difficult to fill in much more for several reasons. There are few traces. His family never stayed in one place for long. His own claims on the subject are tenuous.

In 1917, when he registered with the armed services for the Great War, he informed the draft board that his full name was Albert Weis Harrison and that he was born in New York on April 19, 1897.

That's what he believed to be the truth, even though later, when he grew vain about his age or needed to oblige his sister, he'd say otherwise and edge the years upward. By then he'd changed his name, so it must have seemed natural enough to change the year of his birth, first to 1900, eventually to 1904. Nevertheless, when he tried to make a clean breast of his history, he asserted the earlier date. And yet even then he may have been mistaken. Records show that an Albert Harrison was born on that day in New York City, but that Albert's parents were George and Eliza Harrison and that Albert Harrison died of natural causes in 1988 and was buried in Pennsylvania. That Albert Harrison did not become Harrison Post.

Here, it's not merely a question of trying to draw a line around fog but being careful not to draw a line around the wrong fog. It's possible that two Albert Harrisons were born on the same day in New York City and only one birth certificate remains on file in the city's Municipal Archives. It's also possible that at some point in trying to substantiate his birth, one Albert was given the other's record. To muddy the matter further, the 1900 census reports that Albert Weis Harrison was born in February of 1897, though such archival records are often riddled with discrepancies. April 19 may be correct, but the point remains that even his birth date can't be fixed.

His first home can be. It was a boardinghouse at 248 West Twenty-First Street in Manhattan. It wasn't home for long. By the time Albert was two, the Harrisons had packed up and moved to Manchester, New Hampshire, where Jennie gave birth to a second son, Richard. Then, a few months later, they packed and moved again, farther north, to Portland, Maine. By now it should be clear that Mark wasn't a traveling salesman in the sense of a man who travels from town to town selling clothes. He traveled because he didn't keep a job long.

The *Galveston Daily News* may have been right to bury Jennie's marriage contract with Mark Harrison in the back pages while it raved about her sisters' weddings. Time appeared to bear out the Weis family's apprehensions. Back when she was an eighteen-year-old in a world of Purim balls and military hops, a life with an older, traveled man may have seemed sophisticated and exciting. But reality was different. At twenty-six, Jennie was trapped with an alcoholic salesman, mothering four small children, upping and leaving every year—hardly an easy existence for a daughter of Albert Weis.

At least Portland held promise. The proprietor of a local clothing store, a man named Bernard Kamber, had offered Mark a position as head clerk.

If Mark and Jennie's wedding had been quiet, their marriage was not. Portland, it turned out, also held turmoil, and it's clear that there may have been other factors at play in the Harrisons' transient years beyond Mark's drinking or apparent unsteadiness.

On March 19, 1899, Mark filed suit against Kamber for alienation of affection and sought $30,000 in damages. In contemporary terms and dollars, he sued his boss for more than $900,000 for having an affair with his wife.

"A brilliant man but a drunkard" was how Harrison described his father. Of his mother, he said simply, "She was pretty." It seems that she also had a reckless streak—a young woman given to sudden and ill-chosen romances. Nine months after Mark sued his boss, Jennie gave birth to a daughter named Virginia in Chicago. If the girl was Mark and Jennie's child—and that's a sizable if—she was their last.

Before he was three, Albert had had at least four different homes. The fifth was Gloucester, where his father found a job in the Massachusetts harbor town, but this time when they unpacked there were only three of them: Albert, Gladys, and Mark. The others were in Chicago with his mother.

The trio stayed in a boardinghouse on Main Street, close enough to the wharf to smell the ocean and the haul of fish, to hear the water smack against the boats and the gulls cry overhead. The proprietor was a woman named Chrissy Brown. She ran the home with her daughters. The other boarders were men—a druggist, barber, grocery clerks, harness makers, and two fishermen. The innkeeper, like so many, wasn't born in America. She'd emigrated from Norway some thirty years before. Two of her tenants—the fishermen—were also Norwegian.

During the day, while his father sold trousers and jerseys at the local clothing store down the street and Gladys studied her letters at school, Albert remained behind at the boardinghouse. Manhattan was long gone. It's doubtful he remembered the rented rooms on West Twenty-First Street anyway. Gone also were Manchester and Portland. They weren't places but words—still new things to a three-year-old. "Chicago" was a sound that meant your mother isn't coming back.

Frokost, *middag*. These are the Norwegian words for breakfast and supper. Years later, when he lived in another boardinghouse by the water, he heard them daily. He wrote them in his diaries, but likely he never remembered the house on Main Street where he heard them first.

Gloucester was one stop among many, but it matters because it was the place where he and Gladys became a locked pair. Whether or not

Albert and his sister were full siblings, they were bound by more than blood. They were the two their mother didn't take.

It's an open question as to whether Albert shared the same parents with his siblings. All five children took Harrison for their last name, but at different times Mark claimed anywhere from three to five dependents. For all the census reports and news clippings, the truth slips and slides and never holds still.

Over time, Albert's family ties would fray and fade, but not when it came to Gladys. The bond forged by shared abandonment is a heavy one, an obdurate shackle. Of all his siblings, Gladys's was the only name he wrote years later in his address book. The day would come when he drew a line through it, but that would prove an empty gesture, scarcely enough to truly break free.

3

AN EDUCATION

Three generations of millionaires:
W. A. Clark I, II, and III, 1903.

Will also lived an itinerant childhood. His, however, wasn't a precarious scramble but extravagant flux, meandering from Pullman cars to ocean liners, from Parisian apartments to the elaborate mansion his father built on Granite Street in Butte. Will's parents also lived apart, but this appeared to be a mutually pleasing arrangement that bore no acrimony or turmoil.

He spent summers in Montana, seat of his father's empire, where he learned to fish, hunt, and ride horses, but his world was still oriented around his mother's life. She'd established a home on Long Island, and his education continued there as well as at the Drisler School in Manhattan. He studied Greek, Latin, mathematics, and the classics, preparation for his eventual enrollment at Columbia University.

Through the booming 1880s, the Clark interests had expanded beyond Montana: coal in Wyoming, lead in Idaho, sugar beets in California, coffee in Mexico. In Arizona, W.A. acquired a majority stake in the United Verde Mine. Located in the Black Mountains, the copper deposits there proved even more vast and lucrative than those of the Boulder Batholith.

The copper king continued his tours to Europe, and he continued to expand his art collection, scooping up bronze statues, Delft faience, maiolica pottery, drawings, watercolors, and paintings by Gainsborough, Reynolds, Turner, and Rembrandt. In Butte, people had taken to calling him the "Paris Millionaire." The construction on his opulent redbrick Victorian mansion, completed in 1888, had taken four years. With stained-glass windows, frescoed ceilings, walls textured with plaster painted gold, silver, bronze, and copper, few surfaces were left unadorned. The mirror in the family room was backed with diamond dust. W.A.'s personality might not have sparkled, but the gilt and marble did.

As the boom times swelled to their bursting point, W.A. remained impervious to the miscalculations and shocks that obliterated other once seemingly invulnerable industrialists. On February 23, 1893, after overextending itself through acquisitions and land speculation, the Philadelphia and Reading Railroad, one of America's largest employers, declared bankruptcy. Two months later, the National Cordage Company launched an unsuccessful attempt to corner the hemp market and followed suit. Meanwhile, silver had gone into free fall, depleting the Treasury's gold reserves in the process. Panic flooded the global economic system. Americans fled to their failing banks. Unemployment soared. Businesses and fortunes vanished.

W.A. never flinched. Electricity hadn't disappeared. Buoyed by apparently unending copper reserves—that market barely shuddered—he existed high above the maelstrom ravaging the country. Perhaps the Pullman Strike inconvenienced him, but otherwise the Panic of 1893 didn't breach the walls of the Clark kingdom. He continued to collect Corot landscapes and ormolu furniture and set his sights on a new trophy: a Senate seat.

To many Americans, the Millionaires' Club, as the Senate was often called, wasn't a governing body but an elite trade association for moguls and their agents. Suspicions ran high as to exactly whom the senators were at the Capitol to serve. Did Philetus Sawyer, owner of Philetus Sawyer & Son Lumber, represent the people of Wisconsin or lumber interests? Did Stephen Elkins speak for West Virginia or the railroads where he'd made his fortune? Similar questions were asked of mining tycoons like James Fair, William Sharon, and George Hearst.

At the time, unlike in the House of Representatives, members of the Senate weren't elected by popular vote but by state legislators, who could often be persuaded to elect men who would privilege the interests of industrialists and financiers over those of their constituents. The money spent by the club's eighty-eight members on campaigns and bribery was simply a cost of doing business in Gilded Age America.

Clark, who already belonged to many fraternal orders, could afford the price of admission, but he still faced a sizable obstacle. Marcus Daly had no hankering for pomp or speeches, preferring to deploy his power by bankrolling politicians and leaving the grandstanding to them. Still, as determined as Clark was to seize the coveted title, his rival was equally committed to denying him that pleasure and protecting his own interests. Consequently, their money inundated every corner of Montana.

So far, Clark's results in the political sphere had been mixed. He'd been named grand master of Montana's Masonic lodge, appointed commissioner of the 1884 World's International and Cotton Centennial Exposition in New Orleans, and elected president of Montana's second constitutional convention that same year, though the assembly didn't achieve statehood. In 1888, when Montana Democrats nominated him as a delegate to the Senate, success seemed inevitable. Instead, in a last-minute stealth campaign, Daly directed his own operatives and employees to turn out en masse for the Republican candidate, an unassuming lawyer named Thomas Carter, who swept the vote. The turnabout caught Clark and his associates completely unawares.

A year later, Montana had been finally admitted to the Union, with

Clark again serving as president of the constitutional convention. The Millionaires' Club awaited. Determined not to be bested again, Clark invested liberally in the state congressmen, as did Daly, and even though Clark appeared to have outspent his nemesis, the race ended in a deadlock. As a result, the election was decided not by any impromptu or clandestine efforts but by the Republican majority in the Senate, which swiftly quashed Clark's hopes and chose his Republican opponent instead.

Every setback was a goad. By 1893, as the new Senate election cycle began, the copper kings resumed their positions. At the time, the law required that the legislators cast ballots daily until a senator was elected, and a prolonged, horse-race frenzy took hold as one candidate edged ahead, then the next, and so on, day after day. Money openly changed hands. Both sides hired Pinkerton detectives who lurked in saloons and near the ballot boxes. If a payoff wasn't going to get the job done, then the hired thugs could provide a beat-down. At least, that was the intended message.

On March 2, acceptance speech in hand, W.A. eagerly took his seat as the final ballot was cast, anticipating his moment of triumph, only to discover that despite his brazen bribery, he'd fallen short by three votes. No candidate had received a majority vote and the seat was to remain empty. Once again, he'd paid a lot to lose.

While he nursed his wounds and contemplated his next move, Kate spent the summer touring the West Coast with her youngest daughter. In September, they passed through Butte on their way to attend the World's Columbian Exposition in Chicago. By October, the two women were back in New York City, where the family kept a suite at the palatial Navarro Flats on Central Park South. Soon they would depart for an extended stay in Europe. Their plans were upended, though, when Kate fell ill. Within days, her symptoms worsened. Doctors diagnosed her with typhoid pneumonia, possibly contracted at the exposition. As soon as the news reached W.A. in Butte, he boarded a train, but Kate died on October 19, before he could reach her side.

By all accounts, Will's mother had been kind, attentive, and devoted. His father's wealth had created a boundless and secure realm, and yet for Will the copper baron remained a distant figure. Kate was the one who had ordered his days and overseen his education. He'd lived in her court. Now it was gone.

His older brother had already made the shift into their father's universe. At Yale, Charlie had distinguished himself by spending more in one year than any student had over their entire time at the university—useful training for a role in the Clark political machine. In 1894, the Republicans swept the state legislature, which meant that W.A., a Democrat, had no chance of being elected to the Senate, so he turned his efforts to the battle over the capital of Montana. Again, he and Daly squared off, the Irishman rallying for his base, the city of Anaconda, and W.A. for Helena.

Charlie was the bagman—one among several, but he quickly proved his skill. Some of his methods were indirect, like paying off mortgages, and others blatant, such as pulling up a stool at the saloon and writing checks in return for votes. It was said that during the capital campaign, no one in Montana paid for a single drink. When the results were finally tallied, W.A. at last emerged victorious. The bar bill for the night's celebration totaled $30,000.

Kate, the youngest daughter, found a role as their father's social hostess at the house on Granite Street. In New York, Maizie made her way in upper echelons, having married a society doctor named Everett Mallory Culver. Meanwhile, Paul, a bright student and gifted athlete, was enrolled at Andover. Until now, Will's trajectory had been clear; after prep school, he would complete his bachelor's degree at Columbia—but when the time came, he took a different path.

Charlie had been first to take up the violin, but as with many things, what the first son dabbled in the second pursued with rigor and focus. In 1895, Will traveled to Europe to study under the Belgian violinist Martin Marsick at the Paris Conservatory. For all his tenacity, it can't be said that W.A. was a tyrannical father. Rather, he seemed an indulgent parent, permitting his son to follow a passion instead of submitting to duty.

Reporters had noted that Will stood apart from his siblings in other ways. In their words, the young copper heir was a "very delicate boy" and "extremely nervous." This was code. It was there in plain view for those who could decipher it. If you were trained in the code, you needed no more information to apprehend what the reporters were insinuating about Will Clark, heading off to study the violin in Paris. There were readers who understood that an "extremely nervous" young man was also the kind of young man who'd enjoy the company of another delicate boy. Of course, if the reader was ignorant of such worlds and inclinations—or wished to appear so—the code remained simply words on a page.

Will wasn't the only student his father supported at the Conservatory. That fall, W.A. also sponsored seventeen-year-old Anna Eugenia La Chapelle's study of the harp. A year younger than Will, she'd had a decidedly different upbringing. The story the papers often printed—not so different from the one printed about Harrison Post in the *Cincinnati Enquirer*—was that Anna's father had died working in one of Clark's mines and the kindly capitalist took it upon himself to provide for the bereft family. The facts, however, did not bear this out.

Anna was born in 1878 to French Canadian immigrants in a Michigan mining town. Her family later moved to Butte, where her mother ran a boardinghouse in one of the town's more squalid neighborhoods. Her father sold lotions and ointments and called himself a doctor, though he possessed no medical degree.

Accounts vary as to how Anna and the fifty-six-year-old widower came to be acquainted. A scenario publicized in Marcus Daly's *Montana Standard* portrays Anna as a calculating fifteen-year-old who first targeted a wealthy banker to assist her theatrical ambitions before turning her charms on the copper baron. This seems unlikely. In W.A.'s version of their first encounter, he claimed he spotted Anna at a Fourth of July parade in 1893, where the attractive young girl was dressed as the Statue of Liberty—an auspiciously patriotic origin story. She was further distinguished in her beauty by the fact that her eyes were different colors, one gray-blue, the other brown. After discovering Anna also had a talent for music, W.A. said he was inspired to finance her studies. As his own children had been deposited in France for their upbringing, Clark's new protégée was eventually sent abroad as well, boardinghouse squalor replaced with music lessons, chic Parisian fashions, and French coursework.

When questioned about the propriety of his attachment to a girl nearly forty years his junior, W.A. pointed out that he was often inclined to support children—girls *and* boys—less fortunate than his own. This was true, to an extent. He had also supported several comely young actresses in their careers. Still, there weren't any fatherless boys living at his apartment on Avenue Victor Hugo, studying the harp under the tutelage of Alphonse Hasselmans.

Whether W.A. exhibited such charitable behavior while his wife was still alive isn't clear. They spent enough time apart that he could have. The difference may be that the papers weren't inclined to report on it or perhaps he'd been more discreet. His desire for adulation was well known, and it was certainly evident from his recent political forays that he was willing to pay to be exalted. This appears to have been true of his desire for female attention as well, though these transactions weren't conducted by Charlie in the saloon.

Families are universes unto themselves. A child doesn't question their laws, atmosphere, and mechanics, just as he doesn't question the existence of gravity. As Will was surely learning from his father's example, entitlement, ostentatious display, and the easy acquisition of property and even people were a matter of course. And yet W.A. was a cautious man. Decorum, or its approximation, was vital. The family name must not be impugned and certain pursuits were best conducted overseas. W.A. had sent his young consort to another country, though the word he used for Anna was "ward." No paperwork, however, was drawn up to establish any legal relationship.

From the novels of the Brontë sisters to George Bernard Shaw's *Pygmalion*, the guardian-ward seduction plot has propelled many a fictional romance. History, however, can be somewhat less erotic. The convention of wardship dates back to the Middle Ages when a few men were lords, but most were tenants farming rented land. When a tenant farmer died before his children reached their majority—usually twenty-one for boys, fourteen or sixteen for girls—the lord assumed custody of the property, which included the deceased's heirs, and was accorded the right to arrange their marriage. Through this lucrative custom, the lord could sell his ward to the highest bidder or, if he preferred, marry her himself.

In the nineteenth century, Americans were familiar with variations of this dynamic. After his best friend died in 1876, Grover Cleveland adopted the man's eleven-year-old daughter and then married her ten years later during his first term in the White House. Despite the twenty-seven-year age gap, the marriage was generally celebrated by the populace. Other versions of wardship also existed. In 1871, the US Congress enacted the Indian Appropriations Act, in which members of indigenous tribes were deemed "wards of the state" and denied rights, property, and other assets.

If a man was rich and powerful enough, he could take what he wanted, as could the state. Wardship, however, suggests charity rather than larceny or captivity. Just as the government approved the theft of land, it was also acceptable for a young girl to be delivered to a rich man's apartment in a foreign country. A ward wasn't a person but one of the spoils for those with wealth and power. To be a ward was to be a commodity, and W.A. had a mind for commodities.

Let's agree that the rules are different for the rich, but that they still believe in rules, or at least appearances—enough that W.A. enlisted his sister Lizzie to live at the apartment as Anna's chaperone. Where Will stayed during his time at the Conservatory is unknown. He may have also been at his father's apartment, but even if he stayed elsewhere, say, in a well-appointed hotel suite, he would've been aware that an aspiring harpist was living under his father's roof.

At this point, words like *natural* or *normal* seem irrelevant. It was "normal" for the fifty-six-year-old Clark to bankroll the educations of attractive girls, as it had also been normal for him to rarely see his young children, normal to live apart from his wife, normal to send a six-year-old across the country on a train by himself.

That Will might've shared a home with his father's young charge while she studied the harp and he the violin may have also been normal. At least this was normal in the Clark family, as it would've been in the court of a Bourbon monarch or the estate of a feudalist lord. And while his father didn't have a royal or aristocratic title, or, to W.A's chagrin, a Senate seat, the family possessed that which amounted to same thing in America—wealth and all that it permits.

This was a study in entitlement, but there were still other lessons to be learned about what a man was allowed, where, and with whom. That same year, Oscar Wilde was convicted of "gross indecency." Like Will's father, the playwright had scaled extraordinary heights in the recent decades. While the American mogul distinguished himself through the accumulation of capital, the flamboyant author had come to fame by extolling ephemeral pleasures—beauty, art, youth, love, cigarettes. Both men were dandies—one small and birdlike, the other tall and fleshy with glossy dark hair. Both faced ridicule, scandal, and charges of corruption, and both would leave legacies that lived on through Will Clark.

He'd been a boy of six, making his apocryphal solo journey west, when Wilde, then an eccentric poet, was making his own tour of America, dressed in velvet and silk, lecturing bewildered crowds about Ruskin and Pater, rhapsodizing about the miners in their wide-brimmed hats and high boots in Leadville, Colorado, and begging his listeners to resist the creeping dehumanization of the machine.

Since then, Wilde had married Constance Lloyd and had two sons, Cyril and Vyvyan. He'd authored fairy tales like "The Happy Prince" and essays such as "The Soul of Man Under Socialism" and "The Critic as Artist." He'd scandalized the public with his novel *The Picture of Dorian Gray*, an instant controversy for its decadent aura and homosexual allusions, but it was as a playwright that he triumphed. His most recent comedy, *The Importance of Being Earnest*, which premiered on February 14, 1895, had been a soaring success.

The fall came—shockingly and swiftly—a month later. By then the playwright's open and fraught devotion to a young, talented, and tantrum-prone poet named Lord Alfred Douglas, or Bosie, as his family called him, was well known. The two quarreled, made up, and quarreled more. Combat was a family pastime. Bosie's father, the Marquess of Queensberry, who gave his name to the code of rules on which modern boxing is based, was a churlish man, belligerent beyond the ring. At that point, he was notorious for abandoning his wife and making frivolous lawsuits. Enraged by his son's relationship with the older writer, the marquess had taken to making public scenes and stalking the playwright at his private club, where he left a card reading "For Oscar Wilde, posing somdomite [*sic*]." Rather than ignore the provocation, at Douglas's behest and against his friends' ardent advice, Wilde sued Queensberry for criminal libel. The charge did not hold up in court.

With Queensberry's acquittal, Wilde was then made liable for the defendant's legal expenses, leaving him straightaway bankrupt and subsequently arrested for sodomy and "gross indecency." In a second trial, a parade of tawdry details ensued about Wilde's association with male prostitutes, stained sheets in hotel rooms, and damning testimony from blackmailers. Within a month of his disastrous suit against Queensberry, Oscar Wilde was sentenced to two years in prison.

Wilde was talented and brazen, but he was not shrewd. Although he'd been convicted of "gross indecency," his real crime seemed to be that he'd spoken openly about that which had only been uttered in code. Douglas was the one who originated the expression "the love that dare not speak its name" in his poem "Two Loves," but it was Wilde who broadcast it to the world from the witness stand, and it was Wilde who was now tied to a treadmill grinding wheat inside a cramped prison cubicle. Meanwhile, Lord Douglas had fled to Paris, where he created more headlines and more scandal for his incarcerated lover by publishing poems and challenging people to duels.

Surely Will was aware that the stakes were high for those who tested society's norms, but he was also learning that much was possible with a semblance of propriety—a sister as a chaperone, emphasis on charitable motives—and if one kept out of sight. He returned to Butte that summer, and by the fall he was traveling again, this time with a tutor from Columbia. The two young men stopped briefly in Europe and then ventured south to Algiers, where earlier that year, just weeks before his downfall, Wilde had decamped with Douglas to escape the furious Queensberry. The North African seaport was also a destination for sex tourism, and both Wilde and Douglas had procured Arab boys during their stay. The details of their exploits are recounted in André Gide's autobiography *Si le grain ne meurt* as, by coincidence, the French writer happened to be there at the same time. If Will and his companion traveled to the city with similar intentions, they left no record.

The tour was cut short with tragic news. Will was in Egypt that March when he got the telegram. His brother Paul had died. The cause was erysipelas, a skin infection, also known as St. Anthony's fire. Will returned to the States immediately, as did his father, who'd been visiting Anna in Paris.

At sixteen, Paul had already been accepted to Yale and would've enrolled that fall. The newspapers described Clark's youngest child as "rugged" and noted that he'd held the "promise of a noble manhood." One reporter claimed Paul had been his father's favorite son.

Now it was left to Will to fulfill that promise. He would at least try. If the direction of his life had gone askew after his mother died, in the wake of Paul's death it straightened into a clear line. At eighteen, he resumed his education, not in Europe nor with a private tutor, but at the University of Virginia to pursue a degree in law, picking up one of the few dropped threads of his father's life.

At college, Will formed a tight trio with two other students, John Templeman and William Mangam. Neither "Temp" nor "Buck" would be described as delicate, and neither inclined to pursuits like the violin. Broad-shouldered, strong-jawed Temp was a football player. At six feet, with brown hair and hazel eyes, Buck played catcher for the baseball team.

Meanwhile, Will's father redoubled his Senate ambitions. In 1898, after suffering two humiliating defeats, the copper baron had decided against entering the race, but a cohort of businessmen and associates implored him to block Daly from gaining control over the state's political apparatus, an argument that appealed equally to his financial interests and his vanity. The game resumed.

The first step to determine who would occupy the Senate still began with the election of state legislators, which meant that W.A. and his nemesis were back to buying politicians and taking other extralegal measures. The contest reached new extremes when armed men stormed in on officials who were counting ballots in Dublin Gulch, a Daly stronghold, and killed one of the judges. Although the perpetrators were never identified, suspicions pointed to the Clark machine.

And yet murder wasn't enough to assure victory. When the state legislature convened for balloting in January 1899, the votes were split among W.A., Daly's man, and a rising populist faction. W.A. reached deeper into his coffers for bribes. In Helena, the morning greeting was "What's the price of votes today?" Charlie, philosophical about his father's chances, mused, "We'll either send the old man to the Senate or the poorhouse."

The payoffs were so overt that before the legislators even began balloting, a committee was convened to investigate accusations of corruption. One state senator stunned the panel by producing $30,000 in bills, which he claimed were given to him by W.A.'s attorney, John Wellcome. More damning, he said that when Charlie and other Clark agents got word that he was coming forward to expose the attempted payoff, they responded first with threats, then with an offer of $300,000. Daly's papers crowed that W.A. had been caught red-handed. The Clark papers parried with SET UP!

The Senate impaneled a grand jury. Forty-four witnesses testified while Charlie and his gang continued to court the still-voting lawmakers. The next round of bribes started at $20,000 and topped out at $50,000. W.A.'s odds improved considerably. More votes slid into his bracket. Another boon: the grand jury dismissed the bribery charges; it was impossible to determine who had cheated more, but one thing had become obvious to the rest of the country: thanks to Clark and Daly, Montana, just a decade into the Union, was a cesspool of corruption.

On January 28, the final day of balloting, enough of Daly's holdouts had undergone a change of heart—or received sufficient financial incentive—that W.A. emerged victorious. At last he'd ascended to the Millionaires' Club. At a gala celebration, he gloated and he recriminated, charging his opponent with "treachery, falsehoods, deceit, diabolical conspiracy and almost every crime within the calendar of crime."

But Daly still had another card to play. As W.A. exulted and preened, his stocky rival maneuvered in the context that suited him best, behind the scenes. By March, libel suits had been filed against the Clark newspapers. In May, a motion was made to disbar John Wellcome. That June, as the senator-elect traveled to Virginia to see Will graduate with honors, the charges of corruption continued to pile up.

One of Clark's henchmen offered Supreme Court Justice William Hunt $100,000 and suggested that he go abroad for his health. Hunt wasn't impressed with the advice or with Clark, saying that "if his body were skinned and the skin filled with gold, it wouldn't be any inducement to me." John Wellcome was disbarred in October, a repudiation of W.A.'s claims of innocence. On December 4, W.A. was finally seated in the Senate, but within minutes of the chamber's first session, Senator Thomas Carter, who'd bested him three campaigns earlier, demanded that his election be voided.

New investigations ensued. Although the law restricted candidates to spending only $2,000 of their own money, W.A. acknowledged that he'd spent upward of $150,000 on the campaign. After multiple hearings produced a bounty of documents and testimony detailing, among other things, Charlie's nefarious practices, evidence of boodling, or graft, and the wholesale purchase of the press, W.A.'s removal from the Senate appeared inevitable.

Rather than endure the humiliation, on May 15, 1900, he rose before the body and tendered an aggrieved, tearful resignation, lamenting the persecution he imagined he'd endured: "I was never in all my life, except as by such characters as are now pursuing me, charged with a dishonorable act, and I propose to leave to my children a legacy, worth more than gold, that of an unblemished name." One might suppose he was tempting fate with such words, but the truth is he'd already determined that legacy with his actions.

A third Senate seat had now slipped away, this defeat even more ignominious than when he'd sat awaiting his triumph, acceptance speech in hand. But W.A. wasn't done with the game yet. Instead of slinking back to Montana abashed, he left Washington for New York. He lingered there until Montana's governor left the state for an assembly in Idaho—a ruse devised by allies with Charlie's help. Then W.A. returned, and the Clark-friendly lieutenant governor appointed him to the very seat he'd just vacated.

The coup, however clever it may have seemed to its perpetrators, was short-lived. The governor returned, incensed, and promptly nullified the appointment. W.A. was shrewd enough not to press his luck further.

For nearly a quarter of a century, Clark and Daly had controlled Montana's resources, politics, and press, but now new forces arrived. One was a man, the other an East Coast monopoly. Augustus Heinze, a charismatic young mining engineer from Brooklyn, had come to work for the Boston and Montana Company, but soon set out on his own, a new player in the game.

The other entity was the Amalgamated Copper Mining Company, founded by William Rockefeller and Henry H. Rogers of Standard Oil. Daly had already ceded his Anaconda holdings to Amalgamated along with the Colorado, Parrot, and Washoe Mines. As C. B. Glasscock put it, Daly turned "the 'richest hill on earth' over to 'the greatest trust on earth.'"

W.A. wasn't inclined to welcome a smart young upstart to the field. However, Heinze had taken on Daly, and W.A. saw a new opportunity to capture the Senate seat. Handsome, well-spoken, Heinze was at ease in a saloon, a parlor, and on the campaign trail, where he now served as a charismatic proxy for the tetchy, imperious Clark, who'd become at last more strategic in his efforts to court voters. Instead of throwing money at every state official, he channeled a good share of his funds into entertaining the public. His rallies were elaborate spectacles—marching bands, fireworks, drum corps. He hired a vaudeville impresario to wrangle celebrities who drew even bigger crowds. He touted an openly populist and labor-friendly platform—an eight-hour day and the abolition of scrip system at the company store, a form of peonage that kept workers indentured to their employers.

Not that he didn't still line the pockets of lawmakers, but he took a more surgical approach, directing his bribes to the most powerful members of the legislature. However subtle his methods, no one had any illusions that W.A. was a reformed man. The Democrats put on a great show that year, and in the end, voters preferred the prickly dandy they knew to the East Coast corporation they didn't. The vain little man with the funny head of hair may have been a Paris Millionaire, but he was Montana's Paris Millionaire.

On January 16, 1901, he became Montana's Senator Clark. At long last, W.A. had won the game, though one triumph forever eluded him. Two months before the election, on November 12, 1900, Marcus Daly died from complications of Bright's disease, or acute nephritis. After decades of bitter feuding, Daly still managed to deny W.A. the joy of savoring his rival's defeat.

Within months, W.A.'s alliance with Heinze collapsed. It had been a transactional relationship, and now the deal was done, Daly was gone, and Heinze wasn't a coconspirator anymore but a competitor again.

W.A.'s populist rants against Amalgamated's monopolistic evils would prove just as brief as his allegiance to the Brooklyn transplant. W.A. turned around and sold out to the trust.

W.A. did truly abhor corporations and answering to shareholders. When he did form trusts, they were usually organized with his attorney W. M. Bickford holding one share, Will holding one, and him the rest. One theory for his turnabout, and it seems plausible, is that Amalgamated's agents had amassed evidence of campaign corruption—it couldn't have been hard to come by—and they were prepared to make it public. If W.A. was facing the prospect of an investigation and a fourth disgrace, his actions make sense. He was sixty-two. He had his title. He'd paid dearly for it and this time he wouldn't let it go.

Whatever pain Clark felt at relinquishing his long-held independence was surely alleviated by the spoils the new arrangement offered. Previously, Butte had been a town that made its money from copper. Now it boomed with copper stocks. Clark still retained a number of businesses in Montana, though the profits from those paled next to what was being extracted from his pit in Arizona's Black Mountains, and that March he took his seat in the Senate and held it for the next six years.

Will may have wandered the farthest—Europe, Algiers, Egypt—but he was the one who came home. Maizie and Kate were settled in New York. Charlie had recently made a hasty departure to the West Coast after misjudging his powers of persuasion. He'd tried to blackmail a local judge into siding with Clark interests in a court battle against their former ally, Heinze, and found himself facing an arrest warrant instead. Exile for the family bagman was relatively painless. He decamped to California, bought an estate in San Mateo, built a private racetrack, and spent $125,000 on a colt named Whiskaway.

After graduation, Will returned to Butte. Temp came too and the friends installed themselves at Will's father's home. After passing the bar, they were soon litigating cases, now part of the Clark machine. Buck, who'd gone to Arizona to study mining, as preparation for joining up with the operation too, arrived next. Reunited, the young men availed themselves of Butte's many diversions—society gatherings, prizefights, horse races, juke joints, and baseball games pitting the staff of the *Butte*

Miner against the *Montana Standard*. When the *Miner* team won, Will bought cases of Red Top beer. He hadn't relinquished the violin, though, and from time to time he performed at concerts with local musicians.

Despite the enticements of the town's freewheeling and infamous nightlife, Will remained on the path to propriety. On June 19, 1901, the twenty-four-year-old lawyer knelt beside nineteen-year-old Mabel Duffield Foster in her family's parlor and made his marriage vows. The *San Francisco Examiner* reported that the slender young woman with curly dark hair and a quick smile was known as "the belle of Butte." It also noted that Will had "a habit of twitching his eyebrows, which in combination with his piercing steel-colored eyes, gives him a slightly sinister expression." Despite this tic, Will was considered a respectable young attorney, and like his mother, Mabel was much beloved in Butte, where her father was a prominent merchant. The match was warmly hailed.

With only forty guests, Will's nuptials were a small affair compared with his sister Katie's the year before in Manhattan. There, throngs had attended her opulent wedding to Lewis Rutherford Morris, whose family dated back to the pre-Revolutionary era and had once owned what is now the Bronx and much of New Jersey. Nevertheless, Will and Mabel produced an elegant and festive night for Butte. Onlookers gathered in the street to watch the guests alight from their carriages, the women arrayed in pink silk, yellow satin, black net, and diamonds. Carnations, lilies, roses, ferns, and palms filled the Fosters' house. A string orchestra serenaded the wedding party. Mabel wore a chiffon gown of white taffeta trimmed in duchesse lace. It cost $5,000.

There was much talk about the bride's trousseau, especially one dress made entirely of copper. The Senator—the honorific was his name from now on—had bought it in Paris. The wedding date had been moved several times to accommodate his changing schedule. He also presented the newlyweds with a check for $100,000.

The couple honeymooned for several months in Europe, where they attended Wagner's *Ring* cycle at Bayreuth. They returned to Montana, ready to begin life as one of Butte's most fashionable young couples, hosting dinner parties in the Clark family's Granite Street mansion, where guests drank from crystal glasses that had belonged to the Bourbon dynasty. Yet they were invested in more than frivolity. Will donated $5,000 to establish a library for the inmates of the Deer Lodge penitentiary. At Christmastime he and Mabel handed out presents to the children in the Paul Clark Home, the orphanage founded by Will's father, around the corner from the new home and stables that Will had built on Galena Street. That spring, Mabel was expecting, as was Will's sister Katie.

Even progeny could be a game. The Senator announced he would award a prize to his first grandson: $1 million. Maizie's daughter, his first grandchild, hadn't merited such a trophy.

On December 1, 1902, an exultant Will sent the telegram: "I won." William Andrews Clark III had arrived, a healthy, blue-eyed millionaire.

But the new father's jubilation soon faded. The labor had been difficult, and Mabel suffered severe complications. Surgery followed. Sepsis set in. A specialist arrived from Denver. At first, the newspaper's daily reports were hopeful, but by Christmas the physicians feared the worst. On New Year's Eve, Mabel was said to be resting easily. She died the next day.

The Senator arrived by special train. Mourners streamed through St. John's Episcopal Church to pay their respects. Just over a year before, Buck and Temp had been witnesses at the courthouse when Will and Mabel signed their marriage license. Now his friends shouldered her coffin into the church.

After his mother's death, Will had drifted, studying the violin in Paris, traveling through Europe and North Africa. Then after Paul died, his trajectory had become clear. The way forward was a law degree, then a profession, then marriage, then a son—a steady progression into respectable adulthood. Now, at twenty-five, a father and a widower, Will swerved.

Grief, Buck Mangam believed, accounted for what came next in Will's life. In July, he was arrested for hitting a pedestrian while driving in Denver. Bail was paid, charges dropped, but it was a preview of coming recklessness. Will left his law practice. He turned not to the violin but the racetrack.

Like Charlie, Will spent lavishly on horses. Miss Georgie, Bon Voyage—he followed his stallions and trotters to Seattle, Providence, and Lexington. A reporter noted, though, that the elder Clark brother, in addition to his equestrian pursuits, was also a devotee of the "manly art of self-defense"—most unlike Will, the implication seemed to be.

When he wasn't at the track, Will could be found at the prizefights and the saloons. Sordid affairs ensued with actresses and dancers. Opportunities for dissolution abounded in Butte—parlor houses, burlesques, screened-in stalls at the Theatre Comique where the chorus girls tended to their customers as the revue played onstage. It's possible that Will's liaisons weren't restricted to women. However, Buck, who took close note of this period in his friend's life, didn't suggest this (and surely would have if he so much as suspected it). Still, these were wastrel years, decadent and rash.

Will's sister Katie was living a relatively placid existence in Morristown, New Jersey, with her husband, but his other siblings couldn't be held up as models of decorum. Maizie had proven deft at throwing costume parties at her home in Navarro Flats, including one fête billed as a mock gambling den and another where the guests dressed up as vegetables. That fall, she'd shocked friends and garnered headlines when she began divorce proceedings against her husband.

She made more news when a Mrs. Elizabeth R. Vlasto sued her for $500,000 for alienation of affection from her husband. Maizie, it turned out, was traveling through Europe with the gentleman in question, a Greek national who'd become a favorite in society circles. A photo from one of her parties of "Count" Vlasto, as he was nicknamed, and Maizie gazing raptly at one another, both in "Oriental" dress, had been widely circulated. Upon her return to America, Charlie and Kate rushed to meet their sister at the dock to shield her from reporters. Her indignant father spoke at length to reporters about the impossibility of a romance between his daughter and the so-called count: "Any talk about her infatuation for him is nonsense," the Senator insisted, and then added with no apparent self-awareness, "He is old enough to be her grandfather." The matter was settled out of court, and Vlasto was summarily dispatched as well.

Charlie's dalliances were well known. A notorious womanizer, he was a familiar presence at the gaming tables in Monaco and Biarritz. His capers seemed to belong to a man who knew he'd never measure up to his powerful father, so he might as well drink and spend and debauch. Will's carousing, however, held a darker strain than his siblings' antics. His debauchery may well have been, as Buck believed, the result of sorrow at Mabel's loss. It may also have stemmed from another kind of torment, loathing turned inward. The delicate boy had become a desperate man.

The Senator wasn't pleased. Talking to a reporter, he made the rueful observation that his great wealth may not have been good for his children. He didn't elaborate, but it's not difficult to parse out. He knew how to build an empire. His children only knew how to squander the spoils.

Charlie was an inveterate drunk, gambler, and cheat. Maizie had been sued for having an affair with an older married man. When Charlie and Maizie slipped, the Senator stood by them both. If there were private disagreements, they never surfaced in public. But this wasn't the case with Will. In April 1904, a Minneapolis newspaper reported that father and son hadn't spoken in over a year, a startling rift, especially since the Senator was quite ill from mastoiditis, a now rare but serious ear infection. Will had broken also with his siblings. The Clarks always united against the world—never against one of their own.

Whether Will initiated the break or had been frozen out wasn't detailed. The newspapers followed him to racetracks in Rhode Island, Kentucky, Washington, and California, but his other exploits went undocumented. He may have been discreet, or the journalists may have been toeing the line between what could be exposed and what couldn't. By summer, the Senator had recovered from his illness, and the breach between father and son had been repaired, but the bond would soon be tested again.

Rumors abounded that the Senator was on the verge of announcing his engagement to his protégée, Anna La Chapelle. The rumors were mistaken. A wedding wasn't in the future. It had already happened. Three years earlier, in fact, in Marseille. At least that was what W.A. claimed. Not only was the sixty-five-year-old man married to his twenty-four-year-old ward, but they were also the parents of a two-year-old daughter. Louise Amelia Andrée was born in August 1902, in Spain, six months before W.A.'s millionaire grandson. A year later,

Anna gave birth to a son named Paul, but the infant died after only a few days.

All of this was news not only to the general public, but also to Will and his siblings and even to Anna's own mother. No one believed there was anything proper about the relationship or that the couple had been married before Andrée's birth, but W.A. was rich and he offered a story. It wasn't a persuasive one. The wedding date and place didn't square up with his documented travel in 1901. A state law required people to disclose their marital status when purchasing property in Montana; never in the past three years had the Senator included Anna's name on any contracts. But of course, he'd broken laws before.

People might not believe the trumped-up marriage had ever taken place, certainly not when W.A. claimed it had, but they allowed it. Like the reporters' coded jibes about Will's delicate temperament, the truth could be known and denied at the same time. The world that would tolerate the Senator's patently fake story was the same one that wouldn't abide Oscar Wilde's truth.

The warden at Reading Gaol predicted that the writer would be dead within two years of his release. Wilde outlived that forecast but not by much. He was released from prison on May 19, 1897. Freedom meant exile. He reunited, briefly and disastrously, with Lord Douglas in Naples, and then traveled alone to Paris, where the once insouciant dandy became a grotesque, bloated specter, missing his front teeth. He haunted the boulevards and loitered in cafés to keep warm, hoping a friendly face might pass and pay his bill. A few stalwart friends stood by him, but to most, he'd become a figure for contempt and pity. Prison had broken him. A fall in the gaol had damaged his ear, and untreated, it had grown infected, the infection spreading to his brain. He spent his final days in agony and delirium in a dirty room in the Hôtel d'Alsace in Saint-Germain-des-Prés. He died on November 30, 1900.

The author hadn't survived his transgressions, but W.A. certainly would. Publicly, the Senator's adult children rallied to his defense. Privately, they agonized. Their father was the copper king, and they were the children of the late queen. The mistress was their father's wife now, and in their eyes she was a pretender to the throne. Clark reassured his first family—his imperial issue—that they wouldn't be usurped in the way he knew best, through the transfer of assets. In his will, he stipulated that after his death Anna and her children would have to vacate the mansion in New York. Each son was granted a fiefdom. The Senator installed Charlie as the head of the United Verde Mine in Arizona. To Will, he signed over the deed of the Granite Street mansion in Butte, and made him the director of two Montana enterprises, the Elm Orlu Mining Company and the Timber Butte Mill. Will named his friend Buck Mangam treasurer and secretary of both.

Perhaps sensing her welcome might not be a warm one, Anna didn't rush to join her husband in America. Paris had been her home for almost a decade, and she remained there. Two years later, on June 9, 1906, she gave birth to a second daughter, Huguette Marcelle. She stayed in Paris with her daughters until W.A. finished his long-coveted and mostly undistinguished Senate term.

He'd spent most of it continuing the expansion of his own business, launching a railroad in San Pedro and other ventures. Now with his young family back in Manhattan, he poured his energy into overseeing the construction of a gargantuan mansion of grooved limestone with beaux arts garnishes that rose—erupted, rather—at the corner of Fifth Avenue and Seventy-Seventh Street. When it was finally complete in 1911, "Clark's Folly," as the structure was often called, would cost more than $7 million and house some 120 rooms, including the Salon Doré, an eighteenth-century drawing room with gilded walls that had been transported from Paris, as well as a swimming pool, Turkish baths, and a quarantine suite high up in the domed tower.

Will, too, was looking to make a different life for himself. It may have been the new responsibility that his father accorded him. It may have been that he'd grown weary of his own dissipation. Whatever the cause, Will was thirty now and his episodes of hard living belonged to another, younger man.

As the story went, one day in the spring of 1907, he picked up the telephone and was so charmed by the operator that he inquired further. She turned out to be Alice McManus Medin, a recent divorcée. Will found the dark-eyed brunette as charming in person as she had been at the switchboard, and seven days after Alice patched through Will's call, they were married in a small, private ceremony.

Will and Tertius, undated.

Will and Alice, undated.

However, thanks to a friend of Alice's in Waterloo, Iowa, the paper there gave a very different account of the courtship, reporting that the newlyweds had known each other for a couple years, and that little Tertius had been their matchmaker: "It is said that the million dollar baby made them very friendly to each other by the baby taking a sudden attachment for Mrs. Medin, who is very beautiful, while one day [out] for an airing." The development had not pleased Mr. Medin, a grocer and saloon keeper, and a divorce soon followed.

Whether this was the full story or not—most likely not—it must have been closer to the truth than the telephone ruse. Surely people in Butte knew that was a sham. In any case, Will's new marriage meant that his wilder years were behind him. Now, with Alice, he set out on a new path, not in Butte, nor in Paris, but back to Los Angeles.

4

ALBERT'S CHOICE

Come to California. Begin again. This, as Will Clark knew, is the state's promise. Farther to the north, in Sacramento, young Albert Weis Harrison was about to learn this, though not for himself, at least not yet. In this case, the reinvention was his father's.

Few traces exist of the boy's early years, but what is clear is that his time with his sister in the Gloucester boardinghouse was short, and the two were soon peeled apart; Mark left New England and took Albert with him, while their mother reclaimed Gladys.

In Chicago, Jennie was starting over too. She married a businessman named William Lawrence and briefly called herself Genevieve, before settling on the more subdued Jean. For the rest of his life, her son would refer to her as Jean Lawrence. Only on rare occasions was she "mother."

In Sacramento, Mark found a job at C. P. Nathan, a department store a few blocks from where Collis Huntington and Mark Hopkins once sold shovels to would-be miners, back when the town was a muddy way station between San Francisco and the gold of the Sierra foothills, back before they'd launched the Central Pacific Railroad with Leland Stanford and Charles Crocker. By the time father and son arrived, the frontier dust had settled, the Big Four were gone, and the Gilded Age had nearly gorged itself to completion. The country was rolling into its so-called Progressive Era.

Mark rose swiftly from clerk to buyer to manager until he'd made enough of a name for himself that he put it on a shingle outside a storefront at the Golden Eagle Hotel at the bustling intersection of K and Seventh Streets. On March 30, 1911, with a business partner, he threw open the doors of the Mark Harrison Company. Hundreds thronged across the wooden sidewalk to marvel at the verde marble tabletops, polished oak floor, and gleaming walnut woodwork. In the balcony, an orchestra played jaunty numbers from the latest musicals, and down below, Mark pulled aside a plush green curtain, ornamented with a gold *H*, to reveal a row of handsome suits. On the way out, each visitor received a carnation.

Home for young Albert was upstairs at the Golden Eagle, where he shared corridors with congressmen, lobbyists, salesmen, tourists, and other wayfarers. In Gloucester, he and his father were tenants. Now they were guests, indefinitely. Erected in the 1850s, the four-story Italianate building had survived fires and floods. Its saloon served as the unofficial clubhouse for Republican lawmakers, while across the street, at the Capitol Hotel, the Democrats made the barroom their headquarters. As many, or more, bills were negotiated, compromised, and pork-barreled in those dimly lit drinking establishments as at the actual capital building.

At night the sign for the Pantages movie palace glowed in the dark while trolley cars trundled past. In the saloon, lobbyists and politicians cut the ends off their cigars and ordered another round. Albert moved among chambermaids and bellboys, a child in an adult landscape. In the years to come, he'd be a man accustomed to concierges, at ease in conversation with strangers in lobbies. For now, he was a well-dressed boy wandering the hotel's parlors and billiard room. Downstairs, his father clothed the men who made the laws. Power and money filled the air like the aromas from someone else's meal.

You could enter a higher class, it seemed, by catering to it. The ads for Mark's clothing store featured a coat of arms: *M* and *H* twined above a crown—suggesting a noble line of Harrisons dating back generations—and a banner proclaimed "Distinctly High Class Clothes." The store on K Street saw steady traffic. Trophies for local harness races gleamed in the windows. Mark vacationed in Lake Tahoe, and his fishing successes made the papers. He traveled to the East Coast to replenish his stock with the latest fashions and to see his other children. The once-rootless salesman had become as fixed as he'd ever be.

Although he was well liked, Albert's father had detractors; chief among them was his partner, local merchant Samuel Stone. A year after they opened the store, Mark bought Stone out for $7,500. Soon, though, rumors reached the former partner that he'd been duped, and he subsequently sued Mark, alleging that the salesman had falsely claimed business was falling off and thus had persuaded Stone to sell his stake for less than its value. The plaintiff also claimed Mark had pulled off the con with the help of a friend, who'd told Stone that Mark was "indulging in excessive use of intoxicants."

It's a skilled and self-knowing hustler who deploys his reputation as a drunk for his own gain—a maneuver well suited to a frontier town. Had Mark Harrison arrived in America earlier, had he truly been a contemporary of Clark, as his children once claimed, his schemes might've yielded him more spoils—or gotten him shot. In the latter respect, he was a lucky man. Stone's suit came to nothing, and Mark's business continued to thrive. But his health was poor. He'd developed Bright's disease, the same condition that felled Marcus Daly. During particularly painful episodes, Mark would travel north to the Sierra foothills for mineral bath treatments at the luxury resort in Richardson Springs.

This may be why Albert's time at the Golden Eagle came to an abrupt end in March 1913 and he was packed off to boarding school in Marin County. It's possible there were further reasons for the sudden change. The same suspicions that hovered over Will Clark loomed over young Albert; he, too, seemed to be a delicate boy. The boarding school's blunt mission was to stamp out delicacy of any sort or, in the words of the handbook, "to see that every cadet leaves [the school] better and more manly than when he entered."

It was the middle of the spring term when the sixteen-year-old arrived at Hitchcock Military Academy in San Rafael. Built at the base of Mount Tamalpais, surrounded by groves of eucalyptus and redwoods, the school's lush setting belied the bullies and demerits that awaited. Albert wasn't a guest anymore but a cadet. He made his home in a cramped dorm room, with just enough space for a bed, desk, and chest of drawers.

Every morning at 6:30 a.m. the bugle blared. He pulled on drab olive fatigues and rushed out to the quad with the other cadets for drills in the cold air—jumping jacks, sit-ups, push-ups. The handbook was most emphatic about "the expansion of the chest which is so important to the growing boy."

Breakfast, rushed and clamorous, came next in the mess hall. Then first recitation: *How many changes can be rung with ten bells, taking 7 at a time? From a company of 40 soldiers, how many different pickets of 6 men can be taken? How many permutations can be formed of the 26 letters of the alphabet, taken 5 at a time? How many permutations can be formed of the letters in the word* forming, *taken all together?*

Gone were his derby tweed breeks, wool serge trousers, and double-breasted waistcoat. At least for the Sunday dress parade he got to wear blue dress pants with a black braid. No more one-reelers at Pantages either.

Back to the quad. *Close ranks, march! Present, arms! Order, arms! Parade, rest! Attention!*

Second recitation: *Describe the discovery of gold in California and the rush thither? What difference did* one year *make in the population of California? What doctrine did Douglas apply to Kansas and Nebraska? Was Douglas a patriot? Chase? Sumner? Pierce? A person borrows $5254; how much must he pay in annual instalments in order that the whole debt may be discharged in 12 years, allowing 4½ per cent compound interest? Compare the Panic of 1873 with that of 1837, explaining the likenesses and differences.*

While Albert studied the economic crises of the former century and shivered under a drill sergeant's orders, his sister pursued a different course. Life in Chicago was far more expansive and diverting for the eighteen-year-old Gladys, at least according to a news article that surfaced a couple months after Albert was shunted off to military school.

Their mother's second husband was an executive with Johns-Manville, the leading manufacturer of asbestos during the country's construction boom, which meant that Gladys and her siblings enjoyed a well-appointed home on the city's South Side and that their stepfather traveled frequently for business, often accompanied by their mother.

According to a local reporter, one such afternoon in May when her parents had left town, Gladys and her older sister Claire, who'd taken to calling herself by her middle name, Leicester, had a consultation:

> "Oh, Gladys," said the fair and sprightly Leicester Harrison to her younger sister, also fair and sprightly, as they sat alone in their luxuriously furnished apartments, "let's start something."

Gladys smiled and showed a row of white teeth like pearls in the coral setting of her ruby lips.

"Let's."

Delicious consensus achieved, the weekend began, first with two admirers named Jack and Freddie who arrived in "a low, rakish automobile." From there, they proceeded to various nightclubs. "They cabareted. They tangoed. They turkey trotted." The sisters also fought over their male companions and, later, when a manager refused them a room at the City Hall Square Hotel, one of the owners, a nightlife figure named "Smiley," interceded on their behalf. The diligent reporter tracked their exploits into the next morning when Gladys slipped home alone. Leicester was intercepted by a cop and the girls' mother and stepfather, upon learning of the escapade, cut their trip short.

Surely whatever discipline Gladys and Leicester faced in the wake of their night on the town was less punitive than anything Albert endured in the barracks. He rarely spoke of his time at Hitchcock, but the school and its oppressive atmosphere have been immortalized in the work of the writer Stephen Vincent Benét.

Three years before Albert's arrival, the adolescent Benét enrolled at the military academy. Although Benét stayed for only a year, the experience made such a deep impression on him that he conjured it in his poem "The General Public," published in 1918. Written in homage to Robert Browning's "Memorabilia," about a man's kaleidoscoping memories, Benét recalls a school where "buildings reeked with vapor, black and harsh," and "a howling crowd of boys" set upon a classmate, "his back against the battered door, / His pile of books scattered about his feet," as they pelted him with dirt clods and stones.

A few years later, in his first novel, *The Beginning of Wisdom,* Benét fictionalized the school as Kitchell Academy, a brutish place run by a petty man who brags about his degrees and toadies up to visiting parents in the mess hall while a cadet discovers part of "a pearly worm inside a half-eaten leaf of cabbage." Albert's own experience might well have resembled that of the novel's young narrator, who's terrorized for being dreamy and effeminate. Eventually the fictional boy advances in the school's eyes and comes to possess "the muscles and the bag of dirty stories that will keep him from being bullied at all, that may even permit him to bully some one else."

But Albert didn't grow into a boy with muscles and a bag of dirty stories. Slight, small for his age, the salesman's son remained the kind of boy whose difference—delicacy, if that's the word for it—fills other boys with rage. That he was the target of dirt clods, stones, and mob aggression seems likely. He didn't last a year. It's unclear whether Albert, like young Benét, pleaded to be released, was ordered to go, or if other circumstances led to his departure. In any event, he was gone by Christmas.

With that departure, he vanishes from historical record. Despite Mark Harrison's local success, newspaper reporters weren't inclined to track the Harrisons with the same vigor they applied to the Clarks and their extravagant, often scandalous doings. The merchant bought an electric sign for his store, but he did not, as the Senator did, buy an entire bronze factory out of pique because he believed they overcharged him for the doors he'd ordered for his mansion on Fifth Avenue.

Mark still garnered news mentions when he traveled east to purchase $20,000 worth of new stock in the fall of 1915. The *Sacramento Union* reported that the merchant was "optimistic concerning the company's business." So much so that by the end of the year he'd bid on a house on Third Avenue, a two-story bungalow with eight rooms. After all the boardinghouses and hotel rooms, the Harrisons would have a home.

And yet while Mark had finally found the stability that had eluded him for so long, his health was failing. In early January, the effects of kidney disease had worsened. He traveled to Richardson Springs for more treatments, but these gave little relief. A week later, he returned to Sacramento and was admitted to Sisters' Hospital. On February 1, 1916, Mark died of uremic poisoning. He was buried in the city's Jewish cemetery at the corner of Thirty-Second Street and Alhambra Boulevard. His death certificate stated he was fifty-three.

The store he'd established five years earlier was soon closed. Two weeks after the salesman's death, $17.50 overcoats were marked down to $15, and then $12.50—"all sales positively cash only." By April 1, the sign outside the Golden Eagle Hotel was gone.

Mark did not leave a will. His estate, which amounted to $15,000, the value of his clothing stock, was to be divided among his five children. However, according to his son's terse recollection, this isn't what happened. Years later, his sense of resentment remained sharp, when he wrote, "Gladys got most at the time, she had only seen him but short visits, I had to live with him, I had $50 a month and not for long, I was 'Gypped' out of that." There was much to resent—a stolen inheritance, a harsh stint in boarding school, a precarious existence bound to an alcoholic father.

A family is a cluster of disparate revolving bodies, orbits within orbits, whirling through space. Like satellites, children are caught in the force fields of larger, denser objects. Years before, Albert and Gladys were pulled apart from their mother and siblings. Then the boy was peeled away from his sister, alone with his charismatic, erratic father. With Mark's death, the last bond that tethered Albert slipped away. He'd been named for the esteemed patriarch, but he was now a stray in his own family, a fatherless child who knew his absent mother by her first and last names.

He'd chosen none of it. Not his name, nor his life, nor his family. He hadn't chosen New York, New Hampshire, Maine, Massachusetts, or California, as he hadn't chosen the Hitchcock Military Academy. He did not choose to be abandoned by his family. However, on the morning of June 22, 1916, in a room he'd rented at the Hotel Florence on Taylor Street in San Francisco, he chose to end his life.

The weather that day was fair, light breezes from the bay. He was eighteen. The room was $20 a month. His father had been dead for five months. He swallowed one poison, and then, very certain about the choice he was making, he swallowed a second.

There is no record of who discovered Albert in his hotel room, nor the names of the poisons, which instead of ending his life saved it by contraindicating each other. He was taken first to the Central Emergency Hospital and then to Mount Zion for recovery.

Two days later, an article headlined TWO DRUGS USED BY YOUTH TRYING TO END HIS LIFE ran on the bottom of the second page of the *San Francisco Chronicle*. Its author recorded all that appeared to be known about Albert Weis Harrison in 1916: that he'd taken a room at the hotel on Taylor Street, that his father had died earlier that year, and that he'd briefly attended military school, where he was said to have been "temperamental, moody and morose."

There are so few glimpses of Albert and Gladys in their early years, and yet the two news stories that do exist are a telling study in contrasts. One is a tongue-in-cheek vignette about a pair of "fair and sprightly" sisters having a lark on the town, the other a curt report of a young man in despair.

His sister hadn't been raised by their father, but she seemed to have inherited his instinct for the hustle, for acting on the world rather than being acted upon. Albert, though, had no such self-serving or even self-preserving impulses. Perhaps the stakes for his transgressions were much higher.

In 1916, "temperamental" was code, and its appearance in the article about Albert's suicide attempt was surely not a coincidence. Two years later in a San Francisco courtroom, the word was decrypted during a grand jury trial of some thirty men who'd been arrested in an elaborate sting operation. The police department's so-called morals squad had staked out the home of Hugh Allen, a music teacher who hosted parties in his studio on Baker Street. Salesmen, brokers, decorators, cops, and soldiers were arrested for, among other offenses, violating Section 286 of the California Penal Code, "wherein the infamous crime against nature is made a felony."

Though the word *homosexual*, like *heterosexual*, did exist by 1918, it was never uttered during the trial. *Gay* had been used in the nineteenth century to refer to prostitutes ("gay ladies") and brothels ("gay houses") as well as to male prostitutes, but it wouldn't emerge in its current sense until the 1930s and '40s. Instead, nearly all the defendants were asked whether they were "temperamental," and all were presented with lists and asked to identify others who were.

One, a young man from Germany, was perplexed by the word's sexual connotation:

> **Q:** What did you think it meant?
>
> **A:** Temperamental. What I understand—I don't know if it is. A person is temperamental if they enjoy or love beautiful things, art, music, or any of that kind.

Another, a soldier who was being held on Alcatraz while waiting court martial, lost his patience at the word's deliberate obscurity:

> **Q:** Are the names of all those people that were there on this list?
>
> **A:** A number of the people that were there that night were strangers to me and I could not say. I could tell you how many on that list were there.
>
> **Q:** They were all the same class of people, were they, all temperamental, as far as you could see?
>
> **A:** Well, to use that word—whatever it means—Why don't you use the good old word "perverts" and be done with it?

Pervert wasn't a word to be used in polite company. *Temperamental* was, although of course both the German immigrant's and the soldier's definitions could be true. A man could love art and music and he could have sex with other men, but, as Oscar Wilde brutally learned, the court cared only about the latter.

The legal language for those arrested for sex acts tended to be vague: "social vagrant," "degenerate," and "dissolute person." The behavior was "lewd and lascivious" or deemed "moral turpitude," another shadowy phrase alluding to sex between men. These terms were also used to characterize prostitution and sexual assault, so when reading archival accounts, it's often unclear what has actually taken place. The words mask as much as they reveal.

But the consequences were clear. Violating Section 286, or engaging in sodomy, carried a penalty of five years to life in prison. Even a misdemeanor charge of "conspiracy to commit acts tending to lower the morals of the community" could result in a prison sentence, not to mention public ruin. Hugh Allen, whose home had been the target of the raid, fled to Honduras. When police arrived at the house of an accountant who'd been named in the scandal, the man shot himself in the head. In the face of such disgrace, this was hardly surprising.

In 1914, two years before Albert checked in to his room at the Hotel Florence, a forty-four-year-old bank director named John Lamb walked into a pharmacy in Long Beach and bought a packet of cyanide. He then headed for an outcropping of rocks near Point Fermin, where he swallowed the poison. Unlike Albert, he did not take a second, and later that day two women out for a walk discovered his body. The note he left behind read in part, "I am crazed by reading the paper this morning. . . . I could not endure this publicity as I had not a chance to deny it."

The day before, under the headline LONG BEACH UNCOVERS "SOCIAL VAGRANT" CLAN, the *Los Angeles Times* reported his arrest along with thirty other men and the "astonishing story of a secret society." The paper published the names and the professions of those accused, and after more men were spotted trying to buy cyanide, the health department banned its sale in Long Beach.

News articles ginned up outrage and titillation with alleged details:

> At the functions of this peculiar society all the members on arriving changed street clothes for kimonos, silk underwear and hosiery, and some wore women's wigs. The members made up with powder and paint as for the stage, according to the recital of the officers, and the orgies were attended by at least fifty at each meeting.

A "purity campaign" followed. When the exposé and subsequent trials finally concluded, there'd been one suicide, two acquittals, much newsprint, and over $5,000 in fines collected. Up north in Sacramento, lawmakers enacted Section 288a of the penal code, specifying that fellatio and cunnilingus were felonies punishable by up to fifteen years in prison.

In both the Long Beach sting and the Baker Street raid, two worlds were made visible. In one, men gathered and performed and called each other nicknames; in the other, a web of police officers and extortionists entrapped people in bathrooms, shook them down for ten and twenty dollars.

The Long Beach scandal provides a glimpse into a shadow world, but it tells us much of what we already know: that people will follow desire. They will create codes, go underground, find each other through secret clubs in private apartments and hotel rooms. Sometimes men will dress in women's clothes, put on makeup, sing songs, and call each other endearing names, but this isn't new information. More than a window onto same-sex communities, the revelations from the Long Beach purity campaign and the Baker Street raid lay bare the treacherous and often deadly system of entrapment and extortion that enshrouded those worlds. The criminalization of men who had sex with other men suggested they were a threat to society, but they had more to fear from society—from the state, from cops, from reporters, and a shadow web of extortionists and blackmailers.

Today the words for men who desire men are different from what they were in 1916, when they were already changing from what they had been when Oscar Wilde was on trial. Language is not fixed. The words will change again, but desire continues. It always does—not only for other people but also for one's life to be different from what it is.

In 1916, Albert desired that his life be over. Whatever led him to that moment can only be imagined. In spite of his determination to erase himself, he survived. He would try again, only this time he'd take a different path.

Parents teach their children lessons they never intend. A lesson from Jennie: you can give yourself a new name—if not Genevieve, then Jean. A lesson from Mark: you can make a new home—again and again and again. From Kishinev to Syracuse to Galveston to Manhattan to Manchester to Portland to Gloucester to Sacramento and all the others in between. And each time you leave one place, you can leave behind the person you'd been there.

Perhaps Albert never thought of Jean Lawrence or Jennie Weis or Mark Harrison or whoever his father had been when he realized that there were other choices than the one he'd made at Hotel Florence, but it was his parents who taught him the most important lesson, that you can end yourself by becoming someone else.

5

THE WALL

Will, Alice, and Tertius, in West Adams, undated.

The neighbors did not welcome the wall. Eleven feet high at spots, it was an unfriendly arrival in Los Angeles's exclusive West Adams enclave of leafy streets and elegant Victorians. However, in 1906, D. C. McCan, the young millionaire from New Orleans who'd overseen its construction on his property, was unmoved by the disapproval. As far as he was concerned, his palatial new home at the corner of West

Adams Boulevard and Cimarron Street required a garden, and a garden required a wall, and so the matter was settled.

Four years later, when Will Clark bought the estate from McCan, the 700-foot redbrick barrier was a deciding factor. As the father of an eight-year-old millionaire, Will had to contend with an array of fears, including kidnapping and robbery. The neighbors may have found the looming fortification on the corner inhospitable, but for Will, the wall meant peace of mind. Inside the wrought-iron gates on the hilltop in Kinney Heights, his family was safe.

To be protected, though, didn't mean one had to also be constrained, as evidenced by the hundreds of roses blooming in the garden and by the house itself. A 70-foot arched loggia fronted the fifteen-room mansion at 2205 West Adams Boulevard. Inside, the main staircase rose up to a landing as large as a reception hall. The dining room, paneled with dark mahogany, opened into a solarium. To the south, the view stretched over grasslands and marshes out to the ocean, though eventually that vista would be obstructed by more development, as Thomas Ince, "Father of the Western," moved his film company from the Palisades to the emerging Culver City, later followed by the Hal Roach Studios.

The LA elites were quick to embrace the new arrivals. YOUNG MATRON WHO HAS BEEN CALLED THE MOST BEAUTIFUL WOMAN IN LOS ANGELES ran the 1909 headline above a photo of Alice in the *Los Angeles Herald*. Mrs. W. A. Clark Jr., as she was known in her frequent appearances in the society pages, adapted to her new position, hosting teas for neighboring matrons and visiting figures of note. At Christmas, she threw elaborate luncheons at the YMCA for the "cash girls" who worked in the department stores. Snapshots show her in unguarded moments, lounging with friends on a grassy hill, sitting at the wheel of a toy car, and gamely throwing a stick for Snooks, the Boston terrier, but her predominant image was that of the genteel young woman captured in her many studio portraits, where she's dressed in the latest Edwardian fashions, with bloused bodices, lace and ruffles, her dark hair elaborately coiffed—one charming half of a couple noted for cultural refinement and gracious hospitality.

Will had paid McCan $90,000 for the estate and most of its contents, including lamps from Ceylon, furniture and tapestries from

France, lanterns from Japan, and a lustrous chandelier from Louisiana, but he made two changes. He replaced the billiard hall on the ground floor with a library for his growing collection of rare books and music scores, and he converted the drawing room into a hall for music recitals.

He also hired a local composer and instructor named Edwin Clark to continue his musical education. And he went to Paris to pay $30,000 for a violin made by Nicolò Amati in 1623 that was believed to have belonged to Thomas Jefferson. Will brought it with him for a summer fishing expedition along the banks of Montana's Blackfoot River. The trek included guides, musicians, chefs, waiters, and an upright piano that had to be hauled sixty miles overland. They carried lumber too and built a dance pavilion on a grassy plateau, where the campers hung acetylene lamps and pitched sixteen tents, including one for the piano.

"Capitalist" was how Will identified himself to census takers. This was true in theory. He certainly enjoyed a secure and lofty perch in that system. He belonged to the same clubs as those who presided over the growing fortunes in the Southland—the Los Angeles Athletic Club, the California Club, and the Jonathan Club. LA offered myriad opportunities for the emerging generation of tycoons.

In 1892, a failed prospector named Edward Doheny and his partner, Charles Canfield, sank the town's first oil well, using a 60-foot shaft made from a eucalyptus tree. Hoping to cash in on the new oil boom, a group of investors bought a lima bean ranch several miles west, but they didn't have the same luck, so the men subdivided the farmland, called it Beverly Hills, and sold lots by the acre. Another clutch of speculators formed the Los Angeles Suburban Homes Company and bought the Lankershim and Van Nuys families' wheat fields north of the Santa Monica Mountains, eventually securing more than one hundred thousand acres. Separately and secretly, the developers induced city officials to raise the necessary funds—a final tally came to $25,000,000—from taxpayers to bankroll a 238-mile aqueduct engineered by William Mulholland that would irrigate the arid sprawl.

The water was ostensibly destined for the people of Los Angeles, but the amount that actually arrived there from its source in the Owens Valley was negligible compared to how much was diverted into sluicing the new tract homes of the San Fernando Valley into existence, and thus lining the pockets of the men behind the syndicate. These were newspaper, railroad, and banking tycoons—Moses Sherman, Ned Harriman, Harry Chandler, Edwin T. Earl, Joseph Sartori, and of course Harrison Gray Otis—all perfectly positioned to advertise the land to the people who boarded their trains and took out mortgages from their banks.

Flush with a colossal inheritance from his uncle Collis, railway magnate Henry Huntington saw the opportunity to make millions more by acquiring vast swathes of real estate, chopping those into subdivisions, and populating the fast-spreading suburbs with modest quick-to-build bungalows. Each one came with a lawn, a driveway, and usually a fruit tree, though Jewish, Asian, and Black people needn't have thought those pamphlets rhapsodizing about the sunshine were meant for them. Housing covenants restricted the properties to white buyers.

If the land wasn't divided and sold, then it could be dreamed into someplace else. William Selig, a magician turned film director from Chicago, had come for the weather and because California was on the other side of the country from Fort Lee, New Jersey, where Thomas Edison had patented the kinetoscope and sued Selig several times for pirating his invention. Los Angeles was far enough for the director to shoot one-reelers free from litigation.

Will didn't sell newspapers like Otis and Chandler or rides on the Yellow and Red Cars to housing developments like Huntington. He hadn't been part of the cabal that dammed and decimated the Owens Valley. He sold neither land nor oil nor movies nor fruit. The Clark family did have holdings in the region, including a sugar beet plantation south of LA, where they'd built the company town of Los Alamitos. However, this enterprise fell under the purview of Will's father and his uncle J. Ross, who lived just a few blocks away on West Adams Boulevard.

Will still had his dealings in Montana, though by 1910, the Clarks had sold most everything else there to Amalgamated, and he kept offices in downtown Los Angeles at the Van Nuys Hotel. Erected in 1896, the six-story beaux arts building at Fourth Street and Main was a fashionable spot for well-heeled visitors and a key nexus for Angeleno power brokers, like famed attorney Earl Rogers, a dandy, drunk, and spectacularly brilliant defense attorney, who also kept an office there. Rogers's courtroom antics drew packed crowds and provided the inspiration for Perry Mason.

Though Will rubbed elbows with the titans of industry at the same luxury hotel and in general society, he wasn't possessed by the same ambitions. He kept a close watch on the businesses in Butte, but it was Buck Mangam who inspected the smelters, applied for patents, and kept accounts. Unlike Doheny or his neighbor, the winery mogul Secondo Guasti, a former farm laborer, Will's fortune had already been made for him. And unlike Huntington or, later, J. P. Getty, both heirs as well, he wasn't driven to expand his holdings. This may be one reason Will Clark's name isn't embedded today in Southern California as others are—Sherman Oaks, Flintridge, Doheny Drive, Huntington Beach.

Will Clark and Will Garraway, undated.

While others covered the land with drilling rigs, pored over subdivision maps, and counted ticket sales, Will founded a chamber music ensemble with Eddie Clark—as he called his music teacher. They named it the Saint-Saëns Quintet for the virtuoso French composer. His father helped bring forward the electrical age and, by extension, new and more accessible forms of entertainments, but to Will the flickers coming out of the barns in Hollywood were lowbrow pursuits—traveling circuses that had put down roots. His own passions harked back to earlier forms—boxing, horse racing, literature, and music—none of which required copper wiring.

He branched out in other ways as well. In 1914, after the death of his next-door neighbor, he bought the property and demolished it to expand his own estate. As other houses on the block went on the market, he continued buying and expanding, eventually extending the servants' quarters and the laundry, and building a new garage and a three-story observatory, with the first floor devoted to mineralogical specimens, including a 657-pound meteorite.

While Will and Alice established themselves among Los Angeles's burgeoning elite, the couple remained tied to Montana. Rather than haul a piano sixty miles every summer, Will spent $400,000 to build an elaborate compound on Salmon Lake, which included a grand log cabin—the Mowitza Lodge—as well as guest cabins, a bowling alley, a billiard parlor, tennis courts, shooting range, art gallery, and swimming docks. Every summer, the couple welcomed Alice's siblings and their children, along with Temp and Buck and other friends and longtime family insiders, like Judge William Lippincott, one of W.A.'s earliest legal advisers. A jovial man with horn-rimmed glasses, the judge was credited with having brought the first typewriter to Montana. Photos of gatherings at the lodge show archery contestants, grinning fishermen with strings of trout, swimmers leaping from the docks, and Will the happy host with his charming wife at his side.

Will's bond with Alice proved strong and affectionate. She was a loving and attentive surrogate mother to young Tertius, and the rest of the family, especially the Senator, had warmly welcomed her into the fold.

"My dear sweet Alice," Will called her. In photos, she's often identified simply as "Babe."

Alice McManus Clark and Cora Sanders, undated.

The couple traveled often. They kept rooms at the Hotel Netherland at the southeast corner of Central Park in Manhattan. Photos show them lounging on ocean liners, posing in Venice, and standing beside stone fortresses in Ireland, often accompanied by Cora Sanders, a former schoolteacher and Montana native whom Will had hired as a tutor for Tertius and a kind of lady-in-waiting to Alice. Tall and severe in her bearing, Cora—or Coco, as Will delighted in calling the dour spinster—was a striking counterpart to his petite, cherubic wife.

Whatever rifts had once surfaced in the Clark family had since faded. Will welcomed his half sisters Andrée and Huguette and their mother to the summer home. His father was a frequent visitor to the West Adams mansion. In his seventies now, W.A. remained as attuned as ever to trade and markets. During a trip to Los Angeles in the summer of 1915, the *Los Angeles Times* interviewed the Senator about the Great War ravaging Europe and its implications for America.

A year had passed since Gavrilo Princip, a nineteen-year-old Bosnian Serb, shot and killed Archduke Ferdinand, heir to the Austro-Hungarian Empire, and his wife in Sarajevo, two deaths that would be followed by forty million. The industrialization of combat had arrived with machine guns and tanks. So had barbed wire, trench warfare, and chlorine gas. The possibilities for death and horror had exceeded Oscar Wilde's fears of an increasingly mechanized world.

To the copper magnate, though, war was part of the game. He was not a hawkish man, but W.A. was frank and unsentimental about how the United States had strengthened its hold on markets in Scandinavia, Spain, and South America, which had previously depended on Europe for wire for their industries. As a measure of his confidence, Clark had launched new smelters in Clarkdale, Arizona, capable of producing six million pounds of copper a month, or a monthly gross of $1,200,000.

Will, however, expressed different concerns. The copper heir announced that he would donate all his profits from munitions and other materials, as well as from investments in war bonds, which totaled over $2,000,000, to establish a fund for French orphans. Likewise, Alice threw herself into charity work, hosting events to raise money for the Red Cross, producing a carnival at the Shrine Auditorium to benefit the destitute in France, Britain, and Belgium. Back from a trip to New York in April 1917, just days after America had entered the war, she reported that "social life is at a standstill" and implored Angelenos to make personal sacrifices for the war effort.

They were by all public measures a gracious and cultivated society couple. His dissolute years behind him, Will had proved himself to be a devoted husband, a man of cultural sophistication, a generous philanthropist. And yet there were whispers.

As the juries in Oscar Wilde's trials had learned, hotels can be host to myriad transgressions. The Van Nuys Hotel was no different. It may have seemed ideal for indiscretion, but to keep his affairs separate from the rest of his life, Will would've been smarter to cross an ocean as his father had. There was talk of a porter who'd lingered in Will's suite. Talk of his attentions to a young actor. He and Alice had been married ten years when the talk reached her.

All those summers by the lake, the family they'd made with Tertius, all the society luncheons, all the charity benefits—if the talk was true,

Will was turning their life into a false front. Constance Wilde had stood by her husband, enduring public humiliation and the most private betrayals, but, according to Buck Mangam, Alice had no intention of doing so. She'd been divorced once before and she'd managed. Besides, a divorce settlement from Will Clark wouldn't send her back to the telephone switchboard.

Will's behavior had opened a chasm once before in the family and it now threatened another. This was far more grave than whatever had transpired back when he'd been a young widower. That episode took place in Butte when the Clarks ruled the town, but the family did not rule Los Angeles. The gossip that had greeted the Senator over his marriage to his ward would pale next to the scandal these rumors could unleash.

Alice's plans to leave the marriage hadn't dimmed her work as a society hostess. In early 1918, she gave a reception for Marguerite Chenu, a Parisian film curator who was giving a series of lectures called "The Imperial Honeymoon" about the romance of Napoleon and his second wife, Marie Louise, Duchess of Parma. Alice hosted a dance for friends visiting from Seattle. By April, she was in New York, where she announced she was buying $25,000 in Liberty bonds, but in May newspapers reported that she "had suffered a nervous breakdown caused by war work." Perhaps it seemed less intrusive or more decorous to portray the beloved society hostess's faltering health as a matter of exhaustion rather than print the truth, which was that, at thirty-five, Alice had been diagnosed with colon cancer. This was the first summer they did not spend at the lake, though Alice was well enough to appear at some charity concerts. The senator came to visit that June, relieved to find she was improving. In October, though, her condition worsened. Will summoned doctors from New York to administer radium treatments. The Senator rushed back to Los Angeles.

On November 11, the commanders of Allied and German forces met in a railroad car in northern France to sign the armistice, at last, ending the Great War. In spite of the rapidly spreading influenza epidemic, crowds thronged the streets. Streamers filled the air. While the world cheered, joyful and exultant, those who loved Alice gathered anxiously at her side.

"From time to time she has been able to be carried into the garden," the *Los Angeles Times* reported, "to rest among the flowers in the sunshine and from this fact encouragement is felt." But the illness was too far advanced. On November 17, Alice died at home, attended by her brother, sister, father-in-law, and husband.

For the second time, Will Clark buried his wife. Tertius, now fifteen, was old enough to mourn. The funeral service was short, attended by a few close friends and family members. Alice's body was interred in the J. Ross Clark mausoleum in Hollywood Cemetery. A service in Montana had to be postponed because of fears about contagion from influenza.

In Los Angeles, the first reports of the disease had emerged in mid-September. Within a month, city officials were reporting eight hundred cases a day. The mayor urged Angelenos to wear masks. Schools were closed and public gatherings banned, including the Liberty Day Parade, filming of mob scenes, and funerals.

"Everywhere I look for her," Will wrote to Alice's sister and her niece. "I listen for the sweet sound of her laughter and her gentle voice—but all in vain." His grief was evident and yet there were those who questioned his sorrow. It's an ugly thing to imagine that Will could've been relieved by his wife's death. Buck Mangam believed this to be the case. And though he can hardly be called an unbiased observer, he may have been right, to an extent. With Alice's passing, there was no divorce, and so there was no scandal.

Oscar Wilde loved his wife, Constance, and he was a terrible husband. He was a devoted and kind father—and a devastating one. Like Wilde, Will seems to have been capable of genuine love for his wife but not desire, and in the gap between the two festered pain and betrayal. It's possible that Will both grieved for Alice and was grateful—relieved to be free not only of the prospect of divorce but also of the suffering he'd created, her death both deliverance and torment. In his memory, Alice became the epitome of purity and goodness, and years later he would call her "one of God's sweet immaculate gifts to this sordid world." Even if her death was a ghastly reprieve, it was far from a permanent one. Although he avoided the attention that a divorce would've brought, that didn't mean the whispers were going to stop. Without a wife, they could get much louder.

Over the years, Will had continued buying the surrounding homes on his block in a piecemeal fashion, demolishing them and then extending his own property. After each house was bought and razed, the bricklayers returned to rebuild and extend the wall. No one spoke of kidnapping fears anymore, though. Tertius was away at boarding school on the East Coast. It was Will who needed protection now. Perhaps it had been all along.

6

THE MASK

William Andrews Clark Jr., photographed by Edward Weston, 1919.

At precisely noon on November 21, 1918, the whistle sounded. All across San Francisco, people pulled the masks from their faces and threw them into the streets, at last free. In the Bay Area, unlike in Los Angeles, officials had made the coverings mandatory for anyone in public.

The celebration was premature. While cases of flu had fallen, this turned out to be only a temporary ebb, and by January the infection rate had resurged. The virus continued to spread. In San Francisco, the daily cases reached six hundred and kept climbing. Authorities reinstated the citywide ordinance and the masks returned. As supplies ran low, residents used chiffon and linen. The *San Francisco Chronicle* reported people covering their faces with "fearsome looking machines like extended muzzles."

It wasn't until February, after three thousand people had died and the infection rate had fallen again, that the health department deemed it safe for the city's residents to rid themselves of the hated masks once and for all. Finally, they could breathe freely.

Except for Albert. The gauze was gone, but he still wore a mask, the one that all temperamental men wore. They watched for one another on the streets, lingering at shop windows, glancing back once, and then again. But as the circuit of signals began, they couldn't be certain they weren't stepping into a trap with an undercover cop looking to make an arrest or twenty-dollar shakedown. The shadow worlds, like hotel lobbies and the Sultan Turkish Baths, a seven-story building on Post Street "devoted to the comforts of men," were filled with double agents. It was safer to gather in someone's home, or at least it had seemed so until the stakeout at Hugh Allen's studio.

Albert now lived at 3388 Clay Street, only a few blocks from the disgraced music teacher on Baker Street. San Francisco has always been a small town where degrees of separation can be minimal to nonexistent, and so Albert, who was then working as a clerk in a shop downtown, might have known Hugh Allen and some of the other men who'd been arrested in the raids and were now on trial. He did, in fact, know the wealthy bon vivant Dick Hotaling, son of distiller A. P. Hotaling, whose whiskey warehouse was famously one of the only waterfront buildings to survive the 1906 earthquake and fire. Hotaling was called to testify about the Baker Street raid, though he was never accused of any crimes.

It seemed that fortune had found Albert at last. If he did know Hugh Allen and the other defendants, he was lucky to escape the scandal. He'd also been lucky to have avoided the war and lucky to have survived the epidemic that had killed millions of young people. And then luck struck again. The door of G.T. Marsh & Company swung open and in walked Albert's newest customer, William Andrews Clark Jr.

It's a bitter realization that in excavating queer lives we so often excavate the loathing for those lives. In combing through crime reports and editorials for traces of marginalized existences, we enter a world shot through with scorn and prurience. In trial transcripts, we don't find people but "degenerates" and "perverts." We know the details of John Lamb's death in Long Beach, but we know nothing about whom he may have loved. We know tragedy rather than joy. We know the date that Albert took two poisons to try to kill himself in the Hotel Florence but not the date that Will stepped into the Orientalist boutique at the corner of Powell and Post.

It was sometime in 1919. Three years had passed since Albert's suicide attempt. The despair had broken. Now he lived near the Presidio with an older woman named Mary Post. She was a kindly widow in her sixties with dark eyes and dark hair that she wore pulled back in a bun. Her children were grown and scattered, and Albert had become her foster son. She was, as he recalled later, "a charming old lady and a brilliant one."

How Mary Post and Albert Harrison came together is one of the enduring mysteries of his story. By the time he took the job at "the Marsh," as he called it, he was already living in her house on Clay Street. Many would assume that his later name was a fiction, but "Harrison Post" was the truth of whom Albert had been and whom he became.

He never knew the man whose name he took. Born in Pickering, Canada, John J. Post was a bookkeeper who married Mary "Nettie" Ostrander in Wisconsin in 1874. The couple moved to Seattle, where they lived for thirty years and raised two sons and a daughter. Later, they moved to New York City. After John died in 1908, Mary returned to the West Coast, closer to her children.

By the time Albert had moved into Mary's home, her eldest, Guy Bates, a successful actor in traveling theater, was making the transition into silent film. His name appeared on the marquees for *Omar the Tentmaker*, as well as in the papers for multiple divorces. Her other son, Harold, led a less newsworthy life. An insurance salesman, he and his wife lived in Juneau, Alaska. The youngest, Madeleine, was newly married, living in Los Angeles with her husband, Bob Starrett, whose father had been a founder of the Starrett Brothers, the construction company that built the Empire State Building and other skyscrapers. In later years, Harrison was often identified in newspapers as the foster brother or half brother of Guy Bates Post, likely because he had some degree of fame. However, of all the Post children, it was Madeleine who'd have the most decisive impact on his life.

And yet Albert was still very much his father's son, as well as his grandfather's grandson. Albert Weis, who'd parlayed a dry goods business into a theatrical empire, had died in New York the year before. Young Albert didn't see any inheritance, but the mercantile world was his legacy, and his brief career as a salesman would set the course of the rest of his life.

In Sacramento, his father had dressed state lawmakers and businessmen. Now at the Marsh, Albert tended to another level of power. His customers were the kind of people who saw to it that the men in Sacramento did their bidding. In some cases, the clientele were the children of those elites, and though they may not have amassed the capital, they spent the dividends at places that catered to those who could afford to alight anywhere in the world, provided there were palace hotels, chauffeured cars, and a solicitous staff at their disposal. These were people whose homes were dictated by season, such as the widowed son of a copper baron, who spent spring in Los Angeles, summer in Montana, and winter in Europe.

Surely when Will entered the store, the young clerk already knew his customer's background—knowledge of the rich and powerful was part of the job. Albert likely knew that Will's wife had died the year before and that the Clark family had recently suffered another tragedy. In early August, Will's half sister Andrée was stricken with meningitis. The sixteen-year-old died within a few days. The shocking loss crushed her parents and her little sister, Huguette, and the grief-stricken family had taken refuge at Will's lodge on Salmon Lake.

Whether Albert immediately identified the well-dressed older man with chestnut hair, his new customer may have stood out in another way. That year, Will had broken his arm playing golf and been forced to wear a cast.

The Senator's son wasn't considered an easy man to know. While Alice had been noted for her warmth and easy manner, Will often came across reticent and guarded. A photo taken by Edward Weston shows him, thin-lipped, standing against a wall, holding a cigarette tightly, a recoil in his glance, waiting, it seems, for the viewer to look away. The

Weston portrait Will preferred was of him seated, in profile, not looking at the camera but lost in the pages of a book.

There were many things that put Albert outside Will's orbit—among them his merchant class and his Jewishness. His early years with a peripatetic salesman father bore little relation to Will's opulent childhood. The legacy of wealth that did exist in the clerk's family had closed ranks without him. Albert's existence wasn't secured by mineral assets and land holdings. His life was suspended by slender threads, the fairy-tale benevolence of Mary Post and his position at the luxury boutique.

Albert's employer, George Turner Marsh, was a pioneer in many regards. Born in Australia, he was fifteen when his family sailed for the United States in 1872. They stopped first in Yokohama, where the teenager was so enamored by Japanese culture and art that he persuaded his father to let him stay behind. He found work in an import-export firm, and a few years later, having amassed a collection of fine art and objects, he rejoined his family in San Francisco and opened a "Japanese Art Repository," as the store was often described, in the Palace Hotel on Market Street, the same hotel that had welcomed Oscar Wilde in 1882.

Marsh's legacy endures. He named the city's Richmond district after his childhood neighborhood in Melbourne. He designed an exhibit of a Japanese village for the California Midwinter International Exposition that, along with Makoto Hagiwara's gardens, was converted into today's Japanese Tea Garden in Golden Gate Park.

After the 1906 earthquake and fire destroyed the Palace Hotel and the original store, Marsh reopened at Post and Powell Streets. Often considered one of the first purveyors of Asian art and furnishings in the United States, he was also one of the first retail merchants to bring his wares from behind the sales counter for display out in the open on long tables.

This was a store that invited its customers to linger and touch, to pick up the celadon-glazed charger plate from the Ming dynasty or the teacup of porcelain so thin it would've made Wilde swoon. Albert didn't stand behind a counter but instead at Will's side while the two ambled through the shop, discussing history and craftsmanship. Perhaps the conversation broke into other topics. For instance, that year the Metropolitan Opera was celebrating Enrico Caruso's twenty-fifth year in opera. Albert loved the tenor's voice.

It's the salesclerk's job to draw his customer out. He learns about the patron's life—his travels, the books he reads, what he finds beautiful, what he wants in his home. If two men hold eye contact longer than usual in a store, it's not necessarily cause for suspicion—unlike, say, a second glance in a public washroom.

Although the younger man had been raised in rented rooms, he possessed a distinct worldliness. Will could recognize the clerk's cosmopolitan air, even if it didn't come from living in Paris among tutors and nannies.

Albert was accustomed to admirers—men and women. He enjoyed both, though he preferred men. Of course, like his introverted customer, he was well aware that male attention could come at a cost. They may have belonged to different classes, but they wore the same mask.

When it came time to draw up the bill, if Will in fact bought anything that day, the two men were on opposite sides of the sale. Still, a transaction is a point of contact. Inside the Marsh they were safe. No stool pigeons, no shakedowns. At the intersection of wealth and commerce, shopping offered cover for two men to fall in love.

On October 1, 1919, the shop clerk boarded a train bound for Los Angeles. He was joined by Will and Will's majordomo, William Burgess, along with a society friend named Lillian Kohler and Will's Boston terrier, Snooks. In the years to come, traveling with an entourage would be customary—not only so there was someone to manage luggage, bookings, and other matters, but also to obscure the nature of the relationship between the two men.

The small party arrived at the new Central Station on Fifth Street. The little depot that once greeted six-year-old Will Clark was long gone, as was the Arcade Station, which had trapped exhaust from the locomotives. When he alighted from their car, Albert wasn't greeted by grime and soot but a soaring lobby and fourteen one-ton chandeliers glimmering above.

Will had been reckless after Mabel's death, and now after Alice's, it seemed, he was again. It was unquestionably rash to begin a romance with the twenty-two-year-old shop clerk. But Will's wildness—if that's what this was—took a different form from that of his earlier libertine years. Rather than dissipation, Will had entered a phase of expansion.

He was beginning to make his mark in the burgeoning world of rare books. As with the violin, it was Charlie who proceeded first. The brothers would never outpace their father when it came to making money, but bibliophilia offered them a frontier for conquest. Will had started with collecting law books in his early days as an attorney and since branched out to musical scores, Restoration drama, early modern poetry, and the work of John Dryden, among other areas. Whereas Charlie took a more desultory, hobbyist approach to his interests, Will was driven to establish lasting, substantive legacies. Charlie also introduced Will to Robert E. Cowan, or "Sir Robert" as Will liked to called the winsome, goateed bibliographer, who'd come down from San Francisco to Los Angeles to help index Will's collection after he broke his arm. These ventures were small compared to what came next.

On June 11, 1919, Will had announced that he would spend $200,000 to launch a new orchestra in Los Angeles, followed by $150,000 for each of the subsequent five years to maintain it. This wasn't the city's first. The Los Angeles Symphony had been established several years before, and Will had been invited to join forces with the existing institution, but differences had arisen. Like his father, he preferred to forge on alone.

By 1919, Los Angeles had been through several boom and bust cycles. Land speculation crazes had fallen away before, but the latest growth spurt showed no sign of abating, fueled by a steady influx of immigrants from the heartland.

It's a familiar song, as old as Los Angeles—the lamentation about the dearth of culture, a purported wasteland compared to other cities. Writing for *The Smart Set* in 1913, Willard Huntington Wright bemoaned the refugees from the prairie not because they disrupted an established way of living, spoke in strange tongues, or kept unfamiliar customs, but for failure of imagination:

> These good folks brought with them a complete stock of rural beliefs, pieties, superstitions, and habits—the Middle West bed hours, the Middle West love of corned beef, the church bells, Munsey's magazine, union suits and missionary societies. They

> brought also a complacent and intransigent aversion to late dinners, malt liquors, grand opera and hussies.

If the newcomers filling up the bungalows lacked zest, those coming to make the "flickers" had plenty—perhaps too much. The nascent motion picture industry wasn't populated by the folks but freaks. By journalist Carey McWilliams's count, this included "dwarfs, pygmies, one-eyed sailors, showpeople, misfits, and 50,000 wonder-struck girls. The easy money of Hollywood drew pimps, gamblers, racketeers, and confidence men." Between the provincial Middle Westerners and the outlandish movie colonists, Los Angeles was found wanting. Obviously the town knew entertainment—Sid Grauman had just built the Million Dollar Theatre on Broadway—but Will was determined that it should have culture too, or, to use a term his young lover liked, "tone." They were separated by twenty years, but the two men possessed the same recoil when it came to vulgarians.

That summer Will moved fast. A month after his announcement, he hired Englishman Walter Henry Rothwell, a former apprentice of Gustav Mahler, to be the conductor. (His first choice, Rachmaninoff, declined.) He made Caroline Estes Smith, a stenographer from the Van Nuys Hotel, the business manager.

Buck Mangam contended that the creation of the Los Angeles Philharmonic was a bribe. To the secretary's thinking, it was a preemptive measure on Will's part, a bid to ingratiate himself with the city leaders and to deflect attention from his homosexual life. Buck couldn't countenance that Will might've been acting with the public good in mind, though it seems unlikely that Will would have funded as many free concerts as he did if he didn't care about public good.

And yet Buck may not have been entirely wrong, that Will's new romance was in some ways connected to his sudden cultural efflorescence. Even if Will wasn't spurred by civic selflessness, he may have been acting out of an impulse that had nothing to do with fear and that in making one aspect of his life secret, he was compelled to expand into other realms.

He wasn't a stranger to artistic expression, but he also didn't identify himself as an artist. Despite his passion for the violin, he was quick to show deference to more talented musicians. While he may have wished to be a great conductor, he didn't mistake himself for one, readily ceding artistic decisions to Rothwell and the other conductors he hired. Still, Will Clark did produce the circumstances for artists to create, and he made their work available to the public. In this, his patronage was a creative act. But regardless, he didn't have to be an artist to have a muse. Will was a man in love, emboldened to make grand gestures, like hiring a conductor and ninety musicians, leasing an entire building, and selling tickets to the whole town.

The rain started early on the morning of October 24. It was still coming down that afternoon when two thousand people gathered outside the Trinity Auditorium on the corner of Grand Avenue and Ninth Street for the debut of the Los Angeles Philharmonic. Albert was among those jostling umbrellas and overcoats, pressing their way into the beaux arts building, and yet he was separate.

Just a month ago he'd been attending to the wealthy, an attractive young man polishing their brilliant sphere. Now not only had he penetrated that world, but as the guest of the man who'd financed Los Angeles's new orchestra, he belonged to an even more elite milieu. He floated past the masses, up to the auditorium's luxury loges, taking his seat among the Dohenys, Flints, Barlows, Sartoris, and Clarks, the burgeoning aristocracy of bankers, oil barons, real estate tycoons, and society matrons.

It was a momentous undertaking on Will's part—launching an orchestra, and in only four months. He'd been decisive but hasty, and there hung the unspoken but real possibility that this would be a scorching disaster, a rich man's folly, and not just the usual stumble, like Charlie Clark losing again at the races, but failure on a massive and public scale.

From the back of the stage, a gong rang out, shuddering through the floorboards, and the men, all dressed in white, marched out from the wings. Ten double basses. Violins, violas, cellos. Next, the horns. Ninety musicians in all. Walter Henry Rothwell came next in black tails, spectacles glinting. The applause surged. At the podium, Rothwell bowed to the audience, then pivoted back to the men now seated with their instruments and raised his baton.

The strings came first, then a flourish from a horn. The woodwinds answered, soft, tentative, almost a pause, before the return of the strings and the crash of the kettledrums. They'd begun with Antonín Dvořák's Symphony no. 9.

For a moment, it seemed that the auditorium spun. Onstage, the bows danced and dipped. The music rose again—strings, horns, a ribbed sound, then the woodwinds, soft and gliding.

It's often referred to as the *New World* symphony, but Dvořák actually titled the work *From the New World*—a significant distinction. He'd composed it in 1893, one year after coming to America from Bohemia to direct the National Conservatory of Music in Manhattan. While he was inspired by Black spirituals and Native American melodies, Dvořák dismissed the popular belief that the symphony directly quoted those forms or that he was introducing Americans to their own legacy. He also drew deeply from Celtic and European traditions as well as the Slavic folk music of his native country. The symphony was not so much a celebration of America as it was the reverie of a traveler in a strange and vibrant land, longing for home, with lush and cyclic melodies that give way to an aching solo by an English horn.

A trombone caught the light, a flare flashed across the auditorium. Rothwell's shoulders jerked and his arms spread wide, pulling sound through the air.

Bohemia was gone now. Dvořák's homeland, along with what had once been Moravia, was a new country called Czechoslovakia. The empires—Russian, Austro-Hungarian, German, Ottoman—had shattered into pieces.

The world had changed, and so had Albert. Just a month ago he'd been a salesclerk and now he was something else—anyone he wanted to be. He was twenty-two, beautiful, beloved by a scion of Gilded Age wealth, alighting in Los Angeles on the cusp of Prohibition, the eve of the Jazz Age, as F. Scott Fitzgerald named it—or, in Carl Van Vechten's words, "the splendid drunken Twenties."

The war was over. People were alive. A new game was coming—a giddy, universal, adult hide-and-seek played with secret codes, speakeasies, fake bookshelves, whiskey in teacups, and flasks tucked into garters. The masks were gone—at least most were.

It had been a cruel joke, a glitch in the universe, a young man sensitive to beauty, to finer things, and no means to possess them, as if born into exile. The air he'd breathed his whole life had been suffused with power and wealth, and yet both belonged to other times and other people—his mother's past, his father's customers, his own customers. But that was over. He was done with boardinghouses, done with the family who'd abandoned him, done with despair in a rented room. Now he had a new mask, one that fit him perfectly—wealth.

After the intermission, the Los Angeles Philharmonic performed Weber's overture to *Oberon*, Liszt's "Les préludes," and Chabrier's rhapsody "España." When Walter Henry Rothwell concluded the program and turned to the more than two thousand people who'd gathered in the auditorium, he was met with unstinting applause and bravos.

Albert clapped, too, as the ushers streamed down the aisles bearing floral arrangements, including an enormous horseshoe of garlands—a collective tribute from the symphonies of Boston, Cincinnati, Minneapolis, New York, Philadelphia, St. Louis, and San Francisco. Los Angeles had arrived, and so had Harrison Post.

He slipped into his new self and into the new, loosening decade. He and Will may have been criminals, but soon enough everyone else would be too. Four days after the debut of the Los Angeles Philharmonic, on October 28, the Senate overrode Woodrow Wilson's veto to pass the Volstead Act, enforcing the Eighteenth Amendment, prohibiting the manufacture, sale, and transportation of high-proof spirits. They were all in the shadows now.

It wasn't a question anymore of ending himself but of becoming the man he was meant to be, and so he did. On December 6, 1919, a small item appeared in the *Sausalito News* under "Court Calendar":

> Application for Albert Harrison for change of name—Application is granted.

PART TWO

1919–1934

Harrison Post and unidentified man, circa 1921.

7

THE COPAIN

Later, when he thought back on those early charmed days and glittering nights, it was the parties Harrison remembered—the ones in Alla Nazimova's garden, at Lloyd Pantages's home, and in Prince Troubetzkoy's studio. Will had commissioned the society portraitist and exiled Russian aristocrat to make bronzes of Mabel and Alice, as well as a small statue of himself with Snooks. The prince also did a crayon sketch of Harrison, a relatively subtle note to herald the arrival of the new royal consort.

It was a time of extravagant gestures. Not only had Will launched the LA Philharmonic, but he was also paying to have a moat dredged and an island created for the monumental marble tomb he was having built in Hollywood Cemetery. With a bronze door and a ceiling tiled in gold and pigeon blue, it would be the largest on the grounds—fit for a prince.

Of course, no one called Will a prince, and "royal consort" wasn't a phrase anyone used for Harrison. "Ward" was the term for the young man living in Will's home. It was how the newspapers referred to him that spring when they reported that he'd been cast in a new motion picture.

Will was friends with comedienne Marie Dressler, and he knew Charlie Chaplin well enough to receive a condolence note after Alice's death, but he more or less kept his remove from the bumptious new industry. Not Harrison. He went splashing right in, perhaps assisted by connections through his foster brother, Guy Bates Post, though of course now Harrison was associated with a name that carried even greater weight.

According to the *Los Angeles Times*, the "ward of W.A. Clark Jr."

had joined the cast of *The Barbarian*, starring and directed by Monroe Salisbury, a former stage actor who'd come to fame in Cecil B. DeMille's early films. Salisbury had also launched a production company and named Harrison vice president.

In the Clark family, "wards" have a way of never actually being wards at all. W.A. had referred to Anna as his ward in a bid for decorum and to rationalize why he, an unmarried man in his late fifties, was housing a teenage girl in his Parisian apartments. Will, too, needed cover for his relationship with Harrison, but unlike his father, he did in fact want to establish a legal contract, one that would not only give them a public front but also protect Harrison financially, making him Will's heir. Obviously had Harrison been a woman, marriage would've sufficed. Anna had been young enough for the Senator to adopt her, but he never did. Harrison, however, was too old, and despite the efforts of Will's lawyers, the court deemed him ineligible. He did, however, look the part of a movie star—dark, exotic, openly sensual, and appealingly dangerous. In Hollywood, the outsiders were on the inside now, and that meant Harrison fit right in.

The Italian immigrant Rudolph Valentino, who'd once been Rodolfo Guglielmi, had first made a living in New York City's ballroom circuit and as a "taxi dancer" at Maxim's cabaret, where wealthy women paid for his company. After being entangled in a divorce scandal, Valentino relocated himself to California. He was again paid to dance and to be looked at, but now up on the screen. Although his longing—in film and in life—was for women, Valentino was willing to be the object of anyone's gaze.

Another outsider, a handsome expatriate from Mexico named José Ramón Gil Samaniego, worked part time as an usher at the Los Angeles Philharmonic, chasing bit roles and singing in vaudeville joints until he got his break and ascended into the Hollywood firmament under his stage name, Ramon Novarro.

Success meant the end of the job at the Philharmonic as well as the end of an affair with another usher, a gifted young composer named Harry Partch, who, frustrated with the harmonic limitations of the Western world's paltry twelve tones, would go on to invent a scale with forty-three. Theirs was an early tryst in the sexy, reckless decade.

Hollywood was an industry of interlopers. Certainly hierarchies emerged and power was ruthlessly abused, but there was room for deviance. Women were directors and writers. Jews built studios and became moguls, even if they still weren't allowed to join the Los Angeles Athletic Club.

Alla Nazimova proudly called herself a "Russian Jewess." She wasn't a starlet like Mary Pickford or Bebe Daniels but a star—no diminutive—with dark-painted nails, a throaty chuckle, and, when she smiled, a dimple, which no one expected. She'd arrived in LA around the same time as Harrison and, as the papers noted, she bought "a great big rambling house set among orange and lemon trees with vivid banks of flowers and wide smooth lawn." Soon it was home to her legendary parties.

There was no single path. Frances Marion had come down from San Francisco to look for work as a commercial artist, wound up taking a job as an extra on a film, wrote some dialogue to help the director, and turned into a screenwriter. Blanche Sewell arrived from Oklahoma with dreams of acting, got stuck cutting negatives, and later edited *Grand Hotel*, *Queen Christina*, and *The Wizard of Oz*. Will Rogers started out doing rope tricks in vaudeville and ended up a movie star, airline spokesman, and radio pundit with a 180-acre estate in the Pacific Palisades. This was Hollywood. It was all horizon.

The girls covered their lips with makeup and painted a small red circle in the middle—the "Gish mouth." They weren't called women unless, like Nazimova or Pola Negri, they were dark, mysterious, and from a foreign country or, like Theda Bara, they simply appeared to be. She was from Cincinnati. Out in Santa Monica, Carole Lombard and Marie Prevost cavorted in the surf and showed off their bare knees. These were Mack Sennett's Bathing Beauties and they were "girls."

Bebe Daniels wasn't a girl anymore. The actress had starred in the one-reelers with Harold Lloyd that played at the Pantages Theatre back when Harrison was a boy named Albert. But now she was doing dramas by DeMille and starring opposite Valentino in *Monsieur Beaucaire*. And she was one of Harrison's new friends in his new life. So was Lloyd Pantages, son of the movie theater impresario.

It was at one of Lloyd's parties that Harrison first met Carole Lombard. Her name used to be Jane Peters. He wrote both in his address book.

So many names dropped away. Harlean Carpenter, Douglas Ullman, Lucille LeSueur disappeared into Jean Harlow, Douglas Fairbanks, and Joan Crawford. And Albert—he was finally gone too.

In the previous century, people flocked west to dig, scrape, and plunder the earth for gold, silver, zinc, and copper, but by the 1920s much had been mined. The California Gold Rush was long past. The Comstock Lode had collapsed. The kings of the Gilded Age had faded. Amalgamated, dissolved in 1915 in the wake of antitrust legislation, had re-formed itself as the Anaconda Copper Mining Company and ran Montana now. The Senator had turned his attention to his mines in Nevada and Arizona. In Los Angeles, the fortunes came from oil and the land itself. The boosters kept sending their pamphlets east and the home buyers with their ready money kept coming west. And here was a new resource to be extracted and refined: stardom.

"No mining camp ever equaled it. No mad, lurid, wild and woolly border town ever attracted so many men or women of so high a station in life or so vilely sunk as did Hollywood." So claimed the anonymous author of a 1922 booklet called *The Sins of Hollywood: An Exposé of Movie Vice.*

The copper had been clawed out of the earth and smelted, the arsenic and sulfur gone, never mind the poisons burned into the air and seeping into the water table. Now the purified metal sparked and the current jumped, arcing from one carbon electrode to another. The key lights shone down on the kohl-eyed beauty collapsing in the lead's muscled arms. The copper rushed the electricity through the projector's motor, beaming the gorgeous people out through the curved lens across the dark room and onto the wide, waiting screen.

Outside, the current sped through the lamps, flinging columns of light up to the night sky. The radiant stars stepped out of their gleaming chauffeured cars. They turned to the clamoring crowds, flashbulbs exploding. They smiled and they waved, their names glowing on the marquee above.

Will Clark might shrink from the camera, but not Harrison Post. In a photographer's studio, his double collared shirt open at the throat, he crossed his arms, lowered his head, dark eyes glowering, and nearly smiled when the shutter clicked.

Movie audiences welcomed the dark outsiders to the screen, but Will's siblings didn't want one in his home. A year after Harrison arrived in

Los Angeles, they made their concerns known. This appears to have been the first interference. It wouldn't be the last.

In the fall of 1920, Maizie came out from New York to visit Will. According to Buck Mangam, during her stay she received two letters, both unsigned with no return address. Their origin was mysterious, but the message was not: it was dangerous for Will to associate with Harrison. The writer, or writers, claimed to possess evidence that could substantiate this claim. Alarmed by the insinuation, Maizie turned to Charlie, the family fixer. Between the Bay Area horse-racing set and the wealthy collectors who frequented the Marsh, Charlie may have already heard the whispers that trailed Harrison Post. They wouldn't have mattered before, but now that Harrison was living in his brother's home, they did.

Charlie wrote to Will, acknowledging that, as men of the world, they each knew enough of "human nature to appreciate that a man may have as acquaintances, murderers, second-story men, bunco steerers, etc., without anyone except the long-haired and narrow-minded caring." He noted that "nobody cares much about the ways of a man with a maid." The older brother had spent his adult life running up gambling debts and having affairs with actresses, Floradora girls, and society matrons to whom he was not married. His transgressions may have been ammunition for moral scolds, but that kind of misbehavior was a privilege of wealth. Henry Huntington hadn't required public approval when he married his uncle Collis's widow. Charlie's scruples were fluid if they existed at all, and yet there were lines to be drawn.

He continued: "There is one type of man that one cannot afford to know, and that is the man who is, or even bears the reputation of being, a degenerate." And lest there be any misunderstanding about the exact nature of his reputation, Charlie made it clear: Harrison was "a degenerate of the Oscar Wilde type." What's more, this was known "generally throughout California." If only Harrison had been a murderer instead.

The man who'd described "the love that dare not speak its name" on the witness stand in 1895 had become a stand-in for that very love, though Charlie was hardly contemplating love when he invoked the writer. Oscar Wilde was shorthand for homosexuality and he was a warning: bankruptcy, imprisonment, exile, and ruin.

Will's years of hard living had faded. When he made headlines now it was for his philanthropic endeavors—the Philharmonic, free concerts, Easter services at the Hollywood Bowl. His marriages, marked by tragedy, had been free of scandal, unlike those of Charlie and Maizie. His siblings had sought spouses with social status, but Will's wives had had modest origins. Will married nice people, but whether or not Harrison Post was a nice person was hardly the point.

And as Charlie saw it, it didn't matter if Will wasn't a degenerate. It was damaging enough to know one. Consorting with Harrison Post was a straight path not only to the quicksand of blackmail, endless payoffs, and paranoia but also lasting public humiliation. Charlie knew men—powerful men with public lives—who'd been destroyed by these kinds of associations.

Certainly he'd seen the headlines about the Baker Street raid and the subsequent trial. The details the anonymous tipster claimed to possess about Harrison were exactly the kind of information the family fixer would've gleefully leveraged over a rival. He may not have known that newspaper tycoon C. K. McClatchy kept a list of suspected "degenerates," but Charlie knew such lists existed and he understood their power. He begged Will to consider the consequences of his connection to Harrison, not just for himself but for their sisters, their father, and his own son.

Will's siblings must've believed that once he understood what they knew about Harrison, what the entire state of California apparently knew about Harrison, he'd make an immediate and decisive break. As Charlie hastened to add, Will mustn't "think for one minute, old man, that . . . I would ever attribute any vice to you."

But to attribute it to the so-called ward should've been enough. Charlie invoked their family, their father, and Will's only child to convey the urgency of the matter. That, too, should've been enough, but it wasn't. Will's bond with the younger man proved stronger than duty to family.

Harrison didn't pack his bags and slink back to San Francisco, nor did Will respond to Charlie's letter, at least not directly. Three months later, he paid A. S. W. Rosenbach, one of the era's preeminent book dealers, more than $15,000 for twenty-five letters that Oscar Wilde had written to Lord Alfred Douglas. Then Will gave those letters to his own lover and charged him with the task of transcribing the words of the original degenerate.

It was a logical choice for a collector looking to distinguish himself in the field of Wildeiana. It could also be seen as a brazen riposte to his brother's warning. It was certainly an act of devotion—to Harrison and to Wilde's memory—and it was a way for Will to declare his love through someone else's words, ventriloquism as a means to speak freely.

As bold as it was for Will to bring Harrison so publicly into his circle, the two men still took measures to obscure their relationship, so much so that at times it can be difficult to conjure up the texture of their lives together. Harrison includes a few recollections in his journals and we have Buck Mangam's account, but much of what remains, such as society column mentions, is that which was deemed safe to remain.

Today, at the Clark Library, it's generally believed that after Will's death, Cora Sanders destroyed any material that might've been considered exposing or incriminating. Given that both men were prolific correspondents, it's a remarkable loss, but she was his custodian first, librarian second.

In the library's archives only two letters remain in the files:

Dear Harrison:

I am enclosing a letter which is self explanatory. The books that this person refers to are either first—25,000 Words Often Mispronounced, by Fyfe or Fyf (Miss. Sanders can tell you), or the other—second, is 50,000 Words Often Mispronounced by Vitzatelli. This letter you will find on my desk in the library, as described by her in her letter. Will you kindly give her the required information saying that her letter had been referred to you by me.

With best wishes, I am

Sincerely yours,

Will

Dear Harrison:

Herewith please find a letter from Henry Purdom. When these books come kindly enter the prices in the book as Miss Sanders showed you how to do; check off each item on the invoice and return the correspondence to me as soon as possible.

Books coming in lots such as this should be kept separated from other lots coming from the same or different book-sellers. You may use all the floor space of the library for this purpose.

With best wishes, I am,

Sincerely yours,

Will

More memos than sonnets, these letters deliver little in the way of passion. Will wrote or dictated them while he was summering at the Mowitza Lodge and Harrison had stayed back in Los Angeles. They contain no double entendres, no inside jokes, no pet names, no ardent longing, not even an offhand remark about the weather or the guests at Salmon Lake. The tone is fond but not overly so. There is nothing that would serve as evidence of a romantic attachment in a court of law or public opinion, which is likely why they still exist.

But Wilde's letters were another matter:

> I want to see you—It is really absurd—I can't live without you—You are so dear, so wonderful—I think of you all day long—and miss your grace.

Once fodder for extortionists, these were now historical artifacts. The world of bibliophilia is one in which its inhabitants nurture arcane passions and rarefied tastes, in which oddities and errata like a page printed upside down or twice increases a book's worth. It's a realm in which fetish is accepted, flaws are prized, and unusual or transgressive histories aren't shunned but treasured. Will's attraction to Wilde's work would have been seen as a reflection of his sophisticated if outré literary sensibility, not his own sexuality.

Besides, he hadn't been the first to collect Wilde. That had been

John Stetson, son of the man who invented the cowboy hat. No one thought that John Stetson was homosexual nor does history suggest he was, and when Will bought the full bloc of Stetson's Wilde collection at auction in 1920, he could safely assume his interest wouldn't mark him either. Wilde, who once waxed ecstatic about the sartorial choices of American miners, surely would've relished the fact that his literary reputation was in some measure protected and restored by two heirs to the country's frontier.

And he would have certainly approved of a beautiful young man, head bowed over his own words, transcribing them for posterity in another, older man's library. In fact, there were two attractive young men charged with the work.

Arthur Dennison, a publicist for film director Lois Weber, had joined Harrison in the effort. Tall, with dark brown hair and blue eyes, the twenty-seven-year-old son of a federal judge had arrived in Los Angeles from Grand Rapids, Michigan, with plans of becoming a writer and discovered a cohort of literary-minded men as well as a homosocial haven in Will Clark's library. During travels to the East Coast, the aspiring writer sometimes consulted with Rosenbach on Will's behalf.

It was no small feat for Arthur and Harrison to decode Wilde's stenographic chicken scratch. Also, the playwright rarely dated his correspondence, which made sequencing a challenge. In the library, they labored to transcribe one's man longing for another:

> Dear, dear boy—you are more to me than any one of them had any idea—You are the atmosphere of beauty through which I see life—you are the incarnation of all lovely things—When we are out of tune—all colour goes from things for me—but we are never really out of tune—I think of you day and night.

Wilde's tone in his correspondence differed markedly from Will's. For one thing, he usually addressed Bosie as "My own dear boy." And he was forthcoming, sharing details of his daily life, his work, and his adoration for the young poet. He sends Bosie cigarettes, praises his writing, cautions him to give his poetry shape. He dilates on social outings, gossips about friends, complains of Queensberry's public rampages, and muses about writing a book titled "How to live above one's means."

That was from the letters written before Wilde's prison term. Upon his release, his tone had changed—more formal, longer sentences, more complicated clauses, no blurts of passion. He admonishes his now-former lover to avoid duels and urges him to return to writing ballads. Still, despite the warnings from friends and the conditions of his financial support from Constance, Wilde was seduced by Bosie's entreaties and agreed to reunite. They meet in Rouen. They part. Bosie pleads again and Wilde relents again.

> My own darling boy—
>
> I got your telegram half an hour ago—and just send you a line to say that I feel that my only hope of again doing beautiful work in art is being with you—It was not so in old days—but now it is different, and you can really recreate in me that energy and sense of joyous power on which Art depends—Everyone is furious with me for going back to you—but they don't understand us—I feel that it is only with you that I can do anything at all—Do remake my ruined life for me—and then our friendship and love will have a different meaning to the world—
>
> I wish that when we met at Rouen we had not parted at all—There are such wide abysses now of space and land between us—But we love each other—
>
> Good night—dear—
>
> Evry
>
> Oscar

Of course, Will and Harrison knew the bitter sorrow that lay in store, that the "joyous power" the author so longed for would elude him and that his already ruined life would be ruined more, but this was the last of the letters Harrison transcribed and it preserved the writer in a state of unguarded hope and spared him—for the moment—the lonely boulevards of Paris, the horrified stares, the rotting gums and purulent ear, the dark end in a soiled hotel room.

Will and Harrison likely also knew their true correspondence wouldn't outlast them, but Wilde's letters would. Will consulted John Henry Nash, a fine-art printer based in San Francisco, about the possibility of reproducing the collection for private publication in a limited edition. He'd already hired Nash—upon Charlie's recommendation—to print customized copies of the catalogs from his collection that he'd been compiling with Sir Robert. This was the beginning of a long and fruitful collaboration.

These catalogs, or indexes, went far beyond mere lists of titles. Rather, they are comprehensive bibliographies with in-depth and often opinionated annotations and capsule histories, celebrations of minutiae that brim with the open pride of a new parent and are often marked by a coroner's eye for detail. The first catalogs Nash produced for Will included *The Posthumous Papers of the Pickwick Club*; *Modern English Literature, Vol. I*; *Early English Literature, 1519–1700, Vol. I.*; *The Kelmscott and Doves Presses*; and *Cruikshank and Dickens*. On several, along with Coco, Harrison is credited as "assistant librarian."

Will had ignored his brother's counsel, but he wasn't cavalier when it came to his lawyers'. It had been bold—and costly—to acquire Oscar Wilde's letters to Lord Alfred Douglas, and their opinion was that it would be bolder yet to publish them, even in a private edition.

Wilde was dead, but Douglas was not, and as it had been during Wilde's life, any connection with the aristocrat-poet was a fraught one. Over fifty now, no longer "a gilt and gracious lad" but still his father's son, Douglas remained peevish, vain, and quick to threaten litigation. Although the letters were written to and not by him, there was concern that he might sue if they were published, inviting certain scandal, in true Douglas fashion, and so Will wrote to John Henry Nash: "In accordance with my attorneys I have determined not to publish the Wilde letters, as I would be liable to a suit for libel, which would of course be unpleasant."

He did, however, publish two indexes devoted to his holdings of Wilde and Wildeiana. He also inaugurated a new custom as a way to share his prized titles. Each year he chose one book, poem, or essay from his library and contracted Nash to reproduce an elaborate facsimile, printed in editions of two hundred and fifty or fewer, which Will sent to friends, fellow collectors, and libraries. These came to be known as his Christmas books, as he distributed them at the end of the year, though their themes weren't related to the holiday. They were a kind of royal publication. The work was painstaking, involving specialty papers, meticulous etchings on copperplates, and fastidious typographic planning.

Will spent $8,000 on his first publication with Nash. This was Percy Bysshe Shelley's *Adonais: An Elegy on the Death of John Keats*, the epic poem about the prolific Romantic poet who died at twenty-five from tuberculosis, a celebration both of man's release from earthly suffering and of one man's love for another. Subsequent collaborations would include Thomas Gray's "Ode on the Pleasure Arising from Vicissitude," John Dryden's *All for Love*, and Edgar Allan Poe's "Annabel Lee." These were all private productions, never meant for sale or wider distribution; Will was eager to share his beloved books and incunabula but also vigilant about where they circulated. He could afford extravagant gestures just as he could afford to protect the borders of his world.

In Los Angeles, with its ever-shifting boundaries, Will had learned he could manufacture new realms. He'd watched his father try to join the ranks of the East Coast elites only to be snubbed by the Vanderbilts and others. America was just a century old when W.A. was making his way, but the nation had already constructed its hierarchies. By the time he'd built his looming manse on Fifth Avenue, he'd discovered Manhattan was a small island, with entrée to its kingdoms tightly controlled.

The mining magnate could buy himself a pretty young wife and a Senate seat and Rembrandts and Corots and swathes of land to mine but he never managed to buy entry to the rarefied world of the people who'd made their fortunes a generation or two before him. The line between their class and his may have seemed slender, but it was impenetrable, as W.A. learned when he invited the blue bloods to his mansion in New York to marvel at his ostentatious art collection and no one came.

In Los Angeles, though, Will had positioned himself at the center of a vibrant cultural sphere. Within its first year, the Philharmonic's subscription rate doubled and Will relocated the orchestra to Clune's Auditorium, an eight-story beaux arts structure on the corner of Fifth and Olive Streets, facing what was now called Pershing Square. A onetime movie palace, Clune's was the first building in Los Angeles to be made of reinforced concrete, and it was where D. W. Griffith's *The Clansman*, later known as *Birth of a Nation*, premiered in 1915. Three years after that, it had hosted charismatic preacher Aimee Semple McPherson's first revival in Southern California. Now it was no longer called Clune's but the Philharmonic Auditorium, and soon the opulent Biltmore Hotel would rise as its catty-corner neighbor.

There, Will would hold dinner parties and smaller musicales with local grandees and society matrons who served on the Philharmonic's board, along with his stalwart courtiers like Harrison, of course, as well as Caroline Estes Smith and her husband, George. Previously a concrete inspector, George quickly adapted to the couple's elevated social status, taking the nickname "Chummie" and sporting a monocle.

At the northeastern corner of Pershing Square, a new sphere had emerged for the society columnists. Just a few blocks away, Will and Harrison could stroll through Booksellers Row on Sixth Street, the haven for dealers and collectors, and then press on another block to the Los Angeles Athletic Club, home to power brokers and elites.

Back when Will was a small boy coming to visit his grandmother, the patch of land at Fifth and Olive had been called Los Angeles Park, though over the years it was given other names—Plaza Abaja, Sixth Street Park, St. Vincent Park. When Will moved to Los Angeles with Alice it was Central Park, a proper public square with a tiered fountain, bricked walkways, wooden benches, and lush foliage—cypresses, palms, banana trees. After the war, it was rechristened Pershing Square, in honor of the commander of the American Expeditionary Forces. A leafy oasis during the day for downtown office workers on their lunch hour, the plaza also drew street vendors, preachers, and other soapbox orators. After dark, though, it offered a different kind of sanctuary, a place where men sought sex with other men.

"The number of faggots cruising here is legion," the poet Hart Crane had noted of the plaza during a visit to the Southland in 1927. "Here are little fairies who can quote Rimbaud before they are eighteen."

Will and Harrison may well have been familiar with the darkened groves of Pershing Square, where those who lingered in the shadows faced the threat of shakedowns, public exposure, and prison, but they didn't have to take such risks. They could bring Pershing Square to 2205 West Adams.

Will had continued to buy up the surrounding properties on his block and extend his own walled compound. In previous years, he'd hosted performances on the grounds to benefit war orphans, and Alice had held luncheons for the young ladies at the YMCA. Will continued to host charity events, but there were other gatherings now, which weren't reported in the papers, ones at which naked men gamboled and lounged in the gardens—a detail that's known only because a neighboring judge complained to local authorities.

Harrison didn't mention these parties in his journals, and no pictures of the aforementioned guests exist in his scrapbooks, but one black-and-white photo, taken in 1920, of two women, nude, lounging along a marble balustrade, offers the briefest glimpse of the voluptuous life that was possible behind the high brick walls in Will's shadow court, a world that was both boundless and protected, where they believed they were safe.

In an oral history about Will's collection, Robert G. Cowan, son of Sir Robert, dismissed the idea that Harrison made any significant contribution to the library, insisting, "He was just a figurehead." Nothing more than "a social adjunct."

Indeed Harrison possessed neither Sir Robert's bibliographic expertise nor Cora's organizational instincts. And while he did assist with Wilde's letters and other publications, Sir Robert and Cora were the official librarians, and today their portraits flank Will's in the Clark Library. The younger Cowan rejected the notion that Harrison made any substantive contributions: "He didn't do anything particularly."

This was true. Harrison posed for his studio portrait, but he never did become a movie star, even if *The Barbarian* would've been a fitting vehicle for his debut. The film tells the story of a man living in the wilderness who is swindled out of the rights to his land by a devious agent from a mining corporation. After the agent is found out and punished, the "barbarian" marries the daughter of the head of the corporation, which is then granted permission to mine the land. A happy ending for everyone, with a distinctly Clarkite ethos.

But when the movie premiered in April 1921, Harrison wasn't in it. Nor was his name in the credits as a producer or as part of Monroe Salisbury's company. It may have been that Harrison's screen test did not convince or that when it came time to shoot, he didn't fancy the prospect of spending weeks on location on Mount Shasta.

Harrison looked the part, but he didn't long for stardom and he soon discovered that it's easier to know actors than be one. He didn't have to show up on a set to project glamour, just as he didn't have to foreclose on claims, outbid competitors, or inspect ore samples to accumulate wealth. He didn't even have to inherit it. All that was required of the royal consort was to *be*, to love and be loved.

Harrison didn't do anything particularly, but he did many things generally. He attended dinner parties. He owned a chow chow named Son. He spent afternoons ambling through the Ambassador Hotel on Wilshire Boulevard, a vast city-state of shops and restaurants, including the fashionable Cocoanut Grove nightclub. The sprawling compound also housed a new outpost for the Marsh company, run by Lucien Marsh, the son of Harrison's former employer. No longer the solicitous shop clerk, Harrison had become the wealthy customer.

Will had established a bank account for him with a sizable monthly allowance, and Harrison was generous with his new fortune, quick to loan money, buying as much for others, it seemed, as for himself. He sent his friend actress Carlotta Monterey a Russian snuffbox made of gold topped with an emerald-studded frog. He and Will were often presenting each other books, paintings, and countless bibelots.

He took up bookbinding. He was particularly deft with a fifteenth-century technique involving gold inlay, used on his own palm-sized address book. Weighing no more than a matchbox, bound in calf leather and filigreed with gold crowns, fleurs-de-lis, and curlicues, the tiny socialite hymnal reveals Harrison's new social milieu. In spidery script, Harrison wrote the names of the Hollywood elite: Greta Garbo, Mary Pickford, Norma Shearer, Bebe Daniels, Constance Talmadge, Norma Talmadge, Eugene O'Brien, Lili Damita, Hal Roach, Frances Marion, Salka Viertel, Vicki Baum, Leo Carrillo.

The entries included industry titans, society matrons, political fixers, and hotel managers. For instance, under *P* there was, of course, fellow socialite Lloyd Pantages, but also French coloratura soprano Lily Pons; Jack Pickford, Mary's dashing, volatile younger brother, known less for his acting ability than his drug binges and the shocking death of his first wife Olive Thomas from mercury poisoning; Claude I. Parker, attorney to the stars—back before the "Get me Giesler" era—who'd eventually sell his Palisades holdings to oil baron J. P. Getty; Edna Purviance, the warm-hearted love interest to Charlie Chaplin's

"Tramp" in over thirty films; Ignacy Jan Paderewski, the wild-haired Polish pianist who held sold-out concerts across Europe, owned three thousand acres of orchards and vineyards in Paso Robles, and served as prime minister of Poland after the Great War—possibly the first rock star turned statesman; plus Madame Patteneaude, a beautician renowned for her luxury hair treatments.

There were writers, like his friend Carlotta's husband, Eugene O'Neill, and literary movers such as writer and photographer Carl Van Vechten and the agent Elisabeth Marbury. There were artists, singers, dancers, and aviatrices. There were barons, princesses, and nobles, like Thelma Converse, who'd been the mistress to the Duke of Windsor before he abdicated the British throne for Wallis Simpson. Viscountess Furness was her title and she came from the world of true nobility, where one didn't aspire to be known by fans but by other aristocrats.

The addresses ranged from Paris to Rome to Stockholm to New York to Burlingame to Butte. By now Harrison had made the cut with many from Will's Montana cohort, including his college pal John Templeman, old-timers like Judge Lippincott, and another Clark insider, Judge Sydney Sanner. Even Will's sisters—once alarmed by Harrison's arrival—had adapted, enough so that their names appear in his tiny reliquary of social elites, as does Will's stepmother, Anna. But there were those who remained immune to his charms. No Charlie Clark, no Buck Mangam.

He wrote the names of others like him—those who "didn't do anything particularly." Flamboyant, party-loving Dorothy di Frasso, the leather goods heiress from New Jersey who had married an Italian count and bought the former Medici Villa Madama in Rome. Dark-haired gamine Ann Rork, the daughter of producer Sam Rork and eventual wife of J. P. Getty, who had starred in some movies with Will Rogers and Douglas Fairbanks Jr., amounting to a short career.

These were people who descended from wealth or married wealth, as Harrison had, after a fashion, and they circulated within the interconnected web of capital and fame. Like Ann, they may have been in a few pictures or were somehow in proximity to the industry. Dorothy di Frasso, for instance, romanced both Gary Cooper and Cary Grant. Lloyd Pantages's family owned movie palaces. Neither was a film star. Still, illuminated by Hollywood's glow, they shone brighter than the average swell. The journalist Adela Rogers St. Johns, daughter of Earl Rogers, Will's neighbor at the Van Nuys Hotel, had a name for this species of the new Hollywood aristocracy: the nonprofessional.

They didn't trouble themselves with the work of showing up to set and repeating takes under hot lights, like Bebe Daniels or Zasu Pitts. Nor did they buttress and amplify the movie industry, like gossip columnist Louella Parsons chasing stories and writing copy, though sometimes they visited sets and appeared in news columns.

Harrison went to the races. He went shopping. He went to parties. He threw parties. He traveled in chauffeured cars. He gave orders to servants. He swanned about town delivering rare editions of Chaucer to other handsome young men. He sat for his portrait. He wrote more names in his address book.

Dilettante comes from the Latin *delectare*—to delight—but we finish it off as if it's French, the best language for contempt, the one that gives us *manqué* and *flâneur*—people we can't easily categorize, people without obvious purpose. These are words that allow us to purse our lips, ironic, dismissive, the better not to take these people, whomever—*what*ever—they are, seriously.

An unfixed man, Harrison Post strains our usual terms and so we turn to other languages, strange words to make a strange person even stranger, and in doing so we admit the truth, that it's impossible to be precise about people because being a person is not a precise thing to be. A man exists whether or not the language exists to identify him. Even if he cannot be named, he can still be seen.

Will had a word for Harrison: *copain*. He inscribed it on a photograph of himself at the races, cigar clenched in his teeth, stopwatch in hand, wearing a fedora. Taken from below, the picture makes Will seem a powerful masculine figure, barrel-chested and taller than he was.

In French, *copain* can mean "buddy" or "pal," but it's often used to signal romantic attachment, a more adult expression than *petit ami*. The term comes from *compagnon*, which, along with the Spanish *compañero*, Italian *compagno*, and English *companion*, derives from Latin—*cum* and *panis*—meaning "with whom one eats bread."

The words we use for "with whom one shares a bed" are never so direct. Instead, they're burdened with social norms and contractual obligations, like *wife* and *husband*, veiled in opaque business-speak—*partner*—or recast from platonic terms and yoked to gender, as with *boyfriend* and *girlfriend. Lover* at least draws on a feeling, but none of these words possesses the clarity of the bond established through sharing one of the most elemental acts in life with another person.

They were happy in Rome. They were happy in Venice. They were happy in Paris. They were happy on ocean liners, in staterooms, in private cars, in hotel suites, in bookstores.

Harrison's education had been piecemeal—his father's shop, military school, the Marsh, and now Will's library and at his side traveling the world. He hadn't studied with private tutors. He didn't have his lover's scholarly gravitas. Still, he was an eager student of art and beauty. Part of their bond, especially in the beginning, likely came from the exchange that Wilde had tried to describe to the unsympathetic courtroom—a young man's beauty, his awakening to the world, coupled with an older man's knowledge.

Harrison wasn't a bibliographic expert, but he was a voracious reader. On Will's book-buying expeditions, he acquired work by Dickens, Balzac, Sappho, Ronald Firbank, Rupert Brooke, Laurence Sterne, and Pierre Louÿs for his own growing collection. A library, like a relationship, is built incrementally, an accumulation of discrete moments accruing into something bigger than any one instance or any one book. Harrison's library was an extension of himself—his tastes, his idiosyncrasies, and his history. He'd changed his name. He'd changed his parents. He'd changed his class. He'd changed the place of his birth from New York to San Francisco. He'd changed the year. Everything about him had been an invention, but his library was true and constant. It wasn't what the world made of him but what he made of the world.

Jay Gatsby changed his name and his background. He was a bootlegger who reinvented himself as a society swell on Long Island. He never cut the pages of his expensive books because he never opened them. But Harrison, another invented man, didn't build his library for show, for what it might make people believe about him.

Harrison loved beautiful things and his books were beautiful objects, but he also read them. Much of his identity may have been an invention, a performance, but he never needed anyone to watch him read. That was for himself.

Charlie wasn't wrong about the risks Will was taking. The whispers continued. A time-honored tactic of fighting gossip is simply to produce more gossip, and so in the fall of 1921 a headline appeared in the *New York Daily News*: JUANITA HANSEN BRIDE OF HARRISON POST, COAST RUMOR.

Formerly one of Mack Sennett's Bathing Beauties, Juanita Hansen had since moved on to serious roles and working with directors like Lois Weber and D. W. Griffith. By the time the actress and the socialite were allegedly engaged, she was a reigning serial queen, under contract to Universal. She'd also developed a severe cocaine addiction. Talk was spreading, and the studio executives were unhappy. Therefore, nuptials—or at least rumors of nuptials—were in order.

Between items about Charlie Chaplin dressing as a woman to elude crowds and Nazimova flirting with her husband at the premiere of *Camille*, columnists confided to their readers that Harrison and Juanita had eloped and that the same judge who'd recently sentenced Bebe Daniels to jail for speeding had done the honors.

If in fact there ever was a marriage. For a contrived relationship, the PR effort was paltry—no details about the gifts the newlyweds surprised each other with, the trips they were planning, or other manufactured tidbits. Even the reporters didn't seem inclined to play along, with one in Houston bluntly demanding: "Who is he, 'Buddy' Post?"

Harrison wasn't about to admit the truth, that he was Will Clark's copain. Instead, they offered another term: *secretary*. This was how they explained why Harrison was on Will's payroll, why the men shared a loge at the Philharmonic, and why at the end of the second season Harrison was at Will's side during the orchestra's thirty-three-concert tour of the western United States.

For a wife, none of that would've been unusual, and had Harrison carried out the actual duties of a secretary, it wouldn't have been remarkable either. But he didn't administer Will's library or personal finances—that fell to Cora Sanders. Nor did he handle Will's travel arrangements—William Burgess did that. Nor did he apply for patents, inspect smelters, issue contracts, maintain accounts, or otherwise act as a business agent for Will Clark. This was Buck Mangam's domain. But like the faux marriage to Juanita Hansen, the word *secretary* gave them cover.

They took other precautions. They traveled with an entourage, usually William Burgess in tow, as well as the celebrity priest Monsignor Joseph Tonello, who'd been secretary to Pope Leo XIII and confidant to Enrico Caruso. They also spent time apart. In California, the true nature of their relationship might be plausibly denied, but that wasn't necessarily the case in Will's native state. He continued his summers at the lakeside cabin with the McManus clan and the rest of his Montana cohort. Harrison's name appears only once in the guest book at the Mowitza Lodge.

These were hardly the measures Charlie had hoped for. Harrison had not been cast out, though he did move out of Will's estate and take a suite of rooms down the street at the Holton Arms, a luxury apartment building at the corner of West Adams and Figueroa. But whether Harrison resided in Will's actual home or not was beside the point. By now he was well ensconced in the copper scion's court—enough so that he invited his own sister to stay with him.

Gladys arrived in the spring of 1922. She came from Chicago, where she was known not as Gladys but as Felice. That's the name she used the year before when she married Joseph Barbieri. Little else is known about the marriage except that by the time Harrison's sister got to California, she wanted it to be over.

"Mrs. Gladys Barbieri, who has been visiting her brother, Harrison Post," the *Los Angeles Times* reported, "has gone to Reno for a short visit." After the requisite weeks in Nevada to establish residency and achieve her divorce, Gladys returned to her brother's home in Los Angeles. They were a long ways now from the boardinghouse in Gloucester.

As Will had folded him into his world, Harrison did the same for his older sister. He introduced her to his friends, hosted her at suppers. When he attended the grand opera, she was at his side. When Will threw a birthday party for Harrison, she was there, and why not? He was safe now in the Clark kingdom, protected by wealth and power, and he could afford to share.

8

THE LIBRARY

William Andrews Clark Memorial Library, undated.

Just west of the Cahuenga Pass, Angelenos had found a charming picnic spot in a rounded hollow of the Santa Monica Mountains. They called it Daisy Dell. Visitors had also discovered that the hills rising above the small basin provided excellent acoustics, and in 1918 the Theatre Arts Alliance spent $47,500 to purchase the fifty-nine-acre parcel as a venue for open-air performances. Soon the natural amphitheater became known as the Bowl, so called for the shape of the land, not the now-iconic band shell. The first iteration of the distinctive arches wouldn't arrive until 1926. In the beginning, the stage consisted only of a raised wooden platform. In 1921, an audience of eight hundred gathered on wooden benches for the Los Angeles Philharmonic's first sunrise Easter service. The next year, fifty thousand people flocked to the venue for the occasion. And the year after that, Will made a gift of $50,000 for permanent improvements to the amphitheater, with the provision that the Hollywood Bowl would host an annual series of concerts featuring the Los Angeles Philharmonic, and so established an LA cultural collaboration and landmark for decades to come.

As the city continued to grow and thrive, so did Harrison, and so did the court of Will Clark. By 1923, the wall that D. C. McCan had started building two decades earlier enclosed the entire block. Will had bought the remaining lots—twenty-four total since he'd arrived in West Adams—and had the observatory relocated to the northeastern corner. He gifted other properties in the neighborhood to his employees, installing Sir Robert in a house around the corner, Caroline and Chummie a block away on St. Andrews Place, and Coco on West Twenty-Second Street, where she lived with her sister and two nieces. One assisted at the library, the other at the Philharmonic. But of all the grace-and-favor homes, the consort's was the grandest.

When the neighbor across the way at 2505 Cimarron Street put his house on the market, Will snapped it up for $11,000. Gladys had since moved into an apartment of her own in the tony Westlake neighborhood, the so-called Champs-Élysées of Los Angeles, and taken a position at an antiques store opposite Westlake Park.

Harrison didn't raze the existing structure, but he made enough changes that it seemed an entirely new compound emerged, a stark Spanish Colonial villa among the neighborhood's Victorians and Arts and Crafts mansions. A simpler building compared to Will's stately brick manor with its gabled roof and vine-covered walls, the villa was nonetheless formidable and grand. One shared detail: a white stucco wall rising well over eleven feet encircled Harrison's new home.

Meanwhile, Will broke new ground at his own estate. After a scare from a small kitchen fire threatened his treasured library, he made plans for a separate building to house his collection. He hired architect Robert Farquhar, who'd designed the mausoleum in Hollywood Cemetery. Will would spend more than $300,000 for the marble and travertine in his new library. The English oak cabinetry ran over $100,000, and the final cost totaled nearly $800,000.

Excess was at full tilt. At the Cocoanut Grove, the nonprofessionals and the movie stars dined on figs Romanoff with curaçao and lobster à la Louie. They danced under the mechanical glowing-eyed monkeys dangling from the papier-mâché palm trees that had been repurposed from the set of *The Sheik*. Sometimes the Barrymores brought their own live monkeys and let the animals scramble through the canopies and fake foliage. On Friday nights, Joan Crawford danced the Charleston.

Even railing against extravagance—whether alcohol, sex, motion pictures, or the Charleston—could be its own spectacle. Over at the Angelus Temple in Echo Park, thousands thronged to see Aimee Semple McPherson deliver impassioned sermons, rife with metaphors and props, as when she straddled a motorcycle and drove across the altar to rail about the dangers of speeding to the devil. The charismatic faith healer had also harnessed the new medium of radio, an essential factor in the rise of her massive evangelical empire.

Stocks were booming. "We're All Out Here in California Where the Gushers Are—We Just Ought to Clean Up." This was the sales pitch from Courtney Chauncey Julian, a prospecting oilman who was going to make everyone rich. A populist savior with a gold-lined bathtub, "C.C." had founded the Julian Petroleum Company to fight for the small-time investor. He refused to accept money "Unless You Can Afford to Lose." "Widows and Orphans," he warned, "This Is No Investment for You."

More than forty thousand people bought shares. These included middle-class Angelenos, as well as those who could truly afford to lose, like Louis B. Mayer, Cecil B. DeMille, Charlie Chaplin, and industrialist Joseph Dabney, who'd recently hired a young bookkeeper named Raymond Chandler. They all knew that California was a wonderful place to be rich, and besides, they deserved it.

"We are living a day of great things. We are playing with immensities," proclaimed a *Los Angeles Times* editorial with fervor that would've sent Aimee Semple McPherson quivering. "We are hand in glove with the Titans. With each recurring morn some new magnificence is revealed."

This magnificence could be quantified: "We glow with warranted pride at the realization that a solid mile of new homes is being built within our civic limits every month." And the magnificence could be monetized: "New subdivisions provide more than 80,000 additional sites for immediate or future use."

Still, there was more to consider than bountiful real estate. "It is one thing to be prosperous and enterprising; it may be another to be morally clean and mentally just." The question was: Did citizens of Los Angeles deserve the bounty? There was to be no doubt:

> The conditions which exist here should make for the finest character-building in the land. The hazards of environment are at their minimum. We should have more than the ordinary proportion of patriotism because our citizens are mainly descendants of American pioneers. As a city we have no vast foreign districts in which strange tongues are ever heard.

As if English hadn't recently been a foreign tongue in the settlement with the Spanish name. As if German farmers, Japanese fishermen, and French merchants hadn't arrived before the Middle Westerners. As if the Chumash and Tongva people hadn't lived there for centuries. But the writer wasn't concerned with facts or history. He was committed to the myth of a tabula rasa that had belonged to no one until its rightful owners arrived and carved it into their homeland, into a dream of sunshine, property rights, and people fixed by whiteness. "The community is American to its back-bone," the writer insisted, "American" being code that anyone could decipher: no outsiders, no accents, no "Semitic cast," and no degenerates.

And yet an outsider had slipped undetected into this promised land. In a region where housing covenants prohibited selling or renting property to non-whites and often Jews, Harrison owned a home in West Adams and now also a house on the Gold Coast, the oceanfront enclave for the rich and famous, just down the beach from Bebe Daniels, Norma Talmadge, and Mary Pickford and Douglas Fairbanks. His name was in the Los Angeles Blue Book. Through Will's sponsorship, he'd joined the Jonathan Club, the Los Angeles Athletic Club, and the Bel-Air Bay Club, none of which would've accepted his father or his grandfather (or him, had he identified as Jewish). Nevertheless, he belonged. Like a magic wand, the great Clark wealth had turned him into an insider, and he glided from the wood-paneled sanctums of the gentile power brokers to Nazimova's pool parties to even more exclusive gatherings in his own home.

Harrison's turreted villa was made for entertaining, playing host to gatherings both lavish and discreet. Or as Buck Mangam claimed, "It was the scene of indescribable orgies." Since apparently no one else has attempted to describe these parties, we're left only to imagine what might've been possible when Harrison opened the towering wooden door and welcomed his guests into the cavernous hall with a soaring wood-beamed ceiling and the large stone fireplace.

Here, it was easy to hide from prying eyes. There were two small round windows, each with iron shutters, high up on the wall facing the street. And it was easy to keep the room dark. The only other outside light came from the windows onto the building's atrium. As long as they were careful—as long as there was a wall, as long as the shutters kept out the neighbors—they were safe.

So safe that, in 1924, Will decided to publish Wilde's letters. He'd taken precautions. He'd gotten permission from Vyvyan Holland, the author's son and literary executor, and, in case there could be any doubt, the private edition, produced by John Henry Nash, included a page with Holland's stated approval.

It could be seen as a noble gesture—the restoration of a martyred artist, the rash, brilliant, kind man who spent his final years wandering and broken in abject exile. But those inclined to superstition, wary of tempting fate, might flinch at the decision. If this were a fiction from Poe or Wilde, the reproduction of these letters would be the moment where a reckless protagonist, in his passion and hubris, invokes the spirit that will haunt him forever—the moment when he opens the forbidden tomb, digs up the cursed treasure, makes a ghastly pact with his own portrait to remain forever young and beautiful, or, in the case of the two bibliophiles in Los Angeles, revives a doomed romance that left destruction and exile in its wake.

Soon after John Henry Nash began production, Will wrote to notify Arthur Dennison about the forthcoming publication. The young man had left his position with Lois Weber to pursue a career as a writer in New York, where he lived with the watercolorist Wilmot Emerton Heitland. Arthur's father wrote back to Will with tragic news. His son had gone sailing with the painter in the Caribbean, a research trip for a story, and Arthur had been lost at sea. In his few letters to Will, it's possible to perceive the agility and kindness of the young man's intelligence, his humor and curious mind at work, and a literary career cut cruelly short.

In July, Will published Wilde's letters in an edition of two hundred and twenty-five. Lord Alfred Douglas acknowledged receipt of his copy by sending it back with furious notes scrawled in the margins, correcting spellings and protesting annotations. He belittled and he hectored, but he didn't sue.

And yet scandal still arrived. It came that August, not for Will or Harrison but for Gladys, who suddenly found herself caught up in one of the most sensational crimes and public downfalls of the decade.

Gladys's boss, Albert Moers, hadn't started out as an antiques dealer. He'd sold metals first—copper, zinc, aluminum, and more for munitions. He'd married his stenographer Theresa Weinstein in 1915, and their New York–based company had thrived during the war, but once it was over, they took a new path, importing bronzes, oils, tapestries, porcelains, Persian rugs, vases, brocades, lamps, and silverware. Within a few years, the couple decided to relocate to the West Coast, drop a vowel from their name, and open Mors Antiques across the street from Westlake Park. When Gladys Barbieri joined the company, she was given the title of vice president, though it's unclear what executive experience she might've possessed.

While the store flourished, the owners' marriage did not. In May 1924, divorce papers were filed and two months later the Morses were taking stock of their inventory and preparing to divide their property. Perhaps it was always going to be contentious, but complicating the process was the fact that Theresa had begun a romance with former middleweight boxing champion Kid McCoy.

Born Norman Selby in Moscow, Indiana, McCoy came to fame thanks to his lithe moves, showboating antics, and corkscrew punch. He also gave rise to the expression "the real McCoy," which during the twenties had become shorthand for real whiskey as opposed to moonshine. As the boxer's career had waned, he'd parlayed his celebrity into a film career, playing a detective investigating a jewelry theft in *The*

House of Glass in 1917 and two years later an abusive alcoholic prizefighter in D. W. Griffith's *Broken Blossoms.*

But the acting jobs had dried up and his main occupation appeared to be that of courting wealthy women. Deemed the "undisputed male vamp," McCoy had been married eight times—three of those to one woman. By the time Mrs. Mors hired him to be her "bodyguard," he was a paunchy, balding man with a dark fringe of hair, no longer the sculpted muscular beauty of his champion years but still seductive. At least the new divorcée found him so. As their romance bloomed, Gladys took the role of confidante and helpmate to the lovers.

In July, the couple moved into Westlake's Nottingham Apartments, but it didn't take long for Theresa to have second thoughts. The former boxer was a volatile man, prone to rages, especially as he realized that his new paramour, still extricating herself from one marriage, wasn't eager to start another. Neighbors reported hearing fights and threats. Within weeks, Theresa resolved to leave.

On August 13, McCoy pleaded with Theresa to reconsider, but once he realized she couldn't be persuaded, he shot and killed her. Then he fled to his sister's home. The next morning, increasingly desperate, McCoy sought out Albert Mors for a reckoning. The antiques dealer wasn't in his shop, but a number of customers were and the manic gunman took them hostage, wounding several before running out to Westlake Park, where the police arrived and he quietly submitted to arrest.

The Morses had already caught the attention of authorities apart from their divorce and the boxer's rampage. They'd been under federal surveillance for several months because customs officials suspected that the store was part of an international smuggling syndicate. There were hints of criminal ventures. Two weeks after the murder, federal agents discovered safety deposit boxes containing jewelry, vases, tapestries, and gold bric-a-brac registered to McCoy. Before her death, Theresa had allegedly been on the verge of a deal involving $250,000 of trafficked gems with a diamond broker named Harry Katz.

A bon vivant from Chicago, Katz was doing well for himself, with a yacht in San Pedro and a collection of more than twenty violins. On November 10, he was shot to death in his luxury Wilshire apartment. Despite having a significant number of diamonds in his possession at the time, he hadn't been robbed. That left jilted lovers, jealous husbands, a mysterious heavyset man who'd been seen leaving the building, and the murky smuggling ring as possible suspects.

However, a violent crime of so-called passion committed by a down-and-out boxer quickly eclipsed the mysterious murder of Harry Katz. An early entry in the pantheon of Hollywood trials, McCoy's began in December and featured LA's intrepid district attorney Asa Keyes squaring off against rising star lawyer Jerry Giesler, a protégé of Earl Rogers. The defense claimed that Theresa had been the desperate and unhinged party, threatening to kill herself while McCoy valiantly tried to intervene and the gun went off. In pretrial testimony, Gladys had said that her friend had expressed suicidal thoughts. There were people who'd urged Theresa to leave the unstable boxer, but Gladys hadn't been among them. This made her a crucial witness for the defense's case, and McCoy didn't have many.

And yet when the time came for Gladys to take the stand, she was nowhere to be found.

She'd already given testimony sympathetic to a man whose guilt appeared obvious. At that point, two people had been killed—one from domestic violence, the other a targeted hit. Both victims were suspected of ties to a smuggling ring now under federal surveillance. Perhaps like her father, Gladys believed that flight is often the best move.

McCoy's defense team demanded a delay, but the judge ordered the trial to proceed. The boxer was the only one to testify that Theresa had been the instigator in her own violent end, which he demonstrated by grotesquely reenacting the dead woman's supposed last minutes. The jury was unconvinced. McCoy was found guilty, though for manslaughter not murder, and sentenced to prison in San Quentin.

None of the newspapers that avidly followed the trial mentioned Gladys's connection to Harrison or Will. Nor did they connect her with the murdered Katz. The disappearance of Theresa Mors's friend and confidante was perplexing, but it didn't hold the drama of McCoy's courtroom antics and no one looked closely into the whereabouts of the missing witness. Possibly Gladys had slipped back to Chicago or perhaps she'd gone abroad. Perhaps she adopted a completely new name. In any case, she kept a low profile in the coming years, low enough as to be nonexistent to someone looking today.

Apart from the weekend ramble with her older sister a decade before in Chicago, Gladys hadn't made much news in the previous years. There was, however, one notable exception back when she was still married to Joseph Barbieri. According to local reporting, on October 20, 1921, after attending a performance at the Riviera Theatre on Chicago's North Side, Gladys and her mother emerged to discover thieves had stolen the spare tires from their car. The women drove to pick up Gladys's husband, and afterward they claimed they were headed to the police station to report the theft but before they could make it there, a car blocked them and five armed men descended. The gunmen were more ambitious than the tire thieves, stealing the car and $130 in cash, as well as $7,000 worth of jewels.

In Chicago, home to Al Capone's bootlegging, prostitution, and gambling operations, holdups and burglaries were common. Larceny and brute force were daily occurrences. Just months before, thieves had broken into Enrico Caruso's hotel room and stolen $500,000 in jewels from his safe. The holdup of the Barbieris was one among many in Chicago, yet another statistic in a decade sprawling with crime. The police never did find the gunmen or the stolen jewels. But had there really been a holdup? Or simply the story of a holdup? With Gladys, it's a pertinent question. One assumes the jewels were insured.

It's not hard to imagine that Albert Mors, who, according to his many passports, spent the war selling copper, zinc, nickel, aluminum, brass, and electrical wire all across Europe, might have developed contacts that would be fruitful in other import-export operations, particularly those that wished to evade customs officials. And by coincidence, years earlier, Kid McCoy ran a saloon in Manhattan's Hotel Normandie that was often frequented by jewel smugglers. He'd briefly been a jeweler himself.

But Mors was never put on trial for smuggling. Nor was McCoy. Nor was Gladys. Nor did any leads ever surface in the murder of Harry Katz, a cold case to this day. It's a story of loose ends, one of the loosest being the woman who simply vanished that December, evading federal officials, the district attorney's cross-examination, and whoever paid Harry Katz his final visit.

It's possible to imagine these were all simply unusual coincidences—the reported holdup in Chicago, the murdered jewel smuggler from

Chicago, the suspected trafficking ring at Gladys's workplace, her sudden disappearance during a high-profile trial. It's possible. It's also possible Harrison wasn't the only criminal in his family.

For now, none of his sister's chaos touched him. As Gladys slipped away from danger, so Harrison and Will remained unscathed. The library consumed them.

During their travels, they had toured the estate of Chantilly, twenty-five miles north of Paris. The château had once belonged to Henri d'Orléans, the Duke of Aumale. A distinguished military officer, he was the fifth son of Louis-Philippe, the last king in France, and he might have become king himself except for the revolution of 1848, which sent the duke into exile in England. For more than two decades, he bided his time, collecting rare books and fine art, waiting to reclaim his estate. When at last he was allowed to return to Chantilly in 1871, he set about rebuilding the ruined château, including a bi-level library with iron shelves trimmed in leather to protect bindings of his more than fifteen thousand prized volumes. The duke, who died in 1897, bequeathed the estate to the Institut de France with the condition that the grounds and the collection be preserved for posterity.

Will's own library was considerably smaller, but the traces of Chantilly were evident in his two reading rooms with coffered ceilings and metal shelves, though his were made of copper, in homage to the great Clark fortune. A third chamber—a drawing room devoted to chamber music—was modeled on the Sala del Collegio in the Doge's Palace in Venice. Will commissioned panels for the ceiling to be carved out of English walnut that would detail his favorite play, John Dryden's *All for Love*. He also sent Farquhar to the Morgan Library, the Grolier Club, Harvard Library, and other collections for inspiration. Workmen lined the basement vault with steel to keep the books and papers safe from fire and water. The second floor was designated for Will, Cora, and Sir Robert's offices.

But no office for Harrison. While Robert G. Cowan may have been correct in his view that Harrison was not a skilled librarian, the young man did have a hand in the building's creation. Will charged him with its interior design, and Harrison flung himself into the task, picking out settees, choosing tapestries, and commissioning furniture from the Pasadena designer George S. Hunt. They might not chance living together, but they were decorating together. Just as they had sublimated their love into the transcription and publication of Wilde's letters, they did so again, this time not through books but the library itself.

Initially Will had wavered about publishing Oscar Wilde's letters, cowed by the prospect of being sued, but once he got the estate's approval, he'd gone right ahead. As long as he felt safe, he took risks, extravagant ones. The mural in the marble foyer, for instance, was brazen indeed.

"You should be painted," Wilde had written to his young lover, words that Harrison had transcribed and Will had dared to publish. Now they dared again.

And so, from Wilde's pen to Will's ceiling. He hired muralist Allyn Cox to paint the tableau. Among the emblems of art and science, thirteen naked men slouched and torqued, well-muscled and languorous, each, of course, with the face of his copain—thirteen Harrisons, who would remain young and beautiful in perpetuity. Were they muses or were they omens?

9

JUNIOR

That spring, Maizie married for a third time. First weddings were lavish spectacles for the Clarks, but subsequent ceremonies tended to be subdued. The groom was Marius de Brabant, a traffic manager for Union Pacific with a distant link to Belgian nobility. He was handsome, he was younger, but there was nothing for the gossip columnists to chew over. The couple were married in a small ceremony at the Senator's Fifth Avenue mansion. Will didn't make the trip.

The Clark patriarch was eighty-six now. Will had seen him that past December at Bellosguardo, the oceanside estate in Santa Barbara that the Senator had bought just two years earlier. The old man had lost weight, and there'd been little for him to lose. His ever-restless energy had finally started to ebb. Will noticed. His shrewd father, he said, was "becoming vaguer all the time."

Back in New York, the Senator had stopped traveling to his office down on Exchange Place. He had his cherished reports and mail sent to him at the mansion, but after all the years of calculating, foreclosing, underbidding, and counting profits, the game was slipping away from him.

In the days before Maizie's wedding, he'd come down with a cold. Pneumonia set in. On March 2, 1925, two days after his daughter said her vows, the Senator died at home in his limestone colossus with Anna at his side. All of his children, except for his namesake son, were there too. Will departed immediately for New York. Tertius, now living in Los Angeles, came with him.

The Copper King's death marked the end of one of the nation's most lucrative and corrupt careers, in an era defined by lucre and corruption. W.A. built Montana, ravaged the land for its resources, and degraded its political system to control the profits. After all the cash-stuffed envelopes had been delivered, all the checks written, all the mortgages paid for, all the drinks and all the men bought, and all the humiliation he endured to get his seat in the Capitol building, once there he did very little. He'd gotten his long-craved coronation, but he had no interest in governance—crafting laws, representing constituents, or serving the public. He protected his own interests. He fought to open Indian reservations for sale and development and to expand homesteading initiatives. He opposed President Roosevelt's efforts at conservation. The land—its forests, rivers, bedrock, veined batholiths—was the source of his capital. To W.A., any boundary around what he could take was a shackle.

When his term ended, Clark took his title and returned to New York, where he busied himself with the construction of his mansion. He traveled to Paris and bought more art. He traveled to Butte and reminisced about his prospecting days to members of the Society of Montana Pioneers. He continued to enjoy time at the Columbia Gardens, the free amusement park he'd built in the foothills—a feudalist offering for the serfs. He claimed it was his favorite venture and the only one that was a financial loss.

W.A. never did make his way into the rarefied strata of New York elites, but he'd managed to buy everything else he wanted—Rembrandts, Corots, Renoirs, Stradivarii. He contented himself with creating his own society with Anna, his daughters, his art, and the men who listened to him hold forth at the Union League Club.

After being subjected to one such performance, Mark Twain wrote, "With forty years' experience of human assfulness and vanity at banquets, I have never seen anything of the sort that could remotely approach the assfulness and complacency of this coarse and vulgar and incomparably ignorant peasant's glorification of himself." Admittedly, Twain, who was a friend of one of Clark's industrialist rivals, wasn't a neutral observer.

Unlike many other titans of his or any other era, W.A. didn't try to launder his reputation through charitable institutions. He built an orphanage in Butte named after his son Paul, a home in Los Angeles for young women in honor of his mother, and in Santa Barbara a bird refuge in Andrée's memory. These were less ostentatious philanthropic monuments than they were memorials to people he'd truly loved. Buck Mangam deemed him stingy in this, but it reveals an honesty that, as pretentious as Clark was, he had little vanity about leaving behind an image of himself that was other than who he was. He loved his family and he loved his game. He did not pretend otherwise.

Still, his legacy lived on in ways he didn't intend. In 1913, the Seventeenth Amendment was ratified, stipulating that senators would be elected by popular vote, an effort to curb corruption and keep wealthy men like Clark from buying state legislatures wholesale, one that was effective until 2010, when the Supreme Court handed down the *Citizens United v. Federal Election Commission* decision, allowing unlimited and untraceable contributions from corporations and other entities to flood US elections.

Many courted W.A. Few loved him. His longtime housekeeper Nellie Harrington claimed he was misunderstood, that his seemingly aloof manner was not a deficit of character but the result of partial deafness and that he was in fact warm, considerate, and fond of playing the fiddle, especially the song "I'll Take You Home Again, Kathleen." His children were devoted to him if amused by his mannerisms. Whatever she might've felt as a girl groomed to be the lover of the fifty-nine-year-old man, by the time he died, Anna had spent thirty years in Clark's world. It was hers now too. She did not seek headlines nor did she seem to care when they found her. She and Huguette soon left the much-derided mansion on Fifth Avenue, as required by his will. Two years after his death, the property was sold for $3 million and the building razed.

In 1907, at the end of his Senate term, Will's father rose and gave his farewell address to the chamber, articulating what appeared to be the essence of his personal philosophy, in which greed and hoarding were recast as duty and survival:

> In rearing the great structure of empire on the Western Hemisphere we are obliged to avail ourselves of all the resources at our

> command. The requirements of this great utilitarian age demand it. Those who succeed us can well take care of themselves.

Surely he'd availed himself of enough resources that his immediate heirs would want for nothing. Upon the Senator's death, a Brooklyn newspaper claimed that Will's estimated worth of $40,000,000 would double, making him for the moment the richest man in California.

W.A. may have been prickly, he may have had little charm, but he was still an insightful—a shrewd—man, not merely about money but also about what money could do to people, especially his children.

Once a hack driver in Butte, disappointed at getting a ten-cent tip from the Senator, said, "Why, your sons always tip me a dollar."

"Yes I know," W.A. replied. "Willie and Charlie had a rich father—I haven't."

William Andrews Clark Jr. was always "Willie" to his father. Harrison was one of the few who called him "Will." To employees, he was "Mr. Clark," and to this day that's how the staff at the Clark Library often refer to him, but to most everyone else—his siblings, his Montana friends like Temp and Buck—he was "Junior."

He was never far from his father's shadow, and yet he was not his father, as W.A. had well known. The patriarch could give his son his name, but he couldn't give him the wisdom that a poorer father might have. The younger Clark was born into the empire his father built and he knew nothing else. From birth, his father's name and his father's money protected him, but an empire isn't fixed. Its walls can be breached. It can collapse from its own rot. Clark Sr. had lived without an empire, then he built one. He understood it wasn't guaranteed to last, but Junior did not, at least not yet.

However, the son did become the one thing his father hadn't—a lawyer—and Will distinguished himself through philanthropy. Still, he never tried to usurp his father or directly surpass his achievements. The Senator, small as he was, cast an enormous shadow, and it must've been obvious that Will was never going to step out of it, not while his father was alive.

As with all the deaths before, Will's life changed again. What comes next isn't a clear pivot to expansion or recklessness, but a zigzagging path—a man taking steps of his own and also steps that his father took. When obstacles arose, as they had for his father, Will followed the tycoon's instinct for bribery. The shadow may have disappeared, but the money hadn't.

Nor had the whispers. The item in the August issue of *Photoplay* was a breezy bit of gossip, casual speculation about a starlet's latest romance, but its publication meant there was a crisis to be managed and a charade to be performed.

> The most engaged girl in pictures—we mean Patsy Ruth Miller—has gone and got her name linked up with another chap.
>
> How does she do it?
>
> Seems like every time Patsy has a few weeks between pictures she manages to get engaged—or at least get herself reported engaged. That's a knack that a lot of girls would like to possess.
>
> And Patsy just does it in the easiest, offhand way.
>
> This time the other end of the engagement rumor is Harrison Post, millionaire Los Angeles clubman.

Back when Harrison first arrived in Los Angeles, Patsy Ruth had been a protégée of Nazimova, playing a bit part in *Camille*, but now she was a star in her own right, cast alongside Lon Chaney in *The Hunchback of Notre Dame*. Patsy Ruth didn't have a drug habit or some other scandal that required deflection—or if she did, the dirt has stayed buried to this day. It's possible that she was priming the publicity machine for a new movie, but more likely she was doing a favor for her friend Harrison.

> Patsy Ruth and young Post, while in San Francisco recently, engaged in one of the most thrilling of shopping sprees. If reports from the North are to be credited, the pair bought so much it took almost all the moving vans in town to cart off their staggering burden of loot.
>
> And this sure does look mighty serious this time.
>
> "Harrison is so charming," declares the young lady. "But there is nothing definite about our marriage. I have so much to do in pictures that I don't feel it fair to any man to marry now."

> And that's quite an admission from the clever Patsy Ruth.
> Fair enough, too.

"Sure does look mighty serious this time" was Hollywood's code for "never going to happen." Patsy Ruth Miller would eventually marry—three times—but never to Harrison. Whatever gossip was making its way through town never rose above a whisper, for now. Meanwhile, a new nuisance for Will and Harrison arrived—twelve panels for the library floor were damaged during installation. This calamity, though, was easily managed by ordering another $45,000 worth of marble and travertine.

On October 23, the Philharmonic's sixth season opened with Beethoven's Fifth Symphony in C Minor, the Scherzo from Mendelssohn's music to *A Midsummer Night's Dream*, and Liadov's *Fragment de l'Apocalypse*. The California Club hosted a reception to honor Will and Walter Henry Rothwell. It was announced that the orchestra would tour the East Coast in the spring.

But a month later there was new tumult. Tertius, recently engaged to a Broadway dancer, had been named in a $250,000 breach-of-promise suit by an actress starring in a picture called *Ermine and Rhinestones*. Will hired Gavin McNab to handle the matter. A onetime hotel clerk who'd become a major figure in state politics, the San Francisco attorney had successfully defended Charlie Chaplin, Fatty Arbuckle, and Jack Dempsey. To the press, McNab insisted there was no case against Tertius, who was suddenly on his way to Africa with a party of mining engineers. The scandal faded from the papers, but before long the next crisis arrived.

The key to hiding in plain sight is actually hiding. Perhaps if Will and Harrison hadn't been wealthy men, if they'd been poor or middle class, limited to lurking in Pershing Square, subject to small-time shakedowns, unable to afford walled estates and extravagant parties that scandalized the neighbors, they would've remembered the part about hiding and they wouldn't have believed themselves freer than they were. Discretion requires plausible deniability. Such is the stealth function of a word like *secretary*. A painted likeness on a ceiling can be explained away, but men in women's clothing, endearing words, strains of music, laughter in the courtyard—none of that constitutes hiding. Just across the street on West Adams Boulevard, a neighbor was running a thriving bootlegging operation, but the beat cops never noticed, or at least they were well enough compensated not to.

The high white walls hadn't been high enough. The neighbors may not have seen the doings inside Harrison's near-windowless home, but they'd seen and heard the comings and goings of his guests. In January, after a flurry of nuisance complaints, the DA's office ordered that the premises of 2505 Cimarron be vacated at once.

Squashing this scandal was going to require more than gossip about a shopping binge. As Harrison's father had done so often before, as Gladys had when Kid McCoy's trial threatened to ensnare her, and just as Tertius had months earlier, they simply left town. Will canceled the Philharmonic's upcoming tour of the East Coast. Accompanied by William Burgess and Monsignor Tonello, he and Harrison sailed for Europe.

It was easy enough to mask their sudden departure as the usual seasonal migration, common enough for a man of Will's stature. The men always spent several months out of the year traveling, and for Will, Europe offered freedom. He and Harrison could breathe easier there. Unlike Wilde and Douglas's ill-fated flight through Italy after Wilde's release from prison, they didn't have to scrape and cadge for money to pay for servants and food. As always, they stayed in the finest suites in the best hotels. They dined in high style and visited with their elite friends. They acquired more furnishings for the library.

After three months, mainly traveling through Italy, they returned to the States, believing enough time had passed for the dust to settle. They were mistaken. Now it wasn't neighbors complaining, nor was Harrison involved nor even Will, not directly, but the new crisis prefigured even darker troubles to come.

Charlie may have been right about the risk Will was running with his relationship with Harrison. However, there were others who would prove even riskier for him to know, and yet in the end, the real danger wasn't in knowing those or any other men; it was simply in being Will Clark.

It's possible Will first met Thomas Cowles, the twenty-eight-year-old bibliographer working in the Huntington Library, through their shared literary interests. Cowles had made a series of gifts to the Huntington, including a rare publication by H. L. Mencken, a poem by naturalist John Burroughs, and numerous music scores and books in braille. It was Thomas's other activities, though, that caught the attention of local authorities.

In March 1926, upon returning from their European tour, Will and Harrison learned that the DA's office had charged Thomas with "sex perversion" with another man and "lewd and lascivious conduct" with two boys, both age fourteen. At that point, many would've kept their distance from Thomas, but Will, who wasn't implicated in any of the charges, interceded on his friend's behalf. It's impossible to know what motivated Will to get so closely involved—whether it was fear of further discovery or a sense of duty to help a friend—but Will enlisted his personal attorney, Alfred Verheyen, to defend Thomas.

Verheyen, who'd started out working for the Clark family in Butte and relocated to Los Angeles after the war, proved effective, persuading the judge to put the librarian on probation rather than sentence him to prison, on the condition that Cowles be committed for a period to a sanitarium. Will paid the expenses, totaling $1,000—small change next to the costs to come.

Summer arrived. The new marble panels had been installed, the stone urns placed in the garden, the rose du Barry velvet curtains hung, and the millefleur Laver Kirman rug unrolled. It had cost $16,000. Farquhar deemed the woodwork satisfactory. The thirteen Harrisons gazed down from the ceiling. The library was complete.

Will named the building not for himself but for his father. He also made a surprising announcement. He deeded the William Andrews Clark Memorial Library as well as the surrounding grounds to the University of California. This was a bequest estimated at more than $1 million. Usually the editorials and articles lauding Will's generosity appeared in October—the beginning of the Philharmonic's season—but by June they'd already begun to fill the papers.

As the Duke of Aumale had stipulated about his bequest to the Institut de France, Will specified that his collection could not be dispersed. He made no stipulations about his mansion or the observatory. However, he arranged to lease the property back from the institution, with the understanding that he would reside there until his death. It's common for collectors to make bequests to universities and other public institutions. What's less common is making a gift of your home and its contents while you're still alive and then renting it back. There may have been appealing tax benefits in such an arrangement, but Will didn't need to be alleviated of financial burden.

By extending such a generous gift to the nascent university, Will may have been intent on more than burnishing his status as a public benefactor. Now he wouldn't be the only one at risk if his relationship with Harrison was exposed, his connection to a convict like Thomas Cowles became known, or other associations were uncovered. Will had created a much-admired cultural institution, but he stood alone with the Los Angeles Philharmonic. With this act of charity, he merged with a larger body, a web of an organization that would have something to lose if he ever faced public disgrace. Although the power brokers who oversaw that institution might not necessarily rush to protect Will, they could at least be induced to look away.

The splendid drunken twenties were rolling on, but they weren't quite as splendid as they'd once been. In May, Aimee Semple McPherson had gone for a swim at Venice Beach and vanished, prompting rumors of kidnapping and ransom demands. Weeks later, the dehydrated, bedraggled revivalist appeared in a Mexican border town with a ghastly tale of captivity, drugs, and torture that soon disintegrated. It turned out the preacher hadn't been taken hostage. Instead, she was hiding out with her radio engineer. District Attorney Asa Keyes had a case for obstruction of justice, but it never made it to trial. Rumors abounded that newspaper titan William Randolph Hearst and his checkbook were responsible for the dropped charges.

The charismatic McPherson had been a compassionate presence on the evangelist circuit. Though she returned to her ministry, her fall from grace had left a vacuum and a new voice, that of Bob Shuler, ranting and reactionary, now filled the airwaves, thundering against vice and vagrancy.

The giddy, expansive decade was starting to contract. The backlash was gathering. On July 18, an unnamed writer took to the editorial pages of the *Chicago Tribune* to rage at the presence of an unwelcome contraption in a men's room: "A powder vending machine! In a men's washroom! Homo Americanus!" With the next sentence, the author's indignation slid into a call to violence: "Why didn't someone quietly drown Rudolph Guglielmo, alias Valentino, years ago?"

His honor attacked, Valentino nearly challenged the anonymous writer to a duel until he was dissuaded by H. L. Mencken. A few weeks later, while staying at the Hotel Ambassador in Manhattan, the movie star collapsed from what was thought to be appendicitis but turned out to be perforated ulcers. On August 23, Valentino slipped into a coma and died at the age of thirty-one.

And despite the *Los Angeles Times*' claims of Southern California's innate patriotism and righteousness, there seemed to be other forces at play: greed and corruption. On May 5, 1927, the Los Angeles Stock Exchange halted trading of the Julian Petroleum Corporation. The stock had been over-issued by more than 1,000 percent, and more than $150 million of its investors' money had vanished. The scam tore through the muzzy fantasy that the average American could ascend the ladder of aspirational wealth. If such a ladder did exist, it wasn't there for common folk to actually climb, but for a faux-populist huckster with a gold-lined bathtub to dangle at their expense and his profit.

The original visionary, C. C. Julian, knew his grift was running out and sold his stake to Jacob Berman and S. C. Lewis before the regulators closed in. What had started out as one con—a Ponzi scheme in which the company introduced more than five million illegal shares into the market—had mushroomed into multiple layers of fraud as the executives created new investment pools to purchase more stock, inflating prices for other investors. In creating these multiple tiers, the executives siphoned money from their poorest clients into separate tranches for their wealthiest, which included Louis B. Mayer, Cecil B. DeMille, and Charlie Chaplin, all of whom also lost money, though they could afford to.

Even the Philharmonic and Los Angeles's now-burgeoning music community had taken a sudden shock. Earlier that year, while driving out to the beach, the fifty-five-year-old conductor Walter Henry Rothwell suffered a heart attack and died behind the wheel. In Caroline Estes Smith's history of the Philharmonic's first ten years, she described

Will as the creator of the institution and Rothwell as its builder. It remained to be seen whether Georg Schnéevoigt, the Finnish conductor who opened the 1927–1928 season, would be able to inspire the same accolades.

And yet that wasn't Will's biggest crisis. A new scandal had ensnared him, one that threatened to unmake his entire world. He'd built a name for himself as a philanthropist, establishing one of the pillars of the city's cultural life. His charity extended beyond institutions. He sent his nieces to finishing schools in Grenoble and New York. When his chauffeur expressed an interest in dentistry, he paid the man's tuition. At a dinner party where a young guest demonstrated his talent on one of Will's prized violins, he gifted the instrument to the aspiring musician. And when a milliner named Jack Oray voiced interest in opening a shop, Will provided the funds. He also introduced the young man to his longtime friend Blanche Savoie, a former stage actress from Butte famous for a light opera called *Pink Lady*. Savoie & Oray, their boutique on Wilshire Boulevard, sold gowns, lingerie, and hats. Will had taken such an interest in the young hatmaker that he installed Jack in a home of his own a few blocks away in West Adams, but Will's generosity would come back to haunt him.

Oray was already on probation for driving under the influence when the police picked him up drunk after another traffic accident. In custody, he turned out to be a talkative man, so much so that he implicated Will Clark in a number of offenses that had nothing to do with the California Vehicle Act. As Buck Mangam put it, "Oray was to become the instrument through which the district attorney's office obtained a full statement of Clark's criminal relations, information sufficient to support an indictment on twelve counts."

Buck never specified what the twelve counts were, but presumably they included charges like "lewd and lascivious conduct" or the "infamous crime against nature." It's possible—and troubling to imagine—that, like Thomas Cowles, Will was accused of molesting underage boys. Whatever the evidence the DA had, neither the charges nor the potential fallout could be easily swept away by a stay in a sanitarium. Everything Will had built—his name, his institutions—was at risk.

It may have been a coincidence that Will donated the library to UCLA after Thomas Cowles's trial, and it may have been happenstance yet again that as the DA's office prepared these new charges, Will donated $1 million to support the Los Angeles Philharmonic. The news, announced at one of the first concerts of 1928, was met with thundering ovations and bravos. The musicians stood and sounded fanfares as Will approached the stage. Director Schnéevoigt motioned to the orchestra to begin the overture to *Tannhäuser*, then pressed the baton into Will's hand and left him alone to conduct the Wagner score. The *Los Angeles Times* noted that "it was the first time that so eminent a music philanthropist directed his own orchestra, meeting the sudden occasion most surprisingly."

Days after his performance, Will left town. Accompanied by Harrison and William Burgess, he boarded a ship bound for Europe, and, as before, Will enlisted Verheyen, who'd finessed the Cowles lawsuit, to manage the DA's office while he and his companions waited out the tempest.

Will wasn't the only one buffeted by crisis. For Los Angeles, 1928 was a year full of storms—and at the center of each one was District Attorney Asa Keyes. Angelenos were still reeling from the gruesome murder of twelve-year-old Marion Parker that had taken place weeks earlier. A massive, enraged manhunt had sprawled north to Oregon where the killer, twenty-year-old William Hickman, was arrested. Keyes had built a twenty-five-year career as an aggressive, agile prosecutor. He'd sent Kid McCoy to prison four years earlier, and he made quick work of Hickman. By the end of February, the defendant was convicted of murder and sentenced to hang.

And then, a few weeks later, just before midnight on March 12, the St. Francis Dam collapsed. Forty miles northwest of Los Angeles, twelve billion gallons of water exploded into the dry Santa Clara riverbed, surging all the way to the Pacific Ocean, laying waste to livestock, orchards, bridges, cars, schools, churches, and homes. Between four hundred and six hundred people were killed, some bodies found as far away as the coast of Mexico. Many never at all. Just days before the collapse, a worker had raised alarm about a leak at the base of the dam, but William Mulholland, who'd designed the Los Angeles Aqueduct and its twenty-one dams, examined the spot and deemed the structure sound.

This was the same man who'd famously opened the gates of the aqueduct, watched the water from Owens Valley gush forth, and proclaimed, "There it is—take it." Keyes presided over the inquest, relentless in his cross-examination of the once-lauded architect, who at last broke down and wept, saying, "I envy the dead."

In the past, Will had never been the direct target of the district attorney's office. Harrison had been the first to fall into Keyes's sights, back when the neighbors complained about his parties. He and Will had circumvented that by leaving town. Verheyen's legal acumen and Will's money had mitigated the consequences of Thomas Cowles's crimes. Will expected to deploy these same tools in the wake of Jack Oray's arrest. What he did not expect, though, was another letter from Charlie.

In Buck Mangam's telling, Charlie's intervention wasn't the worst part. That was the news that the last person Will would ever want involved in his secret life had also stepped into the fray: his son, Tertius.

Alfred Verheyen had worked for Will for years. The lawyer finessed many complicated legal matters and likely managed numerous payoffs. However, in the face of Will's twelve counts, Verheyen's confidence faltered. Seeking counsel of his own, he turned to Tertius.

Will's son may have initially believed whatever explanation his father gave him when Harrison first arrived at the West Adams estate in 1919. The mansion was a landing place for countless visitors—musicians, artists, and those who orbited them. Sir Robert was a new occupant back then as well. Will's nieces and nephews often stayed when they visited Los Angeles. In those days, Harrison may have seemed just another member of the ever-shifting court.

If Tertius had been oblivious before, he wasn't now. After his own brushes with scandal, he'd gotten married, though his bride was neither an actress nor a dancer. Born in Big Spring, Texas, Thelma Wyatt Johnson had moved to Helena some years before—long enough to be considered a Montana girl. A grown man, Tertius was capable of seeing the true nature of his father's relationship with Harrison. Besides, it was impossible to misunderstand the DA's complaint. Tertius reacted as Verheyen had. He sought more help. The two men set out for the headquarters of the United Verde Copper Company in Jerome, Arizona, taking the matter directly to the family fixer.

Many times before, Charlie had rushed to his father's aid. Now he lunged on his brother's behalf, hurrying to Los Angeles, where he hired a private investigator, who would claim to uncover at least twenty-four men suspected of being homosexual and all connected to Will. Charlie wrote to Will, alerting him to what he'd found.

Will was not grateful for his brother's intervention or for Verheyen's so-called assistance. He'd expected his attorney to contain the damage, not spread it. That Tertius had been involved, too, was a staggering humiliation. Will had ignored Charlie's counsel before, and he dismissed it again.

For years, Charlie had been an integral part of the Clark machine, but now Will was going to build his own apparatus. Shame may not have been the only reason he rejected the longstanding family network. He sought a new strategy. Or rather, he was going to use an old strategy, but he sought someone new to carry it out. Montana insiders would not do, but California insiders would. Will turned to the son of another senator, also a namesake son, Samuel Shortridge Jr., whose firm, Shortridge and McInerney, was based in San Francisco. The first name signaled wealth, power, and access, but it was the second that would prove more consequential.

For some, power is a blunt object to be brandished, but for Joe McInerney, it was pure liquid—to be channeled, diverted, surfed. A blunt object is effective enough, and Joe, a tall man with a quick and hot temper, didn't shrink from violence. Often he'd instigate it. But he also understood that liquid moves faster, seeps deeper into the ground, making its permanent home in dark cracks and crevices.

Joe hadn't been raised in the West Coast political aristocracy, but he made his way quickly enough. He was born on July 24, 1896, in New York, and his family moved to San Francisco when he was about six. A brief stint at the *San Francisco Bulletin* before turning to law served him well; he would always know which reporters to call whenever he needed an item placed.

Joe worked for bootleggers and politicians. He represented Jimmy O'Connell, the San Francisco Giants outfielder who was banned from baseball after he tried to bribe the Phillies' shortstop to throw a playoff game in 1924. Like Harrison, the lawyer hadn't always had money, but he'd always been near it. In 1919, he married Marjorie Heath, the daughter of a wealthy dairyman from Berkeley, and later represented his wife's mother in a sensational divorce suit against her father.

He'd managed political campaigns and run for a judgeship himself before recognizing that his skills were best deployed in back rooms and men's clubs, amid dark wood and leather chairs, doing business without seeming to do business, the flow of private money to public faces as natural as the waiter putting another cocktail in his hand. Operator, fixer, bagman, and hard drinker, Joe was Will Clark's salvation.

In February, Harrison and William Burgess left Will on his own in Paris and returned to the States. They were greeted by Charlie, waiting for them at the dock in New York. Will's brother wasn't there to offer solace or protection, as he'd once done for Maizie, but to issue a command: Harrison was not to return to California.

A decade earlier, Charlie had wanted Harrison out of Will's life. Harrison didn't leave then. He didn't now. He refused to take orders from Charlie. With Burgess, he boarded a train and returned to Los Angeles.

There, Joe McInerney proved his mettle. In Verheyen's office, he'd demanded the case documents—damning evidence about what the DA had on Will. Joe could be a persuasive man, or rather, he was prepared to resort to whatever form of persuasion a situation required, even if that meant wrestling the sheaf of papers out of Verheyen's hands. Next, Will had an order for Charlie: steer clear of his affairs.

Instead, Charlie enlisted two family associates, the general manager of the United Verde Copper Company and a mining attorney, to travel to Paris to make Will see reason. Both brothers had the same goal—a complete cover-up, which would be an expensive operation, but the Clarks were used to that. They bought silence just as they bought votes. However, Charlie's plan required Will to disavow Harrison and the other men in their circle, and Will refused.

His father and his son had both been accused of breach of promise. Maizie had been named in an alienation-of-affection suit. The senator's marriage to Anna had shocked the country. But the twelve counts waiting for Will in Asa Keyes's office were of a far greater magnitude than anything the family had known before.

Maybe it was the same imperious streak that drove his father to lunge over and over for a Senate seat. Maybe it was the fury and humiliation of having his brother and son sorting through his most intimate secrets. Or maybe he simply could not tolerate the idea of renouncing Harrison or anyone else. Whatever the reason, Will refused Charlie's entreaties and his emissaries. Instead, he readily welcomed Joe. His new attorney had also crossed the Atlantic and, together in Paris, the two men gamed out a plan to put the crisis to rest. Harrison's sister had evaded Asa Keyes by simply disappearing, but that wasn't an option for the founder of the LA Philharmonic. Joe understood that there were always two spheres of operation for men like Will Clark—the public and the shadow—and he threw himself into both.

First the public: By the end of March, the *Los Angeles Times* announced that a tribute concert in Will's honor was scheduled for April 21. The newspapers claimed this was a surprise to greet him upon his return from Europe. The orchestra would use the proceeds from the testimonial to fund a monument to commemorate Will's great philanthropic contribution to Los Angeles.

On April 11, after months of telegrams, lawyers fired, lawyers hired, visitors refused, and harried travel, Will and Joe boarded the SS *Majestic* in Cherbourg. They arrived in New York six days later and proceeded to Los Angeles. But they were late by several hours, missing out on the performances of Tchaikovsky's *Pathétique*, Strauss's *Till Eulenspiegel's Merry Pranks*, and the Overture from Wagner's *Rienzi*. Conductor Schnéevoigt concluded the tribute by encouraging members of the audience to send telegrams to the Philharmonic's founder to express their gratitude. The next step, though—the critical one—didn't involve an auditorium or public adulation.

This was the shadow strategy. The twelve counts against Will remained, but he and Joe had reason to think they might find a receptive audience in Asa Keyes. The DA had been ruthless with murderers like Kid McCoy and William Hickman. Even with William Mulholland, a revered figure in Los Angeles, Keyes showed no mercy. Certainly the tens of thousands of people who'd lost their savings in the Julian Petroleum, or Julian Pete, conspiracy expected justice. And yet the man who'd swiftly brought a conviction of William Hickman and scorned Mulholland didn't appear to be the same man prosecuting the Julian Pete conspirators.

A week into the trial of Berman and Lewis, the DA moved that charges be dismissed. Despite witness accounts and written documentation, including IOUs, Keyes claimed there wasn't sufficient evidence. The judge was unconvinced. The trial proceeded. Keyes rambled, he misdirected witnesses, he contradicted his own attorneys, he appeared distracted, that is, when he did arrive in court. His performance was so baffling, so willfully negligent and meandering, that the judge admonished him.

There were two Asa Keyes. One was a driven prosecutor. The other, the one who dropped charges against Aimee Semple McPherson, was decidedly not, and that was the Asa Keyes who paid a visit to 2205 West Adams Boulevard. In the dark-gabled mansion, with Joe and Will, the district attorney drafted a letter stating there was no complaint on file against Will Clark. This was, in fact, true, but it did not, as Buck wrote, "negative the assertion of Verheyen that the District Attorney had sufficient information in his possession to indict Clark on twelve counts." In plainer terms, Keyes's office had proof to charge Will but never did.

Days later, in the courtroom for the Julian Pete trial, the DA resumed his bewildering performance. During the closing argument, he alternated between exonerating some defendants and shrugging his shoulders at others. The jury acquitted all, citing the prosecution's incoherence and contradictions, as well as the tortured wording of the indictments, which made it impossible to convict. More than forty thousand people had lost over $150 million, and no one was held accountable. A week later, Keyes announced he was retiring to go into private practice.

Joe McInerney had proved his worth, though he may have been lucky in his timing. Who knows if Buron Fitts, Keyes's successor, would've been as amenable to the late-night conference? In any case, the looming twelve counts evaporated. The Will Clark scandal of 1928, the one that could have threatened everything he'd built, never broke.

"I never bought a man who wasn't for sale," his father once quipped. While Will may have rejected his brother's efforts, he still followed the Clark instincts.

The evening with Asa Keyes had not been cheap. The same year, at the booksellers Dulau and Company in London, Will paid $28,000 for the complete bloc of Oscar Wilde's manuscript material. As Clark librarian Bruce Whiteman noted, it was this purchase that "turned his Wilde collection from wonderful to peerless."

Over his lifetime, Will spent more than $683,000 acquiring thousands of rare books, autographed manuscripts, music scores, and incunabula. By Buck's estimate, Will paid roughly $300,000 for a single sheet of paper signed by Asa Keyes.

10

THE SECRETARIES

No wedding rumors for Harrison that spring, but he did make one notable appearance in the *Los Angeles Times*. We'll never know whose idea it was to run an illustrated feature about the espalier trees he was growing in the courtyard of his West Adams villa; surely Joe had approved the article that explored the "Old World art" of training trees to grow against a wall or on a trellis. Ideal for small gardens, they could be shaped in a palmetto form, fan, or double V, and, as the author noted, "espalier apple trees make a flowering boundary between neighbors—definite but delightful."

A trifle of a story, certainly it didn't carry the weight of a payoff to Asa Keyes. Harrison hadn't been enlisted in that transaction, but he too had taken precautions. He'd returned separately from Will to LA. They didn't have to fear outrageous scenes, like the Marquess of Queensberry stalking Oscar Wilde with a bouquet of rotten vegetables, but they'd determined traveling apart was a necessary measure. It seems likely that the brush with the district attorney also figured in Harrison's next move.

While Joe and Will were negotiating the philanthropist's freedom, Harrison installed himself at the Uplifters Club, 120 acres of rambling seclusion in the Pacific Palisades. There, at the edge of the ocean, the Los Angeles Basin bunches up and the land crinkles into wooded canyons, tree-stippled mesas, and red bluffs shearing down to the surf. The rest of the continent—and the people scurrying on top of it with their rumors and whispers—recede. The air is always cooler, softer, cleaner. Maybe it's all the negative ions from the ocean. Maybe it's all the money.

Inspired by the Bohemian Grove, the exclusive, all-male retreat on the Russian River, plumbing mogul Harry Marston Haldeman founded the Uplifters Club in 1913. The group initially held intermittent gatherings at spots like Lake Arrowhead and Del Mar, but once Prohibition took effect, members sought a permanent refuge where they could carouse undisturbed by law enforcement. The roster included financiers, manufacturing magnates, publishing executives, and studio chiefs, as well as actors and writers like Harold Lloyd and Edgar Rice Burroughs. L. Frank Baum coined titles for the club's officers, extolling their various "cup lifting" abilities: Grand Muscle, Elevator, Royal Hoister, and Lord High Raiser.

The compound boasted tennis courts, a theater, trapshooting range, swimming pool, clubhouse, drinking halls, poker parlor, polo field—and privacy. There was so much land that members built bungalows and lodges for themselves as country getaways, all of which were required to conform to code, to be "left rustic" and painted brown, gray, or green. A number of the cottages had been repurposed from film sets, such as the log cabin from the 1923 Plymouth Colony historical drama *The Courtship of Miles Standish*.

The Uplifters exuded an aura of secrecy—more so than the lounges in the Los Angeles Athletic Club or the Jonathan Club. Most buildings included a concealed bar or kegs built into the walls. Everyone there was openly hiding, and Harrison fit right in.

Meanwhile, Will bristled with new ambition. Having dispensed with the nuisance of the DA's office, he directed his energies to what remained of the family empire. A fault line had grown among the Clarks. Despite the acrimony over the Oray affair, it was not between Will and Charlie. The brothers' bond was still strong, and they would remain united by affection and by money.

The issue at hand was how to manage their father's estate, now three years since his passing. The brothers were on one side of the rift and sisters Katherine and Maizie on the other. Eventually, Anna and Huguette stepped in and sided with the men. But the Clarks were a practical clan, and, as family quarrels went, this one was quickly resolved with all agreeing to sell everything and divide the spoils, except, of course, for the Senator's beloved and still lucrative United Verde Mine in Arizona, which Charlie continued to oversee. However, what remained of the original fortune in Montana was absorbed by the Anaconda Copper Mining Company and the American Power and Light Company. Some empires fall noisily, brutally; the Clarks' was chopped up and sold off for parts.

Will, however, had no intention of leaving his home state. That summer, in addition to the usual guests, he'd hosted the still-living members of Montana's Constitutional Convention at Salmon Lake. He also bought the *Montana Free Press* and two other newspapers, as well as a packing plant and several other enterprises. The state was in the midst of a heated gubernatorial campaign, and Will readily jumped into the fray, throwing his newly bought papers' support behind the challenger to the incumbent. He knew well enough from his father that controlling politicians and newspapers was a cost of doing business.

In September, Will announced that after the Philharmonic's 1928–1929 season, he would limit his "active participation in the orchestral affairs" and reduced his annual contribution of $200,000 to $50,000. As Caroline Estes Smith told the *Los Angeles Times*, after a decade of funding the institution, "he feels that now the time has come, when, if ever, the orchestra must stand on its own merit." It's also possible that, like Harrison, he wanted to put more distance between himself and the Los Angeles DA's office.

Perhaps he believed he could have more control in Montana. The Clarks once owned Butte, but they'd never owned Los Angeles. In November, the city's new district attorney, Buron Fitts, charged his predecessor with taking $100,000 in bribes to throw the Julian Pete trial. Three months later, Asa Keyes was convicted and sentenced to prison in San Quentin. It was Will's great fortune that his own payoff activity was never dredged up.

But Will's bid to reprise his father's former glory wasn't met with the rousing welcome he might've hoped for. William Andrews Clark Sr. had been responsible to a large degree for creating the industry that built Montana, but his children had not. Except for Will, they'd spent more time in New York, California, and Europe than in the place that gave rise to their wealth. Consequently, they had come to be seen with disdain—carpetbaggers in their homeland. The rival papers portrayed Will not as a native son coming home at last, but as an interloper, a princeling woefully out of touch.

Besides, Montana wasn't ruled by kings anymore but by one sprawling corporate entity, whose main opponent wasn't a tycoon but a force, the organized labor movement. Will's father had seen the writing on the wall long ago and capitulated, taking his game instead to Nevada and Arizona. Mark Harrison had been a hustler, and so had William Andrews Clark Sr.—on an extraordinary scale—but their sons were not. Will might call himself a "capitalist," but his vocation was for culture, not commerce, and his zeal for his new enterprises soon flagged, especially after his candidate was soundly beaten in the governor's race. He was in his fifties now, not an old man, but too old and too rich perhaps to learn to maneuver and to persevere. Unlike his father, he'd come to the game too late.

In January, he announced he'd had a change of heart and pledged another million dollars to fund the Philharmonic for five more years. And in May, less than a year after buying the newspapers, Will suspended publication and sold the printing plants to the Anaconda Copper Mining Company.

Harrison didn't fancy a himself a business visionary or a hustler. He was a clubman, vetted and protected, both guest and host, ordering meals from a staff he didn't supervise, basking in the ease of hotel service without the burden of travel. The Los Angeles Athletic Club had just finished building the Riviera Country Club, its new outpost in the Palisades with a new polo field and a golf course that'd cost nearly $250,000.

Back in Sacramento, his father had displayed trophies for the local harness races in his shop windows. Now Harrison stabled his own racehorses at the Uplifters. In the Palisades, he belonged to a coterie of socialites, movie stars, and industry players who rode together through the wooded hills and canyons, such as Will Rogers and Leo Carrillo, a onetime vaudeville actor whose family roots extended back to the first Spanish expedition. Today the state park that stretches up the Malibu coast bears his name. Harrison's new equestrian community also included Ann Rork, Hal Roach, and Snowy Baker, the manager of the Riviera Country Club. A sports legend in Australia, Baker started acting in silent films in the United States and also worked as a stuntman and personal coach to celebrities, teaching stars like Valentino, Greta Garbo, and Shirley Temple to swim, fence, and ride horses.

For the past decade, Harrison revolved around Will, but his orbit had shifted. He'd even started making his own philanthropic gestures, paying for the musical education of a talented young singer named John Herring, whom he'd met at a Hollywood party. Though Harrison had seemed at times like a spouse to Will, it's not possible to simply transpose the concept of a monogamous, traditionally heterosexual marriage onto their relationship. They might wear the same ring, they might travel together, but they didn't live together, and if Buck Mangam was correct about the "indescribable orgies," their sex lives were not restricted to one another. Likely they had an understanding similar to the one between Wilde and Douglas—that they were each other's soul mate but not sole sexual partner. While Harrison might have romances and liaisons with other men, his devotion would never falter. He would never develop the type of bond he had with Will with anyone else.

If the early passions had ebbed for Will and Harrison, other connections endured. *Architectural Digest* ran a photo spread that year showcasing the interiors of Will's library, crediting Harrison's work on the furnishings. They were men who loved what the German immigrant on trial after the Baker Street raid had called "beautiful things, art, music, or any of that kind." And they knew what it meant to belong to a despised tribe. They would always be on the same side of the wall, and Harrison would always be Will's copain.

While Will was disentangling himself from his Montana misadventures, Harrison further ensconced himself in the Palisades. He'd sold his beach house on the Gold Coast and bought a home in a new exclusive subdivision designed by Mark Daniels, the engineer and architect who'd planned Bel Air, San Francisco's Sea Cliff, and the gardens at Will's estate in West Adams. Inspired by the Amalfi Coast, Castellammare—castle by the sea—included streets named Bellino, Tranquillo, and Porto Marina Way, where Harrison's Villa dei Sogni was tucked into the coastal hillside.

Harrison was a host again, opening his home to his riding friends, though it's unclear if he was holding more libertine gatherings. He still had neighbors, but they weren't inclined to grumble about, much less report, any debauches. Like Harrison, they'd come for the ocean air and to be left alone. They too embraced the developer's Italianate theme. Up the hill, director Roland West occupied the grand Castillo del Mar. Around another bend was movie star Joseph Cotten at his Villa Romantica, and high above the surf loomed Villa de Leon, the thirty-room mansion that belonged to wool magnate Leon Kauffman.

And Gladys was back. The central figures of the Kid McCoy trial were gone. Albert Mors had returned to the East Coast and remarried. The convicted boxer was serving his term in San Quentin, as was the district attorney who'd put him there and who never did cross-examine Harrison's sister. Will hadn't been able to elude Asa Keyes, but Gladys had. The previous five years of her life are a blank to us—if she intended a disappearing act, it was a flawless performance. Now she was back in Harrison's realm, making herself at home in the Villa dei Sogni. She adapted quickly. She bought a show dog named Sidlaw Trotsky and she took up her brother's hobby of bookbinding. She also began calling herself a countess—if Harrison could be whomever he wanted, then why not Gladys or Felice or whatever name she gave herself?

This was the summer of Robert Ehrmann, the tennis star from Cincinnati. Only speculation remains as to whether or not Harrison was having an affair with the dashing twenty-eight-year-old staying in his beach house. And it's conjecture to suppose that it was Gladys—Countess Barbieri, that is—who initiated the elaborate origin story they told Robert, but surely she provided some of the most ornate touches.

In his journals, Harrison could be quick to appraise but was rarely discursive in his assessments. If he was drawn to people, he usually described them as "attractive" or "amusing," and if he wasn't drawn to them, they were "not" those things. He wasn't a terribly expansive or revelatory diarist like his friend Carl Van Vechten. He made an exception, however, with one person.

This, from 1942, is his description of his sister, written when the summer of 1929 was a distant memory:

> with her indolent life—her inactivity—took form of a grotesque activity of the tongue—she didn't know how things really stand—she lets her phantasy run riot—and that phantasy, nourished by lack of physical exercise indulged in a love of scandal mongering which bordered, and very often trespassed, on the pathological.

> she possesses that priceless of all gifts—she believes her own lies—she looks people straight in the faces and speaks from her heart, a falsehood before it left her lips had grown into a flaming truth—she is an improvident liar. There is no classical parsimony about her misstatements. They are copious, baroque, and encrusted with pleasing and unexpected tricks of ornamentation—never could I hope to rival her technique—nor want to.

But 1942 was still a long way off, and whether or not the fake countess was the first to let *phantasy* run riot with the story of a Montana pioneer father and an exceptional childhood as wards of Senator Clark, it would seem that Harrison didn't protest the fabrication. The truth is none of it was a lie, not entirely. Harrison *was* taken in by a benevolent older figure who wasn't his parent, though Mary Post was hardly a copper baron, and the tale of a poor boy raised abroad lavished with an older man's wealth was real too—just not for Harrison and Gladys. It was someone else's story. They simply stole it.

They also told Robert that Will and Harrison were going to buy Anna Gould's extravagant Palais Rose in Paris, though they never did in fact buy the Versailles-inspired château from the American heiress. Instead, that summer, after selling off his Montana acquisitions, Will spent over $100,000 to buy an apartment at 74 Avenue de la Bourdonnais in the Seventh Arrondissement, just blocks from the Eiffel Tower. Will may not have inherited his father's political and financial drive, but in other ways he was the Senator's truest echo, ever the Paris Millionaire's son.

Raymond Lemire was twenty-five when he moved into Will's new apartment that summer. Passport photos taken years later show an assured young man with a slightly receding hairline, a lively, direct gaze, and a lopsided smile. Raymond gives an impression of ease in his jacket and tie, every bit the "capitalist" he, too, calls himself. He doesn't glower or pout as the young Harrison did, but then again a passport photo is a different affair from a studio portrait.

That people of different ages or generations fall in love or have affairs is not an original observation. That Will Clark was attracted to younger men hardly distinguished him. He was forty-two when he met Harrison, and now fifty-two the summer of 1929.

In a near reenactment of his early years with Harrison, Will showered the young Frenchman with gifts. In addition to the apartment in the Seventh Arrondissement, he gave Raymond money, jewelry, a library, a vineyard on the Riviera, and an estate in Brittany. On passenger manifests, his profession was listed variously as "proprietor," "none," and "secretary." One could accuse Will of cliché: he was aging, but his lovers weren't.

Except that Will didn't meet Raymond that summer. Unlike Harrison, Raymond hadn't been a shop clerk. According to Buck Mangam, he'd been an orphan, one of the beneficiaries of the fund Will had established in France back in 1918, back when Raymond was fourteen.

It would seem when Harrison had told Robert his tale of being adopted by the senator, he was cribbing from Anna's history, but in fact the same scenario was unfolding again on the other side of the Atlantic.

It's possible to assume that Will's interest in Raymond wasn't sexual, that he took a strictly fatherly role with the boy and nothing more. And it's possible to assume that the Senator's interest in Anna La Chapelle had been also purely paternal, until it wasn't.

"After the boy had reached a suitable age," Buck Mangam wrote of Raymond, "Clark initiated him into his mode of life."

Harrison may not have had wealth or power when he met Will, but he wasn't an orphan in postwar France or a thirteen-year-old girl in a nineteenth-century mining town. We can point to the vast imbalance between the power he and Will possessed when they first met, as we could about the difference between Will and his wife Alice. Unless Will pursued Anna Gould, for instance, or Ned Doheny, there would always be a disparity in any relationship when it came to his wealth.

This was the case with most of his friendships as well. He didn't bring Henry Huntington to the Mowitza Lodge. He brought Sir Robert, Coco, Eddie Clark, Chummie and Caroline, Temp, Buck, and other Montana insiders—people who were dependent on ecosystems that the Clark fortune had created. Though they may not have had Will's money, they didn't lack for skill or talent. They were lawyers, musicians, and librarians—people with professions and agency in the world. Likewise, by the time Will stepped into the Marsh in 1919, Harrison had acquired a degree of autonomy. He was twenty-two. He wasn't dependent on the older man for food and shelter.

The histories of the laws that determine when a person is legally allowed to have sex are histories of anxiety. They are snapshots of shifting notions about youth and self-determination, about agency and entitlement, of the desire to protect the vulnerable from predation tangled with terror of sexual expression and autonomy. In 1804, as the Napoleonic Code sought to abolish the feudal privileges of the ancien régime, children under eleven were deemed sexual minors, a reflection of the concept that had emerged in the previous century that childhood was a state distinct from adulthood and that seigneurial privileges were no longer permissible. In 1863, that age was raised to thirteen.

It was still thirteen when Anna La Chapelle arrived in Paris to study the harp and Will the violin. In both Montana and California, it was ten. During the early twentieth century, as the Progressive Era took hold in America, those states revised their laws, and by the time Will bought his apartment at 74 Avenue de la Bourdonnais, it was eighteen in both. In France it remained thirteen.

Likely neither Clark Sr. nor Jr. tracked those legal shifts that closely. They were, though, certainly aware of the governing norms of their times, and they both knew whatever they were doing with their so-called wards, it wouldn't be done in America.

On October 24, 1929, Will attended the opening of the Philharmonic, now entering its second decade. That same day, the stock market lost 11 percent of its value. The Julian Pete financial implosion had been a dry run for Black Thursday, the end of the decade's wild speculation and the beginning of the Great Depression.

Companies went bankrupt. Savings vanished overnight. The crash did affect Will, though of course few people were as secure as he was. Still, he was forced to restructure his financial holdings, but his new plan may have been more a reaction to his recent debacles—in Montana and with the Los Angeles DA—than to the fallout from the Depression.

In January, Will wrote to Buck and instructed the secretary to transfer all his remaining bonds and securities in Montana to his bank in New York. If that didn't make his intentions clear, his next order of business did: "Also," Will wrote, "I want to prepare to sell my Mowitza

Lodge—all except the personal belongings. I am heartily sick of the U.S.—Montana and California. There is only one place to live & that is France."

William D. Mangam had worked for the Clark enterprises in some fashion for nearly three decades, most of that time as Will's manager and proxy in Butte.

He hadn't been raised among tutors abroad, but he came from a well-established Brooklyn family. He was named for his grandfather, a prominent grain merchant. His own father was a successful member of the New York Produce Exchange and active as a deacon in the Washington Avenue Baptist Church in Clinton Hill, at that time considered Brooklyn's "Gold Coast."

He met Will Clark at the University of Virginia. As boys, both had been "Willie." To each other, they were "Buck" and "Junior." Buck transferred to Brown, but their friendship determined the course of his life.

After graduating, he studied mining engineering in Arizona and then proceeded north to the town his friend's father built. With Temp, they were a trio, carousing through Butte's juke joints and saloons. They grew into adulthood together, with professions and memberships at the same eminent clubs. Buck threw punches for Will. He was a witness first at Temp's wedding, then at Will's to Mabel. Later, he was there to carry her coffin. He never married. He seemed instead wed to Montana.

Will was the native, but Buck was the convert, and he had a zealot's passion for his adopted homeland, reveling in its survivalist ethos from inside the comforts of the Clark empire. He founded the local baseball league and managed Butte's own team—the Clarks. He was a boxing enthusiast and intensely competitive, as August Heinze learned in 1902 over a heated game of ping-pong at the Silver Bow Club. Buck, who'd come to renown at the exclusive club as the fastest with his paddle, thoroughly walloped the mining magnate, leaving Heinze sweating, puffing, and swatting air as the ball whizzed past.

While the sprawling Clark apparatus contracted, Buck remained part of it, deeply connected to Montana even as the native son's bond with his homeland started to fray. Now Will was on the verge of dismantling what remained.

For thirty years, the secretary managed Will's business accounts. That meant he knew, for instance, that "[Harrison] had an annual allowance from Clark of thirty thousand dollars, although he was carried on Clark's payroll at a monthly stipend of only two hundred and fifty dollars, reputed to be compensated for his services as a secretary, a capacity in which he never functioned." From Buck's perspective, Harrison belonged to the "Oscar Wilde type." He possessed a "Semitic cast." As far as he was concerned, Harrison was an impostor, a fey Jew who'd infiltrated the privileged bastion reserved for an Anglo gentry.

Harrison had not ascended as a man was expected to in America, through the accumulation of wealth, but as a woman did, through the primary avenue then available to women—a relationship to a man who had accumulated or inherited wealth. Harrison's place in Will's inner sanctum enraged Buck, but the real secretary didn't consider that his own trajectory had been wholly dependent on his relationship to the exact same man. Just as Harrison's connection to Will had given the younger man entrée to elite clubs, so it had for Buck. In this, Harrison wasn't Buck's opposite but his double.

However, Buck did actually work for Will. He knew how the money moved, that it had gone to Paris, to the apartment near the Eiffel Tower, and that more would be going soon to the Palisades. Will's interest in Raymond Lemire still had not displaced Harrison from his inner circle. They hosted dinner parties. They still shared a loge at the Philharmonic. There was talk of the clubman buying another property, a ranch in Rustic Canyon, even in the midst of the Great Depression. Buck had been a beneficiary of Will Clark's wealth, and its custodian. Soon he'd be neither.

Will did not sell the lodge in 1930. He still made the annual trip to the lake that summer. There were new names in the guest book. Joe McInerney arrived with a contingent from San Francisco, including the printer John Henry Nash. There were the usual visitors—Sydney Sanner, Judge Lippincott, John Templeman—but, for the first time, Buck Mangam was not a guest.

On September 27, 1930, after three decades of employment, Will asked Buck for his resignation. He also struck a provision from his will that had included a $50,000 bequest to the accountant. These facts were set out in a lawsuit Buck would file several years later, but there was no explanation as to why he was fired—not in that suit.

In a separate case, Buck would claim that Will fired him because he'd interfered in his relationship with Harrison. But Buck had seen how little success Charlie and Tertius had had on that front. Why would he think that he might succeed where Will's own brother and son had failed? Buck may have been making different calculations from Charlie and Tertius, who were trying to put an end to Will's secret life so it wouldn't be exposed.

Buck had another set of concerns. For years he'd managed Will's accounts and enjoyed a secure position in the Clark operation, but now that Will was retreating from his Montana ventures and moving abroad, there would be nothing for Buck to manage. Another blow: just as the secretary's position was coming into question, Will was making plans to buy Harrison a ranch in the Palisades.

Buck may have protested these developments, and knowing how much Will paid to keep his secrets hidden, Buck may have also threatened to expose what he knew, anticipating a lucrative payout. Whatever Buck's interference did entail, Will's response was sudden and absolute. After thirty years inside the Clark machine, Buck Mangam was out.

Weeks later he was summoned to the Clift Hotel in San Francisco. Buck told the court that he'd expected to meet with Will and be paid the more than $60,000 he claimed he was owed in back pay. But he never saw Will. Instead, Joe McInerney took him to an empty room, handed him a resignation letter, and said that Will was prepared to accuse Buck of misappropriating funds, making unauthorized loans, and failing to keep the books, if he didn't sign.

Though he would describe being subject to "duress and menace," the accountant did have enough leverage to keep Joe padding back and forth between Will's suite and the room where Buck waited, carrying pieces of paper with figures on them, until the parties fixed on one: $54,166.69. The next day he signed the resignation letter and was given a check for $25,000 and told the rest would follow. It did not.

As a child born into wealth and privilege, Will always had a seat at the feast. He could never know the rage of someone who's been at the table and then cast aside. And he was too shortsighted to realize that sending a man into exile was no guarantee that he would disappear, especially a man with thirty years of knowledge. Will had understood the power that Asa Keyes had over him, the ability to prosecute and publicly ruin him, but he'd underestimated his own accountant.

Never once does Harrison mention Buck in his journals, but, as his own book reveals, Buck certainly thought—and agonized—about Harrison. He claimed the younger man played "a more influential part in the career of W.A. Clark, Jr., than any other person." And yet Buck was being modest. In the end, it wasn't the false secretary but the real one who played the most decisive role in Will Clark's life.

The impulse to fire Buck Mangam would turn out to be rash, just as it was rash for Oscar Wilde to sue his lover's pugnacious, irascible father. Like Will, Wilde had underestimated his opponent. Though he didn't have Will's money, the author believed his talent and his wit would vanquish not just the Marquess of Queensberry but the courtroom too.

And it was rash in October when Tertius came to the house and Will fought with him bitterly. There was no truce between father and son. Tertius railed against Will's friends, though he didn't use that word—not for Harrison, not for any of the men Charlie had uncovered, and not for his own father. Years ago, Will had chosen the house with the high brick wall to keep his boy safe, but now enraged, he ordered his only son out of his home.

Over the years, Will remained close to his late wife's family, sending cards and letters to Alice's sister and mother when he traveled. Perhaps they'd never known Alice's wish to leave the marriage, or if they had, perhaps they'd let time bury the knowledge. To them, Will remained the benevolent, welcoming host, a doting son-in-law, a generous uncle. Their love and admiration—unlike his son's—hadn't curdled, and in their eyes he could still understand himself as a good man, or at least a man who wanted to be good. That spring in Paris, he sent a note to his Catholic sister-in-law Margaret on the back of a postcard of La Madeleine, the neoclassical colonnaded church in the Eighth Arrondissement, illuminated by streetlamps. "Sometimes I pray here," he wrote, "but not at night." He needed someone to know he prayed.

In retrospect, it can seem as if Harrison hadn't just copied Oscar Wilde's words onto paper in those quieter days back in Will's library, but that he'd reinscribed the playwright's great love and wretched fate into their own lives. The story of Wilde and Douglas is a romance, full of passion and recklessness. And it's a story of fathers and sons and the breaches between them—not only in the battle between Douglas and his furious father but also of Wilde, living his last years apart from his two boys, a father alone and estranged. Wilde had always been a stand-in for more than queer love, for exile and loss too. Up until now, Will's wealth had spared him from such pain, but it was still coming for him.

11

THE FLUKE

Harrison at "the Farm," 1931.

The night would come, though not just yet, when Harrison sat down beside a fire and threw photograph after photograph into the flames. Even then, as much as he would try to rid himself of memories, there were those he held on to.

For instance, he saved a photo of Will at a ceremony wearing a cap and gown, and another of several men in bathing suits, lined up at the edge of a swimming pool, poised to dive in, one with a tiny party hat perched on his head. He saved a photo of Dorothy di Frasso sitting side-saddle on a camel in Egypt, the Sphinx braced in scaffolding behind her. He saved a photo of himself in a long white robe, loosely belted, strolling arm in arm with Frances Marion along a sunlit walkway. The screenwriter wears a broad-brimmed hat and carries a bouquet of flowers, the two friends in a bucolic bubble of ease.

Many of the pictures Harrison saved are from his time in the Palisades. In these he's usually on horseback with other riders, always well-dressed in a tailored jacket and jodhpurs, reins loose in his hands. This was the world he loved and the person he most wanted to be—a gracious country squire, elegantly attired, surrounded by friends and a beautiful landscape.

In the fall of 1931, in a somewhat unusual but convenient transaction, Harrison swapped homes with Lester Scott, a producer of westerns, trading his villa in West Adams for a thirteen-acre estate on the southwestern edge of the Riviera Club. Compared to the Uplifters Club or Will Rogers's 180-acre compound, it was a modest enclave, but it was enough for him—lush, wooded, and secluded, a haven for a country gentleman. Before Lester Scott owned the property, it had belonged to a beekeeper named William Johnson, and before that it had been part of the Mexican land grant of Rancho Boca de Santa Monica. And for centuries before, it had been home to the Tongva people. Now it was

Mona Goya, Audrey Caldwell, Lillian Sands, Ted Glassel, and Harrison Post, undated.

Harrison's sylvan estate, complete with a running stream and an underground spring.

He built stables for his prizewinning horses. His menagerie also included cows, goats, geese, swans, and at least five dogs. On Cimarron Street, he'd had a cook and a housekeeper. Now he added a butler, two gardeners, a groomsman, and a night watchman. And he brought his library. Though nowhere near as grand or extensive as Will's, it had grown to a respectable four thousand titles. He even had room for a bookbinding studio, but it was life as a genteel horseman that he most embraced. On Sundays, he and several dozen neighbors rode through the canyons and over the mountain ridges along the coast.

"Friday's moonlight ride looms as the top riding event of the season," announced one of the Riviera Club's newsletters. "The party will tour the Will Rogers Rancho and then swing into Harrison Post's Farm, as he calls it, stubbornly refusing to have his beautiful place labelled a villa, an estate, or even a palazzo. A goodly gathering, and gay, is expected to revel in Harrison's noted hospitality."

This was all the fame Harrison craved—to be known among friends for his aristocratic yet rustic generosity. He had his books and his thirteen acres, room enough for a Plymouth coupe and the Rolls-Royce, and ample space for entertaining. It's unlikely that his new neighbors, who now included Greta Garbo and her then-lover Mercedes de Acosta, would ever call the police about men wearing women's clothing. There would be no more visits from the DA, no more shopping binges with starlets, no more harried flight out of the country.

Tucked away on the "Farm," Harrison was at a remove, too, from the poverty and hardship afflicting the rest of the country. More than a million people had lost their actual farms and millions more were without homes and work. And yet while most industries contracted, Hollywood still thrived. More than sixty million people went to the movies every week, respite or distraction perhaps from living on chipped beef and "Hoover stew," a mix of thin broth, canned tomatoes, and sliced hot dogs.

By now the "talkies" were well underway with screwball comedies, Busby Berkeley's swirling kaleidoscopic dance numbers, and Barbara Stanwyck in lingerie. The Marx Brothers rampaged through ocean liners, high society, academia, and a bankrupt country called Freedonia.

Gangsters, bootleggers, chorus girls, card sharps, and rich swells in their swank art deco homes filled the movie screens. The new era of cinema was stylish and sophisticated, full of knowing winks, clever banter, and titles like *Fast and Loose*, *Other Men's Women*, and *Bad Sister.* Audiences clamored for Noël Coward's comedies and Cole Porter's lyrics, two men whose homosexuality informed their distinctly urbane and sly wit.

Lesser known but much beloved by Hollywood insiders was openly gay Bruz Fletcher, the sharp-tongued, tuxedoed singer, composer, and master of innuendo, who headlined at a tiki lounge called Club Bali. His song "Drunk with Love" would be a staple in gay bars for years to come. Cary Grant, Marlene Dietrich, Humphrey Bogart, Louise Brooks, and others flocked to see the stars of the era's Pansy Craze, featuring so-called female impersonators like Gene Malin and Ray Bourbon. They performed at B.B.B.'s Cellar and Jimmy's Backyard, two of Los Angeles's earliest gay nightclubs, which were often raided by the Hollywood vice squad. Conveniently farther west, in the town of Sherman, then an unincorporated part of LA County, Club Bali was safe from the LAPD.

As was Harrison out in the Palisades. Two snapshots taken around this time show a man significantly changed from the matinee idol manqué of 1921. For one thing, he's outdoors, and another, he's on a horse. His focus is on the animal, one hand holding the rein against the saddle, the other against its neck. His face is lean, hair receding but still dark. Taken from the ground, the photos lend him height and power. The former was an illusion but not the latter, at least not for the moment.

One Sunday in late September, Harrison and the rest of the group—nearly forty—went out for their weekly ride. After two hours through the Santa Monica Canyon, they returned to luncheon at Snowy Baker's home. There, the riders dined on chicken à la King followed by pumpkin pie, and then they went over to the Riviera Club to watch the afternoon polo match.

The game was nearly over when Harrison first felt the effects from the meal. He wasn't alone. Thirty-six other people suddenly took ill from what the papers described as ptomaine poisoning. "Several who returned to the Baker cottage for tea were stricken as they walked across the lawn, a number falling on walks and in the shrubbery," reported the *Los Angeles Times*. As Harrison and his friends reeled, ambulances rushed the victims away to local hospitals. City health officials later determined that the sherry cream sauce of mushrooms, green peppers, and pimentos was the culprit, "full of colii bacilli."

While this was a deeply unpleasant end to what had been an otherwise lovely day, for most, recovery came swiftly. But not for Harrison. The effects of his food poisoning were so extreme that the left side of his body was paralyzed.

After several weeks in Santa Monica Hospital, he regained sensation and was released. By December, he was recovered enough to host a party with Will Rogers and Hal Roach after the Mexico-California polo match at the Riviera Club.

In his journals, Harrison complains of rheumatism, a term that medical professionals don't tend to use much today, which generally refers to chronic joint pain associated with rheumatoid or reactive arthritis. Both autoimmune disorders can be triggered by bacterial infections. Guillain-Barré syndrome, with symptoms that include neurological partial paralysis, can also be caused by food poisoning. Whatever Harrison's medical condition actually was, the effects from the attack appeared to last for the rest of his life.

Perhaps it could be considered a fluke when Will Clark walked into the Marsh, or when Gladys ended up embroiled in an alleged smuggling ring, but both of those events could also be chalked up to circumstance or patterns, like wealth or crime. However, it truly was a fluke that Harrison got poisoned by a lunch of chicken à la King, a freak occurrence, much like the storm that January.

Two inches of snow fell across the Los Angeles Basin, a rare phenomenon indeed for the Southland. But it was a welcome, benevolent kind of chance, the familiar world turned beautifully strange—flurries drifting into the surf, settling on the palm trees and the eucalyptus, melting into the rippling brook on his farm.

Maybe the plane crash could've been called a fluke as well, but it seemed more like a curse that had come true.

12

THE PICTURE OF WILL CLARK

George Palé, Will Clark, Edwin Clark, and unidentified violinist, Salmon Lake, Montana, 1926.

Will collected violins. With Tertius, it was airplanes. Months after their ugly fight, he left Los Angeles with his wife for Clarkdale, Arizona, where he pursued aviation in earnest. At that point, Tertius had been taking flying lessons for four years from Jack Lynch, Charles Lindbergh's flying coach. He'd started hosting air meets in Montana. Similar to Will in his early collaboration with Edwin Clark on the Saint-Saëns quintet, Tertius was looking to take his enthusiasm for flying beyond a hobby.

However, his enterprises recalled his grandfather's commercial ambitions more than his father's artistic philanthropy. In the spring of 1932, Tertius and Lynch were awaiting contracts to start a mail and passenger line between Clemenceau, Arizona, and Las Vegas, in preparation for the launch of the Verde Valley Air Lines. While Will had tried unsuccessfully to retrace his father's steps in Montana, as if the nineteenth century never ended, his son actually hewed closer to the patriarch's trajectory, seeing the opportunity available to him in his own era. Tertius had also started a business that manufactured car headlamps, and he'd recently traveled to South America to survey mines for possible investment.

Like his father and grandfather, Tertius was a collector. However, where his elders pursued rare incunabula, music scores, and French masterpieces, he preferred frontier landscapes and statues of cowboys. And like both men, Tertius also loved Montana. He'd built a summer cabin at Seeley Lake, about ten miles north of the Mowitza Lodge. Will relished fishing and camping, though his outdoor excursions tended toward an extravagant form of "roughing it." Tertius, however, orchestrated strenuous and in some cases life-threatening expeditions. A year after leaving Los Angeles, he'd set out with two other men on a 265-mile trek through the South Fork of the Flathead River, a documentary mission to film the landscape and wildlife, and with the goal, as he wrote, of leading "a life in the wilderness with all of 'populous solitude' of the darkness and isolation that yawned on every side." At one point, while cutting back brush to get a better camera angle, he sliced into his left foot with an ax and was airlifted to Missoula, where he got six stitches, and then returned to finish the journey.

Vyvyan Holland was eight when his father was convicted of "gross indecency." His mother changed his and Cyril's surname to hers so that they might avoid the disgrace that trailed Oscar Wilde, but as an adult Vyvyan embraced his father's legacy. An author, poet, and translator, Vyvyan became Wilde's literary executor. He gave Will permission to publish the letters to Bosie. He didn't flinch from seeing his father's genius, deviance, or suffering. But his father was dead. There were no more crimes to commit. Vyvyan hadn't grown into adulthood with the threat that Wilde would wreak more havoc, though perhaps Vyvyan still would've accepted the totality of the living man as he did the one who was buried in the Père-Lachaise Cemetery. There was a history of subversion in the Wilde family that had existed before his father, an awareness that creative spirit and transgression were never far apart.

Tertius was heir to a different world, the American capitalist frontier, material conquest, and a masculinist ethos. His father had deviated from it, though, and for Tertius it seemed there was much to compensate for. Earlier that year he'd drawn up a will. It may have been the result of a man wrestling with his pain or simply the act of a responsible thirty-six-year-old adult with a large fortune.

The conditions were fair outside Cottonwood, Arizona, on May 14, 1932, when Tertius and his flying coach took off over the foothills. That day, Jack Lynch was giving him a lesson in "blind flying," or navigating by instruments only—necessary in the event of impaired visibility. An expert in the practice, Lynch had been training commercial pilots months before.

At two thousand feet, the plane went into a tailspin and spiraled straight down. According to the *Los Angeles Times*, it "landed squarely on its nose, the impact smashing the motor and front back into the ship. It did not catch fire." Witnesses weren't able to say who'd been flying at the time of the crash, though it seems likely it was Tertius. The paper reported that after the coroner's inquest was completed, "the bodies wrapped in their parachutes and tied to a wing of the demolished plane were carried six miles to the road and then transported to Clarkdale."

Will was en route to France when the cable arrived telling him his son was dead. He radioed his wishes that the funeral services take place in Los Angeles and that Tertius be interred in the mausoleum in the Hollywood Cemetery. In the middle of the ocean, unable to reverse course, Will continued to Le Havre, where he immediately boarded another ship and returned to America.

Two weeks earlier, Will had announced that he was donating several rare documents to the Institut de France. These had belonged to the Montmorency and Condé families and included letters addressed to Henry IV, the first French king from the House of Bourbon, as well as to Cardinal Richelieu, the cunning minister of state under Louis XIII who'd founded the Académie Française and guided the country through the Thirty Years' War.

They would be housed at the grand château that the Duke of Aumale had rebuilt in Chantilly, the inspiration for Will's own library. Will could preserve and exalt the past. He could rescue rare letters from obscurity and salvage the vestiges of a vanished monarchy in another country, but he would never repair the breach with his own son.

Perhaps Will and Tertius would never have reconciled, but while they'd both been alive there was always a chance their story could be different. Now the ending was sealed. In July, Will returned to Paris and to Raymond. Perhaps he prayed again at La Madeleine.

Fall was a season of praise. Will had given $350,000 to his alma mater for the construction of a new law building in honor of his first wife. He'd also donated two rare manuscripts that had belonged to Thomas Jefferson. And on October 15, he took his seat on a dais in Pershing Square, where twenty-five hundred people were gathered, along with the orchestra, for the unveiling and dedication of a draped statue looming on a granite pedestal.

Four years had passed since the tribute concert that had been hastily assembled in Will's honor while he waited out the Jack Oray scandal in Paris. Now the funds had finally been disbursed. Will had insisted the memorial not be a likeness of himself. Instead, Glendale sculptor Arnold Foerster was commissioned to cast a bronze statue of the philanthropist's favorite composer, Ludwig van Beethoven.

After the invocation and the orchestra's performance of Beethoven's *Egmont* Overture, Mrs. Leafie Sloan-Orcutt, the head of the Philharmonic's women's committee, took hold of a long white ribbon and pulled the drape away to reveal the German composer, towering over the crowd.

Foerster hadn't cast a conventional bust but sculpted the deaf artist standing with his head downcast, brow furrowed and his hair unruly. His hands are clasped behind his back, overcoat open, waistcoat half-unbuttoned. Articles used the word "heroic" to describe the statue, and its size—seven feet, four inches—was formidable, but the sculptor had also evoked an inner state that was harder to name. The disheveled artist was not a man triumphant, but a man deep in thought. Inspired, absorbed, haunted—whatever mood possessed him seemed as much a reflection of the viewer as it was of the composer.

After speeches from businessmen and the mayor praising Will's selflessness, conductor Artur Rodziński approached the podium and drew the event to a close with the Fifth Symphony. From his seat on the platform, Will had strained, hand cupped to his left ear, to hear the music and the encomiums in his honor. He'd struggled with hearing problems in the past. Like his father, he'd undergone surgery for mastoiditis. He was in his late fifties now, and his hearing had deteriorated so much that that fall he confessed in a letter to his niece that, like his beloved composer, "I am at times totally deaf."

Public opinion was mixed about Beethoven's arrival in Pershing Square. There'd been consternation about the depiction of the artist in such an unkempt state. An article in *The Oakland Tribune* that summer bemoaned the fact that the composer "will wear baggy pants and nothing can be done about it."

Will had no objections to baggy pants or the depiction of an artist enthralled or, as the case may have been, tormented by an unseen muse. Certainly he understood that the act of contemplation wasn't necessarily a placid one. Back in 1926, the author of *Constructive Californians*, a compendium celebrating the state's power brokers, had attempted to capture the essence of the often inscrutable philanthropist:

> He is introspective rather than inconsiderate and when cogitating an abstract subject he is prone to let it ride him, to the banishment of other ideas. That is why he is, occasionally, misunderstood by the undiscerning who see a man almost taciturn, brooding, silent, when beneath his chance exterior functions a scintillant mind, witty, profound, playful or fanciful, in delightful sequence. Those who know him best have learned to refrain from intruding when the corrugated brows suggest a mental pondering of a perplexed problem, satisfied that when the solution is reached the internal delver will quickly dissipate the atmosphere of exclusiveness in which he had temporarily enveloped himself.

Will didn't want a bronze statue of himself in Pershing Square and he was astute enough to know the public didn't either, that a historic figure like Beethoven was far preferable. And yet Foerster's sculpture of the solitary, brooding man did in fact capture something about Will's nature. It was, after all, Will's name on the bronze plaque beneath the composer.

Except for the mausoleum in the Hollywood Cemetery, Will's monuments had other people's names on them. The building at the University of Virginia was dedicated to Mabel, the library at the University of

Nevada to Alice. His own library bore his father's name, though if visitors knew enough about the muses on the ceiling, they could easily wonder if the building's real inspiration was Harrison.

Will always seemed reluctant to be seen, but that November he sat for his own portrait. The painter, Henrique Medina, was a Portuguese artist who'd spent nearly a decade in London as a society portraitist, though his greatest success had been in Rome, where he'd painted Benito Mussolini. Will's portrait was Medina's first commission in California.

Study for portrait of
William Andrews Clark Jr.,
by Henrique Medina, 1932.

Will was thinking of his legacy. Fifty years before, as a boy of six, he had stood beside a pedestal, book in hand, for his portrait. The stockings and breeches were gone now, but the book remained. In Medina's painting, Will is seated, wearing black evening clothes, taking a moment with one of his cherished editions, perhaps before a concert, the stately, erudite philanthropist.

"Those who can succeed us can well take care of themselves," his father had proclaimed, but who would succeed Will? His only son was dead; the natural progression of life had snapped, and in this light, Will's affection for the housekeeper's son was understandable.

Originally from the Basque region of southern France, Martha Palé (pronounced like "valet") was working as a laundress and recently divorced with a nine-year-old son named George when she joined Will's staff at 2205 West Adams in 1925. Will took an interest in the boy's education, paying for him to attend a local military academy. He also arranged for George, whom he nicknamed "General Pershing," to spend summers at Salmon Lake and take violin lessons with Edwin Clark. They wrote often during Will's travels, and the two developed a custom in which Will would write to George in French and the boy would translate the letters into English.

Will was fond of Martha. In letters to George, he asks after her, worries that she is working too hard. However, while he was intent on helping the housekeeper's son rise to a new class, he didn't extend the same efforts to the boy's mother. During trips to the Montana lodge, George signed the guest book, but Martha, still a servant, did not.

George would later say that after Tertius's death, Will treated him as his own son, taking him into his house, where they ate meals together, and giving him a room of his own. Will started signing his letters "your loving Dad" and "Daddy Clark." He offered the teenager paternal advice about his studies, how to prepare for speeches, and reminded him to be good to his mother. Will said the boy filled a void in his heart, and he spoke with Martha about formally adopting George.

At the same time, Will announced that, after fifteen years, he would no longer fund the Los Angeles Philharmonic: "Mr. Clark feels that the orchestra is now a well-seasoned institution and that it should receive the financial support if they desired to enjoy a first-class symphony orchestra in this community." To most anyone else trying to survive during the Great Depression, his situation was more than enviable. He owned a palatial estate in Los Angeles, a luxury apartment in Paris, and he had the lodge in Montana. Still, after three years with no foreseeable end to the financial crisis, he wasn't immune to the effects.

And he seemed to spend as much of his time now in Paris as he did in Los Angeles. He was there that spring when the news came that his brother, sixty-one, had contracted pneumonia and was in serious condition. Will cut his trip short and returned to America. He arrived one day too late to be at Charlie's side when he died in New York on April 3, 1933.

Despite everything between them, "the passing away of my brother has utterly crushed me and has taken from me, for the time being at least, all ambition to do anything," Will wrote to a friend soon after Charlie's death.

Within weeks, Will informed Sir Robert that he couldn't afford to keep him employed. In July, as Will had requested, his beloved librarian formally submitted his resignation. Will also notified John Henry Nash that for the first time since their collaboration began, he wasn't going to commission a gift book for Christmas that year.

Charlie was the only other person who knew how it felt to live in the shadow of William Andrews Clark Sr. The brothers had clashed but always remained close. It was Charlie who'd introduced Will to Sir Robert and the printer. Now he was giving up both. It was Charlie who'd introduced him to the violin. Now he retreated from the Philharmonic. The official reason was the increasing fiscal constraint from the Depression, which was real, but it seems that Will's grief may have been as much a cause as his financial worries. In less than a year, he'd lost his son and his brother.

In the past, after a death, his life had swerved—to Paris, to college, to Harrison. Now, though, it shrank. And yet he still couldn't manage to extricate himself fully from the Philharmonic. When the attempt to raise funds through subscriptions fell short, mustering only $180,000, Will again agreed to fund another year.

And for the first time since moving to Los Angeles, he didn't spend the summer in Montana. He left for Paris in early June, and there he met with the conductor Otto Klemperer and invited him to lead the Philharmonic in the fall.

Born to a Jewish family in 1885 in Breslau—in what is now Poland but was then Germany—Klemperer studied music in Frankfurt and later Berlin, where he directed the Kroll Opera on the edge of the Königsplatz, just opposite the Reichstag, where the lower house of the Weimar Republic assembled. Under Klemperer's tenure, the opera hosted premieres of Arnold Schoenberg's work, commissioned stage sets from artists like László Moholy-Nagy and Giorgio de Chirico, and incurred the ire of the country's rising far-right movement. The government shut down on July 3, 1931, and the building remained vacant as the country slid into fascism.

After the Reichstag was burned down in February 1933, the newly appointed chancellor Adolf Hitler took the fire as pretext to make mass arrests and suspend civil liberties, while the German parliament took up residence in the Kroll Opera, conveniently empty on the other side of the square. There, politicians passed the Enabling Act of 1933, giving Hitler total authority to abolish other political parties, imprison opponents, and begin his dictatorship.

In June, George Messersmith, head of the US consulate in Berlin, wrote with alarm to William Phillips, under secretary of state to Franklin D. Roosevelt: "If this government remains in power for another year, and it carries on in the measure in this direction, it will go far toward making Germany a danger to world peace for years to come. With few exceptions, the men who are running the government are of a mentality that you and I cannot understand. Some of them are psychopathic cases and would ordinarily be receiving treatment somewhere." Klemperer wasn't the only one looking to flee—Messersmith was busy helping others, including Albert Einstein, leave the country.

When the conductor met Will in Paris that spring he'd been disappointed to learn that, as a consequence of the Depression, salaries in America were much lower than he'd anticipated, but Klemperer didn't hesitate to take the job at the Philharmonic. He arrived in Los Angeles that October, the beginning of the migration of European artists and writers seeking refuge in Southern California.

The Philharmonic's horn section was there to greet the conductor at the train station. He was fêted with dinners, luncheons, and ceremonies full of celebrities he didn't know. He wrote to his wife, overwhelmed as much by the social whirlwind as by the landscape: "An enormous village. Lots of small low houses. Distances such as we can hardly conceive of. It takes me twenty-five minutes by car to the concert hall." And though the accommodations at Will's home were luxurious and the staff attentive, Klemperer found it an uncomfortable place to be a guest.

Will was not well. His health had continued to deteriorate. He'd been treated by his physician for what were described as a series of small heart attacks. He suffered from lumbago. He was going deaf. He appeared depressed. He drank heavily and, to Klemperer's shock, he often arrived at the breakfast table undressed and still drunk, or just getting started.

The composer woke up once to discover Will, sitting on the bed, naked, stroking his arm. "He should really be under supervision," Klemperer wrote to his wife. "And I think he is under bad influences."

Will had another disconcerting habit. After his first concert concluded, Klemperer was in his dressing room receiving Charlie Chaplin, King Vidor, and Salka Viertel when they were interrupted by a clash of cymbals and rousing fanfare. Klemperer stormed out to discover Will at the podium conducting the orchestra in John Philip Sousa's "Stars and Stripes Forever" to an empty auditorium, and shouted, "Stop, stop at once!"

Abashed, Will explained that this was one of his pleasures. The conductor's retort was swift: "Not while I'm here."

Still, Klemperer was pleased that the concerts were well attended and that audiences welcomed newer work by Mahler, Stravinsky, and Bruckner. He chafed, though, at his employer's request to play what he considered "a banal piece" by Benjamin Godard, a chamber music composer who'd been in vogue during Will's time as a music student in Paris. It was titled "Serenade à Mabel."

Will's first wife, Mabel, had been dead for thirty years. It may have been tempting, at fifty-six, for him to imagine the other lives he might've led, to lament a bygone innocence or spin a melancholy fantasy about a woman who might've saved him from himself. He may simply have wanted to hear—as well as he could—a melody, however banal, that recalled a young woman whose life had ended at twenty-one, someone he'd never disappointed.

Even before Charlie's death, Will had begun to show the effects of aging and anguish. In the portrait that hangs in the library, Medina gave the philanthropist a warm tone, but the study that the painter worked from offers a starker view. The pale, dark-eyed boy had become a drawn, beleaguered man.

Will was the painter's entrée to Southern California. After Medina finished his portrait along with those of Sir Robert, Cora, and Harrison, he branched out to movie stars like Chaplin, Mary Pickford, and

Norma Shearer. Eventually he returned to Portugal in 1946, but before he did, Medina painted the work that would become his most famous, eclipsing his portrait of Il Duce.

When the producers of Albert Lewin's film adaptation of *The Picture of Dorian Gray* started preproduction in 1943, they hired Ivan Albright to paint both the eternally young version of the protagonist, played by Hurd Hatfield, and the lurid, true likeness rotting in the attic. Albright, who called himself "the master of the macabre," was meticulous in rendering his subject's festering, decrepit flesh, so meticulous that it took him an entire year. Pressed for time, the studio hired Medina to paint, swiftly, the beautiful young Hatfield, the man who looked of "ivory and rose petals."

Of course, Will couldn't have known that one day Medina would paint the doomed fictional aristocrat, but he certainly knew the story of a man grotesquely divided against himself, on an inexorable path of

George Palé, 1926.

self-annihilation while his ageless, unblemished face masks his true and monstrous self.

Maybe it was simply an unusual dynamic, even a heartwarming one: a bereft father who's lost a son finds a boy who needs a father. Except that the boy had lived under Will's roof for seven years now and Will was more than a grieving father. He was also the son of a man who'd sent an innkeeper's daughter to Paris to be sequestered and prepared to be his lover. Will was generous and capable of great kindness, but he'd also been taught that he could use his American wealth for royal entitlements, like concubines, though the word the Clarks used was *ward*.

A familiar scenario: A wealthy, powerful older man sets his attentions on a child's education—French lessons, music lessons. The child's parents are working class, with limited resources, dependent on the man for their livelihood. Martha Palé's ex-husband offered no support and was mostly absent from George's life, though he had consented along with Martha to Will's request to adopt George.

It's possible that a dark calculation had been made on Martha's part that Will's attentions were to be accommodated, given her financial dependency and given what the adopted son of the copper heir stood to inherit.

Here's one of Will's letters from 1934, originally written in French and transcribed by George:

> My dear baby:
>
> You promised to write me. Therefore I expect your letter Wednesday morning. Do not forget. Anyway I have a whip here and your fanny will be well spanked and you will have to eat off the mantel piece.
>
> Your mother will write you a few words. I love you and I kiss you with all my heart.
>
> Sincerely yours,
>
> Daddy

What to make of these few lines written over eighty years ago translated from another language? The pouting recriminatory tone? The inside joke that, at best, rings juvenile? Or was it meant to be erotic? How did it ring to George?

The "dear baby" was eighteen at the time. Whether the housekeeper's son was in on the joke or wanted to be is impossible to say. After Will's death, George submitted the letter, along with several others, to a probate court in Montana as proof of Will's paternal affection. Given that George's translations are the only surviving copies, we can't know how true they are to Will's original correspondence.

In Otto Klemperer's accounts to his wife and in some of the letters to George, a picture emerges of Will as a lonely man, desperate for contact. Another picture emerges too—of a man oblivious, willfully so, to unreciprocated desire, to the possibility that those in his household had no choice but to endure his urges and hope they passed quickly.

Cora Sanders died in 1964, so she wasn't alive to intercept and destroy the letter that Bill Walker, an archivist at the Butte-Silver Bow Public Archives, wrote in 1981 in response to a query from William Conway, then head librarian at the Clark Library, about Will's "sexual preference."

Walker was matter-of-fact about what he knew. He also prefaced that his information came from a man whose father had been a geologist with the Anaconda Copper Mining Company and knew a lawyer at the corporation who'd been a close personal friend of Will's. The lawyer was the source of the information, which makes Walker's account fifth-hand knowledge—or hearsay about hearsay from another era. While Walker's tone is neither breathless nor prurient, the letter has a lurid quality, and this isn't simply because its content was sensational or salacious but because it's written in red ink.

The gossip was this: "[The lawyer] and W.A. Jr were in fact gay and W.A. Jr. was known for his interest in boys and his occasional wild parties at his home on Galena Street when he still lived in Butte. He relationship with Mr. Palé was apparently of this nature."

The archivist included another "tidbit" about Will's friend, the playwright Eugene O'Neill, whom Walker claims was also "erotically interested in young boys" and had shared with Will a poem he'd written about an older man's attraction to a young boy who wets his bed. Walker had salvaged the poem, which was privately published in an oversized bound volume, from a collection that had been donated to the local library, as he expected it would get thrown out—"(obscene you know)."

A startling document, Walker's letter gives voice, decades after Will's death, to the suspicions and whispers that the philanthropist was a pedophile. As shocking, if not more so, is Walker's claim that Eugene O'Neill harbored similar inclinations. I'm not aware that such an allegation has been made before about the playwright. If there is any truth to the claim, it brings a new and unsettling dimension to the torment that marked both O'Neill's work and life.

As for Will, the most benign picture of him in his later years is that he was a grieving alcoholic with an intense attachment to his servant's son, a surrogate for the boy he'd lost. The darker view is that he was also preying upon, grooming, and molesting children.

In Wilde's novel, Dorian Gray attacks the painting, the evidence of his growing moral decay, slashing the portrait with the knife he'd used to kill the painter Basil Hallward. Upon hearing a cry, his servants race to the attic, where they discover the corpse of an unrecognizable and aged man and the portrait of Dorian Gray restored to his youthful beauty.

Will was destroying himself, slowly, with alcohol, but his downfall would come at another man's hand. And yet Buck Mangam was a kind of doppelganger. He had the same name. He'd been Will's proxy in Butte. He'd even started a baseball team called the Clarks. He'd invested his life in their empire. It had faded, but he was going to have his revenge on the one who'd banished him.

Buck Mangam claimed that the Los Angeles Philharmonic was a mask for Will, that it allowed him to play the part of the benevolent philanthropist so he could cover up his transgressions. That may have been true, and yet it was also true that the institution was a genuine expression of Will's love of music, even if, to Otto Klemperer's horror, that sometimes meant a Sousa march or a sentimental tune.

Oscar Wilde understood masks. He knew they were a form of disclosure, but Buck Mangam wasn't interested in such paradoxes. Whether it was a true mask or not, Will's real secretary was going to tear it away.

Years before, when considering publishing Wilde's letters to Douglas,

Will had remarked to John Henry Nash that it would be unpleasant to be sued for defamation. He was about to discover how true that was.

In November, Will abruptly announced to Otto Klemperer that he was leaving for Paris and the conductor would have to relocate to a hotel. Klemperer welcomed the inconvenience.

At first Will had found the crossing calm and pleasant, but midway through the journey they hit rough waters. He was in the "fumoir" when a wave sent the ship rolling, and him crashing with the rest of the passengers across the room. He arrived in France with two broken ribs and a strained shoulder.

Paris had always been a refuge, but even there Will couldn't escape suffering. Two days before Christmas, a train collision killed more than two hundred people who'd been heading home for their holiday. A pall fell over the city.

Then came the news from America. On January 13, 1934, Buck Mangam sued his former friend and employer for defamation. The accountant claimed that Will had slandered him, charging injury to his reputation and grievous mental suffering. The suit didn't mention being subject to "duress and menace" at the Clift Hotel or the remaining $29,166.69 that Buck had been promised by Joe and never received. He was, however, demanding $30,000 for his pain now.

In the past, when Will had been faced with legal scrutiny, he'd fled to Europe. This time he was already there, and there he remained in the company of Raymond Lemire. He left the matter in the hands of his attorneys, including his longtime Montana lawyer Sydney Sanner, who'd moved to Los Angeles, where, with a young lawyer named John Amos Fleming, he set up a practice that catered to one client, Will.

In early February, Will and Raymond traveled to Algiers, but that trip was blighted, too, by snow and rain, and they cut their journey short, taking a boat back to Marseille, as soon as passage was safe on the Mediterranean. Will wrote to George that the sea had been "wild & tumultuous."

He also shared his thoughts on France's presidential election of Édouard Daladier of the center-left Radical Party:

> The new cabinet formed recently by Daladier is already faced with great opposition. He is frank that at today's session of House of

> Deputies the ministry will fall. There will be riots in the streets of Paris tonight & probably very violent ones. It looks to me as if the Republic is doomed. What then, a dictator or a return of Royalty.

Will was right. There were riots and they did turn violent. A scattershot spray of demonstrations led by far-right leagues broke out across Paris. Outside the Chamber of Deputies, police shot and killed fifteen demonstrators. After the uprising and the crackdown, known as six février, Daladier was forced to resign.

Despite the unrest, Will stayed in France for another month. A country on the verge of mob violence and state brutality was safer than what awaited him back home.

13

BUCK MANGAM'S REVENGE

The opulent days of the Van Nuys Hotel were long gone. The once-swank downtown destination for visiting politicians, financiers, and other luminaries had been sold in 1929 and renamed the Barclay Hotel. Now it was a dingy stop for down-on-their-luck transients. And yet while the era of LA big shots like Earl Rogers keeping offices in the building might be over, the hotel's secrets still remained. So did some of the people who knew them, including a man named Stanley Visel. He was Buck Mangam's new lawyer.

Visel had been a clerk to the flamboyant Rogers back in the 1910s, along with Jerry Giesler, who'd gone on to represent Kid McCoy, as well as Errol Flynn, Bugsy Siegel, Charlie Chaplin, and eventually Marilyn Monroe and Robert Mitchum, among many others. The attorney's ruthlessness on his clients' behalf inspired the famous industry catchphrase "Get me Giesler."

Visel hadn't amassed the same celebrity roster as his former co-clerk. He wasn't flashy like Giesler. His reputation hadn't gained him a catchy slogan. Still, he was well respected as a defense attorney. He'd learned much under Rogers's tutelage, especially the art of playing to a jury. He'd worked hundreds of murder cases and could boast of never having a client face the death penalty, but that wasn't why Buck Mangam, a resident of Montana, hired a criminal defense attorney to represent him as a plaintiff in a defamation lawsuit in California. Visel had deep roots in the LA courts, and surely he remembered back when Will Clark had his suite at the hotel, back when the rumors about porters and actors first began, when there was talk that the copper king's son did more than business in his rooms.

Also, Visel was a smart lawyer, and he wasn't likely to take a case against one of the wealthiest men in Los Angeles without the confidence that he would win or, as Buck's ultimate intention may have been, force a sizable settlement.

According to Buck's complaint, since September 1930, when he'd been dismissed by Will without notice, he'd sought similar employment in a managerial capacity in other mining operations in and around Butte. However, he'd been unable to secure any new work, and he claimed that he'd learned that Will had "maliciously and with intent to injure" slandered him to executives at mining companies in Butte.

What were Will's slanderous words?

> Buck is crazy.
> Buck's mania is getting worse.
> Buck can no longer be trusted.

The complaint went on to allege that such remarks had continued over several years since Buck's firing, and that on April 30, 1933, Will was heard to utter "the false and slanderous words following":

> Buck Mangam (meaning the plaintiff) is crazy and I had to get rid of him for that reason.
>
> Also, Buck was so crazy that he tried to break up my friendship with Post and others and I wouldn't stand for that.

At first glance, the complaint seems laughable. Calling someone "crazy" in this context is clearly a form of hyperbole, hardly a grievous injury. Will's words may have borne animosity, but it didn't seem defamatory to say someone wanted to break up a friendship. Will hadn't said Buck was embezzling, defrauding, or committing other crimes. And yet the accusation, tenuous as it may have appeared, was explosive—or rather, it threatened to be.

Because Buck's real charge, lurking behind the talk of mania, was that there was something suspect, shameful even, in Will's relationship with Harrison. It was a clever maneuver. By claiming to be a victim of defamation, Buck was going to lay bare Will Clark's sexual history for the whole world to see. In a courtroom, the issue of whether or not

Buck Mangam was crazy or trustworthy would quickly lead to discussion of why anyone would want to break up Will's relationship with Harrison and as yet unnamed others. It seemed quite possible that Buck was going to resurrect the charges that Will had paid Asa Keyes to bury six years ago.

The true secretary would have his revenge on the false one, who was cantering through the canyons of Santa Monica, drawing a monthly salary for doing nothing, while the other was looking for work. Still, Buck's real target remained Will. If he couldn't be a part of the empire, he could at least have the last word and even some of what was left. Buck wasn't on Will's payroll anymore, but there were still ways to tap into what remained of the Clark fortune. He had years of documentation—all of which a trial would put into public record, that is, if Will didn't settle first.

Back in 1920, Will had been thwarted in his attempt to adopt Harrison, to make a legal, binding contract between the younger man and himself. Now Buck was going to unite the two men in the Los Angeles Superior Court, except he wasn't going to protect them. He was going to unmask them.

14

SNAP

Years later, when he looked back, Harrison would identify two points where his life changed. The first was in 1919 when he stepped off the train at Central Station. The second came the year of Buck's suit.

"In 1934," he wrote, "my life was 'snapped.'"

On March 7, Will arrived in New York. It usually took about three days to get to the West Coast. He may have stayed a day or two in Manhattan before getting on the train, so his exact return date isn't certain, but within a week he was back in Los Angeles. Also not certain is whether he'd told Harrison of Buck's suit before he returned. In any case, by now Harrison knew. Were they going to pack and leave yet again? Those days were supposed to be over.

In different ways, both men had retreated from their previous, more public lives. In the past year, Will had barely spent four months in Los Angeles. He'd been to Paris three times. Harrison, though, hadn't traveled at all. The extravagant flights of the 1920s had subsided. At the farm, the swans glided in the stream. The goats kept the grass short. It was a place of plenitude and stillness. The Santa Monica directory lists Harrison as "bk bndr," but he doesn't seem to have had an official bookbinding business, at least not one that left any traces. He made little mark in society columns that year. An exhibition at San Francisco's Legion of Honor of the miniaturist painter Marion Yoreska included a portrait the artist had done of him, but that tiny rendering was essentially the extent of his publicized appearances.

They weren't young anymore, and though they were still rich, they weren't as rich as they'd been. If Buck's lawsuit went forward, it would surely draw attention from the district attorney's office. How much could Will afford to spend to buy off Buron Fitts, that is, if the DA was open to bribes?

He was—a fact that movie palace impresario Alexander Pantages and others would discover later that year when they were found to be the clients of a sex trafficking operation that involved kidnapping girls from orphanages. The woman who ran it was the only person convicted, and Fitts was later indicted for taking bribes from the men, though his attorney—Giesler, naturally—got him acquitted.

But if Buck's insinuations about Will and Harrison made it into the public sphere, it would be too late for payoffs. Charlie had warned him fifteen years ago. By now, Will had already lost so much, and yet there was still more to lose.

An invented man, Harrison's entire world depended on Will. It had come into being through Will. *He* had come into being through Will. To be exposed was to be disgraced, yes, but it wasn't only that. Along with public humiliation, not only could he face financial ruin and criminal prosecution, but also the return of Albert Weis Harrison, the return of despair in a rented room.

One minute he was a man standing on solid ground, the next the world had gone liquid and so had he.

On March 14, Harrison was admitted to the Chase Sanitarium on Eighteenth Street, several blocks north of his old suite at the Holton Arms.

Without medical records, it's not clear what transpired, except that Harrison again experienced a severe reaction resulting in paralysis. His physician, Dr. Samuel Ingham, who served as chairman of USC's Department of Neurology, described the condition as the result of a "lesion on the brain." This could refer to a stroke or an aneurysm. A lesion could also stem from injury, infection, or an immune disorder, all of which could have been a consequence of the toxic luncheon at Snowy Baker's. In later years, Harrison would refer to having had a "nervous breakdown" in 1934.

As a teenager, he'd attempted suicide. In a 1927 letter to Caroline Estes Smith, Will laments that Harrison doesn't write him more, but rationalizes that it must be because the younger man has been ill. The freak food poisoning incident followed four years later. These are scattershot accounts from a fifteen-year span, hardly a medical history, but a suicide attempt, unspecified illness, and paralytic reaction do suggest a degree of mental and physical precarity such that a harsh shock—the possibility of public ruin, for instance—might lead to a severe reaction.

Well aware of Harrison's fragility, Will had already taken precautions for Harrison's future care. Back in December, before Harrison's collapse, he'd made out his will, which provided Harrison with a cash bequest of $25,000 and the farm. Villa dei Sogni was already in his name. Will also established a $100,000 trust for Harrison that would go into effect upon his death. It was to be administered by Sydney Sanner, Joe McInerney, and John Amos Fleming, with the income on the trust disbursed quarterly. Will added that should the income "not be sufficient to provide for the reasonable needs and comforts of my said friend, Harrison Post, during any period or periods of his illness, or other want or necessity," the trustees were authorized to pay out from the principal of the trust, "up to and including the whole thereof," according to their discretion.

Will updated his will every year, so it's not clear if this clause was a new stipulation or something he'd included in past versions. The "illness" Will refers to is never identified, but it obviously worried him, and if Harrison was living in a vaguely convalescent state out in the Palisades, it may account for why there are so few public traces of him at this time.

Harrison was a meticulous man, but he was not a methodical one. His scrapbooks are haphazard collections from differing eras. Themes do emerge, for instance in a sequence of studio portraits of glamorous movie star friends or a page devoted to Will, but there's no chronological order. Sometimes he dates the photos, sometimes he doesn't. Snapshots from his riding days are scattered throughout. Despite this slapdash approach, it's possible to discern a progression, which is to say a decline.

The earliest photos from the late 1920s show him, always smartly attired, out on the bridle paths with fellow riders. A 1930 shot captures him at his farm, astride a horse, Dalmatian in the foreground, swans drifting on the stream behind. In 1932, noticeably frail, he's seated on an outdoor lounge chair beside a brawny, laughing Snowy Baker. Two years later, he poses with his friend Leo Carrillo. Both men are dressed in riding clothes, the mustached Carrillo still in his polo helmet, with one arm around his friend, smiling devilishly at a gaunt Harrison. A white flower in his lapel, Harrison holds a cigarette and leans against a tree, seemingly for support. He squints at the camera, attempting a smile, but it looks more like a grimace. In his scrapbooks, this is the only photo of him from 1934, taken presumably before his collapse.

Ever the accountant, Buck Mangam observed that Harrison's "expenses at the institution were borne by Clark, to whose conduct with Post the latter's deteriorated mental condition has been assigned." But perhaps Buck was being too modest as to who was responsible for Harrison's "snap."

On April 16, Will attended yet another testimonial concert in his honor at the Philharmonic. This was the last year he would fund the orchestra, and though he'd said it before, it would turn out to be true. After fifteen years, it was only natural that Will should be fêted for creating the Philharmonic and sustaining it through the Depression. And given Buck's lawsuit, it was also a fortuitous time to have movie stars, civic leaders, and the city's elites turn out en masse to celebrate his generosity.

Otto Klemperer opened the program with Hector Berlioz's *Le carnaval romain*. The concert overture, based on themes from the French composer's 1838 opera *Benvenuto Cellini*, begins with a rousing flourish then quickly gives way to a slow, meditative solo by the cor anglais, or English horn, before the orchestra resumes its sprightly course.

Neither English nor a horn, the double-reed woodwind with a curved metal crook at the top and bulb-shaped bell at the end has a lower register than the oboe. In his *Treatise on Instrumentation*, Berlioz described it as "a melancholy, dreamy and rather noble voice, with a somewhat subdued and distant tone. This makes it superior to any other instrument when the intention is to move by reviving images and feelings from the past, and when the composer wishes to touch the hidden chords of tender memories."

Could Will bear to touch a tender memory? A lifetime had passed since he and Harrison listened to the plangent ache of another English horn, the traveler longing for home, in Dvořák's Symphony no. 9. Now

Harrison lay in a sanitarium bed, and did Will have a homeland anymore? Was there a new world anywhere for him?

Perhaps this was part of his fixation on George. Will was invested, literally and emotionally, in his education. He commended the boy on getting good grades. George, who was left handed, had been working to master his penmanship with his other hand, and Will praised him for this: "Would advise you to keep it up." He was disappointed that George had stopped taking a French class but unfazed when the boy got into trouble for playing hooky. "Oh well. What do we care?"

George was to give a speech on chivalry at the end of the school term, and Will offered his thoughts, which were that since women had placed themselves on the same footing as men, the vestiges of the medieval knightly system had vanished: "To be sure, there remains love, respect and comradeship, but chivalry does not exist anymore." He'd signed off, "Affectionately, your dad, who loves you, W.A. Clark, Jr."

George would graduate in June. He'd told Will that he wanted to attend the California Institute of Technology to pursue a degree in electrical engineering and Will approved. There might not be a new world for him anymore, but there was a new person to mold and on whom he could lavish his wealth and need.

Surely no one attending the gala concert at the Philharmonic Auditorium could have imagined Will's isolation. The accolades poured forth. Leo Carrillo rhapsodized about Will's place in California history. Dick Powell, star of *42nd Street* and *Gold Diggers of 1933*, sang. Then, after the encomiums and solos were over, Klemperer returned to the platform and concluded the evening with Beethoven's Overture no. 3 from *Leonore*, an opera about a noblewoman in Seville who disguises herself as a guard to rescue her husband, a political prisoner, from execution.

Will's attorneys were less inventive. Instead, they picked at the details, submitting a demurrer to Buck's complaint, objecting to its ambiguity and absence of specificity—which mining companies Buck was trying to get work at, whom Will had said the supposedly slanderous words to, where he had said them. They argued that Buck's allegation was a general one, therefore inadequate to the plea he was making for special damages. They cited numerous cases to back their objections as well as sections from the Code of Civil Procedure.

They also pointed out that the words *crazy* and *mania* can have different meanings, like "'a strong infatuation' as: a mania for rare books, a mania for movies." In the circumstance with Buck, they argued the word was used to describe "a man who had become so inordinately eager, erratic and out of the ordinary that he sought to interfere with his employer's personal affairs, was becoming a nuisance, and could no longer be trusted for that reason." Furthermore:

> It is likewise manifest that by "Buck's mania" is meant that the plaintiff had an overmastering passion to arrogate his employer to himself, or a mania for interference with his employer's friendships. There is nothing opprobrious in this, nor does it impute any moral turpitude or necessarily expose him to contempt, ridicule, obloquy. Therefore it cannot be slanderous *per se*.

Four days after the gala celebrating Will and his contributions to Los Angeles, his attorneys submitted a motion to dismiss Buck's case, on the basis that the plaintiff had failed to meet the legal requirements in California of securing a bond with competent sureties, necessary to make an action of slander or libel.

Meanwhile, Angelenos assembled for another ceremony to toast the esteemed philanthropist. A collection of civic notables, local businessmen, and Philharmonic luminaries gathered in Pershing Square to plant nine Eugenia trees in a semicircle around the statue of Beethoven. Along with sculptor Arnold Foerster and Mayor Frank Shaw, Otto Klemperer grabbed a shovel and dug into the earth as the crowd clapped and cheered.

But Buck's case wasn't the only pressing legal issue. George's father had given his consent for Will to adopt the boy. Will wrote to George at school telling him the news and that Will would be leaving by steamboat on June 8 for summer at the lodge. Will began the letter by reporting that George's mother wasn't well. "She is suffering and I sent her to her quarters to rest," he wrote. "To tell the truth she works too hard. You will have to reprimand her when you come home Friday afternoon. There is a limit to what a person can do."

Will's concern was kind, and it was ludicrous. At least when his father sent Anna off to Paris, Clark Sr. bought the girl's mother a new home so she didn't have to run a boardinghouse. George would later assert that Will expected the boy to provide for his mother as soon as he was able, though it was obvious enough that Will himself was more than able to do so. But perhaps if she were no longer Will's servant, it would be harder to explain the nature of the relationship among mother, son, and father-to-be.

In any case, Martha's suffering could've been more than a matter of physical exhaustion. Her livelihood depended on a man who may have been abusing her son. Perhaps she worked hard so she wouldn't have any energy left to contemplate what was at stake.

Within a week, she was on the mend and Will appeared to have recovered from his lumbago. He wrote to George that his days were occupied with the library, a visit to the dentist, and seeing "the sick ones." Beyond that, there was no report on Harrison's progress at the sanitarium, though presumably his condition was stable enough that Will was comfortable making plans to spend the summer in Montana.

However, it remains an open question as to how clear-minded Will was in these months. It's unlikely he'd curtailed his drinking binges. After a recent visit from Judge Lippincott, Will wrote to George that he was relieved that the older man was gone, "because he was lonesome here and he lived like a lost soul."

The judge may have been lonely indeed as the guest of a man going deaf who drank too much and wrote letters in French to a teenage boy at military school while his mother cleaned the mansion. If anyone was a "lost soul" at the West Adams compound, surely it was Will.

On May 7, doctors arrived to treat his lumbago, bandaging his sides and his back. He wrote to George, "Your mother is much better, and what is more, she looks better." She'd also seen to it that George sent Will flowers on the second anniversary of Tertius's death.

By now, Buck's lawyer had submitted the bond with the corrected paperwork to the court and on May 15 the deputy sheriff served Will with a subpoena. His lawyers moved to strike much of Buck's complaint for being "sham, frivolous, and wholly irrelevant to the action," but the motion was denied, and Will's deposition was set for June 6.

Regardless, he was still planning for summer in Montana. The cook had placed an order to A.J. Mathieu Company specialty grocers—"A House for the Epicure" was its motto—to be shipped to the lodge: three Virginia hams, five pounds of dried flageolets, five pounds of shelled walnuts, fifteen pounds of rice, capers, anchovies, turtle meat, lunch tongue, crab, shrimp, tarragon vinaigrette, twenty-five tins of mushrooms, thirty-six tins of olives, pineapple, whole apricots, strawberry preserves, peaches, pears, cherries, twelve jars of glacé mints, twelve bottles of maraschino cherries. No Hoover Stew for Will's guests.

Joe McInerney wasn't part of the defense, but he may have had a hand in the surge of good press for Will. A two-column article appeared in the *Los Angeles Times* on June 3, a tribute to Will as well as to the Philharmonic's manager Caroline Estes Smith, who was stepping down. Plans were being made to renovate the symphony hall. It was left unsaid how the institution would survive into a new era without its founder's financial support. The point of the article wasn't the future, though—it was Will's generosity. The author offered an admiring portrait of Will, "a man of few words and quick decisions," and noted that the statue of Beethoven is "the only public acknowledgment of the city's debt to him which has been permitted so far, as he sincerely dislikes publicity of any kind."

Buck Mangam certainly knew that to be true. He also knew why Will so disliked publicity.

"There is nothing certain in this world," Will wrote to George on June 6, the day of his deposition, which was also the same day that the boy was due to give his speech on chivalry. Will sent a check—"for your savings account"—and some words of encouragement. He would be there that night, along with Judge Sanner and Martha.

"Before you go on the stage," Will counseled, "take a long breath, and say 'Slowly old man and I will pull through.'"

Perhaps he'd given himself the same advice when he arrived for his deposition. There's no more paperwork in the case file to determine what took place on June 6—or after. If Will was indeed questioned that day by Stanley Visel, a skilled attorney representing a man who knew Will's secrets, those records have since vanished.

Two days later, Will left Los Angeles as planned. The cook made an additional order with the grocer for Roquefort cheese, two pounds of pistachios, three pounds of almonds, string beans, lentils, ten pounds of macaroni, ten pounds of spaghetti, six pounds of artichokes, six jars of beluga caviar, eighteen tins of shad roe, and more flageolets.

As usual, he traveled with an entourage, accompanied by his valet

Douglas Fenn, William Burgess, Judge Sanner, Caroline Estes Smith, and her son. Four days later, they arrived in Butte. When Judge Lippincott came to see Will at the house on Granite Street, he found Will visibly weary, which the older man ascribed to the long trip. Of course there were other things that had exhausted Will, but he didn't speak of them.

Lippincott would later report that Will didn't speak much at all and recalled that he sat at Will's bedside for more than half an hour, holding his hand, as they planned that summer's expedition, though it was mostly the older judge who was talking.

On June 13, Will and his party arrived at the Mowitza Lodge where the hams and tins of shad roe awaited. The summer staff was already there, preparing the grounds. Chummie and others were due the next day.

Will had paid Thomas Cowles's legal bills, but he hadn't been the one on trial. He'd paid off Asa Keyes and avoided having to go under oath. However, on June 6 he'd been closer to exposure than ever before. The judge ordered that Will return to resume the deposition, but he never did. It seems likely that in the time between the deposition and his departure for Montana, he decided to settle the case to avoid further scrutiny. If he had refused to pay for Buck's silence before, now it must've seemed the best option. The matter would never go public.

However Will managed to wriggle out of the lawsuit and evade the reckoning it threatened, the effort had come at great cost, more than any dollar amount. The torment and grief of the recent years had left him weary, and even with the deposition now behind him, he was tired indeed.

He got to see the morning at the lake, and then around eleven he felt sharp pains in his chest. He'd always loved the lodge for its isolation, but now it meant he was too far for a doctor to reach him. An hour later, Will died of a coronary thrombosis. He was fifty-seven, and he was the only Clark who came back to Montana to die.

His body was taken to Missoula, where he lay in state at a chapel and scores of friends and associates paid their respects. This was the beginning of the memorial rites. On Saturday, his body was transported to Butte by the North Coast Limited train and lay in state at the

Clark mansion on Granite Street, where more people thronged the family home. And then, accompanied by Sanner, Lippincott, and others, his body was taken aboard a private car on Union Pacific bound for Salt Lake City on the way to Los Angeles.

Caroline and Sanner made the funeral arrangements. Thousands of people streamed into Will's home in West Adams on June 18 to pay their respects. Missing among the throngs, though, were those with whom Will shared so much of his life—no Charlie, no Tertius, no Mabel, no Alice, and no Harrison. According to Gladys, her brother wouldn't be leaving his bed anytime soon.

As friends, city leaders, and strangers bowed their heads before Will's coffin, Gladys was at the courthouse downtown submitting a petition to the County of Los Angeles that she be appointed as Harrison's guardian. She attested that the duty should fall to her, given that her brother had been under constant medical care for the past three years, his parents were dead, and he had no other siblings nearby.

It's difficult to substantiate or deny Gladys's first claim. Harrison's illness in the wake of the food poisoning incident had been severe, but he'd recovered enough to circulate among his country club set until his collapse in March. Since then, he'd indeed been under "constant medical care," but it didn't seem that was the case for the past three years.

Jean Lawrence was alive in Chicago. Mary Post was still living at the house on Clay Street in San Francisco. Likewise, depending on whom Harrison counted as his siblings, there were many to choose from. Gladys was the only one of the so-called Harrisons in Los Angeles, but the rest were alive, scattered among Sacramento, New York, and Chicago. And Madeleine Post Starrett and Guy Bates Post were both in California.

Gladys also stated that her brother was thirty-two years old, the one lie that would've pleased Harrison, now thirty-seven.

The following claim from her petition, however, was entirely accurate and prophetic:

> That for more than three months last past he had been in the Chase Sanitarium, 1030 West 18th Street, Los Angeles, California, and by reason of said severe illness, disease and weakness of

> mind resulting therefore, is unable, unassisted, properly to manage or take care of himself or his property, and by reason thereof is likely to be deceived or imposed upon by artful or designing persons.

The next day, blocks away from the sanitarium, hundreds of people filed into St. John's Episcopal Church.

The church rector began the funeral service with a recitation of the Order for the Burial of the Dead. Eight pallbearers, all longtime servants of the Clark family, slowly entered, bearing Will's bronze coffin down the long aisle and setting it down at the foot of the chancel steps surrounded by floral tributes.

There was no eulogy, which Will's friends knew he wouldn't have wanted—just verse and music. After the rector recited Psalms 39 and 96, from the side chapel forty members of the Philharmonic's woodwind and string sections began to play the second movement of Schubert's *Unfinished Symphony*. Verses from Romans and St. John followed, and the orchestra played the Allegretto from Beethoven's Seventh. Once the Litany of the Departed was spoken, a string quartet played Tchaikovsky's Andante cantabile.

The pallbearers returned to their posts at the coffin and proceeded down the aisle out of the church. None of Will's immediate family was there. His sisters were in New York, though cousins and other relatives attended. Along with Will's friends and the musicians, they joined the cortege following the hearse to the cemetery.

The bronze door of the enormous mausoleum had been pulled open. The Shakespearean actor R. D. MacLean read William Cullen Bryant's "Thanatopsis." The rector read the Episcopal committal services, and Will was laid to rest in the tomb with Mabel, Alice, and Tertius. Then, as a reporter from the *Los Angeles Times* observed, "the group of relatives and intimates wandered sadly back across the little bridge that connects the island site of the Clark mausoleum with the rest of the cemetery."

Two days later, Dr. Samuel Ingham certified for the Superior Court of Los Angeles that for the past three months Harrison had been confined at the Chase Sanitarium under his care, due to a "lesion on the brain," and that on June 25, Harrison would not be, "nor for an indefinite time to come, either mentally or physically," able to appear in court.

This was the same day that the newspapers rushed to report that Will Clark had left half a million dollars to George Palé, who was described as the son of "old friends" of Will's. Reporters noted that Will had supervised the boy's education—an echo of the story Harrison and Gladys once told their visiting tennis star friend. Within a week, though, George was identified as the housekeeper's son.

To some of Will's closest friends, like Judge Lippincott, the news came as a shock. "What in the world do you think of him leaving Georgie Palé half a million?" he wrote to Will's nieces Alice and Ethel McManus. "Don't answer that, for I know what you think." Whatever any of them did think is unknown. Only that it must not be uttered.

Will's other bequests were reported as well, which accumulated to about $450,000 to be distributed among some thirty people, including friends, servants, and his various lawyers. He gave all his violins, including the treasured Amati, to Edwin Clark, and all the contents of his home, including his late wives' clothing, to Cora. Of course, Harrison was a significant legatee, well provided for with the $100,000 trust, a lump sum of $25,000 cash, the farm, the house in Castellammare, and all the other assets he'd accumulated over his years with Will.

As Dr. Ingham predicted, Harrison did not appear in court on June 25, and that day, Gladys signed the Letters of Guardianship, in which she swore to "faithfully perform according to the law, the duties of my office as Guardian of the person and estate of Harrison Post Incompetent." She also signed a bond in the amount of $7,000, which she would forfeit if she failed in her obligations to her new ward.

Harrison couldn't hear the wistful chords, much less perceive the tremors rippling through the church as the musicians' bows rose and fell while throngs gathered to mourn his companion of fifteen years. He was stranded in a sanitarium bed, insensible to the music just blocks away, to what he'd lost, and to how much his life was about to change.

PART THREE

1934–1938

Charles and Gladys Crookses' library, circa 1940.

15

THE GUARDIAN

Harrison had been rescued twice in his life—first, when he was a desperate young man and Mary Post had taken him into her home, and then when Will Clark plucked him out of the Marsh and swept him into a world of glamour and ease. In 1934, Harrison needed rescuing again. Los Angeles's Superior Court agreed and appointed his sister to the task. Years before, he'd given her a new life through his own great fortune. Now it was her turn to save him.

Unlike her brother's, Gladys's deep-set eyes were pale blue, her stare hard and glacial. She curled her dark brown hair tightly under at the edges, a stiff frame around her wide, pale face, and kept her eyebrows tweezed and spare. Although she resembled him in other ways—they shared a particular angularity—she lacked Harrison's sensual lassitude and his dark, lingering gaze. Where he was acutely of the flesh, she seemed mostly bone. From a passport photo, one senses she had the habit of looking down her nose when she spoke to others, though like her brother, she was small, about five foot four.

History tells us some things. Sometimes she called herself Gladys, sometimes Felice. Sometimes she called herself a countess. She advised her friend Theresa to leave her husband for a violent much-divorced boxer down on his luck. She may or may not have been involved in a jewel smuggling ring. Harrison tells us others. She spewed "flaming falsehoods." She was an "improvident liar." To put it another way, she would have made a magnificent role for Agnes Moorehead, an actress skilled at contempt and meddling, at playing busybodies and country club snobs.

Mark Harrison had had a tendency toward the flourish—for green velvet curtains—and an instinct for self-invention. Certainly Harrison inherited these traits, as did Gladys, but she'd gotten something else from Mark, a restless eye, always scanning for an opportunity, like a gullible business partner or parents who happen to go away for the weekend.

The recent years had been good ones for Gladys. While Harrison dabbled, she moved with purpose. In his early years in Los Angeles, he'd entered his chow chow Son in a few kennel competitions, but eventually he lost interest. Gladys, however, leapt into the show circuit with alacrity. Her beloved Brussels griffon Sidlaw Trotsky placed reserve at the Ambassador Hotel's annual kennel show and made appearances in *Dog Fancier.* While Harrison toyed with bookbinding, Gladys started a business giving lessons in the craft. Days after her brother had been committed to the Chase Sanitarium, she gave a lecture on "The Art of Books and Bookbinding" at the Foundation of Western Art in Westlake.

She also married a man named Charles Crooks. Fiction wouldn't permit such a development, so obvious, so bald and artless as to be vulgar, but it was the truth. He was a car salesman from Toledo.

Charles Powell Crook Jr. was born on January 2, 1902, though he often simplified his birthdate to January 1, 1900, and added an *s* to his last name. He'd been married before. He started out working at the dealership in Toledo owned by his first wife's father before going into business for himself with Crooks Motor Car Company, which lasted only a year. Three others followed. By 1930, he'd divorced, leaving his wife with a nine-year-old daughter, and moved to Los Angeles, where he rented a room at the Mayan Hotel in the Wilshire neighborhood.

At five foot ten, Charles Crooks wasn't a towering figure, but he was solidly built. With dark hair and a carefully trimmed mustache, he bore a passing resemblance to William Powell, the debonair star of the *Thin Man* detective films, though he seemed closer in temperament to George Raft, the stylish gangster-turned-actor who'd recently starred in Howard Hawks's *Scarface.*

Like Raft, Charles was friends with Eddie Nealis, the handsome mobster who ran the Clover Club on Sunset Boulevard, a swanky destination for Hollywood stars and underworld figures and a front for gambling and money laundering. Prohibition had ended in December

1933, but the web of racketeering it spawned still thrived. Since moving to Los Angeles, Charles Crooks had made his way into the spheres where crime and glamour mingled, and somewhere along the way he met Gladys.

They were married on June 30, 1932, at a Christian Scientist church in West Adams. She gave her name as "Felice Mary Barbieri" and knocked eight years off her age, claiming to be thirty-one. This was her least extravagant lie on the marriage license. She also concocted a father, "W. Nizhueske," from Russia, and a mother, "Maddona Siquet," from France, fitting forebears for a fake countess. Her new husband didn't trouble with such ornate fabrications. Still, the car salesman and the bookbinder shared something else—an instinct for the hustle, for spotting a mark and moving fast.

16

EXILE

It was as if he'd been banished, though he hadn't gone anywhere. It was the kingdom that disappeared.

For the past fifteen years, Harrison had moved through the world, secure in the Clark empire, buoyed upon an ocean of capital and access and servants and chauffeured cars and art and famous names. The affluence hadn't been only a matter of money, but also of love and loyalty. He'd been adored, protected, enshrined, painted on a ceiling.

They'd traveled the world together. He'd grown accustomed to fine meals, beautiful clothes, opulent hotels, friendships with powerful people. He'd grown comfortable with his things—his horses, his Rolls-Royce, his books, his silver, his dogs, his swans, his farm. He'd glided along, suspended by Will's wealth, which had become his as well, and by Will's love. But now the moon had vanished, the tide never to return, and he lay on the desert floor.

His world was fog. Fog from whatever it was that had snapped, like a twig, in his mind. Fog from whatever it was the nurses put in the hypos, fog from his scrambled nerves, from his wounded brain.

He'd been taken out of one room and put in another, all the while motionless, like a thing made of sand. Now another room. It was home, they said.

He didn't move. Others did. They moved and they disappeared. His butler and the housekeeper were gone. The gardeners were gone. The night watchman was gone. But Gladys was there and Him too.

New footsteps, new voices in the hall outside. New staring faces. McFarland. Oliphant. Schenk. Judd—that was the one with the scissors.

Outside, a gate opened and closed. A car sound. A beam of light stabbed the wall. No language for any of it. No language for not having language. Just pale shapes, dark shapes. Something wet, something soft, something hot, something cold. Pins everywhere. Pain then fog then not even that.

Gladys hung new curtains. She drew them shut, and the world outside was gone. He was trapped inside a body that didn't move, in a mind that moved too much in all the wrong directions, and then not at all.

The gate opened. A car. A woman's heels. The fog was back.

He woke. He wanted a book. It had been "misplaced." He asked for another. It too had been misplaced.

He saw and he felt and he heard and yet he could not be seen or understood. He was alive enough to know that he'd been buried.

The gate opened again. Trucks, men's voices. A dog barked. Not his.

It's easier to dismantle a world than to build one. The first moving trucks arrived in August. Weeks later, the Crookses sold the Plymouth. By October, the appraiser was there to go through the library. As Gladys explained to the court, it was necessary to economize. This was why, as Harrison's guardian, she'd initially relocated him from Mildred Chase's high-end sanitarium in West Adams, where, she claimed, the monthly expenses ran more than $2,000. His next home, the Casa Del Mar Sanitarium, charged only $460. Also, it was closer to the Palisades. Never mind that once a patient hanged herself with a stocking there.

Formerly a grand private estate near the coast in Mar Vista, the grounds had been turned into a roadhouse with bungalows and, briefly, a brothel, before being refurbished as a hospital, and then later a sanitarium. The Casa Del Mar advertised treatment for "people suffering from nervous diseases—only milder forms, no insane person admitted." Its more notorious residents included the wife of a mining executive, committed against her will; John Barrymore, ostensibly for a heart condition; and Frankie Bailey, once known as "The Girl with the Million Dollar Legs." Still, despite the efforts of the staff, Gladys reported that Harrison's health continued to fail and an unnamed doctor advised she bring her brother back to his own home.

Back at the farm, Gladys cut costs. She fired Harrison's staff and hired new servants, all paid significantly less and with no prior loyalties to Harrison. Everything—and everyone—would be unquestionably under the Crookses' control.

Gladys's signature was on every petition and every expense report she submitted to the court, but Charles's name was on every invoice from their attorneys—"call to Mr. Crooks," "conference with Chas Crooks." Behind all the decisions, all the firings and hirings, all the trucks that carted away Harrison's belongings, Charles lurked. Of course, the Crookses didn't pay the legal fees themselves. Those bills were charged to Harrison's estate. With the death of Will Clark and Harrison's indefinite confinement, Charles and Gladys had found themselves a near-effortless income stream.

In her petition for guardianship, Gladys submitted an inventory of her brother's assets to the court. This included the ranch, appraised at $60,000, and the beach house in Castellammare, at $19,000, along with the following list:

5 Horses—one worthless
1 Colt
4 Saddles and bridles
1 Sulkey
1 Power Mower
1 Cow and Calf
5 Swans
5 Dogs
Geese and Goats
Approximately 3,500 books
Silver for Main House
Personal Clothing, etc.
Furnishings and studio equipment
Miscellaneous Jewelry
Plymouth Coupe
Rolls Royce

Not itemized were the furnishings in the main house, stables, servants' quarters, guesthouse, and studio, whose value she listed at $3,000. Gladys also tallied up the cash in his bank account as well as various promissory notes, or IOUs, from friends, such as the beautician Madame Patteneaude and Robert Ehrmann. Including the cash bequest and trust fund from Will, Gladys's appraisal of Harrison's estate came to $217,304.54. In today's terms, that's well over $4 million.

After recognizing that the estate was of a higher value than Gladys originally declared when she was first appointed Harrison's guardian, the court increased the bond from $7,000 to $25,000, which she would forfeit if she didn't faithfully perform her duties—a small sum given how much money was at stake.

While the Crookses relished their new fortune, Harrison's former life of comfort and glamour had vanished. The cover page for his case file is styled in the manner of a probate document, much like the one issued after Will's death:

No. 144004
In the Matter of the Estate of
Post

And then just below stamped in bold: **INCOMPETENT**. In more than four hundred pages of filings, the word dogs every appearance of his name. On one form, someone has crossed out "deceased" and written "incompetent"; it was a fine line between the two. Harrison might as well have been dead, because from the court's perspective, he had ceased to exist as a person. And yet he was alive enough that his sister and his brother-in-law could live off him—he was still a host, in the most grotesque sense of the word.

The tale of a nobleman trapped in a cataleptic state, imprisoned by a malevolent scheming sibling, evokes something out of Edgar Allan Poe. The scenario also fits just as easily into the hard-boiled world of the writer's twentieth-century heir, Raymond Chandler: a wealthy drugged-up queer is held captive by his dog-crazy sister and her grifter husband.

It would be five years yet before the former oil executive published *The Big Sleep*, his first novel, about Philip Marlowe, a detective who descends into an underworld maze populated by pornographers, nymphomaniacs, femmes fatales, aging tycoons, book dealers, and homosexuals. However, by 1934 much of the crime and corruption that informed Chandler's books and stories had already taken place—the murder-suicide of Ned Doheny and his valet Hugh Plunkett and its cover-up, the shooting of mob boss Charles Crawford, as well as the many less sensational acts of greed and revenge that proliferated in Los Angeles.

Chandler's career with the Dabney Oil Company had come to a disreputable end. He'd been fired for womanizing, drinking, and roaming about downtown LA instead of working. A habitué of Booksellers Row and the Los Angeles Athletic Club, he could have easily crossed paths with Will and Harrison on his wanders. Surely Chandler knew the rumors that trailed the mining magnate's son, and over the years he lived at several addresses near Harrison's Palisades estate. He knew the shadowy seaside enclave where the wealthy, famous, and desperate hid out among the rambling wooded glens, and he knew the lights of the gambling boats, the same ones visible from Harrison's beach house on Porto Marina Way.

In the writer's world, there were degrees of corruption. Some, like the B-list actors, low-level hoodlums, and even the vengeful young gay man from *The Big Sleep*, wore their dishonor openly. But the truly degenerate were those with money, the ones who pulled the strings and rarely paid for their crimes, which usually involved the cover-up of a family scandal, like the wealthy port-swilling matriarch in *The High Window* who bullies her meek secretary or the reckless daughters of the enfeebled magnate in *The Big Sleep*. In Chandler's world, it's among the rich that real depravity thrives. The rest are pawns in their schemes.

If Philip Marlowe had been called to the farm, what would he have found? At the end of the driveway lay a sun-dappled brook with a few swans floating—an idyllic setting, except for the fact that someone living in a place like this wanted help from someone like him. Maybe the scene would've evoked the cloying scent in Geiger's house from *The Big Sleep*. That was the homosexual pornographer with the book-dealer front who was blackmailing the nymphomaniac daughter of the ailing tycoon. His was the first murder in Chandler's first novel. In noir fiction, the queer ones are easy to kill.

So much of Harrison's life now fit the genre. A German butler at the front door who was hard to understand not because of the accent, but because somewhere a dog was yipping. A bony-faced woman, the kind who owned a dog that sounded like that. A car salesman husband who talked too much, padding around in someone else's wealth. Somewhere in the house, a sick brother, too sick to see anyone. A stroke, a breakdown, "a weak mind," something along those lines. The "secretary" to a copper heir. And then the male nurse, impassive and sinister in hospital whites—a beefy face that never moved, though surely his lips twitched when he drove the hypo in.

Gladys did in fact hire a detective. The expense shows up in her report to the court that September. The records don't say what services he rendered. It couldn't have been much of a job; she paid him only ten dollars. In any case, the scenario playing out at the Palisades ranch wasn't a case for Philip Marlowe or any other fictional private eye. For one thing, there was no femme fatale, and the damsel in distress was a man. Besides, this was a story of character actors.

Once upon a time Harrison might've been a leading man—dark-eyed, seductive, with a vague foreign charm and definite savoir faire—but that era had passed. Rudolph Valentino had been dead eight years. The mysterious stranger who once dominated the screen now lurked in the shadows. In 1934, the year that Harrison's life snapped, a new outsider arrived in America.

One among the many flooding out of Europe, Peter Lorre had come to find work in Hollywood. Born László Löwenstein in 1904, he began his career onstage in Vienna, later rising through the film industry in 1920s Berlin. Dark, diminutive, with large, beseeching eyes, Lorre came to fame in 1931 as a serial killer who preys on children in Fritz Lang's *M*, a man both rapacious and haunted, powerless over ugly desires, which, though it wasn't stated overtly, weren't only homicidal but pedophilic too. In America, Lorre found success playing villains, effete, scheming men who relished male attention, even when it arrived in *The Maltese Falcon* in the form of Humphrey Bogart's fist. That Lorre's perfumed smuggler, Joel Cairo, should be so clearly what he was—a homosexual—and not shrink from the detective's gaze was as great an offense as any theft or other crime, and yet he was still weak and soft enough to be destroyed in the end.

Harrison never wrote about the violence he faced at the hands of the Crookses. Never in his journals does he describe anything "Charles" did to him. He could only write his brother-in-law's name in quotation marks. Whatever transpired behind the new curtains that Gladys hung—and reimbursed herself for—Harrison didn't want to recall any of it. The most he would say was that he had at times been held "in complete physical restraint."

He had no privacy in what had once been his pastoral hideaway. Fearful that he might plot his escape with the help of one of the nurses, the Crookses recorded him with Dictaphones. Few of the medical attendants stayed long. Their names pile up in the monthly reports: Schenk, Lowey, Beckner, Oliver, Hamilton, Oliphant, Sweezey. Some were listed under "ranch help." Most were paid once and then never again. McFarland and Judd were the two that remained. This was the same with the rest of the staff. Butlers and housekeepers came and went. Gone, too, were Harrison's various luxury treatments. No longer did Madame Patteneaude attend to his hair. Now it was Judd who wielded the scissors.

One of the first purchases the Crookses made was barbed wire. They installed a burglar alarm. More than once they repaired the front gate. Were they trying to keep people out or keep someone in? And if Harrison managed to get away, how far could he have gotten? And what condition was he actually in?

Gladys hadn't stinted on drugs. Under her "care," he was heavily medicated. She did eventually bring doctors around. In October, two months after Harrison had been discharged from the Del Mar Sanitarium, Dr. Aaron Rosanoff made the first house call. A renowned alienist, frequent expert witness at trials, and prominent eugenicist, Dr. Rosanoff believed insanity was inherited and that in extreme cases patients should be sterilized. Thyroid specialists and osteopaths also weighed in on Harrison's condition. Gladys paid for him to be subjected to fluoroscopy, a kind of motion-picture X-ray, but she never had Dr. Ingham, the neurologist whom Will had paid to treat Harrison at Chase, come to evaluate him.

Was Harrison cognizant enough to understand that Will was gone? Or did he have to be told again and again, and then mourn again and again? It's impossible to know how much his state was a result of what Ingham had diagnosed as a lesion on his brain, and how much was due to being kept under sedation, a hostage to his sister and her husband, at the mercy of a revolving squad of orderlies. And where had his many famous and powerful friends gone? Bebe Daniels, Frances Marion, Dorothy di Frasso evidently nowhere to be found. Where were the country club friends—Snowy Baker, Ann Rork? Where were Cora Sanders or Judge Sanner or Joe, for that matter? Did they not care? Did they not know?

Harrison always led a double life, but this new one wasn't his choice. For all outward appearances, Gladys was the model of a loyal sister, selflessly devoting herself to the care of her invalid brother. It would certainly be easy to tell a story of poor feeble-minded Harrison convalescing at home, and how she hoped that one day soon he'd be well enough for visitors. Meanwhile the moving trucks kept coming. She rented the property for a film shoot, she sold two of his horses, and she made time for new enterprises.

In November, Gladys announced that she would open a bookstore and bindery on the Sunset Strip with Tone Price. An intriguing and little-remembered figure in the history of Los Angeles bibliophiles, Tone Price was originally from Fort Worth, Texas, where she met book dealer Jake Zeitlin when he lived there in the early 1920s. After he moved to Los Angeles in 1925, she followed and assisted him with his early bookstores. Theirs was never a romantic attachment. Zeitlin was happily married and, in his words, Tone Price was "a mannish lesbian, who wore stylish clothes." She was also the new owner of Harrison's Plymouth, having paid Gladys $450 for the coupe.

Together with Philmore Phipps, a dandy and fellow bibliophile, the women opened Barbieri & Price at 9045 Sunset Boulevard. A formerly rural stretch of country road between Beverly Hills and the studios, the Strip was now in full swing as a nightlife destination, with Cafe La Maze, Cafe Trocadero, and of course Eddie Nealis's Clover Club. It served a daytime clientele too, featuring William Haines's interior design studio and now a high-end store for rare books and a bindery.

Gladys informed *Bookbinding Magazine* that she was going to offer lessons in the craft. "The interest shown in this is really remarkable," she said. "I am almost forced to start the class." The new owners hired architect Lloyd Wright to design the store's interior. The son of Frank Lloyd Wright, he'd made his own mark in LA with the Sowden House, a neo-Mayan mansion in Los Feliz, and the arched band shell of the

Hollywood Bowl, among other buildings. The bookstore included a well-lit back room where Gladys installed the bindery with several hundred hand tools, including those once owned by Grolier. Presumably she didn't need to scrape for funding for this venture. Nor did she need to look far for rare books to sell.

In deeding his library to UCLA, Will Clark stipulated that its holdings would never be dispersed. Harrison's collection was nowhere near the scale of Will's, and though he didn't publish catalogs or indexes, Harrison was passionate about his books, many of which he'd bound himself. Now Gladys was putting them up for auction.

On February 25, 1935, moneyed elites, Hollywood players, and Los Angeles book dealers—many of whom Harrison had counted among his friends and neighbors, like Frances Marion and Salka Viertel—crowded into the new store on Sunset Boulevard. The bidding began with *A Jar of Honey from Mount Hybla*, a slender volume from 1847 by Romantic critic Leigh Hunt about traveling through Sicily. J. P. Getty bought it for fifteen dollars. Paramount founder Jesse Lasky left with collections of Rupert Brooke and Swinburne. Up-and-coming director George Cukor bought William Blake's *Songs of Innocence*, Ronald Firbank's *The Flower beneath the Foot*, and nine volumes of Pater. The crowd included professional bibliophiles like Jake Zeitlin and Merle Armitage, as well as Stanley Rose from the Satyr Book Shop, who bought eight volumes of *Celebrated Crimes* for $15.78. Hugo Kirchhofer, who, with the aid of Will Clark's money, had founded the Hollywood Bowl, won three volumes of Terence's comedies for $7.50. The auction continued.

From the sales report:

Signed letter from Anatole France	K. Thompson	17.50
Petty Worries of Conjugal Life, Balzac	" "	3.00
Trilby, George DuMaurier	Ruth Chatterton	15.00
La Mare, Rupert Brooke	Jesse Lasky	2.00
Silence of Love	" "	2.00
Swinburne	" "	2.00
Bronte, 12 vol.	Albert Lewin	35.00
Pater, 9 vol.	George Cukor	10.00
Song of Innocence, Blake	" "	3.50
The Flower Beneath the Foot, R. Firbank	" "	3.50
Mary Stuart, Swinburne	Salka Viertel	5.00

Arthur Symons on Toulouse Lautrec	" "	3.00
Beethoven's Letters	" "	3.00
The Making of Americans, Gertrude Stein	Merle Armitage	3.50
A Century of Greek Epigrams	Frances Marion	4.00
Madame Recamier and Her Friends	" "	5.00
Psyche, Pierre Louys	E.C. Flynn	4.00
The Life of Benvenuto Cellini, 2 vol.	J.P. Getty	15.00
Little Dorritt, Charles Dickens	" "	20.00
Sergeant Grischa, Arnold Zweig	" "	1.00
Lady Chatterley, DH Lawrence	" "	5.00
Faust	" "	5.00
Child's History of England, Dickens	" "	35.00
Rosenberg, 5 vol	Jake Zeitlin	50.00
In Russet and Silver, Gosse	Hugh Walpole	17.00
Sappho	Merle Armitage	15.00
Tristram Shandy	Jean Dixon	5.00
The Spirit Lamp, Lord Alfred Douglas	J.P. Getty	1.00

A signed letter from Robert Browning sold for fifty dollars. The most expensive sale was a twelve-volume set of Casanova's writings at a hundred dollars. The cheapest were Somerset Maugham's *The Painted Veil* and Ernest Hemingway's *The Sun Also Rises*—fifty cents apiece. Those went to Getty. The most aggressive of the bidders, the oil tycoon bought more than twenty books, including Pierre Louÿs's *Psyche*, a two-volume set of *The Life of Benvenuto Cellini*, and titles by Charles Dickens, Arnold Zweig, and D. H. Lawrence.

Gladys also auctioned other effects—a perfume bottle, a flask, a wooden cross.

Harrison had put his nameplate in all his books, but they were gone now, scattered at the public dismembering. What would those nameplates even mean anymore? This past year under Gladys and Charles's rule, he wasn't Harrison. He wasn't Albert. He was no one.

In his studio portrait, he exudes a certain vampiric aura. Living by night, corrupting others through insatiable, depraved desire, destroyed by exposure to the light, the vampire is a frequent stand-in for the predatory homosexual. It's what an outraged Long Beach mother called the gay men entrapped in the 1914 sting operations.

And yet it was the heterosexual couple, Gladys and Charles, who were feeding on the homosexual. He'd been his sister's entrée to the elites, movie stars, and bibliophiles, and now, in what bordered on a kind of spiritual, psychic, and social cannibalism, she was selling his dearest possessions, collected over the years with Will, piece by piece to those same people.

The total sales that day came to $819.03, one third of which Barbieri and Price took as commission. The rest presumably went back into Harrison's bank account, which Gladys could withdraw from as she liked. And the moving trucks kept coming.

To be sure, it did take work and money to keep up Harrison's estate. There were animals to be fed and curtains to be hung. Gladys kept the piano tuned. She had the fountain fixed. She made sure that horses were shod. She bought shuttlecocks and a badminton net. She bought a croquet set.

She spent fifty-one cents on candy for her brother, for which she reimbursed herself from his funds, a detail that chills in its venality and the glimpse it offers of a man reduced to a child, allotted treats according to his sister's whim. She entered each paltry amount—2.00, 1.50, .80—into her monthly reports.

By May, Harrison's health seemed to have improved enough that he was able to go to a movie, his first in over a year, and to the circus, which cost $4.80. Meanwhile, Gladys advanced herself $1,950, then $5,000. She continued to rent the grounds for film shoots and sell off his books. She never itemized any of the furnishings and never petitioned the court for permission to sell them, so there's no record of what the moving trucks took away, only that they came every month. And yet there was still a bigger payout to come. Why should Gladys and Charles settle for $450, even $1,000 here and there, selling books and bibelots and renting out the property, when they could go straight to the source and take it all? This would be the ultimate heist: the entire trust that Will Clark had established for Harrison.

Gladys had kept her lawyers busy over the past year, suing people Harrison had lent money to, but those had been trifling cases compared to what she and Charles were about to pursue. In July 1935, Gladys and Charles retained the services of a new firm, McAdoo and Neblett. Perhaps the lawyers they'd been using balked at what was coming, or perhaps the Crookses realized they needed a firm with more power. They found it.

William McAdoo served as the secretary of the US Treasury under Woodrow Wilson and succeeded Samuel Shortridge as senator. His partner, Colonel William H. Neblett, it seemed, managed his clients' needs in the style of Joe McInerney. Neblett would end up ensnared in a wide-ranging bribery scandal stemming from the International Alliance of Theatrical Stage Employees. He and McAdoo would ultimately part ways with no small amount of rancor. But that was still to come. For now, McAdoo and Neblett was the firm that was going to help Gladys and Charles dissolve Harrison's trust.

They took the case first to the Montana court, where they argued that an earlier will, made in 1927, in which Harrison was to be bequeathed $150,000 outright, should supersede the one Will signed in 1933. Will drew up a new will every year, sometimes twice a year. It seems highly arbitrary that the earlier will would be considered more valid than any later ones, and bizarre that it should outweigh his final one. Besides, Harrison's health had declined drastically since 1927, and Will clearly established the trust with that in mind.

Gladys also asserted that the farm required maintenance—cesspool cleaning, animal feed, the gate that always needed repair. She cited the financial burden of Harrison's medical needs.

Again, this was the point of the trust. Will had taken pains to specify that should Harrison's circumstances require more funds beyond the quarterly payouts, his executors could draw from the trust. It was antithetical to the purpose of the trust to dissolve it in one fell swoop and yet this is what Gladys was arguing for. The Montana state court was not convinced and dismissed her case. Buck Mangam, however, had more luck there. In December 1934, he'd sued Will's estate for the still-elusive balance of $29,166.69, and two months later the executors settled for the full amount.

The Crookses were undeterred. They took their case to the Los Angeles County Court with a new argument, claiming that, contrary to Gladys's original petition for guardianship, which asserted that Harrison had been under medical care for several years, he'd in fact been in good health when Will drew up the will in 1933. However, it had since become clear that Harrison's care and recovery—which she insisted wasn't imminent—would require in excess of what the trust would provide. She also claimed that the fund would be exhausted in a few years and that those monies should now be turned over to her, as the person most sympathetic to Harrison's condition, so she could better invest them with Harrison's future financial and medical well-being in mind. Given the medical attention that Harrison required, the matter was urgent. Therefore she requested the full amount be distributed to her at once.

The court agreed, and on September 18, 1935, it was ordered that Harrison's trust be liquidated and delivered to Gladys. She promptly withdrew $5,000. She also bought Harrison a pair of tennis shoes from Montgomery Ward's.

In November a new doctor came to the farm. Dr. A. A. Kosky wasn't trained in neurology or thyroid disorders but in "human catatonia." The condition's causes range from psychotic disorders to encephalitis. Dr. Kosky had first studied people in catatonic states when he served in the Canadian Army, where his patients suffered from post-traumatic stress disorder, more commonly known in 1935 as shell shock. Harrison hadn't been in combat, but he had suffered a brain infection and for the past year been subject to prolonged shock and distress.

According to Gladys, though, he was making extraordinary strides, when only months before she'd claimed his recovery wasn't imminent. Maybe Dr. Kosky had prescribed the one treatment Harrison needed, but that's unlikely. Harrison's supposed return to health seemed most certainly dependent on the fact that Gladys had now gained unrestricted control of his entire fortune.

For Gladys and Charles, life would be much simpler if they didn't have to record and submit expenses to the court, if they could dispense with all the bureaucracy. Gladys had simplified other parts of her life. Whether she'd wearied of the work or sold all the books she wanted to sell, the book-dealing venture had come to a quick end, and that December the sign at 9045 Sunset read "Tone Price Books."

Gladys moved swiftly. By the end of January she had a letter in hand from Dr. August Hromadka of the Santa Monica Hospital stating that he'd found Harrison much improved and "capable of transacting business for himself." Never, though, did his original doctor, Samuel Ingham, who'd confirmed that Harrison required a guardian, examine Harrison or offer his assessment to the court. In February, Harrison appeared to be well enough because, along with Gladys, he signed a petition requesting that he be restored to capacity and that she be discharged as guardian. Shortly after, Gladys requested that the court proceedings be transferred from Los Angeles County to Santa Monica. Surely Philip Marlowe would've raised an eyebrow over that move.

On March 9, 1936, the petition was granted: "Harrison Post is now sane and competent and capable of taking care of himself and his property." No longer was Gladys her brother's guardian. Two weeks later, the court allowed her to withdraw from his bank account without a countersignature. Another development that would've given Philip Marlowe pause.

By the end of March, Gladys was relieved of all liabilities and exonerated of the bonds issued when she was appointed Harrison's guardian. Her final expense report as "Guardian of the person of Harrison Post, Incompetent," was dated April 1, 1936. Years later, Harrison gave a very different version of events. In fact, he'd not recovered and he hadn't understood the document he'd put his name on. Gladys had told him it was a form that would allow the Crookses to rent property from him.

The court had been a nominal protector, a mark Gladys had easily outwitted. She didn't have to ask permission anymore to take her brother's money. She'd sold much that was precious to him, but the real value lay in what was left. The beach house. The farm. And she didn't have to keep records on what happened next.

After his father's death, Harrison had foundered alone, lost in a tailspin of despair. He'd been taken in by Mary Post, but she wasn't going to save him now. The kind widow had died just months earlier at her daughter's home in San Francisco. Will, who'd protected Harrison for the past fifteen years, was gone. None of his friends had come to the rescue. Possibly none of them had any idea how dire his circumstances were. Only those on the inside could know.

Over the past year and a half, Gladys had cycled through nurses, new names every month. On her last expense report submitted for that March, there was yet another. This was under ranch help: "O Tringstad."

Harrison had suffered abuse under many of the men Gladys hired, but some had been sympathetic, enough so that the Crookses had spied on them to make sure they didn't help him escape. The nurse Gladys hired that spring was kind and he was going to rescue Harrison. At last, a true savior had arrived, a new player in the noir world at the ranch: a tall, blond masseur from Norway.

Once upon a time Harrison had been a handsome young shop clerk and then Will Clark had stepped into the Marsh and changed his life. Now he was a traumatized invalid, and the man coming to liberate him wasn't a wealthy American philanthropist, but, just like Will, this man was going to save Harrison from one danger and deliver him to another. His name was Oscar.

17

ESCAPE

Will was gone, but he'd left a map. When the neighbors complained, when the DA ordered Harrison's home vacated, when their friends got arrested, they'd fled to Europe. They'd always been freer there than in their own country. Now Harrison made the journey again, this time with a new companion.

In all his travels, Harrison had never been to Norway. It must've been the masseur's idea. It was Oscar's hometown they traveled to and his family's hotel where they would stay.

One year older than Harrison, Oscar Tryggestad was born in Ålesund and grew up in Hellesylt, a small village on the northwestern coast of Norway, near the great Geiranger Fjord. He came to America in the 1910s, where he worked as a baker in Minnesota, before moving to Los Angeles and training as a masseur.

Home to a handful of farmers, Hellesylt was also a stop for sightseers from the visiting cruise lines and a few small businesses, including two hotels. One was the Grand Hotel. The Tryggestad family ran the other. After his father's death, Oscar inherited the business, though his sister Margit managed it in his absence. Harrison called the Norwegian masseur "Trygga," but most people back home knew him by his middle name, Birthing (pronounced "bear-ting"), because his brother-in-law was an Oscar too.

The story they told was that Harrison had had a stroke and Trygga was bringing him to the quiet town to recuperate, away from the parties and the guests who crowded his home back in Santa Monica. They left out Gladys, Charles, and the gothic treachery of the past two years. Harrison would later claim that he'd remained debilitated after Gladys had stopped being his guardian, but photos on this trip show him engaged and alert. While he looks notably frail—thinner, worn—and older than his thirty-nine years, he doesn't appear to be paralyzed. His health certainly wasn't strong. He continued to suffer from rheumatism and would always fear getting a "reaction," but he wasn't in a catatonic state anymore.

The Crookses still hadn't succeeding in finding a buyer for the farm, but they had transferred the deed for the beach house to Bank of America, a transaction they'd managed to execute the same month Harrison and Trygga left on the cruise. Whether Harrison approved or even knew was beside the point. Gladys now had the leverage and the purse strings.

To the newspapers and in court documents, Harrison would assert that she sent him to Norway for a rest cure. However, his diaries don't refer to being forced to go, and indeed it seems he wanted to, perhaps for his ailments, perhaps for other reasons. With Harrison, as with Gladys, there was always a story behind the story. It's all but certain that he was being subjected to another type of pressure, one he could never accuse his sister of in a court of law. The Crookses didn't need drugs or straitjackets anymore. He had taken Gladys in and she knew his world—all of it. They had the truth to keep him cornered. It was safer for Harrison to say he was physically ill or mentally incompetent than that he was being blackmailed by his own family.

During his confinement, Gladys had spied on him, recording him with Dictaphones, to make sure he wasn't trying to flee. Now he had escaped, more or less, with her apparent approval. With the trust dissolved, the Crookses didn't need to tend to Harrison to have access to his bank account. Even if he had any inkling of what they might do in his absence, Harrison was desperate to get away.

Liberation came in October 1936. After two years of being trapped in his own home, hostage to his sister and her husband, constrained to thirteen acres, he and Trygga left Los Angeles on a cruise. Now he was free on the open sea.

While Harrison kept his scrapbooks in an erratic fashion, Trygga was methodical, carefully captioning photos and sequencing them in chronological order. He traced their route on a map with precise, thin red arrows around North America and through the Caribbean. Their tour took them to San Francisco, Costa Rica, Panama, Belize, New Orleans, Havana, and up the East Coast. Along the way, Harrison reunited with old friends. He and Trygga spent several months as the guests of the Langdales, who owned a coffee plantation in Pleasant Hill, Jamaica, and on April 30, 1937, they sailed from Kingston to Copenhagen. France had been Will's refuge, but Harrison would find sanctuary farther north.

Norway is part of an old rock. The belts of granite and beds of gneiss in the Baltic Shield go back as far as the Archean Eon, when the earth's crust had cooled just enough to harden into continents. But the fjords are young, left over from the last ice age ten thousand years ago, when the retreating glaciers twisted and gouged new chasms into the ancient slab.

Hellesylt means flat, wet ground. Nearby is the town of Stranda, the word for "coast," and on the other side of the sheer mountain rising to the south lies Myskredal, which means avalanche valley. Here, the land was named for what it was, not for saints, angels, or the men who carved it into tracts and sold it. Among the fjords, it's obvious the earth doesn't need us. The staggering cliffs don't. The vast waterways don't. It's not a question of dominating the land, but of making peace with it and with the seasons, with the midnight sun and the endless winter dark.

Henrik Ibsen set his first play in Hellesylt. *Brand* is the story of a man of extreme virtue, never swayed from his principles, even when his rigid sense of morality leads to his son's death. The play ends with his own demise in a rockslide. This wasn't a metaphor. A few years before Harrison arrived, an avalanche destroyed a neighboring village.

Bordered by the Atlantic and Arctic Oceans, as well as the Norwegian, Barents, and North Seas, and interlaced with more than a thousand fjords, Norway is a country that seems as much water as land. Harrison and Trygga came by boat, threading through the narrow canyons to the small village at the end of the Sunnylvsfjorden. It was May, and the surrounding wheat fields were lush and green.

In the Pacific Palisades, he'd lived on a "farm," but in Hellesylt there were real farmers who tilled real soil. They harvested crops, baled hay, and worried how long the snows would last before they could plant again. It was calm. It was breathtaking in its beauty. It was as far from Gladys and Charles Crooks as Harrison could get.

It was also a preliminary visit. They stayed only for the summer, and in September, Harrison returned with Trygga to California and discovered that the Crookses had made their way into the ranks of the rich who trade property among themselves and that his home was gone.

Just a few years before, he'd swapped his Cimarron Street home for the Palisades estate, and that April, while he was in Jamaica, Gladys had followed suit. She traded his beloved ranch to Courtland Hill—son of James J. Hill, who'd built the Great Northern Railroad—and his wife, Blanche, previously married to George Hearst. In return, the Crookses moved into the Hills' mansion at 626 North Arden Drive and received $130,000. The Monterey Colonial mansion with the wraparound terrace in Beverly Hills was designed by Paul Revere Williams, who also designed homes for the likes of Frank Sinatra and Lucille Ball. There was room for Harrison, but he hadn't come back to stay.

Other negotiations ensued. He and Gladys came to an agreement, which was that while he was recuperating in Norway, he would receive an allowance of $175 each month; today that would be a bit more than $3,000. At least this is what he later told reporters, which means it was only a fraction of the real story.

The rest is murky. It doesn't appear that there was any legal document drawn up to solidify this arrangement, if indeed this was the understanding, but a lawyer was involved, one skilled at shadowy handshake agreements and undocumented financial transactions. Will had named Joe McInerney an executor to Harrison's trust and though the old fixer had no fiduciary obligation now that it'd been dissolved, he managed the disbursal of the funds. As long as there was Clark money, there was still a Clark machine.

When Will was alive, $5,000 had arrived every month in Harrison's bank account, through no effort of his own. Even before his illness, his finances had been managed by other people, whether by Will or his intermediaries, and this continued. Admittedly, $175 was a much smaller monthly allowance than what Harrison had been used to, but he also didn't need as much in Hellesylt. And besides, what really mattered was that he would be free of the Crookses, that he would be safe.

Harrison, unidentified friend, and Oscar Tryggestad, 1938.

In hindsight, it's hard to fathom that anyone could imagine Norway—or any corner of Europe—as a place of safety in the late 1930s. And many wouldn't have needed hindsight to know the danger, but perhaps for those accustomed to wealth, totalitarianism is something that happens to other people, to the poor, to the middle class, to immigrants, but not to courtiers, not to aristocrats, not even the invented ones. As beneficiaries of hierarchy, they're already accustomed to the fact that their protected sphere requires exclusion, so it may be natural to believe they'll remain untouched as a despot lunges for more power.

In Germany that Christmas, people hung ornaments shaped like grenades and topped their fir trees with swastikas instead of the Star of Bethlehem. There would be no celebration of a Jewish child born in a manger. On Christmas Eve, brown-shirted storm troopers assembled in Berlin at midnight. They didn't sing carols but nationalist hymns. They lit bonfires and threw wreaths into the flames to commemorate their fallen comrades and they pledged their fidelity to the Führer.

That same month in Romania, the leaders of the National Christian Party decreed that those who'd arrived in the country after 1920—which included hundreds of thousands of Jews who'd fled Poland and Germany after the Great War—would be expelled. Borders were closing. Bulgaria wouldn't permit refugees. Nor would Hungary or Yugoslavia. A campaign in Austria advocated "to close the gates against foreign Jews—we have enough."

Harrison may not have been oblivious to the looming threat. Still, even though he'd just emerged from a harrowing state of captivity, he'd lived too long in the Clark empire to think such danger could be meant for him. Besides, none of that was happening on the Scandinavian Peninsula. Berlin and Bucharest may have seemed as far from the small town nestled at the end of a Norwegian fjord as they did from Los Angeles. After Christmas, Harrison and Trygga set sail from San Pedro on the M/S *Laurits Swenson* bound for Oslo. They would travel by way of the Panama Canal.

Out on the deck, they lounged, Trygga shirtless with his white pants rolled up and Harrison in white wide-legged trousers and a snug white polo. He tanned quickly.

A black-and-white snapshot taken aboard the ship shows them reclining on deck chairs on either side of a younger, shirtless man. Their blond friend smiles at the camera, as does Trygga, jolly and relaxed, arms outstretched above his head. Wind lifts his fair hair.

Harrison sinks back in the white canvas of his chair, his torso slightly angled toward his handsome companion, hands in his lap, though his face is turned away, eyes closed, smiling. It's a fleeting moment, his head tossed, white shirt collar flaring against his dark neck, a twist in his body as he gives himself over to laughter, pleasure, maybe even peace. A man at last released, free and happy under the sun.

PART FOUR

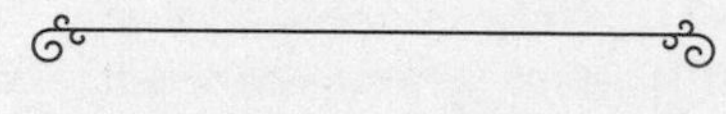

1938–1945

Postcard of Hellesylt, from Harrison's journals.

18

HELLESYLT

Tryggestad Hotel, undated.

Harrison arrived in Hellesylt that January wearing a full-length fur coat. He'd left the world of sun for one of snow.

Here, life was calm and simple. Down the road from Tryggestad Hotel, a woman made a living by selling knitting. Children earned money shoveling snow, gathering hazelnuts, and carving wooden spatulas. One boy had a job pumping the bellows for the church organ. The drama didn't come from people but from the land—the narrow valley rising up into massive granite cliffs, the waterfall rushing down the rocky ravine through the middle of the town and out to the fjord.

A large white wooden building, the hotel stood in the center of town along with a handful of businesses—bakery, grocery, tailor, mechanic, print shop, café. Farther up the hillside were the small white church and the schoolhouse. Enough visitors passed through for two hotels, though the other, the Grand Hotel, usually closed during the winter. A nexus for the town, Tryggestad Hotel was a frequent stop for traveling merchants, and Margit welcomed a steady stream of tourists, some from nearby towns, some as far away as Turkey. Norwegian names and addresses soon filled Harrison's address book alongside the Hollywood elite.

For a small village, Hellesylt had an active social life and Harrison quickly became a part of it, befriending Olav Gausdal, the lensmann, or police chief, and local farmers like Anton Larsen. Harrison liked to stroll down to Larsen's pond where the two men would smoke and talk together. He struggled with the language, though he soon mastered some words, the ones for meals—frokost and middag—and for party—selskap.

In photos from his early months in Norway he often holds a cane, and in some instances, grips other people for support. His health improved, though he remained delicate. Later snapshots show him out in a rowboat, lounging at picnics, drinking beer near the banks of the fjord, feeding goats on a hillside, always impeccably dressed, in a suit and tie, as are most men in the photos. He remained vain about his appearance, fastidious in his dress. Seventy years later, villagers from Hellesylt could recall how exacting he'd been with the local tailor about the length of his shirtsleeves, how it was imperative that the cuffs hit his wrists just so.

As he regained his strength, Harrison took up skiing. He didn't have his horses anymore, but he found a new way to glide through the countryside, and he readily embraced the Nordic concept of friluftsliv, or "open-air living." Despite his frailty, Harrison could be vigorously physical, elated after a long walk or hours on the slopes. Sometimes he paid for these exertions, the next day sore and depleted, but this was part of his character—bursts of exuberance followed by anguish. A day spent sunbathing on a rock by the water's edge meant a week throbbing from the burn, coated in salve. A night of drinks and more drinks became a dour string of dark days.

There was no getting around it. The past four years since Will's death was lost time, a quicksand of horror and helplessness. He was free now from Gladys and Charles but not from grief. At least in Hellesylt there could be no reminders of how much he'd lost, no shared histories, no one to know his secrets, except for Trygga.

The two made a curious pair—Harrison, slight and dark, next to Trygga, tall and blond. Both men were understood to be homosexual, though such a thing was never said aloud. Trygga was Harrison's servant, but at the same time, Harrison was a guest in Trygga's hotel, where the two men shared a room. Never in his journals does Harrison express romantic feeling for the Norwegian, but Harrison was often full of other feelings—exasperation usually—for his masseur turned manservant, and frequently beset by the kind of grievance that accumulates through confinement in close quarters. Whether they ever were lovers, or even friends, is a mystery, but they were, on some level, intimates, bound in a complicated twist of mutual dependency and secrecy.

Harrison Post,
Nordfjorden, 1938.

Both men's albums include photos from the same picnics, hikes, and other outings. Although Harrison was happy to pose for the camera, Trygga also snapped pictures of his American charge caught unawares, enraptured by the landscape. On a trip to Tystigen, a glacier on the Nordfjorden, Harrison, cloaked in his long fur coat, gazes out from the deck of the ship. In another picture, the coat is gone, he's wearing sunglasses, standing on a grassy slope, water in the distance. He's dropped one hand to his side, the other is half raised, mid-gesture, as he stares at a vista that we can't see, his jacket bunching up in the back. This detail might have displeased him, but the photo caught him in something like awe, and it caught Trygga in the act of watching, of taking pleasure in Harrison's pleasure. Whatever the nature of their relationship, Trygga was devoted, and he wanted to remember Harrison in moments of wonder. He gave Harrison a new home, he nagged him, he protected him—at least he tried.

As an American, possibly Jewish (though this, like his sexuality, wasn't discussed), Harrison was an obvious outsider, but he was a glamorous, alluring one, encircled by the aura of wealth and Hollywood, a welcome novelty. By now he'd lived nearly half his life as Harrison Post, clubman, socialite, art collector, millionaire. The invention was real enough. And yet it was becoming increasingly clear that it didn't matter what a man believed about himself. In the Third Reich, the law now decreed that if a man had three Jewish grandparents, he was a Jew, even if he didn't practice the religion. If he did follow the faith, then only two grandparents had to be Jewish. If he was a Jew, he wasn't a citizen of the Reich; he was a subject. He couldn't have a job in the civil service. He couldn't be a journalist. He couldn't practice law. He couldn't marry a so-called German.

Three months after Harrison arrived in Europe, Hitler's empire annexed Austria. Weeks later, German forces invaded Czechoslovakia. In October, all Jews in the Reich territories were ordered to surrender their passports, and on November 8, armed mobs swept through cities and towns, looting and burning Jewish stores and synagogues. Kristallnacht, or the Night of Broken Glass, had arrived. Days later, all Jewish businesses were banned. By January, three hundred thousand Jews had fled.

Back in Harrison's old neighborhood, an émigré community was emerging. Bertolt Brecht, Thomas Mann, Lion Feuchtwanger, and Christopher Isherwood, among other European artists and writers, had found refuge in the Santa Monica Canyon. But over in Hellesylt, Harrison remained a diaspora of one. He'd already escaped danger. He'd known his persecutors and perhaps he believed he had to fear only them, not a faceless empire, and that as a foreigner he was safe, that being an outsider meant he would somehow remain outside the forces sweeping the continent.

On September 1, 1939, Germany invaded Poland from land and air, bombing railroads, munitions factories, and airfields. The next day, the Einsatzgruppen, paramilitary death squads, arrived. Using lists that had already been compiled with the help of Germans living in Poland, they carried out mass executions, targeting political leaders, scholars, priests, actors, doctors, lawyers, aristocrats, Jews, and homosexuals.

The doctrine of appeasement having decisively failed, Britain and France declared war. Norway declared its neutrality, and in November when the Soviet Union attacked Finland, Norway declared it again. As a trading partner with both Britain and Germany, the nation was desperate to remain clear of the hostilities, but Norway was simply too close to Sweden's iron ore and too strategically positioned to remain on the sidelines.

Still, it was a shock on April 9, 1940, a sunny morning, the beginning of the spring thaw, when German forces invaded Norway and Denmark. Twenty-four hours later, the Wehrmacht had occupied the towns of Trondheim, Bergen, Narvik, and other key points on the coast. Denmark surrendered within six hours, but Norway fought back, aided by British forces.

The Germans bombed Hellesylt on April 21, and both British and German planes strafed the town. Resistance fighters stationed themselves in the hills, battling until May, when German troops swarmed and seized the village. More than a hundred soldiers and officers were billeted at the Grand Hotel.

On May 10, Germany invaded Belgium, France, the Netherlands, and Luxembourg. Its forces strained, Britain retreated, and on June 10, after two months of fighting, Norway surrendered. The country's royal family, cabinet, and parliament had escaped just days earlier so as to never legally surrender to Hitler. Nazi sympathizer Vidkun Quisling was installed as head of state, though he would remain a puppet of Josef Terboven, the Reichskommissar.

The Jewish population in Norway was around twenty-two hundred when the Germans invaded. Most lived in Trondheim and Oslo. All were ordered to register as *J* for jøde, and Jewish shops were initially marked, but once officials realized this might create sympathy, they had the signs removed. In other occupied territories, death squads massacred whole communities as part of the Fuhrer's plan to exterminate Jews and non-Aryans. In Norway, however, the hysteria for so-called racial purity took a different form. Here, the Reich leaders promoted Lebensborn, meaning fountain or wellspring of life. The SS program had been initiated in 1935 to increase the falling birth rate in Germany. Lebensborn homes were established for mothers, many of whom were unmarried, to give birth to and house "racially pure" children. The Nordic countries were considered especially desirable for Nazi breeding purposes, and soldiers were encouraged to impregnate local women. In Norway, somewhere between eight thousand and twelve thousand children were born as part of the eugenicist campaign, the largest outside Germany.

The Nazis also established an extensive system of slave labor camps in Norway populated by the hundreds of thousands of Slavic soldiers who'd been taken captive on the Eastern Front. Many of the Polish, Serbian, and Slavic prisoners who weren't killed were brought north and forced to build Festung Norwegen, Fortress Norway, an elaborate barrier along the entire coastal perimeter to defend against an Allied invasion.

By September 1941, the occupying forces had declared martial law, banned alcohol, shuttered newspapers, confiscated radios, and started inventorying Jewish property. In October, Gerhard Ernst Flesch, Kommandeur der Sicherheitspolizei und des Sicherheitsdienst, arrived in Trondheim to head the Gestapo and oversee the vast network of prisons, which included Vollan in the city and Falstad to the north. By then, all Jews had been forced to wear the Star of David.

In Hellesylt, the villagers reached an uneasy stasis under the Tyska—German—occupation. They'd been issued new passports and required to carry them at all times. The Germans requisitioned the locals' trucks and the former owners were offered work as drivers, though all refused.

German troops marching through Hellesylt, undated.

Fuel was scarce and some converted cars to run with wood-burning stoves.

The occupying forces set up camouflaged guns on either side of the fjord in anticipation of submarine invasion. Sometimes the townspeople could hear the machine guns firing across the water—they guessed it was practice.

As the lensmann, Olav Gausdal was charged with keeping peace between the occupiers and the locals, frequently stepping in to defuse tensions. The Nazis had ordered the police chief to shut the mills by the waterfall so the villagers couldn't get access to the grain. Gausdal made a show of sealing the doors but in fact left them unlocked.

Acts of resistance took other forms. Under the guise of choir practice, the townspeople gathered to sing patriotic songs. The baker refused service to a German until the soldier cocked his pistol and pressed it to the man's forehead. A group of soldiers offered two young men drinks, which each declined, one saying, "I don't drink Hitler's cat piss." Gausdal wasn't able to spare him the beating, and both were sent to the Falstad prison camp. Life under the Tyskas was grim, but the villagers—and Harrison—had been spared the Einsatzgruppen storming into homes and rounding up citizens for mass execution.

For the Tyska soldiers, Hellesylt was a peaceful, bucolic spot to land, especially for those coming back from the Eastern Front. Shell-shocked, easily panicked, and prone to violence, they were the ones villagers tried to avoid.

At the head of the Sunnylvsfjorden, the town was far inland, a good distance from the skirmishes between Britain's Royal Air Force and the Luftwaffe along the coast. This was fortunate, though the villagers weren't spared the dread, terror, and other miseries of life under occupation, like boredom.

Harrison tried to occupy himself. He skied. He walked. When the weather was bad, he read or he played dominoes or he did cross-stitches. It was odd to see a man so deft with a needle and thread, but what wasn't odd about Harrison Post in Hellesylt? He was a Hollywood socialite trapped in a fjord town occupied by Germans. He'd ended up there because his masseur owned a hotel in the village. He used to be a patient. Now he was a perpetual guest.

On November, 12, 1941, he wrote in his diary, a stiff-backed notebook with a mottled black-and-white cover:

> Today a very sweet letter from Maud Chaffey—and it has helped—
> Bitterly cold.

A year and a half after the Germans invaded, this is the first entry from Harrison's journals, of which four remain. On the front page of each, he quoted Robert Browning: "And yet those blottings chronicle a life."

Harrison had been photographed, sketched, and painted. He'd been documented in census reports, society columns, news clippings, case files, and a bilious biography. Buck Mangam had finally managed to reveal all his inside knowledge about the Clarks with the publication of his book in 1939, though it doesn't seem that Harrison knew of its existence. In any case, the point is that for years others captured him. Now, at last, he speaks for himself.

> Thursday, November 13
>
> My new sun lamp arrived this morning. I mailed a letter to Maud Chaffey—and I hope it will reach her.

Friday, November 14
dull day

Saturday, November 15
a long walk

Some days he wrote more than once, as if updating a friend on his whereabouts. After nearly four years in Hellesylt, the natural beauty still dazzled him: "This morning all the world was blanket of snow—very beautiful."

In spidery script, he tended to itemize rather than explore, noting the weather, the letters he wrote, walks he took, villagers he greeted, meals he ate, and books he read. He was a voracious reader, though terse in his observations. In the past month, he'd finished Hermann Sudermann's *The Dance of Youth* ("rather good"), Johan Bojer's *The Last of the Vikings* ("I have yet to find interesting—dull, dull"), and Ole Edvart Rølvaag's *Pure Gold* ("not bad").

He wasn't inclined to reflect deeply on the war. This may have been an act of delusion, wishful thinking, or self-preservation. If he thought too much about the invasion and the danger the Germans posed, the threat would become that much more real. (Harrison used the term "Tyska," never "Nazi.") He had few interactions with the troops. At least he never writes about any. The soldiers weren't billeted at Tryggestad Hotel, though they were a constant presence throughout the village.

By now he felt pride in his adopted country. He pasted "Ja, Vi Elsker Dette Landet," the Norwegian national anthem, into the front cover of his journal. After first trying to appropriate the song, the Germans had banned it. Harrison does mention occasional arrests but never writes about resistance efforts. He was elated when he saw that one of the men who'd refused "Hitler's cat piss" had survived Falstad and returned home. The other had contracted tuberculosis and died in prison.

Every day he wrote in the composition book. On some occasions, he made tiny crosses next to the date. Sometimes he made more than one and circled them. These curious notations have no explanation. They don't follow any pattern and they appear on days where nothing of particular importance is mentioned. They are one of the puzzles of the diaries, one more mystery in his mysterious life.

Some entries are less coded, but still oblique. For instance, on August 2, 1942, he wrote, "red letter day," with no explanation. Another day, following a string of fairly unremarkable entries, which included walks and various meals, he described writing a long letter to Trygga. "I hope he quite understands," he reflects, but there is no context, no sense of what prompted his need to make Trygga understand or even what it was that Trygga should understand.

What emerges from Harrison's diaries are the rhythms of daily life in a small tourist town surrounded by farms, at times prosaic given that he was under siege. Villagers go about their routines, travelers arrive and depart, and the American watches with a gimlet eye as the cycle of life makes its rotations:

> Padeo Lym called to come and see his new baby—it is very attractive—all babies are.
>
> A wedding at the church—the bride and bridegroom were so young and so good looking—I was envious of them.
>
> Last evening tante Maria Tryggestad died—a sweet old lady—I went to her every day on my walk—and she liked me very much—but she was ill—and a painless death—something to be hoped for.

Other entries capture Harrison's elation at a long day of skiing or his continued frustration with learning Norwegian: "The language eludes me." Still others reveal more complicated feelings:

> Snowing all day—and very cold—took a short walk—arranged my several photograph albums—I put many into the fire—I don't want so many—just the old friends—and some views of Norway—very dull these days—so little to do—and talk with.

Harrison seems to have feared his own mind and moods more than the Tyska soldiers making their rounds. Depression beckoned constantly. He understood this, and one of his recurring cautions to himself is not to think too much.

While the diary offered a place to deposit his fears and worries, if he wasn't careful, he could end up consumed by panic and dread. Harrison mentions rheumatism, but more than that he feared having a "reaction." A fight with Trygga could prompt a "reaction." Anxiety could lead to a "reaction." Too much liquor could give him a "reaction."

The diaries contain intimate glimpses into his daily life, and yet they are also protected documents, written by a man who still evaded many things, even when he was alone. He fed his photos to the fire. The past could be a painful place. Dwelling on it could give him a reaction.

The cold days continued and he grew restless and depressed. He lamented the growing scarcity—especially when it came to cigarettes. As to the Nazis, he seems to have considered himself more inconvenienced than endangered. He bristled at his dependence on Trygga. He'd been a guest at the hotel for three years now, if such a person can be called a guest.

As winter crept on, he made small attempts to assert some kind control over his life. He wrote to Frances Marion. It was important to stay connected to old friends. He ordered new skis. He bought himself a new knit cap, brown and white. He went out to buy Christmas presents for Trygga. Shopping cheered him. A plan had formed in Harrison's mind. He was going to buy a home of his own in Norway.

On December 4, 1941, he wrote to Joe McInerney with instructions for transferring the money in his account. Sometimes he considered living in Oslo, but mostly he pictured himself tucked away in one of the valleys or up on the Korsbrekke hill with a view of the fjord. He would have a dog, and a small but comfortable house where the skiing was good, his Norwegian Dream. He would have to go back to the nightmare in America, though, to get his things, what was left of his furniture, bibelots, silver, and books. It would mean facing Gladys, but once he did, he'd be free and, after seven long years, he'd have a home of his own again.

Monday, December 8, was cold. He took a brisk walk up the Korsbrekke hill where he saw Peter Fröyas, who told him there'd been a conflict between the United States and Japan—a base in Hawaii had been bombed.

When he got back to the hotel, his new skis had arrived. That night there was a small selskap and he talked and drank with the guests until three in the morning. The next days were wonderful, full of snow, and inside, he played dominoes by the fire. And then on Sunday the newspapers arrived, three days late. Germany and Italy had declared war on the United States. "It is hell," he wrote.

The next day, he saw Gausdal, who told him that as an American, he was now considered an enemy of the state and would be required to submit weekly reports to the authorities. This amused them both. They already saw each other every day. It would require no change for Harrison to stop in and talk with the lensmann about his walks, skiing, and the usual business of the town. As Gausdal had made a spectacle of locking the mills while actually leaving them open for the villagers, these reports were another performance for the Tyskas.

Back at the hotel, to Harrison's great delight, a parcel with nine packs of cigarettes arrived from a friend in Copenhagen. That night, some farmers stopped by as well. Harrison bought a box of apples and they all had drinks. A pleasant evening by the fire.

On Saturday, December 20, Harrison went to make his first report to the lensmann, but Gausdal was away. His son Jon, home from pharmacy studies in Oslo, took the briefing. Harrison often met with the young man to practice his Norwegian, though usually they ended up drinking and talking in English. Jon was confident the war would be over by spring. One thing he didn't say was that he was working with British intelligence. That would come out years later.

On Christmas Eve, Harrison, Trygga, and Margit sat around the Christmas tree and opened presents with the Bjørdals. Trygga gave Harrison a mug for coffee, some underwear, ski stockings, and a silver ashtray.

It was lovely the next morning to see everyone at the little white church up the hill, though Harrison was troubled that he'd gotten no telegrams, no word from Joe, nothing at all from America. Harrison tried not to dwell on the matter. He would hope and pray, but "to try to think these days would drive me mad," he wrote.

Three days passed and still no wires. News came that a British warship had attacked the base in Molde and there'd been much damage. In the village, the Germans were worried, a hopeful sign.

And then a week later his letter to Joe came back unopened. Next, a letter to a friend in Germany came back. And then more mail returned from America.

"It is like bitter deaths," he wrote.

He tried to keep himself active. He paid a visit to the tailor. He skied—when the weather allowed. When it didn't, he read. He was finishing the last book in Sigrid Undset's trilogy. Set in Norway of the Middle Ages, the books promised "forgetfulness in an unhappy time."

His next read was Norman Douglas's *South Wind*, a comic novel from 1917 about millionaires, mystics, aesthetes, and other expatriates living in languorous dissipation on a fictionalized version of the island of Capri. Harrison found it "quite human."

If Harrison was ever forced to choose between cigarettes and books, it would be difficult. Of course, a book could last forever, so the choice should've been obvious, but as Lord Henry Wotton observed in *The Picture of Dorian Gray*, "A cigarette is the perfect type of a perfect pleasure. It is exquisite, and it leaves one unsatisfied."

If he had to choose one book, it might be the one he read every morning, the *Book of Daily Thoughts and Prayers*, written by Swami Paramananda, one of the first people to bring the Vedanta philosophy to America. Structured like a daily missal, the book was divided according to monthly themes—September was "Selfless love and devotion," December "Redeeming power within." Each page presented a sequence for the day: a "salient thought," lines to memorize, a lesson, and a prayer.

On February 17, he opened his journal, made a tiny cross, and began to write about his dream of living in Norway, which of course meant he would first have to go back to America. The thought sent him into the past and to a recent verse from Swami Paramananda.

> I think of the old days in my first home of my own—the Cimarron house—it was beautiful—but so useless to me—in that Will's house was just next door—and I had a bedroom and a salon there—then my Beach house—and 905 Ocean Front—Santa Monica—very lovely place—but it was a mad house. Then a house and a stable at the Uplifters' Club—then my Porto Marina place at Castellammare—then my farm adjoining the Riviera Club—that place cost a whole fortune—Will and I got the

> place—and I had hoped to live there forever—and what a tragedy it has been—and for seven years I have had no home at all. I do hope that soon that I shall have a place of my own—today I thought of these words:
>
> "The ramparts of this dwelling where I live
> Are built with faith, hope, courage and love
> There four walls stand all weather and storm"
>
> I will remember this day—and it will be interesting to me—to see if I will have my dreams.

He went skiing the next day, though it was more ice than snow. When he got back, the newspaper had arrived and with it a shock. Carole Lombard had died in a plane crash. The last time he'd seen her it was 1929—a party at Lloyd Pantages's. So long ago. A dim future.

On January 20, 1942, in Wannsee, a suburb of Berlin, leaders of the Gestapo, the SS, the Race and Resettlement Office, the Department of Justice, and other agencies met to draft a plan, or "final solution," for the Jewish people in the Reich. Rather than continue to rely on the death squads to carry out massacres in newly conquered regions, which distressed local populations and had become a strain on the mobile units, it was decided that they would transport Jews, Romani, homosexuals, and others to killing stations in Poland. At Chelmno, they'd already experimented with gassing prisoners. Majdanek, Auschwitz, Treblinka, Belzec, and Sobibor would soon follow.

As for the captured troops, they would be worked to death. Many were sent to Norway, where more than five hundred prisons had been established, and though these weren't extermination camps as in Poland, hundreds of thousands of prisoners succumbed to diseases like diphtheria, tuberculosis, dropsy, and pneumonia, while others died from abuse and starvation.

On February 21, Harrison wrote, "Tomorrow it will be G.C.'s birthday." He couldn't bear to spell out his sister's name. That night, he read some detective stories, and the next day he realized he'd been mistaken.

"I find that G.C.'s birthday is in March," he wrote. "However, it will be the same at any date."

Jon Gausdal had predicted the war would be over by spring, but spring arrived and peace did not. Still, Harrison's spirits lifted with the weather. He went skiing ("sliding down the hills at Stadheim"). He still took pleasure in his evenings with the guests at the inn. He read Joseph Conrad and played dominoes. On March 7, more skiing—"some good hills." On the way back, he ran into Gausdal: "I had forgotten to see him for my weekly report for the German officer, but he laughed. It was all right. I am realizing how contented I am these days."

But the next day there was news of food shortages and more than two thousand Tyska soldiers arrived in nearby Ålesund. He worried for his friends there, yet he seemed unconcerned for himself. In spite of the dread and malaise, there were moments of near-contentment. From March 10, 1942:

> I was tired today after eight hours of ski, but it was worth it. And the hills and beauty everywhere. These beloved mountains. We took some good mountain tops—a good *middag* [supper]—then an hour of sleep—then coffee and the end of Margit's birthday cake. I am happy these days. Almost.

Skiing and reading, skiing and reading. He read essays by Francis Bacon, Arnold Bennett's *The Old Wives' Tale*, and Sylvia Townsend Warner's *Lolly Willowes*. He reread Poe's "The Gold-Bug" and "The Purloined Letter."

More mail came back unopened: "No word from America, Denmark, or France. I am disappointed. No news. But I am becoming partially reconciled. Time does this to anything. Contented. Dogged contented. As wild animals in cages. . . . we played dominoes all day."

In March, Norway reestablished an 1814 constitutional prohibition that forbade Jews from entering the country. Jewish businesses and estates were declared bankrupt and liquidated. The Gestapo confiscated gold, silver, wristwatches, and jewelry.

Meanwhile, new tourists arrived at the hotel. One, a teacher from Hvalstad, said there was talk of more arrests in Ålesund. Germans told the minister in Hellesylt that he and his wife had to vacate their house. Now there was no more church and no more school.

On March 29, Will would have been sixty-five. Harrison hoped Joe had taken flowers to the mausoleum. He felt rage on Gladys's birthday, grief with Will's, and then April 19 arrived:

> My birthday
> Today am very sad—for ever so many reasons—but I shall try my best not to overreact.

A neighbor gave him a kitten as a present, but Margit and Trygga refused to let him keep the pet. He walked to Larsen's pond and smoked by himself. The brand of the cigarettes was Madina. This made him think of the painter Medina and the portrait of him Will had commissioned. He wondered where it was now.

The cold days had stretched on and on, longer than usual, but it seemed now that they were truly over. At least there'd be no more birthdays to face—not for a while.

On Tuesday, May 12, a letter arrived from the Swiss legation in Berlin, along with a questionnaire for him to fill out so he could travel to America and return with his furniture, his silver, and of course his books. This cheered him immensely.

May 17 was Flag Day. He walked through the village. Not a single flag.

Harrison walked up to his hill. He thought of it as his now. It would be beautiful in the summer and perfect skiing in the winter. The people who lived in Hellesylt were good and old-fashioned. A simple life now—that was what he wanted. "If I want to go 'harloting' again," he wrote, "I can always go to Oslo or Ålesund."

A few days later, several hundred soldiers arrived. His best pullover disappeared, probably swiped by one of the Tyskas. Never mind, he'd be sailing soon for Lisbon, and then New York. That night, he packed many of his things in a trunk for safekeeping while he was gone.

It rained steadily that first week of June. He loved the countryside even in this weather. He would miss it when he went back to America.

On Sunday, June 7, as usual, he went for a walk. On his way back to the hotel, he stopped in to see Gausdal and told the police chief he'd be leaving soon.

Gausdal shook his head. It was impossible. There was nothing but bombs from here to Lisbon. It seemed to shock him, as if it'd never occurred to him the darkening tide could reach him too.

At least by Tuesday the rain had stopped, but Harrison felt ill. He walked to Stadheim and watched Anton Larsen work a fish on his line.

He tried to contain his frustration and his impatience, but he simply could not. He hated being "broke." He put the word in quotes, because, of course, he was not broke. He was only broke here, not in America.

His anger at the overwhelming injustice of his situation welled up inside him, big enough to burst, and it would've been cathartic if it had, but before that could happen, the feeling collided with the knowledge that there was nothing he could do. It was all so futile. As he so often did in these moments, he sat down and wrote to Joe.

It seemed a summer of endless rain. He grew tired of walking, tired of the tourists at the hotel. He dreamed of Cimarron Street, of Will, "whom I shall never see again."

He argued with Trygga and then worried about a reaction.

He'd read so many books these past weeks, but they didn't help. "Stupid books." He wanted his own.

> Sept 22
>
> I am so anxious to begin some work of some sort—preferably bookbinding—and I could do that at Oslo—perhaps J. Mc will advise these things—If I ever see him again—
>
> Last night two soldiers came down to the hotel—that it was important to hide the lights at night, you see. Planes and tanks are all about—it is not a healthy place these days. What will happen—the lord only knows—Norway is really hungry—the people are beaten—no food—no work—no money—and the winter in the cities—it is pitiful. Here we eat—the best we can—but the future—it is best not to think too much. And these days even the Germans do not sing as they used to—

He was aggravated with Trygga, more than usual. He didn't say what it was that made the valet so disagreeable, but "I feel it is congenital," he wrote. He wanted desperately to go, but he was trapped. "It is not a happy arrangement. I wonder that I cannot forgive Gladys." He closed the journal and did not return to the thought.

It took a few days, but the dark mood finally lifted. Tuesday arrived: "A perfect day. Like summer—and all the mountain tops have taken the snow." He went for a walk and visited with villagers. One of them gave him some turnips.

The next morning, Harrison transcribed Swami Paramananda's lesson of the previous day:

> It is beauty I love
> Though like the foolish moth
> Oft I burn my limbs in the flame,
> Yet evermore my soul craves its attainment
> In love and with love
> I seek the Maker of the Beautiful.

He made his usual rounds that afternoon. He tried to read a book of Will Durant's philosophy in Norwegian. Eventually he gave up and got in bed with *Gone with the Wind*.

It was September 30 and he was coming to the end of the notebook he'd started almost a year before. He paged back through the diary. Days of snow, days of cold, days of rain. It didn't add up to anything. Just a collection of little incidents. In truth, none of it was interesting. Tedium gave way to worse: "Such loneliness. No word from old friends . . . some dead. Life is strange. There must be some reason."

On October 25, 1942, in Oslo, Norwegian police officer and Nazi collaborator Knut Rød led hundreds of German and Norwegian security forces on a blitz going house to house, arresting Jewish males over the age of fifteen.

They started at four thirty in the morning, barging into homes, dragging people from their beds and then to the harbor, where they were boarded on the steamer *Donau*, which sailed for Stettin, or Szczecin, a transit hub in Poland. From there, they were then transported by rail to Auschwitz-Birkenau. Five hundred and thirty-two people were kidnapped that night.

The Swedish minister in Berlin said the remaining Jews in Norway should be allowed to come to Sweden, but he was rebuffed. A month later, a second raid seized three hundred people, men and women of all ages.

Olav Gausdal had hoped the weekly reports would satisfy the authorities, but by fall the lensmann was unable to stall the officials any longer. Harrison was taken into German custody and interned at Vollan prison in Trondheim.

19

MEXICO CITY

While Harrison dreamed of a home of his own, the Crookses built one, with his money.

After he left for Norway, Gladys and Charles took a two-month cruise through the Virgin Islands. When they came back, they sold the Beverly Hills mansion and spent $38,000 to buy a lot on San Vicente Boulevard in the Palisades and to hire architect Cliff May, the eventual creator of the California Dream House. Although the building May designed for the Crookses was more formal than his now classic postwar ranch house, it included many of the features he'd make popular, such as a living room oriented toward the backyard and integrated outdoor spaces, like a lanai.

Set back from the street, the house at 1123 San Vicente Boulevard was a low-slung, rambling home, tucked away in wooded seclusion overlooking the Santa Monica Canyon. A less imposing affair than the white Colonial on North Arden Drive, the home was still lavish in its casual rancho effects. It had two bedrooms, an expansive central living and dining area, a four-car garage, and servants' quarters where the watchman from the farm lived with his wife and their five-year-old son. The walled garden included a greenhouse, aviary, vegetable garden, and kennel for the Brussels griffons. Sidlaw Trotzky had company.

Photographs from one of Cliff May's promotional brochures offer glimpses of the property, including Charles's bedroom, handsomely furnished with a four-poster antique bed, befitting "a retired gentleman," as the marketing material described the homeowner. Harrison had reinvented himself with Will's money, and now Charles would do the same with Harrison's.

The couple kept separate rooms, common enough at the time. In Gladys's chamber, a tondo painting of the Madonna and Child hung above an antique Italian labor bed, a strangely pious effect, and gothic, too, and yet it wasn't the eeriest room in the house. That was the library.

Compared to the vast living area, it was fairly small, with space enough for a fireplace, reading chair, book stand, backgammon table, and two walls of bookshelves. On another wall, framed letters and papers were hung gallery style. These included a photograph of a full-bearded Walt Whitman, likely from Harrison's collection, as it was likely that most everything in the house—the dark heavy furniture, the grand piano, and the antiques—were his. Certainly the large oil portrait looming above the library's fireplace belonged to Harrison.

It was a familiar pose. It was in fact a re-creation of the glamorous studio photograph taken of him in the early Los Angeles days. It's possible this was the very painting that Harrison had wondered about at Larsen's pond, the portrait by Medina, but Cliff May's brochure doesn't identify the artist. It would be fitting indeed, though, if the man who would eventually paint the ageless Dorian Gray had produced this image. In it, Harrison floats, arms crossed, eternally young and beautiful, before a mountainous landscape. Meanwhile, the actual aging man remained trapped in another country.

Was this a trophy room for the Crookses, with Harrison's image mounted to boast the hunters' prowess? Or was it a shrine? He was after all their benefactor, if an unwilling one. Did it reveal that, in spite of everything Gladys had taken from him, she still felt a sense of devotion? And did they expect him to return? Surely not to this home. Cliff May hadn't designed a third bedroom.

For such a vulnerable man, Harrison's image exerted incredible power. This was often the case with him—the dueling impulses to conceal and display. Will hadn't wanted the nature of their relationship made public, but he'd still had his lover's face painted thirteen times on the library ceiling. Gladys had kept her brother hidden away, drugged and incapacitated, and yet she hung his portrait in her home. She wanted to preserve his likeness but not him, to erase Harrison while retaining the traces of him that pleased her, and she'd succeeded.

They'd built their dream home with his money, and it seemed they intended to stay, but in October 1941, just a year and a half after hiring Cliff May, the Crookses put the house on the market. The ad in the *Los Angeles Times* said the owner was going east. A quick sale was necessary. They asked $39,000, only a thousand more than what they'd originally paid. Within a few weeks, the destination in the ads had been changed to South America. In fact, though, the couple never left the continent. Two months later, just days before America entered the war, Charles Crooks arrived in Mexico City.

Gladys may have remained behind or perhaps they had an agent handle the sale of property and assets, because the ads in the paper continued: "Brussels Griffons. black. very rare. The only black puppies in the U.S." By May it was the books—"first editions, press copies." In July, the price on the house dropped to $35,000. The next month, a 1937 Zephyr sedan—"never off city streets"—was up for sale. In October, the mahogany Steinway grand piano was going for $750 and a full-length mink for $450. By the fall of 1942, as Harrison was taken prisoner yet again, the Crookses were starting a new life in Mexico.

They were not alone. Charles's friend Eddie Nealis made the journey after provoking Bugsy Siegel's ire when Nealis refused to let the gangster edge in on his various underworld enterprises. Harrison's fellow non-professional A. C. Blumenthal—"Blumey"—had also recently crossed the border rather than testify against Joseph Schenck, the former head of United Artists and a founder of 20th Century Fox, who was on trial for tax evasion. The story given to the court was that Blumey had taken ill during his travels. Six different doctors had diagnosed him with six different ailments, all of which prohibited him from returning to testify against the movie mogul, who was eventually convicted. Meanwhile, Blumey recovered enough from his illnesses that he was able to pursue new ventures. With the financial support of the then secretary of the interior and later president Miguel Alemán Valdés, he invested in the upscale Hotel Reforma and launched an outpost of Hollywood's swanky Ciro's, which quickly became a fashionable destination for Mexico City's burgeoning nightlife.

Schenck's trial wasn't the only dustup between the federal government and Hollywood that year. Back in March, the ringleaders of the million-dollar extortion scheme involving the International Alliance of Theatrical Stage Employees and industry moguls had been convicted and sentenced to prison, but the scandal wasn't over, as William Bioff, one of the convicted felons, would end up incriminating other figures in the conspiracy, including the Crookses' lawyer Colonel William H. Neblett, accused of taking a $5,000 bribe to quash an investigation into the payoff racket.

Mexico City might feel like Hollywood on the lam, but the industry wasn't movies. It was deals—the international kind best made without scrutiny, like arms sales or J. P. Getty shipping barrels of oil to Germany. Here, the shadow industry of war could thrive, though it wasn't Casablanca with refugees scrambling to escape the fascist forces engulfing Europe. While Mexico City of the 1940s didn't inspire an iconic film with Humphrey Bogart and Ingrid Bergman, it was memorialized in *Mexican Hayride*, a Broadway musical with a Cole Porter score, about a racketeer on the run, and later adapted into an Abbott and Costello comedy. A destination for high rollers and those pretending to be, the city was a perfect haven for Gladys and Charles.

Soon the Crookses were familiar faces at Blumey's club, the Mexico City version of Rick's Café Americain. On Charles's World War II draft card, under the "person who will always know your address," he listed the hotel's manager. One of their newest friends at the fashionable nightspot was Hilde Krüger, a German expatriate who'd also found it necessary to make a fast move.

Krüger's route had been a circuitous one from the Third Reich to the Distrito Federal. Back in 1935, the aspiring model and actress played a bit part in a movie called *Nur nicht weich werden, Susanne!* (Don't Lose Heart, Susanne!), about a young woman in the German film industry trying to fend off the malicious, scheming machinations of two Jewish producers. As hungry as the audience might've been for anti-Semitic fare, it also couldn't be ignored that the movie was tremendously bad, and the premiere was met with resounding boos, much to the dismay of Minister of Propaganda Joseph Goebbels, who was in attendance that night.

What did please him, though, was Hilde Krüger's blond, voluptuous presence and soon she was starring in Nazi propaganda films and appearing on posters brandishing swastika flags and proclaiming Aryan supremacy. However, once Goebbels's wife discovered he'd begun an affair with the actress, the roles swiftly evaporated. Hilde left Berlin first for England and then settled in Hollywood in 1940, poised to break into the industry. And yet her film career didn't take off.

She may have left Germany, but she never left the Reich. Hilde's real work wasn't on-screen, it turned out, but working for the Abwehr, the Nazis' civilian counterintelligence agency. She swanned through Hollywood, attended parties, and had a few high-profile romances, most notably with Errol Flynn and J. P. Getty. The oil baron bought the actress jewelry and paid her bills at the Beverly Wilshire Hotel—details that piqued the curiosity of the Federal Bureau of Investigation. Toward the end of 1941, as Getty realized that the United States would soon join the Allied Powers, he saw to it that his German mistress made it out of the country. In Mexico City, Hilde moved among the city's cosmopolitan elite, befriending politicians, reveling in the glamorous and growing expatriate community, conducting industrial espionage, and of course dining at Blumey's nightclub.

Racketeering, espionage, fraud—there was plenty of crime to go around in Los Angeles, and Mexico City offered sanctuary for those who'd tested their luck. Years before, Gladys had skipped town to avoid testifying at the trial of Kid McCoy. Whatever she and Charles had been dabbling in, by the end of 1941 they had something to hide or someone to flee. They hadn't sold off their assets and run across the border to take in the sights. But they weren't inclined to keep a low profile in their new home. Charles had been heard "bragging"—the bureau's word—about his various high-powered connections. The FBI characterized him as a "known prevaricator" and a "promoter type." He may have fancied himself a savvy dealmaker with big profits on the horizon, but he was still what he'd been back when he made himself at home on Harrison's farm—a hustler.

His schemes abounded. At various times, Charles presented himself as an exporter, a broker, and a cattleman. He claimed to be an agent for Southwest Airways who was developing aviation schools with investors like Hollywood agent Leland Hayward and other power brokers. He said he was going to buy a ranch in Tabasco that had belonged to the province's former governor, now living in exile in Costa Rica because he was running guns for the Germans. He said he was going to start an import-export business selling mahogany. Next it was horses. Then automobiles. Seeds. Oil. The FBI kept watch.

They weren't the only ones. George Messersmith, the same diplomat who'd warned of the militant pathology infecting German society back in 1933, was now the American ambassador in Mexico, and his instincts were sharp as ever. Messersmith was well aware of the latest grifter who'd shown up at Ciro's, and he knew, too, that the Crookses were often in the company of Hilde Krüger. What he couldn't have known, though, and what Gladys and Charles surely didn't know either, was that while they, thanks to Harrison's money, were carousing through Mexico City with a Nazi-spy poster child for the Third Reich, across the ocean, he was being forced into the role of her counterpart, the despised Untermensch.

20

TRONDHEIM

In the prison's attic, Commander Flesch called the inmates to order. The Nazi was tall and fair, with a small mouth often on the verge of a smile, though not a nice one. His eyes were bright and watchful, and he had pale, nearly colorless eyelashes, which made him appear even more alert. He stood before the prisoners, some hundred men awaiting transportation orders. First, though, he was going to give a lecture about the hierarchy of race, comparing himself, a "pure" German, to a man with Jewish ancestry. He'd brought a prop. Next to the blond Gestapo leader stood Harrison Post.

The three Norwegians assigned to Cell 17 had been astonished several weeks earlier when the slight American first appeared at their door, smiling, a bit dazed. One of them, Kaare Viken, wrote a memoir of his time in captivity, *More Than 1,000 Days: Among Prisoners and Guards in Vollan Circuit Prison 1942–45*, and Harrison's arrival, late in the book, strikes an unexpected note in a chapter titled "Harrison Post, internert dobbeltmillionœr fra Santa Monica."

No stranger to the winds of fate, and perhaps still believing in his Clark armor, Harrison seemed more mystified than alarmed by his new circumstances. A welcome novelty to the other inmates, the American opened his suitcase and unpacked tools for bookbinding, a gold watch engraved with Enrico Caruso's autograph, and a set of ivory dominoes with gold inlay. The men soon discovered Harrison always won.

Each morning, after the prisoners pushed their hard mattress up against the wall to make more space in the cramped cell, Harrison used it as a kind of mantelpiece, setting out a framed photo of his friend, the actress Carlotta Monterey. Harrison showed the men photos of his farm in the Palisades—Harrison with a Dalmatian, Harrison on a horse. He showed them photos of himself with Charlie Chaplin, Marlene Dietrich, and other stars.

Back in California, he said, he used to host horseback-riding parties and he described mornings when he'd look up and see sixty riders coming over the canyon ridge, many of them movie stars. But he'd had a stroke, and Trygga, his "body man" or valet, believed Harrison would be better able to recuperate in Hellesylt. There was no mention of his sister.

Harrison explained that his wealth had come from William Andrews Clark Jr., that he'd worked in Clark's library, where he'd first used the bookbinding tools, and that he'd inherited a great deal of money from Clark—$200 million, according to Viken's memoir, either a miscommunication or a fantastical inflation—but the money was gone. No reason for this was offered. Harrison wasn't bitter about the loss as much as melancholy: "Think of all the good you could do with that money."

Still, he told them he was secure with real estate investments back in Los Angeles and other funds. After the war, he planned to buy a farm, perhaps near Lillehammer, where he'd have a dog, a horse, and a car.

Viken doesn't say if Harrison was assigned to a work detail, but he was still a captive, sharing a hard woolen mattress with three other men, eating the same spare portions of potato and herring. As far as they could tell, he wasn't bothered by the privations, except for the hard, doughy bread, which gave him stomach cramps.

At night, Harrison read to the others from his leather-bound Bible. His favorite passage was Psalm 23. Viken marveled at hearing the man who'd known Charlie Chaplin and owned racehorses read, "The Lord is my shepherd. I shall not want."

He told them his dreams for the future—the farm with the dog and the horse—and yet he had no sense about how to prepare for the next day. He was incapable of rationing cigarettes, instead smoking one after the next. When his were gone, he would turn to Viken, expectant.

Once, the Norwegian scolded him, "You must learn to save."

Harrison frowned. "You are very pinelus," he said, turning away in a huff.

A harsh insult meaning "stingy," it was a shocking word to use in an exchange between friends, though it was clear from his ease with it that the American had no sense of its power, like a child blurting profanities. Another man might've gotten enraged, but Viken, amused, offered Harrison a cigarette from his reserve.

In so many ways Harrison came off like a child to the other prisoners, a strange naïf in their harsh world. When Christmas came, he wrote up a list of the presents he wanted Trygga's sister to get him for the guards and prisoners. It amazed Viken that the American could imagine Christmas lists in the middle of a prison, but for Harrison it was possible, because soon care packages arrived from Trygga. He opened them gleefully, calling the others to gather around: "Now we will have a selskap!"

In Viken's telling, Harrison is a kind, sprightly, impulsive figure, prone to a playfulness that's absent from his diaries. Of course, like so many diarists, Harrison probably didn't turn to his journal when he was happy as much as when he wasn't. Besides, the notebooks didn't bring him joy. People did that, like Brun and Eriksen, the two young men who sang during their work detail.

They were students from the technical school and had been arrested for resistance activities. They'd also been in a choir and both had beautiful voices. Even the guards didn't bark at them to stop when they sang. Harrison often scoured the barracks for the men, imploring them to come to the cell and sing, and when they did, Viken watched the little American, enchanted, enrapt, and wondered if he was happier than he might've ever been, even back on his grand estate with his movie stars in California.

Still, Harrison suffered. Once, seeing him newly shorn after a visit to the barber, Viken complimented his cellmate on his haircut, to which Harrison replied bitterly, tears in his eyes. "It's awful. Fengsel haircut." Perhaps it was easier to cry over a "prison" haircut than their true circumstances, or perhaps it was a reminder of how yet again he had so little control over his life. Viken wouldn't have known that there was another time not that long ago when Harrison had been subjected to haircuts he hadn't wanted.

For the most part, though, he was a good-humored presence, a welcome oddity to the other prisoners among the oppressive barracks. Even the Germans were intrigued. August, a guard with an ugly temper, was especially magnetized. Most of the men kept their distance from the brusque German, but Harrison understood he held an allure to August, who lingered outside the cell, eager to glimpse the millionaire from Hollywood.

With a smile, he deployed his best mix of Norwegian and German: "Har du ein sigaretten for min, August?"

Happy, flustered, the guard fumbled through his pockets and produced a cigarette.

Harrison thought of the doughy bread that made his stomach hurt. "Hast du ein Schwartzbrot for min, August?"

The next day, August arrived at the cell with a lump under his uniform—a mouthwatering hard-crusted loaf of dark German bread for the socialite in Cell 17.

Commander Flesch was not charmed, but he too wanted a closer look at Harrison Post, and he wanted his prisoners to have one too, and so he ordered that the little American be brought up to the attic for his lecture.

Flesch had joined the Nazi party in 1933, readily embracing Hitler's mission for Arisierung or "Aryanization," and by 1936 he was a member of the Gestapo. He headed one of the Einsatzkommando units during the 1939 invasion of Poland. Afterward, he returned to his hometown of Posen, where he ran a death squad that killed three thousand Jewish citizens. In 1940, he joined the 3rd SS Panzer Division Totenkopf, or "Death's Head," march into France. Now he'd come to Norway.

The commander was skilled in torture techniques that left no visible marks. He was also practiced in "verschärfte Vernehmung"—sharpened or enhanced interrogation—which involved subjecting victims to stress positions, simulated drowning, and prolonged freezing baths. Earlier, when he'd been stationed at the Falstad prison, where prisoners from the Eastern Front were systemically brutalized, starved, and executed, Flesch was called the Evil Spirit.

Vollan, however, wasn't a labor camp. It held actual criminals as well as political prisoners. The conditions weren't as severe as Falstad, where there appeared to be no discernible system behind the torture and killing, only whim and savagery.

Still, sadism thrived at Vollan. Once, when one of the prison's section leaders celebrated his birthday, each of the officers got to hang a Russian prisoner in the basement. The gallows had been constructed by placing a wooden board on a raised platform; while two officers stood on one end, their weight holding the board in place, a prisoner was blindfolded, a noose tightened around his neck, and then prodded to the end of the plank. When one of the officers shouted, they both hopped off and the blindfolded man fell to his death. At the section leader's birthday party, thirteen men had been killed.

Harrison was in the attic now, but he could end up in the basement when Flesch's lecture was over. To the Nazi, Harrison wasn't a man. He was a specimen, and that meant the commander was entitled to probe and pummel him for the spectators' edification and his own amusement as he derided the very things about Harrison that Buck Mangam had loathed, that he was "small, dark, and with Semitic cast."

Harrison spoke no more German than he did Norwegian. As anyone in a foreign land learns, he knew to appear amenable and blank when confronted with words that made no sense, for instance, when Flesch pointed to himself as an example of "ein Herrenvolk," and Harrison as "ein Untermensch." If Flesch laughed while using Harrison as a prop in his call to genocide, the American prisoner may have responded in kind, the better to seem a willing party to the grotesque vaudeville routine unfolding. It may have been that Flesch sought no levity, that the tenor of the room was bleak and airless, or the commander may have tried to rouse the prisoners with his own fervor, an echo of the Fuhrer. But the attic wasn't an arena and the crowd of men awaiting their transit orders weren't the fanatical Volk but prisoners forced to endure the extended taunt of a smirking bully who'd cornered his prey and was now simply prolonging the torment.

Harrison knew his father was buried in Sacramento's Jewish cemetery, and he knew he was descended from a prominent Jewish family on his mother's side, though that wasn't something he touted in the letter outlining his family history. His aunts were married in Galveston's B'nai Israel Temple, but his own parents made their vows at city hall. They didn't stand under a chuppah or finalize the ceremony by breaking a glass. It's possible Harrison never experienced any of the rituals of his parents' faith—no bar mitzvah and, crucially, now that he was in a Nazi prison camp, no bris.

Decades later, villagers from Hellesylt speculated that Harrison couldn't have been Jewish, because if he had been, he would've been circumcised, a fact that would've been discovered once he was taken prisoner and subjected to physical examinations. Surely such a revelation would've led to his execution.

It seems surprising that Harrison's parents wouldn't have observed such a fundamental custom, especially for their first son, but considering how scattered and turbulent their marriage was, Jennie and Mark Harrison may have neglected most expected conventions for raising their children. Harrison's siblings don't appear to have identified with their Jewish heritage either. Certainly Gladys didn't.

Harrison's family ties frayed early in his life and so, it seems, had his sense of his ancestry. He appeared to have no urge to reclaim his Jewish faith or culture; they were like a pair of gloves that had been forgotten somewhere along the way and never missed. It had been convenient to forget. He wouldn't have been able to join any of the exclusive clubs or own the property he had back in Los Angeles if he'd identified as Jewish, even with Will's wealth.

Finally Flesch came to the end of his rant. He didn't send Harrison down to the basement. Instead, he dismissed the American to his cell and then turned to the task of deporting prisoners. Harrison may not have considered himself Jewish, but Flesch clearly did, and yet somehow, Harrison Post survived the Evil Spirit.

By the time Harrison returned to Viken and the other men, they'd already heard about the lecture. But when Harrison asked them what it was that he'd just endured, each man feigned ignorance, leaving him to speculate as to what had taken place during Gerhard Flesch's incomprehensible tirade.

Why didn't Flesch have Harrison killed? Or do it himself? He clearly would've relished it. Viken didn't ponder this. The commander may have foreseen that the death or torture of an affluent US citizen with an array of important connections could lead to bureaucratic or diplomatic furor. Even in the midst of a genocide, customs were to be observed. In the Nazi camps, prisoners of war from the United States and the United Kingdom were treated demonstrably better than their Slavic and Serbian counterparts, who were systemically brutalized and treated as savagely as the few Jewish prisoners who hadn't been deported to death camps. However, when it came to the American and British prisoners, even if they were Jewish, the Nazis observed the Geneva Convention, which forbid the very conditions in which they forced the Russians, Slavs, and Poles to live—those who did live.

Another theory as to why Harrison didn't end up blindfolded in the basement is that there could've been higher-level diplomatic concerns at stake, such as the delicate orchestration of prisoner exchanges. A vicious harangue about racial inferiority may have been the furthest Flesch was permitted to indulge his contempt for the "internert dobbeltmillionœr fra Santa Monica."

The irony remains that Harrison wasn't what he seemed. From one angle, he wasn't a member of a global and powerful elite but a defrauded Jew living off his Norwegian masseur. This, of course, wasn't at all how Harrison understood himself, and it may have been this belief and his embodiment of a Hollywood aristocrat that saved him. His wealth might not exist anymore, but its aura remained.

For a man with no real profession, Harrison was practiced in one of America's most durable and robust industries—mythmaking. He wasn't a deliberate scam artist like his sister or her husband, but an accidental one. And this talent may well have spared him from the Evil Spirit. If so, Harrison pulled off the most important con of his life and never knew it.

A few weeks later, Anton Schwenk, the Oberscharführer, came to the cell with good news for Harrison. Viken translated: orders had come for Harrison to be sent to a camp in Germany.

Harrison shook his head. He didn't want to go.

"Tell him there will be other Americans there," the warden said, but this was no incentive for Harrison.

"I want to stay." His voice broke. He'd made friends at Vollan. He'd survived Commander Flesch. He could persuade August to bring him the good bread.

For the next days, Harrison lay on the mattress, pained and sickly.

He was ill, he said. Too ill to get up, too ill to travel. The transit order was delayed.

But after several days of languishing on the hard mattress with no company, he grew restless and bored. He slipped down to the cellar where Viken and the others were working in the carpentry shop. They warned him to stop running up and down the stairs, that he would attract attention, but just as he shrugged off Viken's counsel to ration his cigarettes, Harrison ignored these cautions, and soon enough he'd undermined his own charade and it was obvious to the prison authorities that he was healthy enough for travel. His transit order was issued.

There was still time to get news to Trygga, who sent a large package of food. One last selskap. As usual, Harrison wanted to share, but Viken, picturing the long, uncertain journey ahead, cautioned Harrison to save some of the food, at least some slices of bread.

Harrison saw no need, saying he'd buy what he needed at the railway station. Viken pointed out that he could hardly rely on that. He was more likely to find himself pressed inside a car with hundreds of others and no food whatsoever. Harrison dismissed his friend's caution, determined to enjoy his last party at the prison. Viken and another prisoner took it upon themselves to hoard some of the food and prepare a package for Harrison to take with him.

That last night, Harrison packed his things, but when he lay down on the hard mattress with the other men, he couldn't sleep. He didn't let Viken sleep either, nudging him awake when the others started to drift off. They whispered about what the next day would bring.

Vollan was a bleak place with harsh conditions, but by then Harrison knew its stairways, its grounds, the other men, and the students singing in the yard. And he and Viken both knew that, in Trondheim, grim as it was, they were on the very outer edges of the war, and that Harrison was being sent straight into its heart.

21

GRINI

On January 30, 1943, Harrison arrived with his suitcase at Grini, a former women's prison outside Oslo. After commandeering the facility, the Nazis had expanded the compound. Electrified fences and barbed wire surrounded the grounds. Sentries stood watch with machine guns.

This wasn't a labor camp, and there wasn't one Evil Spirit who haunted the complex, but rather a faceless, highly organized system of repression, scarcity, and dread. Punishment was meted out in the form of "exercise," pointless sprints up and down a steep hill until the prisoners dropped from exhaustion and the guards set upon them, kicking and stomping those who didn't scramble to their feet. If one person tried to escape, the prisoners were told, the guards would shoot ten. Food portions were a potato and a few slices of bread. No herring. Sometimes there was something called soup; this was a dirty gruel from boiled potato peelings that made the prisoners sick and they soon learned to avoid the buckets when they came around.

Over the course of the war, Grini held more than twenty thousand prisoners. Many were Norwegians who'd been caught in the resistance movement, planning sabotage or helping Jews escape to Sweden.

At night, screams from the interrogation room hung in the dark.

A week before Harrison arrived, five British pilots had been walked out to the woods, blindfolded, and shot in the back of the head. His journals reveal nothing about his time at the camp, though he did later tell a newspaper reporter that it was the worst of all the prisons. At Grini, he said, the Nazis "broke arms, legs, heads, and gouged out eyes." He was lucky. He spent only two weeks there. On February 15, Harrison was transferred.

A week after he left, a group of prisoners at Grini was sent to Oslo to board the steamer *Gotenland*. These were the last remaining Jews in Norway. The others who'd survived the raids—about eight hundred—had managed, through underground resistance efforts, to cross the border to Sweden. Those on the *Gotenland* were bound for Stettin, Poland. It was a three-day journey by ship. From Stettin they were sent south, then east to Auschwitz. There were 157 of them. Six survived.

Harrison, too, had been shipped from Oslo to Stettin, but he was put on a different train. A small figure, suitcase in hand, he traveled south through a landscape of death.

22

LAUFEN

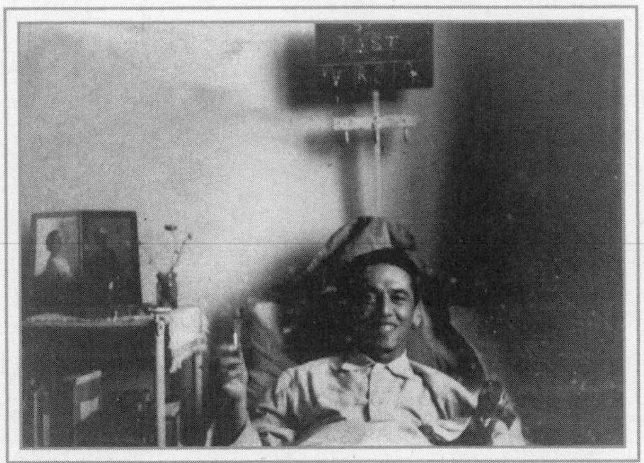

Harrison in the infirmary at Laufen (Ilag VII), Christmas 1943.

The relentless, sprawling Nazi machinery carried him not to Chelmno, not to Dachau, not to death-camp horror but to a castle in Bavaria. It was February and the ground was covered in snow when he arrived in Laufen. Built in the fifteenth century near a bend of the Salzach River, it had been a summer retreat for the archbishop of nearby Salzburg. A stocky square fortress, this was nothing like the turreted colossus the word *castle* often conjures. It had a single tower and an interior courtyard—easy to convert into a prison. The grounds had been ringed with barbed wire.

Ilag VII, as the castle-turned-prison was designated, wasn't an extermination camp like Treblinka or Auschwitz or a slave-labor camp like Falstad or Mittelbau-Dora or nearby Flossenbürg. It was a prisoner-of-war camp for nearly one thousand British and American citizens. Amid the terror and depravity of the Reich's systematic network of death and torture, Laufen seemed an incongruous enclave of something approaching humanity.

About five hundred of the prisoners had come from the Channel Islands, the British dependencies of Guernsey and Jersey off the coast of Normandy. The rest were Americans like Harrison who'd been living abroad and trapped when war was declared—or they claimed they were.

Many were Polish Jews who'd managed to buy US passports through legations in Honduras, Cuba, and Panama. The American section also included men from Italy, Greece, Mexico, El Salvador, and Brazil. Few of the "Americans" actually spoke English. When the camp was liberated in 1945, the Allied forces discovered that only seventeen people were in fact from the United States. The rest were men who'd been fortunate with their paperwork.

The prisoners didn't tell each other much about their personal histories—it was less complicated that way. In the American section, there was a Spaniard who'd fought for the Republican side and one who'd fought for Franco. Some men were Oswald Mosley fascist sympathizers, others conscientious objectors, and still others suspected informants for the Germans. Josef Nassy, a Black painter, had been living with his wife in Brussels when the Germans arrested him. Like Harrison, he claimed to have been born in San Francisco, though he was in fact born in Suriname, and like Harrison, he also was of Jewish descent. In Vollan, Harrison had been a novelty. Now they all were.

He wasn't free, but he wasn't going to end up as a prop in a sadistic show-and-tell. Here, there was a canteen, not a gallows, in the basement. And once the Poles volunteered to run the kitchen instead of the British, the meals improved. The Swedish YMCA sent books, playing cards, carpentry tools, sunglasses, one hundred pairs of ice skates, and art materials. As long as he could get cigarettes, Harrison was content enough.

At Laufen, there was no shortage of music. The prisoners included violinists from a conservatory in Poland and a band of musicians from El Salvador who'd been touring in Europe when the war broke out. Several men formed a group called the Swingternees and played '30s and

'40s dance numbers, along with Mozart and Bach. They sometimes broke off into smaller combos and played "Tea for Two" and "Saving Myself for Bill," but Harrison's favorite was a baritone named John Belland, especially his rendition of "Daybreak," a dreamy reverie about sunrise and love.

By spring the snow had melted and the men were allowed to walk through the town unsupervised. On the other side of the Salzach River, Harrison visited the small chapel that had been built to commemorate the song "Silent Night," composed here in 1818. He bought postcards too.

Some men took jobs with the local mechanic and the butcher. One internee from the Channel Islands turned down the opportunity to repatriate because he enjoyed the work he was doing at a nearby farm and wished to remain permanently in Germany.

Harrison found there were privations, though. Some mornings, the prisoners were forced to stand at attention for hours on end. Food could be scarce. Circumstances improved with the arrival of Red Cross packages, which gave the prisoners currency with the guards, but even so their treatment usually depended on what the Germans had faced in combat. Those who'd seen action in the Caucasus were to be avoided at all costs. And there remained the psychic toll of captivity, of having no sense when the war might end, just hope being dulled away.

Still, in the heart of the Third Reich, he was safer than he'd been in Norwegian camps, though he was closer to the horror of the Nazis' Final Solution. There were men at Laufen whose family members had been sent to the gas chambers. One prisoner, a Red Cross doctor, knew firsthand what was taking place at the death camps. He'd gone to inspect the prison at nearby Tittmoning. Outraged at the conditions, he began to prepare a formal condemnation and was arrested on the spot by Heinrich Himmler, leader of the SS and architect of the Reich's concentration camp system.

Whatever the men did or didn't acknowledge to each other about the cattle cars rattling over the train tracks, they were still prisoners, this was war, and that they were alive at that moment was no guarantee for the next, which may have been a factor in Harrison's decision on the Octave of Corpus Christi.

On July 1, 1943, four months after he'd arrived, a group of ten men, including Poles, Americans, and Islanders, gathered to witness Harrison's conditional baptism, a Catholic sacrament granted for someone who cannot verify whether or not he's been previously baptized. Harrison made his vows. He professed his belief in God, the Father Almighty, Jesus Christ, and the Holy Spirit, the holy Catholic church, the communion of saints, the forgiveness of sins, the resurrection of the body, and life everlasting. He renounced Satan and his empty promises. And then he took a new name: "Stanislaus Casimir."

The next day, on the Feast of the Most Sacred Heart of Jesus, he made his First Holy Communion. As usual, Harrison was loose with his facts. The certificate claims that he was born in San Francisco in 1904 and that his parents are John Post and Marie Moreno Ostrander.

Will had been raised in the Episcopal church, though according to Buck, he was not a religious or devout man. Buck claimed that despite his great friendship with Monsignor Tonello, Will viewed Catholicism with contempt, but then Will hadn't sent the accountant postcards of the church where he prayed in Paris. In any case, whatever Will's relationship to faith may have been, Harrison was a believer, even if he wasn't bound to any particular denomination.

In his journals, Harrison never mentions his baptism nor the men who witnessed the ceremony. Nor does he profess any belief or uphold any tradition specific to Catholicism. He was moved by Kahlil Gibran. He found comfort in Ecclesiastes. He treasured his Bible as he treasured the *Daily Book of Prayer and Thoughts* and likely shared Swami Paramananda's belief that "there is no difference in the great saints anywhere."

By now Harrison had been in three prisons. He'd been transferred before. He could be again. Will once paid Asa Keyes $300,000 for a piece of paper that he believed would keep him safe. Harrison may have sought his own insurance in writing. Back in 1919, when he changed his name to Harrison Post, he'd stepped into a world of wealth and ease and status. Stanislaus Casimir opened a different door.

Still, his declaration of faith may have come about for other reasons. Illness was common at the prison. Men had died of meningitis and diphtheria. Harrison certainly had had time these past years to contemplate his own mortality. Perhaps he shared Oscar Wilde's belief that "Catholicism is the only religion to die in," a quip that foretold the writer's own conditional baptism on his deathbed in Paris.

When Harrison arrived in Norway in 1938, he was recuperating from the dire conditions in which his sister and her husband had held him captive, as well as from the effects of what appear to have been a stroke and post-traumatic stress disorder. In Hellesylt, he'd made a significant recovery. He skied. He took vigorous walks.

Now, however, he'd spent two years in Nazi prison camps, and it was evident. A photo taken that Christmas shows him in the infirmary, smiling painfully, notably gaunt. Whether the sacrament was an act of faith, self-preservation, or both, Harrison traveled with the piece of paper for the rest of his life.

In February 1944, the Associated Press reported that 350 Americans who were being interned as "enemy aliens" would join a diplomatic party in Lisbon to be exchanged, along with several wounded soldiers, for German prisoners held by the Allied Powers. Priority was given to those who were ill. Despite the empire's systematic mass murder, the Nazis didn't want POWs dying in their custody. Harrison was lumped in with the other Americans to be repatriated.

Again, he packed his bags. They were heavier than when he first arrived at Laufen. Ever the collector, even in prison, Harrison had bought several watercolors from a British painter named Henry Barnett and commissioned the artist to do his portrait in oil. He gave the painter an IOU for $350.

Two years ago, Harrison had stowed away his belongings in a trunk at the hotel, thinking he was going to board a ship bound for Lisbon and then return to America, so he could reclaim what was left of his estate and begin again in Norway. Nothing had happened as he'd hoped. Now a ship was ready to take him home, but Harrison never boarded it.

He was released from Laufen on February 24, 1944. Instead of going back to the States, he returned to Norway.

Many of the Black Americans who'd been living abroad when the war broke out didn't want to go back to the States now that they had passage. Harrison had his own reasons for thinking he'd still be safer in Europe. He may not have trusted his strength after the years in the camps, and though he resented being tied to Trygga, he must've known he couldn't manage without him. Gladys claimed he'd been restored to competency in 1936, but eight years later, he wouldn't risk making the trip alone.

23

THE NORTHERN LIGHTS

Harrison Post with Gynt, 1944.

It was the summer of 1944 and the helmeted soldiers still marched through Hellesylt, but the villagers could feel it—the war was turning. By the end of August, the Germans surrendered in Paris.

Out in the sun, Harrison and Trygga lounged, shirts off, grinning at the camera. He'd gained back some weight and he was well enough that summer to hike and picnic with Trygga and others. He'd also taken to wearing a soft cap even on warm days, a new fashion perhaps.

In November, with Soviet forces advancing on Poland, Himmler ordered the destruction of the gas chambers and crematoria at Auschwitz-

Birkenau. Meanwhile, the snows had arrived in Hellesylt and Harrison was back on the slopes. Seven years had passed since he first arrived in Norway, and he still held tight to his dream. Now, though, his vision was far grander than the Korsbrekke hill or a farm in Lillehammer. He was going to buy the hotel in the neighboring town of Øye, about fifteen miles northwest of Hellesylt, through the narrow winding valley of Norangsdalen.

Built in 1891, the Victorian hotel had been a destination for European aristocrats, heads of state, and other luminaries, like Ibsen, Edvard Grieg, and Sir Arthur Conan Doyle. Harrison would have his mountains and he wouldn't be lonely for his friends. They would come to him. Harrison had a new vision, an echo, whether he realized it or not, of Will's own expansive endeavors decades before. Maybe he wouldn't start an orchestra, but he would build a stadium for the locals, a place for the townspeople to come together, and he could be the benevolent patron.

In the spring of 1945, he shared his plan with a young teacher named Olav who was visiting from Øyelandet and who later described their exchange for a 1991 newspaper article on the occasion of the hotel's one-hundred-year anniversary. Laid up in bed, recovering from a sunburn, Harrison was happy for the teacher's company.

The American told his visitor he'd traveled the world and seen bigger mountains and deeper valleys in his lifetime, but when he stood in the valley of Øye he felt a harmony that touched more than his senses. He told Olav, "The voice inside me was clear: Here you shall settle down and be a happy old man."

The hotel wouldn't be a common tourist spot, he explained, or even a functioning hotel in the normal sense. He would have his own suite and then the other rooms would be for his friends from America, England, Italy, and elsewhere.

The teacher was a pragmatic young man. He asked what they would pay.

"Guests don't pay!" Harrison laughed. "But I presume they won't come with empty pockets."

Olav was curious and blunt. He asked how much money Harrison had.

"To be honest, I don't know myself. You have to ask my accountant." He went on to say he owned a large amount of real estate in Los Angeles, worth somewhere between $18 million and $20 million, he guessed. The schoolteacher recounted this anecdote some forty years after it had happened, so it's possible he misremembered the figure Harrison gave him, but it's just as possible Harrison came up with the outrageously inflated amount himself.

The interview came to an end, and as Olav got up to go, Harrison fumbled about with his bedside drawer. When he turned around, he had three cigarettes for the teacher. Each came with instructions.

"This one you smoke as soon as you are outside," he said. "And this one you enjoy this evening, and this one you save for tomorrow." He pressed them into his guest's hand. His old cellmate Kaare Viken would have been touched to see that the "dobbeltmillionœr fra Santa Monica" had finally developed some common sense. The "sunburned immigrant," as Olav recalled Harrison, was a naïve man, not entirely earthbound, it seemed, but moving in his exuberance and generosity. The teacher stood in the doorstep, three cigarettes in his pocket, and felt like crying.

In time, Harrison's sunburn healed and he was off again on his daily walks. He had a new companion now, too, a whippet named Gynt. Often called the "poor man's racehorse," the deer-like and regal dogs are known for being spectacularly agile, prone to sudden bursts of balletic speed followed by lazy stretches. They don't bark much, and they're too friendly to be guard dogs.

Gynt came with Harrison everywhere—on walks to visit with Anton Larsen fishing at his pond, to the local café where Harrison snuck off to have a beer with the owner, though inevitably Trygga tracked him down and scolded him for drinking, worried for his health.

Dependent as he was on his host and servant, Harrison still groused at Trygga's mood swings, though it's just as likely that his own moods were responsible for the frequent strain. Villagers sometimes spied the little American and his whippet striding through the landscape, Trygga trailing fifty feet behind.

With spring came more hope, and then joy. On May 8, 1945, the German forces capitulated, and in Hellesylt, for the first time in five years, they raised the Norwegian flag. Harrison stood on Main Street, Gynt in his arms, and cheered the marching band and the villagers parading past in their traditional Norwegian costumes. Later that day they burned the blackout curtains and the signs in German.

The end of the war meant at last an end to those years of isolation

Liberation Day in Hellesylt, Harrison and Gynt in the foreground, May 8, 1945.

from friends. Finally contact with the world. On July 4, a letter arrived in the post from Joe McInerney. With the lawyer's help, Harrison would at last be able to organize his finances and get the hotel, his dream of peace never closer.

Harrison opened the letter, and his joy soon faded:

> For the first time I realize what I have before me—Gladys and Charles Crooks have defrauded me of everything—my fortune in cash—my farm—and other properties and town house—poor Joe in all these years has been in the dark—he cannot understand that I could not get to America—account of the war—but with many wires and many letters he will understand things thoroughly
>
> I am really shocked at the news—to think twenty odd years of supporting her—ten years for him—it is really unbelievable—however I will be very clear—and I will do the best I can. they sold all my personal belongings—my library—lovely silver and antique furniture—in fact, everything—I shall, when I get to America I shall put them in order—if necessary to put them in jail—I am "soft" and I have been all my life—but this time they will not get away with it. What a hell of a life.

Later he took a long walk and went to bed after "a strong bromide—find since many years I needed it."

It's difficult to overstate the impact of this news, not only in the shock of Gladys's betrayal but also the blow to Harrison's dreams of his new and tranquil life, a vision that had sustained him over the past years. He wired Joe straightaway and sent his power of attorney, authorizing the lawyer to take whatever measures necessary to recover his fortune. Over the next several days, he wrote more letters, providing written testimony and urging Joe to act quickly. The effort exhausted him.

"It has been ghastly—the whole thing—the day I have lived somehow—I find as though I am half dead—perhaps I am."

Joe's response was swift. The attorney assured him it wasn't a lost cause. They had legal recourse, and Joe, of course, had connections that could give them extra-legal leverage. Harrison had known his return to America would not be an easy one, but this was far worse than what he'd imagined. And yet it was necessary to his ultimate goal: a quiet life in the country he'd grown to love.

On Sunday, July 7, he traveled to Oslo with Trygga and Gynt, expecting to leave straightaway for America, only to learn that his passport was no longer valid. Despite that frustration, it was a wonderful change to be in the city, to reunite with friends there and to attend an evening at the National Theatre. The royal family was present too. After all this time: glamour and tone. "I feel so gay here," Harrison wrote. "I talk to everyone I like—at the movies everyone excited with Gynt."

Several more days passed. He expected to be on a plane to San Francisco, and yet there was no progress with the American embassy about his passport. There was nothing to do, it seemed, but wait. They returned to Hellesylt, and Harrison resumed his walks.

The days were full of rain. He preferred that to the heat, but what he would prefer most of all was to get to San Francisco. He admonished himself not to drink too much. He wanted to be fit for the trip ahead and his new life in Øye when he returned, but he was rattled, nerves alert.

> and then—a long talk with myself. for I have been worried to death—full of doubts and fears—and—I realize—I am middle-aged and how stupid to be upset—with my vast collections of

> experiences—so, again my old philosophy—that did so well—in the past—and in Trondheim—and Grini—and Bavaria—to know that I have only one day—enjoy and die each evening—no past—and no future—just an eternal "now" it is the only thing for me—and perhaps I can laugh again—and perhaps seem new again.

He soon got help feeling "new." Several British parachutists arrived in town, including a handsome blond soldier named Gordon Pritchard, who lifted Harrison's spirits considerably. He and Gordon developed an immediate rapport—obvious in photographs taken during the soldiers' short stay. After a few days, they were gone, and Harrison's mood plunged again, until the post arrived with a package from Bergen. Gordon had sent a hundred Player's cigarettes and Harrison flushed with happiness: "He did like me—after all. he was so cool—and collected."

On July 27, news of a different sort arrived. Harrison opened the paper and saw that Commander Flesch had been arrested trying to escape the country with several gold bars smuggled in his suitcase. "Hope he dies," he wrote. "A terrible man." Whether or not Harrison ever did fully understand how the commander used him as a prop, he knew

Harrison with Gordon Pritchard, 1945.

he'd come close to death at the other man's hands: "He would have shot me if he could have." But this wasn't his only impression of the Nazi officer. "Very handsome man—but cruel," he wrote.

And yet as much as he tried to follow his own counsel—to live in the "eternal now."—he still strayed into the past. Trygga told him that Nazimova had died. The news sent him into a reverie. Those early years in Los Angeles, the parties, another lifetime.

> I remember twenty years ago—at Crystal beach at Santa Monica—she was so lovely—with a boy's figure—her black hair brown skin and marvellous brilliant green eyes—full of fun—she earned $7500 a week—she was married with Charles Bryant—English actor—they were later divorced—her "girl friend" was Consuelo Flowerton—she was very beautiful—she had a lovely voice—Nazimova gave me many photos—I trust Gladys hasn't destroyed them—about ten years ago she built a beautiful apartment house at Sunset Boulevard at Hollywood. "Garden of Alla." What an interesting career—she was a Russian Jewess—a refugee—came to New York and played at the famous Yiddish Theater—later became the mistress of Gilbert Miller—he made her famous and starred in Ibsen's plays—she became a great artist—later the films—and became very famous and rich—was always—simple and kind—and charming—God Bless Nazimova—my old friend.

More news of America and his friends filtered in. He read that Charlie Chaplin was married to Eugene O'Neill's daughter. "She must be very young," he wrote, and then reminded himself to write to O'Neill's wife, his friend Carlotta. "Life does go on!"

He reconsidered his plan for the hotel. For one thing, he wasn't sure the owner would sell, and if they did, it'd be a fortune. Harrison didn't directly link his reluctance about the hotel to the news about Gladys ransacking his estate, but in the wake of the letter from Joe, he seemed to be taking stock of his circumstances in a new way. "I am not so young as I have been."

Now he had something simpler in mind. Jan Nordang, a political official, had a summer home on a hill in Øye. If the diplomat sold him the property, Harrison reasoned, he could live there on very little, hire a cook for seventy kroner a month and maybe staff for housekeeping. "A tiny villa" with Gynt. The thought lifted his spirits.

On September 1, he woke to a gorgeous morning and the mountain peaks covered with snow. Cold, but the sunshine was brilliant. He wrote many letters that day to friends.

He continued his hikes. He ate a steak for the first time in five years. He read. He quoted Swinburne to himself: "Sleep, and if life was bitter to thee, pardon. If sweet, give thanks."

Anton Larsen's birthday came and Harrison and Trygga attended the party along with Gausdal, the Bjørdals, and many more. A good dinner, dessert was fruit and whipped cream, then coffee, then crème de menthe, and many cigarettes. The evening was lovely, but by ten he was tired and "a wee bored."

He slipped away and walked home alone. The night was dark, the air cool. He could see the mountains rising around him, and above the northern lights swirled in the sky. The land was solid. The people were good to him. He would be happy here.

Gynt leapt up, tail wagging, when he got to the hotel. "Then to bed, writing this." Harrison had stepped into the "eternal now," recording time as it was passing. "And now to read a bit—and then to sleep—life isn't too bad!"

If only he could stay in that contented place, but the month crept on and with it came an anniversary and he wasn't thinking of the present but the past. On September 30, he remembered back to 1919, when he took the train with Will and Snooks and the others to Los Angeles:

> and then began my real worries—worries until this very day—I am hoping to get to San Francisco in a few days—settle all affairs—what is left—and begin all over—in Norway.

PART FIVE

1945–1946

24

THE ALIEN

"I eat like a pig," Harrison confessed after his first dinner aboard the *Stavangerfjord*. Potage à la grecque, fried halibut, roast leg of lamb, biscuits, and caramel pudding. A long way from boiled potato peelings. It was October 13, and at long last, he was bound for America.

There'd been many people waiting to board in the cold, gray harbor the day before, but Harrison was likely the only one in a full-length fur coat, accompanied by a valet and a whippet. He'd prepared for the crossing as best he could—Seconal, seasickness pills, and a bottle of spirits, though he hoped he wouldn't need any of that. He'd traded two of his suits to Oscar Bjørdal for 250 Gold Flake cigarettes, and a villager had given him two packs as a gift, so that brought him to 300 total—enough, he figured, to last ten days.

He'd forgotten one thing, though, or rather, he hadn't considered it until the purser knocked on the cabin door to inform them that they'd neglected to pay the three hundred kroner for Gynt's passage. This was a matter for Joe to handle, and a telegram soon was dispatched. Such things were beyond Harrison.

The dog was a sensation. Harrison made friends easily as they strolled the decks, the friendly whippet delighting fellow passengers. Five months had passed since the Allies' triumph, and the rolling giddiness and camaraderie continued aboard the *Stavangerfjord*. Harrison's new acquaintances included a *Times* correspondent from Minneapolis and an American from the embassy in Moscow, but he was most enamored of a group of Swedish travelers. They were young, attractive, and happy, and being with them filled him with a sense of liberation and joy. One night, they all ventured down to the ship's "Turist" salon, though Harrison wasn't impressed. "No grandeur," he noted.

There were several days of rough seas, and the ship pitched and rolled, but he had the stomach for that. It was what awaited him in America that made him queasy.

He was still reeling from the phone call from Ted Glassel, an old riding friend who now lived in Copenhagen. They'd spoken just days before Harrison boarded the ship. It was Ted who delivered the bombshell: Gladys and her husband weren't in California; they weren't even in America.

"What horrible people they are," he wrote after he'd absorbed the news that the Crookses were now living in Mexico City. "I intend to arrest them at once—unless they do something in my favor." But he didn't have an address for them nor did he know what if anything remained of his estate. "I hope they haven't made away with everything. How cruel they are."

Despite the looming confrontation, he was hopeful and happy on the ship. "Thank God I am able to be with young and happy people." The last night at the captain's dinner he danced with his Swedish friends until three in the morning.

And then, after eight years, Harrison had his first glimpse of America: fog. The Brooklyn harbor was socked in with it. They were supposed to dock at eight o'clock that morning, but the ship slowed to a crawl, and the hours ticked by.

It was after three that afternoon when the *Stavangerfjord* finally inched into the dock. And then "torture at the passports and the purser and then to the customs," but the most excruciating part was still to come: putting Gynt in the kennel. "It made me sick," Harrison wrote.

He and Trygga checked in at Hotel St. George in Brooklyn, and then he called Joe. It was wonderful to hear his old friend's voice, but the lawyer was candid. Their task wouldn't be an easy or simple one. Harrison took a pill to sleep that night.

The next morning, on October 24, he got Gynt from the kennel and then, with Trygga, they taxied to Manhattan. His first stop was Gimbels near Herald Square. Nearly a decade had passed since Harrison had walked through the doors of a department store. He bought himself a brown coat. Later, they took a long stroll up Fifth Avenue, and that evening he went to bed without any pills.

The next day, they were on the move again, boarding a night train for the West Coast, but Harrison didn't sleep at all. Like the Atlantic crossing, it was a gleeful, rollicking journey, this time with cars full of happy soldiers. These were men who'd gotten lucky in the war—as Harrison had—and they were coming back for their new lives. Liquor and bonhomie flowed as the train sped through the dark countryside.

But they were brought up short in Chicago. Joe had forgotten to pay for Gynt's passage on the ship, and now it turned out he'd also forgotten to book them all the way through to the West Coast. All the compartments were reserved for the next two weeks. Still, their luck hadn't run out. One of Harrison's new friends from the train—a naval officer—was in the same predicament, and he and a sailor had managed to hire a car to take them to the coast.

Ever since Will's death, Harrison had been trapped—first by illness, then by his sister. When he did manage to get free, he was trapped again—by the Nazis—and again, held hostage and terrorized. After the war, it'd been one ordeal after the other—the passport, waiting on funds, a hideous sunburn, boredom, waiting for a flight, and then when that didn't come through, waiting for the boat. But now, something had shifted. There were still obstacles, but Harrison wasn't stuck anymore. He had momentum. He had options. If he didn't have a seat on a train, he could jump into a car and drive off into the night.

It was one in the morning when they left Chicago, and for the next sixteen hours they sped across Illinois and through Iowa, spent the night in Columbus, Nebraska, and then up at five the next morning. Fifteen hours that day, until Rock Springs, Wyoming. Then they were up again and on the road before dawn, speeding through Utah and Nevada.

It was after midnight when Harrison, Trygga, and Gynt tumbled out of the car on Powell Street in San Francisco. They'd arrived at the Sir Francis Drake. Happy, exhausted, Harrison deemed it "the smartest hotel I have ever seen—every service and consideration."

When he woke the next morning, it seemed that all the mail he'd longed for had arrived—letters from Bebe Daniels, Frances Marion,

Carlotta Monterey, and many more. And then, in the hotel lobby, there, at last, was his old friend Joe, in the flesh. The lawyer presented him with a handsome wristwatch and a check for $250 to tide him over.

Phone calls came next. So many voices Harrison hadn't heard in years. Every hello, every handshake, every embrace, every card carried with it gratitude, relief, and joy, and even if they didn't say it in these words, the message, simple and clear, was the same: "I am glad you are alive."

Like her mother had done years ago, Madeleine Post Starrett threw open her home. She and Bob lived in a grand brown-shingled house on Lake Street just south of the Presidio. Bob had aged—balding now. Madeleine looked well. She'd always had a marvelous style, always a natural host, and Harrison learned she had an impressive position now as vice president at the City of Paris department store on Union Square.

Bob poured the cocktails. More friends arrived. Madeleine served a wonderful meal, and Harrison was flooded with a tremendous sense of well-being. In the Starretts' home, he understood that he was cherished. It'd been a long time since he'd had that feeling, and it stayed with him through dinner and the drive back to the hotel.

Light from streetlamps jeweled the windows. It was dark as they passed the Presidio—no houses, just trees, but it was the kind of dark that felt safe. He felt in his pocket for the paper that Madeleine had slipped him on the way out the door and unfolded the check: $250.

Back in his hotel room, Harrison wrote her name and the amount next to the others in the back of his journal—soon he'd be able to repay all their kindnesses. When he sat down several days later to write in his diary, he marveled at how different the city felt, and how he still found it so beautiful. Considering the wear of the past weeks, he thought he looked well enough, but he admitted to himself that his nerves were jumpy. Los Angeles was next.

The Harrison Post who stepped off the train in Central Station in the fall of 1919 was young and beautiful, with every advantage and protection of wealth. Twenty-six years later, it was fall again in Southern California, but little else was the same. Even so, tired and older, this Harrison Post was content.

"I am so happy—it is like a dream—swimming twice today." Again, he'd been swarmed with goodwill and friendship. Bebe Daniels and Ben Lyon had opened their gracious mansion on the beach, a few houses from his old Gold Coast home. "I will never forget my welcome," he wrote on his first night.

With the war over, the Lyon-Daniels family concluded their BBC radio (and later TV) sitcom of cheerful family mayhem and returned to life in the States, and now Harrison had stepped into the real-life version. He joined Bebe at the studio where she was writing gags for her old boss Hal Roach, and later they lunched with the actress's good friend, gossip maven Louella Parsons.

The reunions continued. "What can I do for you?" Snowy Baker said when Harrison saw his old riding pal for luncheon at the Riviera Club. "Moral support," he replied, warmed by the club manager's concern.

Everyone asked. Famed costume designer Orry-Kelly, Norman Kerry, Zasu Pitts: again they said, "If you need anything . . . ," and again, he said, "Moral support." He'd have his own money soon.

Of course Harrison wasn't the only one changed. His dear friend Ann Rork wasn't Ann Rork anymore. She'd become Ann Getty, wife of the oil baron and mother of two boys, and then Ann Light, mother again to a daughter, Donna. Now she had a new romance—his lawyer, Joe McInerney. Life was full of surprises.

In Norway, Harrison went for hikes and played dominoes. Here, he shopped at Bullock's, sat in on Louella's broadcast at the studio, had cocktails at the Savoy, dined at the Brown Derby, drank silver fizzes at the Ambassador, and had more cocktails at Randolph Scott's home. He bought red roses for Bebe, yellow carnations for her mother, Phyllis, and cartons of cigarettes to send to his friends in Norway.

He cheered when Bebe's son Richard arrived home with news that he'd been cast in *Anna and the King of Siam*. Later, they went out to see *State Fair*, the Rodgers and Hammerstein Technicolor musical about the adventures of a Midwestern family, a small-town variation of the merry, glamorous world he'd landed in. "I would love to live with this happy family always," Harrison wrote. Still, he knew his worries belonged to a different genre.

Joe arrived and they went out for drinks at the Trocadero with Ann. But the evening took a sour turn—a small quibble between the two paramours erupted into a furious row that Ann ended by storming out of the club. She phoned the next morning, apologizing for the drunken misunderstanding. It was the kind of thing that was easy to laugh off, and so they did. "She is a good egg," Harrison wrote. His concerns were larger than a spat at a nightclub, and all the silver fizzes and moral support hadn't changed the reality of his situation. They still didn't have an address for Gladys.

Monday after Thanksgiving, Harrison was ready to get down to business. He met with Will's longtime adviser, Judge Sanner, who was confident it would all be settled in Harrison's favor. It was a relief to know that the Clark machine still worked—and to get a check for $500. Harrison wrote the judge's name in his journal below Madeleine's, and then he gave $400 to Joe and $50 to Trygga.

In the early weeks back in California, the Norwegian rarely figures in Harrison's journal entries. It seems he accompanied Harrison to Los Angeles, but he did not stay at Bebe Daniels's home. Oscar Tryggestad had arrived in Southern California well before Gladys hired him as a "ranch help" in 1936. Presumably he had friends and a social cohort that preceded Harrison. While Harrison was gadding about Bullock's and the Ambassador, reconnecting with his gang of socialites and film stars, Trygga was likely having reunions of his own. Harrison may have given little thought to Trygga's life beyond him, but it's certain that the masseur had one.

What consumed Harrison was Gladys—when they would have her address, when Joe would make headway, when he would have his affairs in order at last. He dreaded making contact but knew he couldn't start his new life until he did. He called Mrs. Rosanoff, the wife of the alienist who'd treated him during his confinement, to see if she had his sister's address, but this yielded nothing. Nor did Blanche Hill have any leads; the new owner of his old home was gracious when he called, but she had no news and certainly wasn't going to restore the land to him.

Joe had told Harrison that the Hills paid the Crookses $130,000 for it. The property was worth far more. In any case, he hadn't seen a penny. "It broke my heart—my dream home." That one's heart could break again and again was a lesson he kept learning, even though he knew it well enough already.

It doesn't seem that Harrison set foot on the property, but a few days later he did revisit Will's home in West Adams. With Bebe and Phyllis, he drove past the walled estate, circling the block where Will had built his compound, the gardens where Harrison had been young and safe, laughing and dancing in the splendid kingdom. In the library up on the ceiling, his thirteen painted selves were still young and safe, still there with the settees, tapestries, bronzes, and the books. Now he stared at the grounds through a car window. He didn't get out and knock on the gate at his old home across the street. They drove on.

If Harrison understood himself to be performing rituals of mourning, he didn't indicate this in his diary. In 1934, he'd been stranded in a sanitarium while others memorialized the philanthropist. He hadn't been part of the sad little group that wandered over the bridge to the mausoleum where Will was laid to rest.

In Norway, Harrison had pictured the grave and hoped Joe remembered to place flowers on Will's birthday. But now that he was back in Los Angeles, he didn't visit the cemetery. It had been easier to imagine his copain's tomb from another country than to stand before its bronze door now.

"I feel that Will is always with me," he'd once written in Hellesylt. Here, it was harder to be certain of that. Perhaps part of the reason Harrison pined for the other country wasn't simply its sublime landscape or because he could leave behind all the hideous things that had happened to him in America—after all, hideous things had happened in Norway too. However, in a foreign land, he could hold on to Will and all that he loved from the past. In Los Angeles, everything was evidence that Will was gone, that the world they'd known had slipped away and was being forgotten by those who remained.

More than a decade had passed since Harrison's life had snapped. Los Angeles was a different place. There were freeways. His friends were fading movie stars. The library belonged to UCLA. As soon as Joe got the Crookses' address, he could make plans for his real life in the country where he was truly himself. "It's foolish to think of the weather—it is perfect here—but I am not happy—I long for Norway."

Like the Duke of Aumale recuperating scattered vestiges of a lost empire, Harrison tried to reclaim what he could of his past. He wrote to Lawrence Clark Powell, the new head of the Clark Library, and requested the return of several items, including the statue of Pan that Troubetzkoy had done, a jeweled miniature of Empress Josephine, and a silver tea set. He wrote to Mary Pickford to ask if she still had a pair of cuff links he'd once given her brother Jack. Of course these were trifles compared to the restoration he was due.

Still no word from Joe on Gladys's address. Harrison was restless and worried. He wasn't sleeping well. He was tired of the sunshine. When his old friend Henry Trumbull, a former actor now married to the daughter of a shipping magnate, suggested he join him in his chauffeured car for a drive up the coast to his home in Burlingame, Harrison jumped at the change of scenery.

The visit was a disaster. The first night was delightful—the welcoming friend, a lovely wife, a luxurious home, attentive servants, champagne, a game of dominoes—but Harrison soon discovered his old friend had grown into a mean and jealous drunk whose wife, exhausted by his binges, was beginning divorce proceedings. Harrison fled to Madeleine and Bob, who'd been looking after Gynt, and took refuge at their home on Lake Street.

While the Trumbulls appeared to be dissolving their marriage, other friends were embracing the institution. On December 5, he phoned Joe and learned that his attorney and Ann had tied the knot that morning. He congratulated the newlyweds, but he was dubious: "They are no children—Ann has 3 children—same with Joe—God bless them." Everyone, it seemed, had gone a bit mad. He wanted none of it. He went back south but this time he stayed alone at the Hotel Miramar in Santa Monica.

Harrison was impatient. The pleasures of return had faded. He was learning, as he did in Burlingame, that not all reunions were heartwarming ones. In some cases, old friends weren't the friends he believed them to be. A rift—never explained in his journals—transpired with Snowy Baker. Mary Pickford responded to his inquiry about her late brother's cuff links with a typed note explaining she knew nothing of their whereabouts. It wasn't a snub, but she didn't invite further contact. Frances Marion had dropped him completely—the result, it seemed, of a disagreement over the brooch that he'd requested from UCLA. Set in gold with two large diamonds and a pearl, and studded with diamond chips, the miniature of Josephine had a storied provenance. The empress had presented it to Napoleon. Prince Philippe de Bourbon had given it to Frances Marion, and years ago the screenwriter made a gift of it to Harrison, who then put it on display in the library. Now apparently she wanted it back. He didn't even have it to give. Besides, he barely had anything to his name as it was.

For all the so-called moral support he'd been offered, the tide of good wishes that'd swept him forward appeared to be receding. Perhaps the novelty of the socialite who'd survived the Nazis had worn thin. Perhaps an affluent clubman has only a small window before a seemingly transitory bout of poverty is considered a fixed state. Will's money had given him entrée and secure footing in the world of wealthy elites, but Harrison's position was slipping, and he'd stumbled into a new twilight existence—that of the aristocrat awaiting restoration of his fortune.

Also, he was sagging under the weight of anxiety. "I am not very well," he wrote. "With Gladys' disappearance—worry in finances—annoyance of money—has made me a 'louseworthy' subject. and yet I must keep going on—I can't fail—my old friends are sticking to me—but sometimes I feel as though I could not go on."

And then word got to Dorothy Taylor that Harrison Post was back in town. In turn, his fellow nonprofessional, the extravagant party maven, put out the word that he was invited—no, he was summoned—to her oceanfront home in Malibu. Delighted, Harrison readily accepted her command.

In his journals, Harrison referred to Dorothy by her maiden name, as he'd first known her back in the 1920s, but in gossip columns she was Countess Dorothy di Frasso. Her title came from a short-lived marriage in Italy and her wealth from her father's dry goods fortune in New Jersey. Over the years she'd been romantically linked to Gary Cooper and Cary Grant, though it was her relationship with Jewish gangster Bugsy Siegel that drew the most headlines. That, along with her enthusiasm and support for her now late friend Benito Mussolini, had piqued the interest of the Federal Bureau of Investigation.

In 1939, both the tabloids and the bureau had avidly followed the bizarre misadventures of a cruise organized by the countess with Siegel, to search for supposed buried treasure near Costa Rica. The captain had mutinied, and there were suggestions that the point of the trip had been something other than rich people larking about the Pacific—perhaps a cover for smuggling. The bureau's file on the American countess also included reports of her attempts, unsuccessful, to bring explosives into the United States from Mexico, as part of a plot directed by fascist operatives.

Harrison had begun his stay in Los Angeles with friends who'd been beloved figures in the Allied propaganda effort on British airwaves. Now he, a former prisoner of war, was staying in the home of a woman who'd counted Mussolini among her dear friends and had attempted sabotage on the dictator's behalf.

Likely Harrison didn't know this last detail, but Dorothy's political leanings were no secret. In any case, whether oblivious, unfazed, or incurious about his hostess's fascist sympathies, he was eager to wash away the bitter taste of false friends. Besides, class solidarity trumped other allegiances. Like Bebe, Dorothy still recognized Harrison as part of an upper echelon, a member of the elite Hollywood tribe, and he happily glided from one seaside compound to another, secure within the protected bubble of wealth.

Dorothy, like everyone, was older now, grayer too, but still the raucous dynamo of their earlier years. She showed him to his rooms, a suite with a private entrance, and insisted he use her chauffeur and car whenever he liked. She also had a ferocious Scottish terrier named Inky who appeared to approve of him. She'd told him that he should have Gynt come stay as well. They spent their first afternoon together talking for hours, and Harrison shared his plans for the hotel in Norway.

"[She] wants me to stop with her as long as I like," he wrote. "I think it will be good for me." After nearly two months of bouncing around California, he'd found a harbor that was safe and calm.

Still, it was relative calm. In Hellesylt, he went for long walks, he read books, he sewed cross-stitches by the fire. "I can think in Norway," Harrison wrote, and it was surely harder to think now that he was buffeted about by shopping, lunches, cocktails, and phone calls late into the night from Joe about how the case was proceeding.

"Case" is a loose term here, since Joe hadn't filed any type of legal motion. Although he'd enlisted an attorney, Bruno Newman, in Mexico, so far no petitions had been filed either there or in California.

But the court wasn't always Joe's first recourse. He specialized in planting news items and off-the-record negotiations. The Crookses had taken Harrison's fortune through underhanded and nefarious means, and it seemed that Joe's intention was to respond in kind. Once he had an address for the Crookses in Mexico City, he assured Harrison, they would see results.

What Harrison didn't seem to consider was that for years he'd benefited from the Clark machine but wasn't actually involved in its operation. Will was the one who'd dealt with Joe and the other attorneys while Harrison had retreated to the Uplifters Club. He'd never managed anyone else's affairs and barely his own. His homes had been bought for him. Trygga booked his passage.

There was a lot Harrison didn't consider, especially when it came to Trygga. They'd shared Christmases for years now, but not this one. Harrison celebrated it with Bebe and her family, exchanging gifts and welcoming friends who dropped by. He sent cables and made phone calls. When he spoke to Joe on the phone, the lawyer was confident he'd have finessed their problems soon. Back at Dorothy's, Harrison kissed her good night and went to bed. No mention of Trygga, though.

The next day, the Norwegian arrived. He gave Dorothy a massage, and then he joined Harrison for a walk on the beach where the two men argued bitterly. Harrison didn't record the cause of their quarrel, but Trygga would've had any number of reasons to be angry. He may have been hurt not to be included in the holiday. He may have resented being treated like the help when he wasn't being paid like the help. And if he wasn't the help, then maybe he was a friend. But this would've crossed a line that Harrison couldn't tolerate. Despite everything, to him, Trygga was a servant. But it's possible the Norwegian understood himself differently, to be playing the role of chaperone, not the subservient one after all. And though Harrison may have chafed at this attitude, Trygga wasn't necessarily wrong. It did seem that Harrison needed looking after.

As it turned out, life in Malibu had not delivered the serenity he'd hoped for. Harrison was grateful Dorothy was so generous, and it'd been thrilling to rekindle their friendship, at first. She was so taken with his plans for the hotel in Norway that she talked of joining with him. At one point, a visiting friend speculated about them getting married, a development which would likely have delivered Harrison into a realm of financial security.

Certainly he had reason to be anxious about money. He was still cadging checks from friends—"wrote Whitey for a touch." He'd seen Cora Sanders, who said she'd send him $500, which turned out to be only $100, sent to him in care of Bullock's. Marriage to a wealthy countess might've solved some of his problems, but if he did entertain the idea, it hadn't been for long. Friends had cautioned him—over drinks, naturally—not to get a "snootful" while he was staying at Dorothy's. At the time, the warning amused him. It didn't anymore, though. He'd discovered that Dorothy lived on whim and bourbon and frequently erupted into raging tantrums—at the maid, at "pinkos," at perceived slights. Every day brought a new affront, a new rant.

A pattern emerges in Harrison's reunions. At first he's euphoric to be reconnected with his old friends, suffused with well-being and security, but soon his effusive gratitude wears thin. Next comes recoil. His stay with Dorothy was the most extreme of this cycle.

Some of this was certainly due to his own fickle character and perhaps a readiness or expectation, learned from the years with Will, that others would rescue him. And he did have people ready to take him in or guide him, but in several cases—as with both Dorothy and Joe—his would-be saviors also had severe alcohol-use disorders. The splendid drunken twenties were gone, but the drunks remained.

And, as he'd been in Hellesylt, Harrison was still a guest. Thankful though he was for his friends' generosity, he was dependent, and he'd been so for nearly a decade now. The days wore on and he grew lonely, exhausted by Dorothy's drinking and by her friends, who arrived at all hours and seemed to encourage her rampages. He tucked himself away in his room with Gynt—at least he had the dog with him now. Madeleine and Bob had brought the whippet during a visit to Los Angeles.

Bourbon, roses, more bourbon, rants, sunshine, sunshine, sunshine. He longed for Norway.

He wrote letters and sent cigarettes back to his friends there. He took his fur coat, useless in Los Angeles, to be repaired. He bought himself some new ski goggles and more handkerchiefs for more friends, and then admonished himself: "And no more for anyone until I find out about my affairs—for I am really 'flat'—and no prospects for some time—also weary this evening."

Three months had now passed since Harrison had returned to the States. In that time, he'd gotten wisps of information about the Crookses, but otherwise Joe had accomplished little. Every time Harrison called the lawyer, he was recovering from a hangover.

And then a glimmer of hope. On Friday, February 1, letters arrived from Bruno Newman, the contact in Mexico, alerting them that there was a lead on the Crookses. It was only a glimmer, but it was enough to feel like progress, and Harrison gave Trygga $600 to book their return passage on the *Stavangerfjord*.

At the Ambassador and the Riviera Club, Harrison's friends lavished their sympathy on him. They all said it was terrible, that Joe should be on the "up and up," that it should've been *done* months ago. "I agreed," he wrote.

On February 9, he started out making the usual rounds—breakfast with Bebe, a stop at the Riviera Club, then back at Dorothy's, where he braced himself for the inevitable scene, but he was in for a shock—the good kind, for once.

First, he discovered his hostess "was less drunk and in good humor," but the true surprise came in an envelope. It was from Mexico, presumably from Bruno Newman. Harrison had been craving results, and at last they'd arrived:

> Dear Mr. Post
>
> Below I trust will give you information desired—
>
> Charles Crooks
> 1105 Calle Alpe Lomas
> Chapultepec
> Mexico City, D.F.

And with those few lines, the blur of binges, shopping, and cocktails evaporated and a clear path lay before him. Elated, he called Joe—still in bed, of course. Harrison went to Bullock's and bought a suede jacket. He wouldn't be "flat" for long now.

On Friday, Joe had more news. He'd brought a law firm in on the case, Dalton and Goodrich. A well-respected American attorney who'd been living in Mexico City for years, Jess Dalton apparently knew how to navigate the legal system there, and he'd already suggested a course of action: they would have the Crookses charged with fraud and embezzlement and the villains would be detained. Harrison would need to submit a complete account of his personal assets. Thrilled, he called Madeleine, his faithful ally, to share the news, and then went to bed, contented and hopeful.

The phone jangled him awake. It was two o'clock in the morning. It was Joe, drunk. Ann was away on a trip and the lawyer wanted to talk. Mostly about the fees that Harrison owed him. One third of everything. "It seems like a 'hold-up' to me," Harrison wrote.

He tried to go back to sleep. The phone rang again. "More rambling stupid conversation." Now Joe was talking about the things Harrison was going to get from the library, what they could pawn. The trip to Mexico was going to be expensive. The lawyers too. They needed funds. "As of old," Harrison wrote. "Wanting—and more wanting."

A big man, Joe had a big presence. His moods swung quickly from jovial to bellicose. Massive, doughy, strong, with large dark eyes and a bulbous nose—that's how he seemed to Ann's daughter Donna, who was around nine when Joe married her mother. Donna remembers the lawyer as a devoted San Francisco Seals fan, shirtsleeves rolled up, porkpie hat shoved back on his head, cheering raucously during baseball games. She remembers him, too, barging through the front door of their Beverly Hills home, a looming, raging figure, running from room to room, waving a .45 pistol, while her mother frantically tried to call the police. It took at least three men to finally subdue him.

Harrison hadn't faced that level of fury, but it was becoming clear that the man he expected to stabilize his life kept creating chaos, not order. Harrison must've believed Joe would be as effective as he had been back when Will was alive and the lawyer finessed newspaper mentions and paid off the DA, but it wasn't playing out that way.

At least he had Madeleine to turn to. Their phone call the next day put him at ease. She told him that she and Bob would help with the money. Harrison was grateful but maddened that it had gotten so tangled. "A good lawyer would have finished the whole thing—it would have cost a fortune—it would have been easier." Still, he hadn't lost sight of what mattered to him most now:

> I am happy enough that soon (god willing) I will be on my way with my mountain tops and fjords and rivers.

Dorothy's drunken rampages continued. "Polluted" was the word Harrison used. He was desperate to leave. "After all, a binge is a binge, but for daily life I want a semblance of decency." And even when he didn't get phone calls in the middle of the night from the alcoholic who had his power of attorney, Harrison still had trouble sleeping. On February 21 at 3:45 in the morning he opened his diary:

> A resolution—that should have been done many, many years ago—that God willing—will help me on my way. Another thing that is important—to try to forget the horror of the last twelve years—it has been ghastly—Emmet Fox's book *Power through Constructive Thinking* has helped no end.

A former Catholic and significant figure in the New Thought movement, Emmet Fox had become a touchstone for Harrison. Drawing inspiration from metaphysics, psychology, and Mary Baker Eddy, Fox published a series of pamphlets with titles like *Be Still* and *The Seven Day Mental Diet* that were collected in *Power through Constructive Thinking*. Harrison often turned to the book, which included a close analysis of the Good Shepherd, the psalm that he had read aloud to his cellmates at Vollan.

More and more, Harrison struggled with insomnia. When it struck, he wrote letters or read. Sometimes he pasted postcards from Norway in his journal. A shot of the Geiranger Fjord, soaring crags above a gleaming inlet. A town dotted with red roofs nestled beneath snow-capped mountains. Reminders that life could be calm and simple. In a way, he enjoyed the quiet and the solitude of those hours, though it meant a dull headache the next day, and if he wasn't careful, he knew it could lead to a reaction.

Amid the waiting, he found peace where he could. They had two days of fog and he was glad for it. He drove to see Cora Sanders in her magnificent home in West Adams. She, like Sanner, was still living comfortably off the Clark fortune, and she would for the rest of her life, in the house that Will had bought her, among Will's things, as if she were his widow instead of a dutiful attendant.

If Harrison opened Cora's closets, he'd have seen the dresses that had belonged to Mabel and Alice. She had survived both women, and, in a way, him too. The consort had returned from exile to find a barren world. He hadn't been a wife, a child, not even a real ward. He hadn't been Will's lawyer or his librarian. A "secretary," forever in quotes. *Copain* was a word that had mattered only to Will, and with him gone, Harrison was left to scavenge.

Cora had the crystal candlesticks out that he'd given to Will. The brush box too. They should've been his, but Harrison said nothing. "Cora is as she is." He was taking a long view of things: "This will perhaps be the last time I shall ever see her."

On February 27, a package arrived from Dalton and Goodrich with the complete file on Charles and Gladys. "It will not be long," Harrison wrote. He didn't use their names. "The man will be apprehended. The woman is a dope addict. We know the doctor who gets the drugs for her. It is pitiful. And it upsets me frightfully—but I must be calm—it is difficult with Dorothy about one."

Small progress. Another call from Joe with more details on the Crookses. A picture of their life in Mexico emerged. They were living well—a grand house, a grand Packard, and a chauffeur. By now word had reached them that Harrison was back in the United States. Joe said they were nervous.

"As they should be," Harrison wrote. At least he could have that satisfaction.

And he was closer now to drawing the ordeal to an end. He was full of hope and so he went shopping. He bought ski trousers, a ski hat, woolen socks, mittens, ski boots, and sheepskin-lined overshoes. It was early March now, and if he got back to Norway by the end of the month, there'd still be snow.

Then, with an end to his strange ordeal finally in sight, Harrison slept through the night. "That helps always," he wrote. "I am weary of lapses (Thank God no doctors this time) and I long to stop at San Francisco and then soon Norway—and then establish a home of some sort—I am really an alien in the United States."

25

LAKE STREET

At last he was out of the sunshine.

Of all the places Harrison stayed when he came back from Europe, he was happiest at Bob and Madeleine's house on Lake Street in San Francisco. By mid-March he'd fled Dorothy and her sodden tirades.

Here, he had quiet afternoons in the garden and long walks with Gynt. The house was a block from the Presidio. The Starretts told him to stay as long as he liked, and Madeleine insisted that Harrison take the master bedroom with the fieldstone fireplace. This may have been a favor to Madeleine, since it meant she and Bob would sleep in separate bedrooms.

The Starretts hadn't had children. Likely this was because they were first cousins, but it also seems that their marriage wasn't rooted in passion. Once upon a time it may have been, but it wasn't that spring when Harrison arrived.

Back when Madeleine's mother first welcomed Harrison into her home, the Starretts were newly married, living in Los Angeles where Bob worked for a construction company. His father, Theodore, had been one of five brothers who formed Starrett Brothers, Inc., the engineering company that had helped usher in the skyscraper boom and built the Empire State Building, the Flatiron Building, Penn Station, and the Plaza and Biltmore Hotels. A highly successful and extremely combative man, Theodore died in 1917 before the company's peak years, but he was a significant figure in the industry's rise and expansion. His legacy loomed oppressively large in his son's life, and Bob never seemed to carve his own path.

By the time Harrison arrived in Los Angeles in 1919, the Starretts had moved to Nevada City and then briefly to Japan, where Bob took work for the George Fuller Company. But he never held a job long and was often out of work, as he was when Harrison arrived that spring. He was also an alcoholic, and though initially welcoming, his moods swung quickly. Harrison found him "peppery."

Madeleine, meanwhile, had built a significant career as an executive at the City of Paris department store at Union Square, a San Francisco institution that hailed back to the Gold Rush, when Félix and Émile Verdier first arrived from France with a stock of dry goods. The brothers never made it to shore, though. Before their ship, *La Ville de Paris*, docked, they'd sold out of their inventory of wine, brandy, silks, and lace, and so they headed back to Europe, restocked, and returned to establish a brick-and-mortar store named for the ship. Now, almost a hundred years later, Émile's grandson Paul oversaw the beaux arts emporium crowned with a glass rotunda depicting the illustrious first voyage.

And Madeleine was one of the vice presidents, unusual for a woman at that time. Stylish, with dark brown hair, and, according to Harrison, "a good figure," his foster sister drove a Cadillac, played the piano at dinner parties, and was innately generous, warm, and loyal. In a story marked by greed and dissipation, she remains steadfast and kind.

She was also incensed by Joe's demands and the fact that he hadn't made any real progress on Harrison's behalf. While the attorney wanted a list of what he could pawn, Madeleine was prepared to mortgage the house on Lake Street to get Harrison the funds he needed.

His first day there, he arranged his room. He wrote letters. After a dinner—Madeleine was a marvelous cook—he brought out his photo albums and they talked and looked through them together. When he went to bed that night, he felt the happiest he'd been in years. No sleeping pills. The next morning, he was calm and rested in a way he'd forgotten he could feel.

After a few days of respite, he got a call from Joe and Ann. They'd just arrived in San Francisco from Los Angeles. As usual, Joe had nothing of substance to report but still talked and talked. They inquired about having Trygga stay with them as a house servant. Harrison was glad the Norwegian took the job—it meant he'd be in San Francisco—but he also felt badly for Trygga being stuck in Joe and Ann's volatile home.

For those first weeks at Lake Street, Harrison finally had a sense of stability and ease. He "pottered." He went for drives. He took Gynt on long walks in the Presidio and then took a trolley car back to the house.

Some days he went to the City of Paris with Madeleine and stopped in at her office and chatted with Madame Raymond, another executive there. One of the illustrators did a sketch of Gynt. There was talk of running it in an ad.

Sometimes he and Madeleine went to the movies, then stopped for Chinese food. They drove to the St. Francis Riding Academy and rode horses through Golden Gate Park.

It's unclear how open Harrison was with his foster sister about his sexuality, but Madeleine had no illusions and introduced him to Jordan, a window designer at the department store. Within a few days Harrison had a routine of going out with Jordan and his "young friend Wallace," making a circuit of the bars—usually first to the Tonga Room at the Fairmont, then the Zebra Room at the Huntington, and finally to Finocchio's for a midnight show with drag performers.

Harrison and Jordan spent days visiting art galleries or watching horse races at Bay Meadows. They drove down to Monterey and Pebble Beach and dined at the Mission Ranch. Their connection was a platonic one and Harrison was grateful for it. "Jordan has been really kind to me," he wrote.

Back in the Gold Rush days, San Francisco had been a city of single men, and in the wake of World War II it was again, though this era wasn't marked by fortune-seeking but the reprieve from war and death. The soldiers had been decommissioned. The hotel bars were usually packed with men interested in other men, though these weren't gay bars in a contemporary sense but public spaces where gay men could congregate without drawing police attention. With Jordan, Wallace, and their friends, Harrison also ventured out to spots like the Chi-Chi Club, the Black Pansy, Mr. Chips, the Chinese Cellar, and other "low-down places," as he called them.

March 29 arrived—Will's birthday. As he did every year, Harrison made a note of it in his journal. Beyond that, the day passed with little ceremony.

Meanwhile, Joe had at last taken some steps. He'd arranged for Harrison to meet with the society editor at the *San Francisco Chronicle* and give an interview—a preemptive strike, getting Harrison's story out first. This pleased Harrison. "I shall not be 'besmeared,'" he wrote.

For a time, Harrison appeared to be more settled. His anticipated return to Norway gave him new confidence. He still got riled by Joe and Ann but he also had a new level of equanimity. "Talked with Ann and then Joe—they are steadily developing a 'grandeur complex,'" he wrote. "However, the end should be near—we can beautifully get on apart."

On April 19, Madeleine and Bob woke him at seven in the morning singing "Happy Birthday." They gave him a bookplate and clock. He took a walk with Gynt. Jordan arrived with a beautiful wallet and they went for a drive across the bay in Marin. Trygga called to wish him happy birthday. Harrison knew he wasn't happy with Joe and Ann, and he reassured him that it would be over soon and they'd be on their way back to Hellesylt.

Later, he took a nap and then went for dinner at Joe and Ann's. Her sons, Paul and Gordon, were there, and Harrison was charmed by the boys and the whole evening: "Grand food—grand drinks—good conversation." But these were rare times with Joe and Ann.

Usually they started with highballs. Then wine with dinner—several bottles. In San Francisco, there were many nights like this, or rather, there were many days that turned into nights like this.

Ostensibly Harrison and the Starretts kept meeting with Joe and Ann to discuss the case against Gladys and Charles, though at some point the group would adjourn to the Tonga Room or other nightspots, and more often than not, these so-called conferences devolved into nasty, drunken spats. Despite or because of their shared history, Harrison and Ann's clashes were the harshest. Reconciliation usually came a day or two later.

It was during one of these "huddles," as Harrison called them, that Joe made a jibe about Harrison needing carfare. Considering what he'd pawned to get Joe money, it was an outrageous insult, which was likely Joe's intention. Harrison took the bait. The evening quickly degenerated, and in the aftermath, wounded and indignant, he decided to set Joe straight. Harrison rolled a sheet of airmail paper into the typewriter.

The letters we write but don't send. Beseeching, strident, aggrieved declarations of love, apology, injury in voices that are so clearly, so embarrassingly our own. In his journals, Harrison admonished himself to stay calm, to take things coolly, and he was likely telling himself those same things when he began to write, but in sentences that go running, comma after comma, his letter to Joe is hardly the expression of the calm, measured voice Harrison wanted to possess. Instead, it's a wounded blurt that threatens to go on and on.

And so began his story of himself, jumbled, misspelled, acerbic, and lofty. He laid out his mother's background in Galveston, his grandfather's theater empire, but he soon digressed:

> you spoke belittling? and spoke of my "background" and that I didn't have carfare for street cars etc. etc. and I told you directly that my background is alright, only I am ashamed of Gladys and with me, at least, I don't lie (I do evade many things fo rth reason I thought it wa s no bodys business, and I dont steal, I resented that evening, more because I invited you, and my sister cooked the dinner and I washed the dises, and unfortunately, I cant change my self, any more than you can, I am hype r-sensitive, mostly at this time, do you under-stand?

There were older injuries too. These stretched back before the Crookses had betrayed and cheated him, before he'd even known Will, and he spilled this out, too, for Joe:

> At school, it was then the Hitchcok Military Academy, my father died, Gladys got most at the time, she had only seen him but a short visits, I had to live with him, I had $50 a month and not for long, I was "Gypped" out of that, then the adoption of Mother Post, a charming old Lady and a brilliant one, then "the Marsh," I worked hard, they did nothing for me at any time, it was when I become rich and they liked me then, you see the charming way they do things for me. The only happiness I have every had has been in Norway, and I shall go back there as soon as possible as I am an Alien here, an d this time here I will not be "sweet". At the same time I do not want to be embittered, we will take this whole

> case as a Laugh, and results, all that I have told you you can look up I have not needed street cars(figurately) thenortoday and I hope not in the future, I hope to walk in Norway.
>
> I hope we will have no further misunderstandings of any sort, we have much to do, both of us, also it is hardon the nerves, but it is better than being stepped upon, no one likes that.

It's possible that Harrison wrote a second draft, one that was more polished and cogent, and sent that. But whatever the sequence of events was that led Harrison to sit down at the typewriter, the night of drunken outrage was one among many, one more rotation in the highly fraught and seemingly endless cycle of insult, indignation, recrimination, and reconciliation that marked the men's relationship.

After the dinner at Madeleine and Bob's, it would've been dark. So when Harrison looked out the kitchen window, he wouldn't have seen the street. He would've seen himself reflected in the glass, standing at the sink. That night on Lake Street, smarting from the jab about carfare, shirtsleeves rolled up, hands in soapy dishwater, he was still a man dreaming of home.

It was nearly May. Eight months now since he'd arrived in the States. Harrison was no closer to Gladys, his money, or getting back to Norway. The ski season was over. And still Joe called late at night, drunk, with no plans.

Madeleine, though, took action. On April 25, she drove Harrison to the Mexican consulate and they got their visas. Later they drove out to the Cliff House for cocktails and gazed out at the ocean.

The next day, Harrison and Gynt walked all the way to the Legion of Honor and watched the ships pass under the bridge. Then he went to see *My Reputation* starring Barbara Stanwyck as a widow whose romance with an army officer scandalizes her friends and family. Back at Lake Street, Harrison spent the rest of the day writing letters. By now this was routine—a walk with Gynt, a movie, and then letters, but this day was different. He wrote to Gladys.

They hadn't spoken in nearly a decade. Never once during the war had she tried to find out if he was dead or alive. Possibly, she'd hoped for the worst for him. He'd sent her cables when the war ended and never heard back, and then he'd learned why. Over these past years she'd become an abstraction, a villain certainly, greedy and cruel, but with the visa in hand, he was drawing closer to the actual person.

What, after all this time, could Harrison have written? Maybe he pleaded for her to take pity on him. Maybe he marshaled a sense of autonomy and demanded she make restitution. Maybe he wrote that he loved her.

Whatever he wrote, he regretted it as soon as he put the letter in the mail.

"I feel I was stupid to write 'G.'" Even that was too much to see in his diary and he scratched out her initial. "I realize she has no feeling for me—her life has been 'on the make'—however there is nothing to do about it—I must think first—my impulses cause me much trouble."

On May 6, Joe called from Mexico City.

Harrison packed his bag. Joe was supposed to arrange for Harrison to fly to Brownsville, but he didn't, and again the trip was postponed. Now Ann was coming, too, which he knew would only complicate the plan. And then, instead of Brownsville, he was supposed to go to El Paso, and then that plan was scrapped.

He was glad to have a home to come back to and for Madeleine's garden—the roses were blooming—but he'd wearied of his nights in San Francisco. Zebra Room, Chi-Chi, Finocchio's. It was pleasant and yet so very futile and stupid. "And I will become very old—definitely—I want my funny Hotel."

He went out to clear his head and made the rounds at the bars alone, but he was still anxious when he got home, still up at three in the morning writing in his journal, and still woozy from his cocktails. "I feel as though I was in air—and passed out with Gynt beside—me."

The next day, a hangover awaited him, but finally so did his flight. Harrison and Madeleine touched down in Burbank where they fortified themselves with martinis, but they weren't able to find a second flight together, so she boarded a plane to Tucson and he to El Paso. After months of false starts, at last Harrison was in motion. He checked in at the Hotel Cortez. Overlooking the San Jacinto Plaza, it reminded him of an old Spanish castle. The elderly woman at the front desk told him that he would be happy with his suite and he was.

Now, after so many disappointments, he felt a surge of hope. Tomorrow he would fly to Mexico City. "Everything is perfect, but the 'villains'—very real ones," he wrote that night. "I think I thrive on excitement. It is life."

26

THE EMPEROR'S PALACE

The plane out of El Paso was supposed to leave at six that morning, but they didn't have a seat for Harrison. He would have to wait until the next day—ever more waiting. The airline offered to pay for his taxis, the hotel, and his food, which pacified him. Still, he was eager to get to Joe and meet his new lawyer and "hurry up the grief."

But for now he was stuck. Yet another setback in a long line. He took a taxi to the bridge at the border and walked across to Juárez for lunch. Later, he went to a movie, and then back to the hotel. He was in a reflective mood. He wouldn't be able to live in a town like this with the sun relentlessly beating down and the dry hot air. "I cannot be happy with warm weather," he wrote. "I am only really happy on a mountain top—snow-capped." But to get back to his beloved ski slopes, he needed to steel himself first for the coming days in Mexico City. "I shall win out if I will be 'cool.' It will not be easy—for in 1934 my life was 'snapped'—and now—pillar to Post—and above all, what to do? I am terribly alone."

He went out looking for company that night and crossed the bridge to Juárez a second time. He was coy about what he found there, though nonetheless emphatic: "It was very amusing."

The flight the next morning was full, but Harrison got a seat. Madeleine was waiting at the airport with Jess Dalton, and after the belabored routine with customs, they set out for the hotel.

Harrison pegged Dalton as a "square shooter"—a relief after all the double-talking and soft-soaping from Joe, who was waiting in his room when they arrived at Posada del Sol on Calle Niños Héroes.

With Ann, they all got in the car and the group drove straightaway to the Crookses' home.

As they wound through the wide curving streets, past grand houses with large walled gardens, it was clear that Gladys and Charles still had money—Harrison's money. The car turned from the Paseo de la Reforma onto a small side street in Lomas de Chapultepec.

Harrison got out with the others and walked to the door. Joe took the lead, stepping forward, pounding with his fist. Someone answered on the other side. Harrison couldn't make out the words, but he knew the voice. He would know it anywhere.

Two men had brought Harrison close to death—Gerhard Flesch and Charles Crooks. The Nazi prison commander who'd taunted and mocked Harrison was in a Norwegian prison now, awaiting trial, but Crooks was free—right there on the other side of the door.

Harrison couldn't speak. Joe banged again, shouting: "Here is the man who wouldn't dare come to Mexico City. He demands his money and possessions. At once." There was a scuffling, and then silence. The door stayed shut.

They went back to Dalton's car and waited. Another car arrived. A man got out—this, Dalton said, was the doctor. And then another car, another man. This was their lawyer. The two men went into the building. Outside, Harrison and his party waited. No one else came out. No one else went in. Eventually, admitting defeat for the day, they left and went out to dinner and then back to the hotel. They would try again tomorrow.

The next day was hot. Harrison and Joe went to Dalton's office and talked for nearly four hours. After Joe's alcoholic clubman antics and his calls to society editors, which had yielded few results, Harrison was grateful to have someone on the case who had a sense of order and process. Jess Dalton was well established in Mexico City. He'd represented Sylvia Ageloff, Leon Trotsky's secretary, and gotten her cleared of being an accessory to the murder of the Russian revolutionary in 1940.

Like Joe, Dalton appeared to understand the tools necessary to obtain police cooperation, but that wasn't his only area of expertise. He was also skilled at bringing actual cases to trial and reaching settlements. He knew the expatriate world, the law, and how to make things happen in Mexico City.

His plan was simple. First, they'd bribe two policemen to put the Crookses in jail, and then they'd search the house. Harrison would go through and identify all the things that would be returned to him. It was like something out of a novel, but so much of Harrison's life had been like that. This would be no different.

The next morning, their driver, Maja, took Harrison and Madeleine to tour the Chapultepec Castle. They strolled the grounds where Emperor Maximilian, the puppet sovereign of the Second Mexican Empire, had his short and tragic reign during the last gasps of the French monarchy.

Napoleon III installed Maximilian in Mexico in 1864, a disastrous attempt to establish a foothold for France in the Americas. During his rule, the emperor oversaw the neoclassical renovation of the castle perched on Chapultepec Hill, as well as the creation of a wide, imposing thoroughfare, Paseo de la Emperatriz, in honor of his wife, Charlotte. But as France's military came under increasing strain with faltering campaigns in Italy and elsewhere, Napoleon III withdrew his troops from Mexico, abandoning Maximilian to Republican forces, who then captured and executed the forsaken emperor in 1867. In the new republic, the boulevard became Paseo de la Reforma. Back in Europe, Empress Charlotte descended into paranoia and depression. She spent her remaining years in a Belgian castle under the care of doctors and her brother-in-law Archduke Karl Ludwig of Austria until her death in 1927.

In his scrapbook, Harrison collected news clippings about exiled aristocrats and displaced royalty, companions in limbo and dislocation. If he reflected on his own parallels with Empress Charlotte, the widowed consort whose mind had snapped, he made no mention in his diary. He was deeply awed, in any case, by the castle's expansive view over the rippling canopy of green.

Later, he and Madeleine passed by the Crookses' home again. They saw the car, a gleaming Packard, and drove on to the Ritz for drinks.

The next day, Maja took them again to the Crookses'. Even in the morning the heat was strong. It's unclear what Harrison hoped to obtain from these stakeouts. He may have been stalking the Crookses so he could report to Dalton on their doings. He wasn't about to barge in on them himself and demand his furniture and books, but it seemed to be the only way he knew to order his days, to feel that something was being accomplished.

For four days now, they'd driven over to Calle Alpes and parked and waited. He was worried and hot. He missed the snow. He was tired and he missed his hill. Sometimes in Norway it had been too quiet, too dull, but he would be happy just to be bored. He was ready to be done with all of it—Joe, Ann, the lawyers, the police, the huddles, the drinks, the heat.

And then, after all those years, there *he* was: not a memory Harrison was trying to suppress, but the actual man who'd terrorized him. Charles Crooks walked across the yard in his bathing trunks. Harrison watched his brother-in-law settle himself on the chaise, eyes closed, nothing between his bare chest and the hard sun. In the hot gloom of the car, Harrison stared, frozen in place.

That was Thursday. Now it was Saturday, the day that Charles and Gladys were supposed to be taken into custody. But the Crookses were still inside their home with Harrison's money and his things, and he was outside in the back of the chauffeured car waiting.

After a couple hours, he returned to the hotel, where he found Joe in an ebullient mood. Dalton had gotten them passes to the Reforma Club, the University Club, and the Bonham—all very exclusive. Only three Americans were members at the Reforma, Joe crowed, and Harrison could be made an honorary citizen of Mexico.

"All this is charming," Harrison wrote, "but doesn't make shoes for the baby."

More days, more sightseeing, more late nights out, and more, many more, drinks. Joe and Ann fought at dinner. They fought in their hotel room. They fought in Harrison's hotel room. There was more back and forth with the police and the lawyers and more fights.

He continued the stakeouts in the mornings and sightseeing in the afternoons. With Madeleine he ventured out to the pyramids at Teotihuacan. He collected postcards and snapshots. It all would've been fascinating but for the heat—and the dread.

Round and round it went. El Patio, the Ritz, the Waikiki Club. At

Ciro's, Harrison saw Blumey doing fine for himself, presiding over the swanky nightclub. "He looked like a parakeet," Harrison wrote.

He wired Judge Sanner for money. There was more back and forth with the police and more lawyers, more fights between Joe and Ann, both of them keeping Harrison up until all hours. The next day, Joe dragged him to the races. All Harrison wanted was sleep.

Sanner wired back $500 and with that they returned to the police, now more sympathetic than the day before. An official at the American embassy said they'd be content to see the Crookses rot in jail. It was promising and yet Harrison was no closer to his money than he'd been when Joe banged on their door.

Then, nearly two weeks after he'd arrived, Gladys called him at the hotel. She asked to see him. Harrison didn't want to see his sister. He wanted the police to see her.

Even if all of it—the drugs, the nurses, the Dictaphones, the theft—had been Charles's plan, and even if Gladys had been sorry for any of it, she'd signed every form, stood by as the movers packed up his antiques and silver, sold his books off, and she'd let Charles and the men in white do whatever they wanted.

Nine years had passed since Harrison had boarded the M/S *Laurits Swenson* with Trygga and sailed for Norway. In all the time he'd been trapped by the occupation, held in the camps, hoping to recover and return, she'd never tried to reach him, never tried to make sure he was safe. His death would've been a relief to her.

The next day, he sat for an interview with a reporter from the United Press and then went for drinks at Dalton's house. Gladys called again. He picked up the phone and there was her voice. Already, the "sob story" began. She wanted him to come see her, but not with Joe.

Harrison was tired of his terrible quest, of being trapped with his drunk friends careening through Mexico City. He was tired of the dread and the waiting. He wanted to be back in Norway. If he wanted to get back, he was going to have do this.

He agreed to go. Gladys's lawyer arrived and took him to her home.

It'd been almost a decade. Of course, he was changed, and so was she—gray, but she looked well enough.

His diary entry about their meeting contains few details. That wasn't unusual, but it stands out from other entries. Rarely did Harrison quote people. However, in this case he transcribed the exchange with Gladys.

> the same story—Harrison, what are you doing to me—I said Gladys what have you done to me? Then I said is Crooks here?—I don't want to see him at all—and she said "he is a crook, a real one"—and then she said I know I owe you some money—but we haven't any—so, I said Gladys what have you done with all my money?—she said I only owe you a little—you spent all your money

It was preposterous. He certainly hadn't spent all his money. She was living as if there was still plenty of it, plenty of *his* money.

They knew each other's lies. They'd shared each other's lies. Once upon a time they'd told them together, their fabulous tale of being orphaned in Montana, adopted by a wealthy senator, how they'd been sent abroad to savor the riches of the world. She'd been a countess and he a country gentleman.

But Harrison had been circumspect. His name wasn't a lie. He'd never given himself a false title. He'd never dared his sister's fictions. He'd always had more to lose, and she had always counted on that.

Now, though, her lies were so outrageous that they didn't even make sense. He wondered if she was on drugs. She left the room and when she came back she had a ring, a cigarette lighter, a pocket watch, and more of the sob story. This, she claimed, was all she had to give him, all that was left. It couldn't possibly be true, but she was someone who believed her own lies, and perhaps she believed this one now.

After all the time it'd taken to find her, to reclaim the life she'd stolen from him, here she was handing him a few stray trinkets. He took them. They fit in one pocket—the sum of all those years. He didn't seem to feel anger or even shock. Fatigue swept through him like a wave. He asked her lawyer to call him a taxi.

Harrison left Gladys with her lies and got in the cab. It took him back to Dalton's. Joe was there. He had nothing to offer, except to say that Harrison should ask Madeleine for fifty dollars.

The US embassy didn't trust the Crookses. A 1944 FBI memo on Charles reported: "His actions have resulted in considerable embarrassment to the Embassy in Mexico inasmuch as he has made statements running down the Embassy and American government officials. He is known to have some excellent connections among Mexican officials."

Crooks had arrived in Mexico touting a scheme to build an aviation school. It never materialized. Next he made calls to oil executives and talked about buying hotels and bus lines. None of it happened. Now he was trying to get an export license so he could bring used cars from America over the border for resale.

Ambassador Messersmith had no illusion about Charles Crooks, an obvious con man. The diplomat wanted Mexico to declare him persona non grata, but for all the shadiness of his connections and dealings, Messersmith couldn't find real cause. In some of his pitches, Crooks allegedly impersonated members of the American embassy, but there was no evidence. Crooks had violated regulations for petroleum rations, using gasoline for an unauthorized purpose, and he'd misrepresented his credentials to the State Department to get priority treatment on a flight from Mexico City to Washington, DC. He'd delayed submission of his draft card. Still, none of these offenses was so grave as to warrant expelling him from the country. And so he'd remained, palling about with Hilde Krüger and other shadowy figures of the cosmopolitan elite, ingratiating himself with Mexican authorities while denigrating the American State Department.

In 1920s Los Angeles, the shadow world had existed in plain sight. Harrison thrived in that giddy, reckless decade. He'd been young and glamorous, and with Will Clark's money, he'd walked into any club he wanted, owned beautiful homes, traveled the world, lived among the fashionable and the powerful, but all that was gone. So were the shadows. They'd drifted down to Mexico City, along with Will's money.

With that fortune, Harrison had transformed himself from shop clerk to Hollywood aristocrat and country gentleman. And now, with what was left of that same money, Charles Crooks, too, parlayed himself into someone new. His invention, though, was a coarse one, still bearing the traces of a grandstanding car salesman. With Harrison, it'd been an act of refinement, and yet both men had crafted their personas thanks to the same source.

A crude bully and a braggart, Crooks was the one thing Harrison Post couldn't bear: a vulgarian. But that didn't matter to the police.

Sydney Sanner might wire Harrison $500 and the police might take it and turn friendly for a few hours, but after five years in Mexico City, Crooks's network was an extensive one, and Harrison had stepped into the vulgarian's world.

The plan to take the Crookses into custody had evaporated. At least, unlike Joe, Dalton spoke plainly. From the hotel, Harrison called the lawyer and asked what there was for him to do if Gladys wasn't going to make restitution. Dalton replied that Joe needed to have the Crookses extradited to the States. Here, there was no way to get to them.

"I am weary unto death," he wrote. He wanted to leave the next day. Just as he was getting into bed, Ann showed up with a bumper of bourbon, obviously untroubled by the disaster the trip had become. To her it all seemed a lark—a band of socialites trying to solve a crime.

Pause for a moment to review: Ann was Harrison's old friend from the riding club days. She'd been married and divorced to an oil magnate who happened to buy many of Harrison's beloved books and then later took a Nazi spy for his mistress and then smuggled her to Mexico where she, in turn, befriended Harrison's sister and brother-in-law. As if those connections weren't convoluted enough, now Ann was married to Harrison's lawyer. The web of wealth and status that had suspended Harrison for years had become a sticky, smothering snarl.

Ann insisted Harrison stay on in Mexico. He wanted out. "I don't know what to do," he wrote. "So I think I will try to rest—and hope that Lord will direct me. Golly: I am weary."

The next day, Joe made calls but they weren't for extradition orders. He was back to his usual methods, phoning reporters. He set up an interview with the Hearst papers. Harrison stopped at Dalton's house for some drinks, and then he placed a call to Gladys.

For another person, this might've been a calculated move to disarm one's opponent with a faux naïve show of goodwill. Harrison wasn't a strategic thinker, though. He relied on others for power and protection. Perhaps he thought it would be easier to get what he wanted if he was "soft," the very thing he'd claimed he wouldn't be back when he was aboard the *Stavangerfjord*. Perhaps by now submission was a reflex. Certainly wishful thinking was, and that may have been what spurred him to phone his sister. He'd always been an easy mark for her.

Gladys arrived at eleven. In her gleaming car, they drove through the park up to the castle. There, Harrison roamed the palace grounds with the person who'd sabotaged his life, stolen his fortune, and showed no remorse, no fear that he might be killed during war. Gladys had been jailor, extortionist, and thief, but as much as she'd hurt him, he seemed to still love her and he still wanted to think she might love him. For Harrison, their bond, poisonous as it was, remained.

As children, they'd been nomads together, bouncing up and down the Eastern Seaboard, left with their alcoholic father in Gloucester. Later, they were fabulists together in the Villa dei Sogni, inventing a childhood that knew loss but never poverty. He was unable to vanquish his sister, the person who'd known him—Albert—since his beginning.

The former consort and the fake countess strolled the palace of the doomed emperor. From the marble terrace they gazed out over the treetops. How far they were from the boardinghouse by the sea, and yet Harrison was still a vagabond, still aching for a home.

Afterward, she came to the hotel and they met with Joe. It was the same as before: "Complete confession of guilt—she then said that we would be received in a few hours—'Charles' telephoned." He could not write his brother-in-law's name without quotation marks. Whatever Harrison might've hoped from his afternoon at the castle with Gladys, it was obvious nothing had changed.

Over the next couple days, the phone calls continued: "More lies—and today more lies from Gladys and Crooks." Joe made his calls to the press. "etc. etc. etc.," wrote Harrison. "I am weary enough to die."

With Joe at the lead, Harrison was being yanked through nightclubs and racetracks by a quarrelsome alcoholic, not a mastermind. Still no plan, only chaos.

Previously, Dalton had sketched out a scenario that involved paying the police to arrest Gladys and Charles, a common-enough practice apparently. It would've been a poetic reversal of fortune indeed to have his sister taken prisoner, but now weeks into this folly, it was evident that the Crookses were the ones with leverage, with more means to bribe the police, and, to follow that logic to its grim conclusion, this meant that if anyone was going to be taken captive, it would likely be Harrison.

He often counseled himself not to think too much, and if he thought about the chance that he could be a hostage again—if he ever allowed that possibility to bubble into his consciousness—he didn't put it down on paper. Still, whether or not Harrison articulated the risk to himself, he knew well enough by now that *any*thing was possible, no safety was guaranteed, certainly not while he was within his sister's reach.

On Wednesday, May 29, he woke at four in the morning with chills, a fever, and a sore throat: "Bronchial tubes—laryngitis." The strain of all these futile days in this hot city, the phone calls, the drinks, the lies.

And perhaps the thoughts—the ones he tried to keep at bay—had arrived after all. He felt ghastly, terrified the aches would worsen, that a reaction was coming next. His mind had already snapped once, his life more than that.

Flight. He knew that much. He got out of bed and packed his things. He left Mexico the next morning.

27

"SCHÖNER GIGOLO, ARMER GIGOLO"

His bungalow at Hotel Miramar in Santa Monica had a view of the ocean. After several hypos from the doctor and two days of rest, he felt human—enough to sit in the sun with reporters and talk and drink and smoke. He remembered the *Herald*'s cameraman from a party years ago at Will's home.

Joe had orchestrated the press blitz. Harrison felt a momentary pang at its effects on his sister, but that quickly faded. He owed thousands now—Trygga, Madeleine, Judge Sanner, Joe. So many other friends had loaned him money these past months. Above all, he hated that this would drag Will's name into the fray.

"I feel he knows I am trying to do the right thing," Harrison wrote. "God help me."

Gladys said the money was all gone, except for the ring, lighter, and pocket watch she'd given him, and he showed these items to the journalists now. They took photos and he told them it was obvious more remained.

In the wake of the disastrous trip to Mexico City, there was at last movement in Los Angeles. They met with the district attorney and an extradition order was filed for the Crookses to be remanded to the United States to appear before court on charges of fraud and false imprisonment. Then Harrison got on a Greyhound bus. It was crowded, but he was grateful to leave Los Angeles, a place that no longer felt like home.

Back at Lake Street, Madeleine, Bob, and Trygga greeted him, and he fell asleep that night with Gynt beside him.

On Sunday, June 9, the news broke: TWO ASSERTED SWINDLERS SOUGHT IN $500,000 CASE. And SWINDLE STORY INQUIRY SLATED. And NAZIS' CAPTIVE CLAIMS FRAUD. The radio was full of it as well.

Finally he was telling his story, and despite his earlier apprehension about bringing Will's name into the press, Harrison was relieved. *The New York Times* quoted the petition he'd filed at the courthouse, which asserted that Gladys had called on him "at his hotel in Mexico City and informed him that her husband had persuaded her to use his monies, that she and her husband had spent most of the money and they would endeavor to make restitution."

Photos showed him holding out the paltry remains of his once-vast estate. In most articles he was identified either as Guy Bates Post's half brother or as the secretary and confidant to William Andrews Clark Jr. An *Examiner* story described him as "an aging art connoisseur." In his scrapbook he underlined the words in blue ink.

Two days later, Charles Crooks fired back. BROTHER-IN-LAW CALLS POST COMPLAINT SMEAR was the headline. "Mrs. Crooks and Post are devoted to one another and someone only is trying to drive a wedge between them," Crooks claimed. "When he came to Mexico a short time ago, she left a sickbed against her doctor's orders just to see him."

With all the headlines, Harrison began hearing from old friends. The names in his journal piled up again.

Richard Harrison called. Harrison's younger brother lived in Sacramento now and had opened an insurance company. "He was very nice," Harrison wrote, "but I would rather not see him for I think at last I am hard-boiled, at least I hope so."

Some friends, though, had stopped returning his calls, presumably keeping their distance from any scandal, even if Harrison was the victim.

Still, the public pressure had an effect. Joe called to report that Charles Crooks had phoned Jess Dalton and offered $10,000 and whatever was left of Harrison's effects. Harrison's response was unequivocal: "I told Mc he could stick it up his ass—the hell with him—we will see in court." He busied himself making Dalton an inventory of the things that Gladys and Charles had taken. And, for the first time since he'd returned to the United States, Harrison considered a new avenue. "I am going to get a job in a couple weeks—and in a year or so—I will have enough money to live in Norway comfortably—and that's that."

He was forty-nine. He hadn't worked in any professional capacity in more than twenty-five years. It was a sobering prospect, but a realistic one, long overdue. "I need to be 'aware,'" he wrote. "I am dreaming too much."

A few days later, he wrote to Lucien Marsh, the son of his former employer. The Marsh company had expanded beyond the shops in San Francisco and Los Angeles, with thriving boutiques in Monterey and Santa Barbara.

Harrison had a glimmer now of what it might look like to stand on his own, without the dreams of Clark wealth saving him. He'd inherited two homes and $125,000 from Will in 1934. All of it was stolen from him, but he'd had another inheritance, and as he once claimed, he'd been "gypped" out of that—$50 a month from his father's will. Still, Mark Harrison left more behind than a stock of clothing. His father had begun again and again and again.

There was a person Harrison had been years ago: a shop clerk, the son of a merchant. Briefly, before Harrison left Norway, he'd entertained a thought about working as a bookbinder in Oslo, though he never returned to the prospect. However, now he considered getting a job with the very company he worked for before he met Will—before, as he once admitted to himself, his real worries began.

Working for the Marsh family offered a path that Harrison had known long ago, before the hideous years and even before the charmed ones. For all his childish naiveté and fantasies, he was capable, at last, of seeing things as they were, and, for once, relinquishing the enfeebling entitlement he'd learned in the Clark empire. It had been a grand and expansive world, and it had also been a cage.

For the first time, he saw that his freedom didn't have to come from a settlement with Gladys or an allowance doled out by Judge Sanner, but from himself. He'd been shackled to Gladys through the bond of family, of shared history, and over these past listless, frenzied months, the demand for restitution, for what was rightfully his, had bound him ever more tightly to his sister, even as he'd strained to break free.

And yet there was a way out and forward. It wasn't dramatic. It didn't involve lawyers or elaborate schemes. He simply had to take one step on his own and then another.

He went to see Charles Vidor's new movie *Gilda*. Set in Buenos

Aires, the film stars Rita Hayworth and Glenn Ford in a love triangle that plays out among a small-time gambler, a nightclub singer, and a casino owner who's using his operation as a front for an illegal tungsten cartel run by German gangsters. Rita Hayworth is on the movie poster, but the real love affair, unspoken yet always simmering, is between the two men.

The film opens with a hold-up in a dark alley and the casino owner saving the gambler, an encounter that gives rise to the movie's iconic line.

"I was born last night when you met me in that alley," Ford's Johnny Farrell says to his rescuer. The phrase returns throughout the film, as the men battle over and scorn Hayworth's Gilda, a pawn in their not-so-latent desire for each other.

Harrison might as well have said those same words to Will Clark when the copper scion plucked the young shop clerk out of the Marsh and swept him into a new life of wealth and glamour. But the line that lingered now was the film's last one, Rita Hayworth's final plea: "Let's go home."

The days were full of fog that summer. He was happy for that. In Norway, he'd been a tiny figure in the landscape, and he was again now, strolling out to the edge of the Pacific with Gynt at his side. He let the dog have a good run along the surf, and afterward, at the Cliff House, a hot dog and ice cream for himself and a hamburger for the whippet.

On Sunday, June 23, he finished inventorying his assets and then he joined the Starretts for a drink. Bob was already well sloshed by the time they started, full of bitter jabs, and it dawned on Harrison that even though Madeleine seemed happy to have him there, Bob was not. "It takes a barn door before I 'get' the facts." It depressed him, but for now he was trapped.

The press flurry had faded, and though some friends had disappeared after his weeks of publicity, others hadn't. Einnim McNear Train, a divorced socialite and daughter of the late George McNear, once known as "grain king" of California, was one of his newest companions. They spent afternoons together, which turned into evenings and late nights and then mornings. It seemed an affair had developed.

Meanwhile, he was back to making the rounds with Jordan and Wally at the Zebra Room and the Camellia Room. As much as he may have longed for quiet, Harrison couldn't embrace it. Perhaps he couldn't let himself be still, knowing that soon he would have to face the Crooks. September 13 was drawing close.

It had all been much harder and taken much longer than he'd expected. At this rate, he'd be getting back after the winter snows began. Still, there were happy signs of progress. Lawrence Clark Powell had agreed to the requests Harrison submitted for his things at the library. In early July, a parcel arrived with the miniature of Josephine, the brooch that Frances Marion had demanded. He gave it to Madeleine and she was thrilled.

A few days later, a second delivery came with his statue of Pan, a silver tea set, and a pair of seventeenth-century Spanish candlesticks. These arrivals cheered him, but he was still nervous. "Jittery" was the word he used. He was glad to get a call from Dorothy. She said she'd been worried about him, and later he tried to master his nerves by taking Gynt for a long walk, "in my usual Norwegian stride."

The countess wanted him to come south for Van Johnson's birthday. She was throwing a party for the former matinee idol at the Bel-Air Bay Club with two orchestras and 250 guests—Cary Grant and everyone else in pictures. It would cost $6,000. He couldn't summon the interest. Years ago he would have jumped, but now it all seemed foolish. He wanted to rest, to sit at home and read Epictetus and Schopenhauer. Cigarettes weren't scarce anymore, but he still bought fifteen hundred at the City of Paris.

"I long for Norway," he wrote. "Definitely this is my last American tour."

Trygga had returned from visiting relatives in Minneapolis and was staying now at Lake Street, indefinitely, same as Harrison. The Norwegian kept busy helping Madeleine run the house, but Harrison knew they were a strain on the Starretts.

A letter arrived from Jess Dalton and it perturbed him. It seemed to Harrison that the square shooter might have ended up in the Crookses' pocket, though he didn't indicate what gave him that impression. He may have been right. However, it's also possible that Dalton was advocating for the best settlement he thought Harrison could get given the circumstances, which were becoming more urgent.

"Today came some bouncing cheques," he wrote in his diary. "A new thrill—I don't enjoy it." Joe said he'd cover them, but it was a reminder of how precarious his situation had become, how little he could be certain of.

Gynt chewed up a $90 dress Madeleine had bought for her sister-in-law. She was visibly upset. He felt terrible. He couldn't give the dog up. It was clear Harrison needed to go, but where?

He called Lucien Marsh. There was a position at the store in Santa Barbara, but Lucien said it must be definite, not a short stop. "I have much to think on," Harrison wrote.

He returned to the bars. One night in late August, he met a young man named Dan at Mr. Chips. "A pleasant chap," recently back from his tour of duty in Paris and Frankfurt. In his late twenties, Dan was handsome with blue eyes and brown hair. The attraction seemed mutual.

Dan picked him up the next day and they went for a drive. "Drove a long way," Harrison wrote, and then: "'X X X.'" This was a new code, though easy to decipher. He was notably more interested in the young soldier than in Einnim. It remains vague as to how romantic he was with the divorcée—no *X*'s next to her name. He did keep seeing her, and endeavored to keep the two from meeting one another.

A shipment arrived from the Crookses—a case of his bronzes and a number of books. He was glad to have them, but for every step forward, Harrison still seemed inexorably stuck.

Worse, he was out of money. He pawned the last of his jewels, and even as he grew to deplore his aimless nights, he continued: "Straggling home . . . several bars . . . was very drunk." They knew him now at Mr. Chips. A familiar refrain set in:

> Home at five am. A very expensive evening.
>
> Finnochio's, the Chinese place, and after 12, a drink a dollar. Got home at 3 am sober enough.
>
> Just a day—at night—the Richard bar—almost a tragedy.
>
> We got quite stinko.
>
> I got home at 1 am terribly drunk
>
> Drinks and more drinks.

Joe called him two days before the court hearing. Harrison was adamant about his terms: "$250,000 in settlement from the Crooks." He also expected an allowance of 1,000 kroner a month from Sydney Sanner, which would've been roughly $100 then or $1,500 today.

Other people had always controlled his money, and he seemed to assume that would remain the case, and yet there was no sense of where that allowance would come from. A $250,000 settlement was unlikely, even though the Crookses had squandered that much and more with the sale of his home.

Again, his grasp on the realities of his situation seemed tenuous. Will had provided him a salary for a job he never did, but Will was gone and so was the payroll and so was the trust he'd established. Like Buck Mangam, Harrison hadn't prepared himself for life outside the Clark empire.

Julius Brammer was a Jewish librettist born in Moravia in 1877. Trained as an actor, Brammer moved to Vienna, where he found success as a leading figure in the city's Silver Operetta era. After the Anschluss in 1938, he fled to France, where he lived in Juan-les-Pins until his death from a stroke in 1943.

One of Brammer's most famous songs is a tango he wrote in 1924 titled "Schöner Gigolo, armer Gigolo." We know its English version as "Just a Gigolo," about a man who wanders nightclubs as a dancer for hire, singing ruefully, "When the end comes, I know / They'll say 'Just a gigolo' / As life goes on without me."

But Brammer's original verse is far richer in history and compassion than its English derivation. For one thing, the title doesn't condescend. The actual translation is "Beautiful Gigolo, Poor Gigolo," and it tells the story of an Austrian hussar in the wake of the Great War, adrift without his empire, devoid of purpose, still dressing in his uniform, while he mourns his youth, reduced to walking dance floors, hoping for a few francs, and pretending that his heart isn't breaking.

Bing Crosby's rendition hews close to Brammer's original, using the third person to preface the story of the melancholy soldier, though it transports him to one of the victorious nations: "Was in a Paris cafe that first I found him / He was a Frenchman, a hero of the war / But war was over."

In her version, Marlene Dietrich didn't bother with the introduction or the safety of the third person. She didn't keep her distance from the forlorn, wandering soldier. Dietrich understood what it was to live in a world that was unfixed. She was born in 1901 in the German Empire, and by the time she came to America thirty years later, it no longer existed. She understood power, too, about how to wear a tuxedo and how the world around her rippled with electricity when she swaggered, confident and amused, through a nightclub in *Morocco* and kissed a woman on the mouth. She didn't want to understand time, though, which knows the body can't be fixed, that flesh goes slack, the heart grows tired, and youth fades.

Beautiful Harrison, poor Harrison.

On Friday, September 13, he arrived at the superior court in San Francisco. His journals lack the urgency that marked the weeks running up to the trip to Mexico City. Perhaps he felt more assured in his position, or perhaps he already knew what awaited him.

The Crookses weren't there. A new extradition date was set for November 9. He made no reflection in his diary on the matter. He returned to Mr. Chips.

"I am not well," he wrote. "I look like hell."

He wrote again to Lucien Marsh. By now he seemed to truly recognize that the matter with the Crookses would be a drawn-out one, and he told Lucien he was prepared to begin work on October 1.

Letters from friends bolstered him. Carlotta Monterey dutifully sent him books. He seemed happy with Dan. They went to see *A Stolen Life*, a film in which Bette Davis plays twin sisters, one an unassuming painter, the other a con artist who impersonates the good sister to seduce her love interest played by Glenn Ford. In the end, the bad sister dies in a boating accident and the good one is reunited with her love.

"Not bad," he wrote. Afterward, they had drinks at Trad'r Sam's on Geary, and then he walked home, "tired and peaceful."

But he admitted to himself that he was lonely. "Not for one person, just that I could for some moments forget the hideous past, at least the last thirteen years."

A creeping horror attends these entries—a feeling that some essential thread had come unwound, the elastic gone slack, and the events of his life were running on without him.

October 1 came and went and he hadn't started working for Lucien Marsh. Maybe it was too late to try his father's way. He caught himself getting depressed. "I have had for several days the 'all alones.'"

As he had before, he turned to Emmet Fox. On October 4, he resolved to begin a seven-day treatment, a week-long diet of positive thinking.

The next day he took stock, recognizing that he might not be up to the task of owning the hotel in Øye. Whether because of limited funds or stamina, he didn't say, but he was back to considering the modest house on the Korsbrekke hill. "It would cost me very little with a good maid—four hours (really lovely trip) to Aalesund—drive direct to Oslo."

Around five that evening, Trygga gave him a haircut. They had cocktails with Bob and Madeleine and then went out for Chinese food and a movie. Writing on the last page in his notebook, another diary filled, he was reflective: "not one good day in the States—I hope I shall be able to get 'home' some day." And then perhaps before a grim mood could take hold, he remembered he was on the Seven Day Mental Diet. "I hope I have a happy time in the new journal of mine————here's hoping!"

28

LEGACY

Harrison Post died at 6:20 in the evening on October 30, 1946, two weeks before Gladys was due in court. The cause was a heart attack. He was at Bob and Madeleine's house, the last home he knew.

He was forty-nine, eight years younger than Will when he'd died of a heart attack at the Mowitza Lodge. Twenty-seven years earlier, Harrison had traveled to Los Angeles to attend the premiere of the Philharmonic and began his life with Will, buoyed by the Clark empire. It was snapped in 1934. He'd spent his last twelve years trying to find his way through the wreckage. On the funeral record, Madeleine listed his occupation as "booksalesman" and "none."

His foster sister kept a journal too, a small leather-bound book divided by week with four lines allotted to each day. She wrote down the names of the people who attended her foster brother's funeral. There were ten total, including Einnim, Dan, Joe, Ann, and of course Trygga.

No one read "Thanatopsis." No one performed Schubert's *Unfinished Symphony*. There was no string section, no bronze coffin. Harrison wasn't interred alongside Will in the largest mausoleum of Hollywood Cemetery. The expenses for the services, including cremation, totaled $156.13. Tax was $1.16.

Several weeks after Harrison's death, Joe was severely injured in a car accident. He never resumed the case against the Crookses. It was Madeleine who saw Harrison's suit through after his death. She and Bob continued to pursue the Crookses for restitution, replacing Joe with the law firm of Erskine and Tully. In 1949, a court settlement for $17,500 was finally reached, only a couple thousand more dollars than what Mark Harrison's store had been worth in 1916.

"A man who pays his bills on time is soon forgotten," Oscar Wilde had quipped. Harrison would not be forgotten for the following debts:

O.B. Tryggestad	12,000.00
H.E. Edwards	6,955.90
B. Gladstone	450.00
Henry Barnett	350.00
Oviatts, Inc.	49.88

In March 1949, the court advised the estate and the claimants to compromise, given the settlement sum, and ordered that the following amounts should be dispersed:

O.B. Tryggestad	3,859.31
H.E. Edwards	1,659.47
B. Gladstone	111.68
Henry Barnett	63.42
Oviatts, Inc.	14.59

However, Madeleine and Bob Starrett didn't receive a payout for the estate until 1957, at which point the court again advised a compromise, with the following final amounts to be dispersed:

O.B. Tryggestad	564.73
H.E. Edwards	327.75
B. Gladstone	22.06
Henry Barnett	12.52
Oviatts, Inc.	1.88

Trygga remained in San Francisco, returning to visit Hellesylt almost yearly. He naturalized as an American citizen and worked as an assistant manager at the St. Francis Hotel until his death in 1968. He was seventy-two.

Joe died in 1954 from complications from cirrhosis of the liver.

Buck Mangam never seemed to find work again in Butte. He never married either. Not long after the publication of *The Clarks*, he moved back to Brooklyn, where he lived with his sister. He died on November 29, 1955, and is buried in Green-Wood Cemetery.

Harrison was right that Charles Crooks would go to prison, though it wasn't until 1974, when he was arrested in Mexico City for fraud.

On the charging papers obtained from the US State Department's archives, his next of kin was Felice Mary Barbieri. That was the last trace I found of Gladys. Just as Mark Harrison emerged from tantalizing archival wisps—like a marriage license with a scribbled caution—so his daughter also slips away. But as history has shown, after every vanishing act, Gladys always returns, and I'm certain more traces are bound to surface.

Another lost thread: Raymond Lemire. Records show that the young man remained in Paris for a few years after Will's death and that he managed to evade the Nazis, arriving in Rio de Janeiro in the spring of 1939. His trail stops there.

Bob Starrett died in 1966. Madeleine lived to be eighty-six. When she died in 1971, she bequeathed the house on Lake Street and its contents, including Harrison's scrapbooks and journals, to her niece Sue Lombardi, who would become yet another custodian of Harrison's story.

It was a dry, hot day in July, but inside the tomb the air was cool. This was the summer of 2011, when I was trying out life in Los Angeles, before I would move back to California two years later. My parents had come down from Chico to visit. We were all trying out new ways to be that summer.

We'd spent the morning at the Clark Library, whispering in the reading room, paging through the guest books from the Mowitza Lodge and photographs of my grandmother as a child with her aunt and uncle. We continued the pilgrimage—if that's the word for it—to Hollywood Forever Cemetery, driving through the wrought-iron gates on Santa Monica Boulevard and parking beside the green lawn.

The official line was that only direct descendants were allowed in William Andrews Clark Jr.'s mausoleum, but someone in charge was persuaded by my mother's explanation of our circuitous family connection and agreed to take us inside. There aren't in fact any direct descendants, and I wondered if the employees, curious like us, welcomed an excuse to pull open the big bronze door. In any case, we piled into a golf cart and sped past several peacocks preening on the lawn.

Inside the cold tomb, we were quiet, but this was different from the hush in the library, where archivists pad through the carpeted reading room to deliver manuscripts to waiting scholars. Our footsteps echoed against the marble. Only four people are interred here: Will, Mabel, Alice, and Tertius. The man who'd opened the doors broke the moment with a nod to one of the still-empty marble sarcophagi: "There's room if anyone wants." My mother shook her head. None of us wanted to stay.

"Everyone's going to die." Of course we know this, but Kris Kardashian reminds us in the seventh season of *Keeping Up with the Kardashians.* In this particular episode the matriarch of the reality TV empire attempts to address the subject of mortality with her family. She calls her daughters to discuss the topic, but each one hangs up as soon as she can. Her son, Rob, recoils too.

"Cremated or buried?" she asks him.

"Buried," he says. End of conversation.

Kris turns to her husband, who also deflects. He's Bruce in 2012, having not yet emerged in public as Caitlyn Jenner. Kris wants to make plans, but nobody else does, so she seeks out someone who will take her seriously: Noelle Berman, spokeswoman for Hollywood Forever Cemetery. In the offices on Santa Monica Boulevard, Kris and Bruce wait for the others to arrive. Kim comes in first, and Noelle tries to suppress her giddiness, but a small smile still flits across her face.

Finally the rest assemble, and, just like my parents and I did the year before, the Kardashians pile into a golf cart, on their way to Will Clark's tomb. The family is full of plans.

"We should build a mausoleum by a lake."

"We want our own lake."

"And we want, like, a moat."

The Kardashians are not direct descendants of Will Clark either, but the cemetery opened the mausoleum for them. They walk across the bridge to the island and soon they're inside, voices bouncing off the marble. Kris muses about how each Kardashian would have their own section of the mausoleum and then, to try this out, she clambers up onto my aunt's coffin and lies there.

Until then, I'd been on Kris's side, agreeing that conversations about death are hard but necessary. However, once she's up there on my aunt's tomb, my rage comes fast and hot. It's the first time I think "*my* aunt," and it's the first time I feel the distance between all the generations collapse, and I am furious.

Kim is the one with dignity, rushing out of the mausoleum: "She is ridiculous! She's, like, disrespecting the dead people in there." My outrage lasts longer than Kim's, who gets distracted and chases after a goose.

And yet the Clark legacy, one of excavation and empire, belongs as much to me as it does to an American dynasty that mines celebrity rather than metals in our own Gilded Age.

More legacies remain. The bronze statue of the brooding Beethoven still looms in Pershing Square, though the Philharmonic Auditorium was demolished decades ago. So were the Victorian mansions of neighboring Bunker Hill, replaced by high-rise apartment buildings. Now up on the hillcrest, the Walt Disney Concert Hall rises at Grand Avenue. Frank Gehry's monumental sheaths of stainless steel curve and billow, gleaming sails against the downtown skyline, a twenty-first-century counterpart to another iconic LA landmark, the Hollywood Bowl.

Will spent millions of dollars to build the orchestra, but he left no endowment, taking his father's dictum to heart: "Those who succeed us can well take care of themselves." And they did. The mining magnate Harvey Mudd stepped into the void Will left and, with the efforts of a hastily assembled committee, managed to secure funds to keep the institution afloat in the immediate years following its founder's death. More than three hundred thousand people attend concerts at the Philharmonic each year. And more than a million go to the Hollywood Bowl. In a city often criticized for lack of public space, two of its most cherished sites for music and collective experience owe their existence to the same intensely private man.

The Will Clark who founded the Philharmonic in 1919 would surely have thrilled at its longevity and worldwide acclaim as the institution enters its second century. But he wasn't the same man at the end of his life. By then, the once-expansive philanthropist seemed to fold in on himself, as if that was the only place left to hide, abandoning his grand literary and musical ventures, his attention reduced to the education of his housekeeper's son.

George Palé and family, with
Clark George Palé seated at lower right, undated.

After Will's death in 1934, George Palé became a millionaire. A year later, he married the daughter of a trombonist from the LA Philharmonic. They'd first met in 1933 at a party for Will. The couple had five children. Their first son was born on March 11, 1942. They called him Clark George, namesake to both his father and his father's benefactor. In photos, the young, dark-haired Clark, usually with a toothy smile, bears a resemblance to George as a boy in pictures taken at Salmon Lake.

The Palé family lived in California for several years, until George discovered that his wife was unfaithful. His time in the Clark world had left its mark; by then George knew something about leveraging power and money over other people. He hired private detectives to photograph his wife with her lover, and then once he had the evidence in hand, without her knowledge much less consent, he packed up their kids, moved to Arizona, and demanded she relinquish any claims to custody if she wanted

Clark George Palé, with siblings Ron and Susan,
at Encanto Park, Phoenix, Arizona.

to see her children. George had the means to prove she was an unfit mother, and so she had no choice but to comply. Nor did she have any money, and it was nearly impossible for her to travel to see the children. George remarried, got involved in local politics, and started several businesses, including a citrus farm.

By the time Clark Palé was a teenager, it was clear that he was a delicate boy. His effeminacy incensed his father, who hounded and tormented Clark, ordering the namesake son to parade around the family pool in drill formations. George was a product of military schools—paid for by Will Clark—and his cruelty may have been learned there. Or it's possible his rage came from somewhere else. He'd named his son after the noble patron, but maybe that was a myth and maybe the boy reminded him of what lay behind the myth. Or maybe it was retribution when George shouted at Clark marching around the pool, even if by then the actual villain was long gone. In any case, the father inflicted pain that was not the son's to bear and yet he was forced to.

Clark didn't choose his name, just as he didn't choose to be the target of his father's fury, but when he was old enough, Clark chose to leave and he fled back to his mother in California. He was in his early twenties, at her home, when he took the first poison. She found him in time to revive him, though he cursed her for it. On March 25, 1965, Clark drove out to a motel in the Mojave Desert, where he took the second poison. He was twenty-three.

It was Clark's nephew, Stephen Gruse, who told me this. Stephen also told me that none of the tremendous mining wealth passed down to George's children or their children, that George had poured most of it into his businesses, which had little success. What was left his second wife spent. The great Clark fortune vanished from the family, but one boy had borne its name, a legacy with more shadows than light.

Will put the name on three buildings—the Clark Library of UCLA, the Clark Law Library at the University of Virginia, and the Clark Administration Building at the University of Nevada, Reno—but none is named for him. They are dedicated to honor, respectively, his father, his first wife, and his second wife.

Cora Sanders and Buck Mangam were the first custodians of his legacy, though they diverged in their approaches. Having lost the opportunity to sue Will for defamation after his death, Buck published the most damning information he knew in *The Clarks: An American Phenomenon*, while Cora, as the story goes, destroyed anything remotely personal. What remained was that which was considered safe to remain—thank-you notes, inquiries about editions, instructions to his staff. From these emerges the picture of a kindly and learned if sometimes stuffy man, who voices concerns for his employees' health, sends flowers on their birthdays, and raves about the food in France. Two Will Clarks remain, one through erasure, one through exposure—one upstanding, scholarly, and benevolent and the other tormented and corrupt.

Harrison didn't found a Los Angeles institution, create a library, or build the largest mausoleum in Hollywood Forever. Even in his own day, Harrison was an ephemeral man, known for parties, shopping sprees, and espalier trees. He left behind scrapbooks, journals, ship menus, snapshots, newspaper clippings, and a small Norwegian flag. No monuments, only mementos. He was a man who measured time not in eons or empires but with cigarettes.

At Sue Lombardi's house, a sculpture by Troubetzkoy sits on the mantelpiece and the bronze of Pan stands in the corner. Her son has the pocket watch that Harrison once displayed for newspaper reporters and photographers. The tea set is in the dining room.

The house where Harrison hosted "indescribable orgies" still stands across the street from the Clark Library. For the past fifty years, it's been the home of the Rinzai-ji Zen Center founded by the late Joshu Sasaki Roshi. The Buddhist teacher arrived in America in the 1960s and is credited as one of the major figures to introduce Japanese Zen teachings to the West.

Harrison's salon is now a zendo, and today under the dark-beamed ceiling, the monks and devotees sit on black zafu cushions, attuned to the breath as it rises and falls away. In the courtyard where he once tended espalier trees, they walk in silent meditation, moving through the eternal now.

Joshu Roshi died in 2012 at 107. He established the Mt. Baldy Zen Center in the San Gabriel Mountains and dozens of other centers. His legacy is vast—and tainted by revelations that over the years the powerful teacher coerced female students into sexual encounters and then threatened them to maintain their silence.

No inheritance is pure—not in this tangled saga. It's easy to find villains and victims. Heroes are harder to come by. Yet they exist. Despite all of Gladys's venality and manipulation, Harrison did know a sibling's loyalty and devotion. In the glamorous, strange, and tragic swirl that was his life, there are two pure strands, finer than any metal, and both held strong. One was Trygga, steadfast, devoted, trying to guide and protect Harrison but ultimately trailing him throughout the world. The other Madeleine.

Harrison's foster sister never swerved. She never gave herself a title or a fake name. She'd come from a middle-class family and worked her way through the merchant trades that Harrison and Gladys had abandoned.

Of all the people he reunited with when Harrison returned to America, Madeleine was the most stalwart and kind, taking him into her home, even offering to mortgage her house to pay his legal expenses. If his biological sister had been his downfall, the foster one appeared to be his salvation, for as long as she could be. Madeleine never faltered in her generosity, support, or moxie on his behalf. He died in her home, where he had known some small measure of calm and true kinship, had taken pleasure in simply sitting in her garden and walking to the ocean in his Norwegian stride where he could watch Gynt race across the surf. After Harrison died, Madeleine and Bob kept the dog.

Madeleine loved her vagabond brother unreservedly. She found him companionship. She took him horseback riding in Golden Gate Park. She cooked him dinner. She saved his photo albums and his journals. She paid for his funeral. After his death, she pasted a clipping into his scrapbook headlined HARRISON POST DIES DURING SUIT TO RECOVER $500,000. At the bottom of the page, she wrote, "The End. We're Sorry."

29

THE PICTURE OF HARRISON POST

Painting of Harrison Post by Henry Barnett, 1943.

It was the police chief's daughter-in-law who saved the painting.

In 1985, Tryggestad Hotel was torn down. Now an empty lot sits next to the large wooden white house that was once the Bjørdals' grocery store and home. Across the street is a white modern building with sliding glass doors and a pitched roof. This is the Kyrkjelydhus, Hellesylt's church community center.

Upstairs under the sloping ceiling is a room for people to gather. It's a cozy space with grandmotherly clutter—decorative plates and lace-curtained windows. In the adjoining room, a series of framed oval photos line the wall; these are the faces of the town's former medical staff, including Dr. Torgersen, who once prescribed salve for Harrison's sunburn.

Against one wall stands a hutch filled with cups and saucers, and next to that sits a large boxy television. A painting of the Madonna and Child hangs nearby. A group of chairs suggests AA meetings, a borrowed space, as much for storage as for fellowship, but a tiered rack, stacked with skeins of colored yarn for knitting, reveals a different kind of community.

Someone has stashed an electronic organ in one corner. A large freestanding red cupboard stands in another, and beside it, a chair stacked with boxes. Above those hangs the painting that Anne Pernille Gausdal rescued from the trash.

After the hotel was torn down, the village held a flea market to sell off what was left of its furnishings, and Henry Barnett's oil painting of Harrison Post remained, unclaimed. Margit had hung it in the hotel after he came back from the war, but that was gone now, and his portrait had no home. So Anne, the daughter-in-law of his old friend Olav Gausdal, the town lensmann, took it across the street to the community center. Upstairs in the cluttered room, she put a nail in the wall and hung it there among the lamps and chairs.

Women keep saving him after he's gone—pasting his clippings into his scrapbook, hanging his photograph in their homes, salvaging his painting from the trash.

Harrison was forty-six when Henry Barnett painted his portrait at the prison in Laufen, but he looks like an older man. He is dressed for the cold—a soft black cap, a heavy brown coat. He was happiest in the cold.

ACKNOWLEDGMENTS

First, I am grateful to my mother, Noël Doyle Brown, for beginning this story, for treasuring her family, and for her love and support. To my sister, Holly, and my brothers, Tom and Scott, I am more thankful than I can say. To my cousin George Marchand, thank you for the days at Avenida Farralone, for the wine, and everything else. I will be forever grateful to my uncle Richard Doyle and sorry that I did not get to share this book with him. Nor was I able to share it with my father, Clark Tait Brown, the one who first taught me to love books, the Clark I carry with me always.

I still marvel that Sue Lombardi agreed to pick up a complete stranger at a BART station and bring me into her home. Thank you, Sue and Dave, for your generosity and friendship. I am also grateful to Aase-Turid Husøy for sharing her memories of her uncle Oscar Birthing Tryggestad and for the extraordinary gift of the cross-stitches that Harrison made in Tryggestad Hotel. I am indebted to Stephen Gruse for trusting me with his uncle's story. I will always be grateful to Kåre and Oddhild Stadheim and to Knut and Madeleine Carayan Stadheim, who made me welcome in Norway and offered guidance and good company.

For their counsel and assistance, I thank Melissa Anderson, Marianne Bacigalupi, Joseph Bristow, Richard Bucci, Kateri Butler, Kate Coe, Richard Daly, Bill Dedman, Masa Fox, Dr. Michael Haas, Jan Habberstad, Toril Hanssen, John Howell, Marissa Marchioni, Charles McNulty, Rory Mitchell, Alan Lucien Øyen, Anahí Parra, James Polchin, Lisa Reynolds, Alex Ross, Gwen Strauss, Abraham Trejo Terreros, Fredrick Tucker, Matt Tyrnauer, Chris Wells, Esther Wenger, Tom Zoellner, and the Invisible Institute.

I am profoundly grateful to Lauren Sharp of Aevitas Creative Management, Patrick Nolan of Penguin Books, and Sam Raim, formerly of Penguin Books. I am thankful also to Travis DeShong, Matthew Klise, Julia Rickard, Susan VanHecke, and Margaux Weisman, and for the inspired work by Penguin's production, design, and publicity teams.

This book was supported by a Wallis Annenberg Research Grant to use the Special Collections at the University of Southern California Libraries, as well as a Brown Foundation Fellowship at the Dora Maar House in Ménerbes, France.

For inspiration, hospitality, and companionship along the way, I am grateful to Thomas Ades, Marina Ancona, Hilary Birmingham, Nayland Blake, Russell Brown, Heather Byer, Scott Cameron, Patty Chang, Clifford Chase, Lisa Cohen, Jim Conley, Sarah Kielt Costello, Todd Downing, Anne Etheridge, Jory Felice, Caitlin Gallagher, Noah Glassman, Joe Hardesty, Colleen Hennessey, Cliff Hon, Adele Horne, Anne Ishii, Luis Jaramillo, Justine Kurland, Steve and Vera Lawrence, Lawrence Levi, Melissa Mendonca, Sharon Mizota, Sean Moor, Beth Morgan, Laura Nix, Silvana Nova, Cara O'Connor, Alison O'Daniel, Fil OK, Jeanine Oleson, Dawn Osborne-Adams, Lisa Jane Persky, Yann Philipp, Joy Press, Fabrice Ravenel, Kelly Rudis, Amy Sadao, John Sanchez, Ariel Schrag, Sarah Schrank, Craig Seligman, Michael Stabile, Dave Vamos, Jonathan and Sarah Veitch, Karin Wandner, Stef Willen, and Kristine Woods. For her light and love, I thank Lisa Connaughton.

AUTHOR'S NOTE

Harrison Post's journals, scrapbooks, and letters constituted one of the main sources of information for this book. I also relied on correspondence from William Andrews Clark Jr. and Judge William Lippincott to my grandmother Alice McManus Doyle; my aunt Ethel McManus; and my great-grand-aunt Margaret Doyle, as well as scrapbooks that belonged to Alice McManus Clark and Oscar Birthing Tryggestad.

I am indebted to Rebecca Fenning Marschall of the William Andrews Clark Memorial Library of University of California, Los Angeles, for her expertise and countless consultations. In addition to the staff at the Clark Library, I am grateful to many other curators, archivists, historians, and institutions: Ellen Crain, Butte-Silver Bow Public Archives; Stacey Behlmer and Kristine Krueger, Margaret Herrick Library of the Academy of Motion Picture Arts and Sciences; Kathy Gordon, Los Angeles County Hall of Records; Knut Sivertsen, Justismuseet/Norwegian National Museum of Justice, Trondheim; Laurie Thompson, Anne T. Kent California Room, Civic Center Library, Marin County Free Library; Sue Luftschein, Marje Schuetze-Coburn, and Dace Taube, Special Collections, University of Southern California Libraries; Kim Cooper and Richard Schave, Esotouric; Julia Larson, Architecture and Design Collection, Art, Design & Architecture Museum, University of California, Santa Barbara; Ljiljana Grubišić and Selena Chau, Los Angeles Philharmonic Association; Dr. Kevin Clarke, Operetta Research Center Amsterdam, Dale Ann Stieber, Bill Henry Room, Special Collections, Occidental College Library; Stephen Tabor, Huntington Library; David A. Langbart, Textual Records Division, National Archives at

College Park, Maryland; Michele L. Brann, Maine State Library; Alex Gilbert, Center for Sacramento History.

Additional institutions provided critical material: Beinecke Rare Book & Manuscript Library, Yale University; Maine State Archives; Montana Historical Society; National Archives at Kansas City; New York City Department of Records and Information Services, Municipal Archives; ONE National Gay & Lesbian Archives at the USC Libraries; Pacific Palisades Historical Society Collection, Santa Monica Public Library; Sacramento Public Library; Book Arts and Special Collections, San Francisco Public Library; and Regional State Archives, Trondheim.

I am thankful to those who took the time to speak with me: Carol Bagshaw, Svein Bjørdal, Anne Pernille Gausdal, Peggy Guccione, Aase-Turid Husøy, Stephen Gruse, Donna Wilson Long, John Mallen, Caterina Marsh, Robert Mason Jr., Kåre and Oddhild Stadheim, Knut Stadheim, Roger Tryggestad, and Bruce Whiteman. Guided tours and interviews with Rolf Olaf Haavik of the Grini Museum, Carolyn O'Brien of the Riviera Country Club, and Gento Steve Krieger and Myoren Yasukawa of the Rinzai-ji Zen Center provided essential information.

For newspaper articles, birth and death certificates, census records, city directories, draft cards, marriage licenses, passenger lists, prison records, and other archival materials, I relied on databases: Ancestry.com, California Digital Newspaper Collection, Fold3.com, Los Angeles County Office of the Assessor Online Property Database, Media History Digital Library, NewspaperArchive.com, Newspapers.com, Online Archive of California, and ProQuest Historical Newspapers. In an attempt at concision, I do not include citations for widely known or uncontroversial facts.

SOURCES

INTRODUCTION

Books

Bill Dedman and Paul Clark Newell Jr., *Empty Mansions: The Mysterious Life of Huguette Clark and the Spending of a Great American Fortune* (New York: Ballantine, 2013).

Wayne R. Dynes, ed., *Encyclopedia of Homosexuality* (New York: Garland Press, 1990).

Meryl Gordon, *The Phantom of Fifth Avenue: The Mysterious Life and Scandalous Death of Heiress Huguette Clark* (New York: Grand Central, 2014).

William D. Mangam, *The Clarks: An American Phenomenon* (New York: Silver Bow Press, 1941).

HOUSE OF DREAMS

Articles

"Random Notes," *Cincinnati Enquirer*, June 23, 1929.

Books

C. B. Glasscock, *The War of the Copper Kings: Builders of Butte and Wolves of Wall Street* (Indianapolis: Bobbs-Merrill, 1935).

Sam Watters, *Houses of Los Angeles, 1920–1935* (New York: Acanthus Press, 2007).

Documents

Harrison Post letter, unaddressed though likely intended for his attorney Joseph McInerney (n.d.).

PART ONE, 1882–1919

1. A TRAIN TO LOS ANGELES

Articles

"Greatest and Most Colorful Mining City in the World," *Montana Standard*, March 14, 1943.

W. M. Underhill, "Historic Bread Riot in Virginia City," *Washington Historical Quarterly* 21, no. 30 (July 1930).

"Death of Mrs. W. A. Clark," *Butte Miner*, October 20, 1893.

"The Boulder Batholith and the Richest Hill on Earth," Montana Department of Transportation, www.mdt.mt.gov/travinfo/geomarkers.shtml.

Butte Weekly Miner, January 15, 1878.

Greg Fisher, "The Long Arm of the Clarks," *Downtown Los Angeles*, August 16, 2012.

Michael Malone, "Midas of the West: The Incredible Career of William Andrews Clark," *Montana: The Magazine of Western History* 33, no. 4 (Autumn 1983).

Books

John Astle, *Only in Butte: Stories off the Hill* (Butte, MT: Holt, 2004).

Scott Cummings, *Blue and Green: The Drive for Justice at America's Port* (Cambridge, MA: MIT Press, 2018).

Glasscock, *The War of the Copper Kings*.

Lewis Hall, *The William A. Clark Collection: Treasures of a Copper King* (Billings, MT: Yellowstone Arts Center, 1989).

Mangam, *The Clarks*.

Michael P. Malone, *The Battle for Butte: Mining and Politics on the Northern Frontier, 1864–1906* (Helena, MT: Montana Historical Society Press, 1981).

Documents

"Early Days in Montana: Being Some Reminiscences Dictated by Senator William A. Clark and Written Down by Frank Harmon Garver," Montana Historical Society Research Center, 1917.

William Andrews Clark Sr., address to the Society of Montana Pioneers, Deer Lodge, 1923.

"A Self-Guided Tour of the Mines of Butte," Butte Historical Society, 2010.

2. THE BOND

Articles

"Victory in 19 Games Wins Title," *Miami Herald*, January 6, 1946.
"Remembered Their Clerks," *Galveston Daily News*, December 25, 1892.
Galveston Daily News, March 14, 1892.
Galveston Daily News, May 9–14, 1888.
"Brilliant Nuptials," *Galveston Daily News*, January 21, 1891.
"A Quiet Wedding," *Galveston Daily News*, September 6, 1892.
"A Happy Wedding," *Galveston Daily News*, October 17, 1892.
"$30,000 Damages," *Daily Kennebec Journal*, March 30, 1899.

Books

Gary Cartwright, *Galveston, A History of the Island* (New York: Atheneum 1991).
William Richard Cutter, ed., *American Biography: A New Cyclopedia*, vol. IX (New York: American Historical Society, 1921).
Andrew Morrison, ed., *The Port of Galveston and the State of Texas* (St. Louis and Galveston: Geo W. Engelhardt, 1890).

Marriage License

I have not cited individual birth certificates, census reports, draft cards, and other public records. However, given the secrecy and subterfuge that attends the Harrisons' marriage certificate, a noteworthy document indeed, I cite it here: Mark J. Harrison to Jennie Weis, Houston, September 1, 1892, County Clerk's Office, County of Harris, Texas.

3. AN EDUCATION

Articles

"W. A. Clark, Jr. & Miss Mabel Foster," *Butte Daily Post*, March 2, 1901.
"Death of Mrs. W. A. Clark," *Montana Standard*, October 20, 1893.
"Culver-Clark," *New York Sun*, April 22, 1891.
"Reception at Home at Bride's Parents after the Ceremony," *Butte Daily Post*, June 20, 1901.
Independent-Record (Helena, MT), November 13, 1895.
"Paul Clark Dead," *Independent-Record* (Helena, MT), March 11, 1896.
"Buck Mungam, Old Mines Leaguer, Dies," *Montana Standard*, November 29, 1955.

Butte Miner, July 24, 1900.
Anaconda (MT) Standard, December 2, 1900.
"The Romance of the Little Innkeeper's Daughter," *San Francisco Examiner*, March 3, 1901.
Anaconda (MT) Standard, June 20, 1901.
Butte Daily Post, June 20, 1901.
"Wears a Copper Dress," *Washington (DC) Bee*, August 24, 1901.
Ravalli Republic (Helena, MT), June 14, 1901.
Anaconda (MT) Standard, June 28, 1901.
"W. A. Clark Jr.'s Latest Gift," *Great Falls (MT) Tribune*, December 14, 1901.
Anaconda (MT) Standard, December 25, 1901.
"Wins a Million," *Los Angeles Examiner*, December 3, 1902.
"Specialist Has Been Summoned," *Butte Daily Post*, December 23, 1902.
"Mrs. Clark's Condition," *Anaconda (MT) Standard*, December 31, 1902.
"Death Ends Long Sufferings of Mrs. Williams Andrews Clark, Jr.," *Butte Daily Post*, January 1, 1903.
"Mrs. Clark Laid to Rest," *Anaconda (MT) Standard*, January 6, 1903.
"W.A. Clark Jr. Arrested," *Los Angeles Times*, July 5, 1903.
"Will Race in Seattle," *Anaconda (MT) Standard*, July 31, 1903.
"Outdid Her Own Record," *Anaconda (MT) Standard*, March 23, 1902.
"The Senator Will Not Agree to Any Compromise Out of Court," *Butte Miner*, November 28, 1903.
"Modern Croesus a Very Sick Man," *Minneapolis Journal*, April 22, 1904.
"Senator Not to Wed," *Fall River (MA) Evening News*, June 7, 1900.
"Will Clark Married to Mrs. Alice Medin," *Anaconda (MT) Standard*, May 8, 1907.
"Married and Ran Away," *Butte Daily Post*, February 10, 1902.
"Married a Millionaire," *Waterloo (IA) Daily Courier*, May 27, 1907.
Malone, "Midas of the West."

Books

William E. Conway and Robert Stevenson, *William Andrews Clark, Jr.: His Cultural Legacy* (Los Angeles: William Andrews Clark Memorial Library, University of California, Los Angeles, 1985).
Dedman and Clark Newell Jr., *Empty Mansions*.
Glasscock, *The War of the Copper Kings*.
Malone, *The Battle for Butte*.
Mangam, *The Clarks*.
Robert Megarry et al., *The Law of Real Property* (London: Sweet & Maxwell, 2012).
Oscar Wilde, *Decorative Art in America: A Lecture* (New York: Brentano's, 1906).

Documents

Corks and Curls Yearbook: 1899, University of Virginia Library.

4. ALBERT'S CHOICE

Articles

"Beautiful Store Opens Its Doors," *Sacramento Union*, March 30, 1911.
"Ready for Call for Starter at Charity Meet," *Sacramento Star*, July 14, 1914.
"Personal," *Sacramento Star*, July 30, 1913.
"Sues Clothing Shop Man for $12,500," *Sacramento Union*, May 9, 1912.
"Personal," *Sacramento Union*, June 5, 1913.
"Hitchcock Notes," *Marin (CA) Journal*, March 6, 1913.
"Then Dad Looked for a Slipper," *The Times* (Munster, IN), May 9, 1913.
"Personal Mention," *Sacramento Union*, September 5, 1915.
"Redmond Home Sold," *Sacramento Union*, December 12, 1915.
"Well Known Merchant Passes," *The Sacramento Bee*, February 1, 1916.
"Two Drugs Used by Youth Trying to End His Life," *San Francisco Chronicle*, June 24, 1916.
"Rooms to Let," *San Francisco Examiner*, February 6, 1916.
"Salesman Caught in 'Vice Ring' Net," *Los Angeles Times*, March 15, 1918.
"Two Policemen Are Implicated in Vice Ring," *San Francisco Chronicle*, March 3, 1918.
"Vice Fugitive Allen on Way to Honduras," *San Francisco Chronicle*, May 24, 1918.
"Takes His Life Through Shame," *Los Angeles Times*, November 15, 1914.
"Long Beach Uncovers 'Social Vagrant' Clan," *Los Angeles Times*, November 14, 1914.
Earl O. Coons, "Homosexuality in the News," *Archives of Criminal Psychodynamics* 2 (1957).

Books

Stephen Vincent Benét, *The Beginning of Wisdom* (New York: Henry Holt, 1921).
William Burg, *Sacramento's K Street: Where Our City Was Born* (Charleston, SC: The History Press, 2012).
Edward Channing, *A Short History of the United States for School Use* (London: Macmillan, 1908).
Webster Wells, *A Short Course in Higher Algebra: For Academies, High Schools, and Colleges* (Boston: Leach, Shewell and Sanborn, 1889).

Court Cases

"Testimony and Proceeding before Grand Jury on Indictment of William Hatteroth," City and County of San Francisco, April 29–May 27, 1918.

Documents

Post, letter (n.d.)

Hitchcock Military Academy Yearbook, 1912–1913, Anne T. Kent California Room Collection, Marin County Free Library.

5. THE WALL

Articles

"D. C. McCan's Home," *Los Angeles Times*, May 27, 1906.

"M'Can Home Sold to W.A. Clark Jr.," *Los Angeles Times*, November 1, 1910.

Duncan Maginnis, "2205 West Adams Boulevard," *Adams Boulevard: An Inventory of Its Houses*, 2017, adamsboulevardlosangeles.blogspot.com.

"Yuletide Feast Makes 200 Cash Girls Happy," *Los Angeles Herald*, December 29, 1910.

"Program Enjoyed," *The Oakland Tribune*, July 9, 1911.

"A Refreshing Outing Story," *The Missoulian (MT)*, July 30, 1911.

"Past Times: William Clark III in The Bob," *Montana Magazine*, July/August 1998.

"Dedication of the Clark Observatory," *Los Angeles Times*, January 30, 1917.

"Germany Saw War's Coming," *Los Angeles Times*, June 15, 1915.

"Big Profit on War Will All Go to France," *San Francisco Chronicle*, October 6, 1916.

"Sons of Wealthy First to the Front," *Los Angeles Times*, April 8, 1917.

"For Madame Chenu," *Los Angeles Times*, February 21, 1918.

"Society Leader Breaks Down from Overwork," *Los Angeles Times*, May 22, 1918.

"Mrs. W.A. Clark Jr. in Serious Condition," *Los Angeles Times*, October 4, 1918.

"Friends Mourn the Death of Mrs. W.A. Clark Jr.," *Los Angeles Times*, November 18, 1918.

"New Orchestra Is Organized," *Los Angeles Times,* June 11, 1919.

Books

Robert Fogelson, *The Fragmented Metropolis: Los Angeles, 1850–1930,* (Berkeley: University of California Press, 1993).

Mangam, *The Clarks.*

Documents

W. A. Clark Sr., letter to W. M. Bickford, July 5, 1918, Montana Historical Society.

W. A. Clark Jr., letter to Margaret and Alice McManus, September 22, 1919.

W. A. Clark Jr., letter to Alice McManus, September 21, 1927.

6. THE MASK

Articles

"George Turner Marsh—San Francisco Jewelry Icon," *What's On Blog*, Watson & Son, https://watsonandson.com/george-turner-marsh-san-francisco-jewelry-icon/.

Woody LaBounty, "Naming the Richmond District: George Turner Marsh and the Birth of a Neighborhood," *Western Neighborhood Project*, April 2, 2010, www.outsidelands.org/gt-marsh.php.

"At the Clark Home," *Montana Standard*, August 31, 1919.

"Sponsor of New Orchestra," *Los Angeles Times*, October 19, 1919.

"Philharmonic Makes Debut," *Los Angeles Times*, October 25, 1919.

Douglas Shadle, "Did Dvorak's 'New World' Symphony Transform American Music?," *New York Times*, December, 14, 2018.

Sausalito News 35, no. 49, December 6, 1919.

Books

Conway and Stevenson, *William Andrews Clark, Jr.*

Dedman and Clark Newell Jr., *Empty Mansions.*

Gordon, *The Phantom of Fifth Avenue.*

Mangam, *The Clarks.*

Carey McWilliams, *Southern California: An Island on the Land* (Salt Lake City: Peregrine Books, 1973).

Caroline Estes Smith, *The Philharmonic Orchestra of Los Angeles: The First Decade, 1919–1929* (Los Angeles: Press of United Printing Company, 1930).

Kevin Starr, *Material Dreams: Southern California through the 1920s* (New York: Oxford University Press, 1990).

Documents

Robert G. Cowan, *California Bibliographers: Father and Son*, transcript of interview conducted by Joel Gardner (Oral History Program, University of California, Los Angeles, 1979).

Bruce Whiteman, "'With These Philistines We Have No Quarrel': William Andrews Clark, Jr. as Collector and Public Benefactor," *Gazette of the Grolier Club*, no. 59/60, 2008–2009.

Interviews

Caterina Marsh and Bruce Whiteman.

Websites

Influenza Encyclopedia, influenzaarchive.org.

PART TWO, 1919–1934

7. THE COPAIN

Articles

"Post with Salisbury," *Los Angeles Times*, May 16, 1920.

"Nazimova," *Oroville (CA) Daily Register*, January 15, 1920.

Floyd Bossard, "A Look at the Copper Kings, Amalgamated, Anaconda," *Montana Standard,* March 15, 2015.

"Juanita Hansen, Bride of Harrison Post, Coast Rumor," *New York Daily News*, September 5, 1921.

"Water Sprite," *The Houston Post*, October 23, 1921.

"Over the Teacups," *Picture Play Magazine*, December 1921.

"Los Angeles Philharmonic Orchestra Spring Tour Makes East Sit Up," *Montana Standard*, May 4, 1921.

"In Reno," *Los Angeles Times*, September 22, 1921.

"Birthday Dinner," *Los Angeles Times*, April 21, 1921.

Books

Michael Ankerich, *Dangerous Curves atop Hollywood Heels: The Lives, Careers, and Misfortunes of 14 Hard-Luck Girls of the Silent Screen* (Albany, GA: BearManor Media, 2015).

Lillian Faderman and Stuart Timmons, *Gay L.A.: A History of Sexual Outlaws, Power Politics, and Lipstick Lesbians* (Berkeley: University of California Press, 2009).

Gary F. Kuretz, *Sir Robert E. Cowan and the Genesis of the UCLA Library Californiana Collection* (Los Angeles: UCLA Library, 2012).

Emily Leider, *Dark Lover: The Life and Death of Rudolph Valentino* (New York: Farrar, Straus and Giroux, 2003).

Frances Marion, *Off with Their Heads: A Serio-comic Tale of Hollywood* (New York: Macmillan, 1972).

Alex Ross, *The Rest Is Noise: Listening to the Twentieth Century* (New York: Farrar, Straus and Giroux, 2007).

Caroline Estes Smith, *The Philharmonic Orchestra of Los Angeles.*

Catherine Parsons Smith, *Making Music in Los Angeles: Transforming the Popular* (Berkeley: University of California Press, 2007).

Court Cases

Los Angeles, California, probate case file no. 144004, Harrison Post INCOMPETENT (1934–1949).

Documents

W. A. Clark Jr., letters to Harrison Post, June 9 and July 5, 1922.

W. A. Clark Jr., letter to John Henry Nash, March 4, 1922.

Cowan, *California Bibliographers.*

Arthur Dennison, letters to W. A. Clark Jr., 1922–1923.

Harrison Post, address book.

Harrison Post, journals, 1941–1946.

The Sins of Hollywood: An Exposé of Movie Vice (Hollywood Publishing Company, May 1922). Originally published anonymously, the booklet's author was later identified as *Photoplay* editor Ed Roberts.

"Some letters from Oscar Wilde to Alfred Douglas, 1892–1897: <heretofore unpublished> with illustrative notes by Arthur C. Dennison, Jr. & Harrison Post; and an essay by A.S.W. Rosenbach, Ph.D.," San Francisco: printed for W. A. Clark. Jr. by J. H. Nash (1924).

Whiteman, "'With These Philistines.'"

Interviews

Bruce Whiteman.

Note

The account of the unsigned letters and Charlie Clark's letter to W. A. Clark Jr. comes from Mangam's *The Clarks.*

8. THE LIBRARY

Articles

"Early Views of the Hollywood Bowl," *Water and Power Associates*, waterandpower.org/museum/Early_Views_of_the_Hollywood_Bowl.html.

"To Accept Gift for Bowl," *Los Angeles Times*, March 30, 1923.

"The Soul of the City," *Los Angeles Times*, July 24, 1923.

Dan Cuoco, "The Curious Case of Norman Selby," *International Boxing Research Organization*, October 8, 2011, www.ibroresearch.com/2011/10/the-curious-case-of-norman-selby/.

Cecilia Rasmussen, "The Violent Life of Boxer Kid McCoy," *Los Angeles Times*, April 14, 1997.

"Officers Seize Gems of Victim," *Los Angeles Times*, August 15, 1924.

"Smuggled Gems Believed Key to Mrs. Mors's Death," *The Indianapolis Star*, August 22, 1924.

"Coast 'Lone Wolf' Leaves Trail of Jilted Women," *Minneapolis Star*, November 24, 1924.

"Mors Seen at Killing Spot, M'Coy Defense," *New York Daily News*, December 9, 1924.

"Bandits Rob 2 Women and Man of $7,000 and Car," *Chicago Tribune*, October 20, 1921.

Wendy Moonan, "The House That Grief Built," *New York Times*, May 6, 2019.

Books

Robert Cantwell, *The Real McCoy: The Life and Times of Norman Selby* (Princeton, NJ: Auerbach, 1971).

Conway and Stevenson, *William Andrews Clark, Jr.*

Mangam, *The Clarks.*

McWilliams, *Southern California.*

Watters, *Houses of Los Angeles.*

Court Cases

Los Angeles, California, probate case file no. 144004, Harrison Post INCOMPETENT (1934–1949).

People v. Selby, 198 Cal. 426 (1924).

Weinstein v. Moers, 207 Cal. 534, Cal. Supreme Court (1929).

Documents

"Arthur C. Dennison: Lost at Sea, February 1, 1924," obituary privately published, April 12, 1924.

Cowan, *California Bibliographers.*

Arthur Dennison, letters to W. A. Clark Jr.

Receipts and other materials related to the construction and design of the Clark Library, including correspondence with Allyn Cox, Robert D. Farquhar, George Hunt, and various contractors and suppliers.

Interviews

Bruce Whiteman.

Websites

Domaine de Chantilly, domainedechantilly.com.

9. JUNIOR

Articles

"The William Andrews Clark Legacy," *Montana Standard*, August 4, 1978.
"Clark Home Sold Under $3,000,000," *New York Times*, February 2, 1927.
"Senator Clark's Son May Be the Richest Man in California," *Brooklyn Daily Times*, March 4, 1925.
Cal York, "East and West," *Photoplay*, August 1925.
"Patsy Ruth Miller Object of Barrage Directed by Cupid," *Bakersfield Californian*, August 18, 1925.
"Ex-Oakland Girl Charges Broken Troth," *San Francisco Examiner*, November 23, 1925.
"Eastern Tour Plan Canceled," *Los Angeles Times*, January 21, 1926.
"Pink Powder Puffs," *Chicago Tribune*, July 18, 1926.
"W.A. Clark, Jr. Conducts Number," *Los Angeles Times*, January 2, 1928.
"W.A. Clark Announces Betrothal," *Los Angeles Times*, August, 25, 1926.
"MacDonald to Begin Term in Prison Soon," *San Francisco Chronicle*, January 23, 1921.
"May Stop Scandal Probe," *Los Angeles Times*, June 30, 1925.
"Mrs. Heath Agrees to Transfer," *The Oakland Tribune*, June 20, 1927.
"Sounding Board," *Los Angeles Evening Express*, March 31, 1928.

Books

Margaret Tante Burk, *Are the Stars Out Tonight? The Story of the Famous Ambassador and Cocoanut Grove* (Los Angeles: Round Table West, 1980).
Writers Project of Montana, *Copper Camp: The Lusty Story of Butte, Montana, the Richest Hill on Earth* (Montana State Department of Agriculture, Labor and Industry, 1943).
Gordon, *The Phantom of Fifth Avenue*.
Leider, *Dark Lover*.
Mangam, *The Clarks*.
Starr, *Material Dreams*.
Mark Twain, *Autobiography of Mark Twain*, vol. 2 (Berkeley: University of California Press, 2013).

Jules Tygiel, *The Great Los Angeles Swindle: Oil, Stocks, and Scandal during the Roaring Twenties* (Berkeley: University of California Press, 1996).

Court Cases

People v. Cowles, no. 27578 Cal. (1926).

10. THE SECRETARIES

Articles

"Espalier Trees Solve Small Gardeners' Fruit Problems," *Los Angeles Times*, March 28, 1928.
"Riviera Riders," *Pictorial California*, April 1927.
"Clark Family Reunion," *Helena (MT) Independent Record*, July 12, 1928.
"Clarks to Sell Mines to A.C.M.," *Helena (MT) Independent Record*, August 19, 1928.
"Clark Jr Plans to Buy Paper to Fight Enemies," *Helena (MT) Independent Record*, August 22, 1928.
"Clark Reduces Orchestra Gift," *Los Angeles Times*, September 14, 1928.
"Philharmonic Saved from Rocks," *Monrovia (CA) Daily News*, January 14, 1929.
"Suspends His Papers," *San Bernadino Sun*, May 21, 1929.
"Random Notes," *Cincinnati Enquirer*, June 23, 1929.
Stephen Robertson, "Age of Consent Laws," *Children and Youth in History*, chnm.gmu.edu/cyh/items/show/230.
"Buck Mangam, Old Mines Leaguer, Dies," *Montana Standard*, November 29, 1955.
John Astle, "Heinze Loses Ping Pong Match in 1902," *Century of Butte Stories*.

Books

Mangam, *The Clarks*.
Paula A. Scott, *Santa Monica: A History on the Edge* (Mount Pleasant, SC: Arcadia, 2004).
Betty Lou Young, *Pacific Palisades: Where the Mountains Meet the Sea* (Santa Monica, CA: Casa Vieja Press, 2001).
Betty Lou Young, *Rustic Canyon and the Story of the Uplifters* (Santa Monica, CA: Casa Vieja Press, 1975).
Betty Lou Young, *Santa Monica Canyon: A Walk through History* (Santa Monica, CA: Casa Vieja Press, 1997).

Court Cases

Mangam v. Estate of William A. Clark Jr., Deceased, no. 35307 Mon. (1935).
Mangam v. Clark, no. 368069 Cal. (1934).

Documents

Harrison Post, journals, 1941–1946.
W. A. Clark Jr., postcard to Margaret McManus, April 1, 1931.

11. THE FLUKE

Articles

"Deals Made in Lands at Beach City," *Los Angeles Times*, October 2, 1931.
"Luncheon Guests Stricken," *Los Angeles Times*, September 29, 1931.
"40 Poisoned at Club Luncheon," *Modesto (CA) News*, September 28, 1931.
"Baker Food Poison Test Completed," *Los Angeles Times*, October 1, 1931.
Riviera Club newsletter, 1932.
"Snow Mantles All Southland," *Los Angeles Times*, January 16, 1932.

Books

Young, *Pacific Palisades*.

12. THE PICTURE OF WILL CLARK

Articles

"Past Times," *Montana Magazine*.
"Crash Kills Clark Son," *Los Angeles Times*, May 16, 1932.
"News of Fatal Place Crash Comes as Severe Shock to Residents of Mining Community," *Montana Standard*, May 13, 1932.
"Announce Services for W.A. Clark III to Be Held on Coast," *Billings (MT) Gazette*, May 17, 1932.
"France Receives W.A. Clark Gift," *Los Angeles Times*, May 2, 1932.
"Two Sets of Jefferson Papers Presented University Library," *Richmond Times-Dispatch*, March 15, 1932.
"Beethoven in Baggy Pants to Grace L.A. Park," *The Oakland Tribune*, July 8, 1932.
"High Tributes Paid Clark," *Los Angeles Times*, October 15, 1932.
"Charles W. Clark, Head of United Verde, Passes in New York," *Montana Standard*, April 9, 1933.

"Henrique Medina," *Los Angeles Times*, November 5, 1932.
Robert Cozzolino, "Ivan Le Lorraine Albright (1897–1983)," *Illinois Historical Art Project*, www.illinoisart.org/ivan-albright-c1mnq.
"Orchestra Will Lose Clark's Aid," *Los Angeles Times*, January 12, 1933.
Philip Drew, "Big Surprise," *Los Angeles Times*, February 23, 1947.
"W.A. Clark Jr. Sued by Former Employee," *The Oakland Tribune*, January 14, 1934.

Books

Sam T. Clover, ed., *Constructive Californians: Men of Outstanding Ability Who Have Added Greatly to the Golden State's Prestige* (Los Angeles: Saturday Night, 1926).
Peter Heyworth, *Otto Klemperer, His Life and Times* (New York: Cambridge University Press, 1983).
David Wallace, *Exiles in Hollywood* (Pompton Plains, NJ: Limelight, 2006).

Court Cases

Mangam v. Clark.

Documents

W. A. Clark Jr., letter to Alice McManus Doyle, August 31, 1932.
W. A. Clark Jr., letter to Albert Bender, April 24, 1933.
Robert E. Cowan, letter of resignation to W. A. Clark Jr., July 29, 1933.
G. S. Messersmith to William Phillips, under secretary of state, June 26, 1933.
Mowitza Lodge guest book, 1915–1932.
Bill Walker, letter to William Conway, June 12, 1981.
George John Palé, affidavit, Los Angeles, May 21, 1936 (includes copies of correspondence between W. A. Clark Jr. and G. J. Palé).

13. BUCK MANGAM'S REVENGE

Articles

"Last Rites Held for Stanley Visel," *The Signal* (Santa Clarita, CA), May 22, 1952.

Court Cases

Mangam v. Clark.

14. SNAP

Articles

"Paintings on Ivory at Palace," *San Francisco Chronicle*, April 10, 1932.
"Testimonial Gala Event," *Los Angeles Times*, April 18, 1934.
"Philharmonic Staff to Plant Memorial Trees," *Los Angeles Times*, April 20, 1934.
"W.A. Clark Jr.'s Support of Philharmonic Reviewed," *Los Angeles Times*, June 3, 1934.
"W.A. Clark, Jr., Taken by Death," *Montana Standard*, June 14, 1934.
"W.A. Clark, Jr., Summoned by Death," *Los Angeles Times*, June 15, 1934.
"Body of W. A. Clark at Old Butte Home," *Montana Standard*, June 16, 1934.
"Thousands View Body of Clark in Los Angeles," *The Missoulian (MT)*, June 19, 1934.
"Clark Rites Conducted," *Los Angeles Times*, June 20, 1934.

Books

Hector Berlioz and Richard Strauss, *Treatise on Instrumentation* (New York: Dover, 1991).
Mangam, *The Clarks*.
John Steven McGroarty, *Los Angeles from the Mountains to the Sea: With Selected Biography of Actors and Witnesses to the Period of Growth and Achievement*, vol. 2 (Chicago: American Historical Society, 1921).

Court Cases

Mangam v. Clark.
Los Angeles, California, probate case file no. 144377, William A. Clark Jr. (1934).
Los Angeles, California, probate case file no. 144004, Harrison Post INCOMPETENT (1934–1949).

Documents

Judge William Lippincott, letter to Ethel McManus, June 24, 1934.
George John Palé affidavit (including copies of correspondence between W. A. Clark Jr. and George John Palé).
Harrison Post, journals, 1941–1946.

PART THREE, 1934–1938

15. THE GUARDIAN

Articles

Myrtle Frank, "Just Dogs," *The Sacramento Bee*, March 12, 1932.
Dog Fancier, July 1931.
"Art of the Book," *Los Angeles Times*, March 11, 1934.

Document

"Charles P. Crooks," US Department of State case no. F-2018-02566, Office of Information Programs and Services.

Marriage License

As with Mark and Jennie Harrison's hushed-up marriage certificate, the Crookses' baroque document deserves its own mention: Charles Powell Crooks to Felice Mary Barbieri, June 30, 1932, local registered no. 7744, Country of Los Angeles, California, County Recorder's Office.

16. EXILE

Articles

"Los Angeles Bookshop-Bindery Arouses Western Interest in de Luxe Work," *Bookbinding Magazine*, February 1935.
Richard L. Olsen, "The Mob and the Movies," *Los Angeles Times*, July 5, 1987.
"Catatonia Curable," *Los Angeles Times*, June 21, 1941.

Books

Raymond Chandler, *The Big Sleep* (New York: Vintage, 1992).
Tom Hiney, *Raymond Chandler: A Biography* (New York: Grove Press, 1999).
Ravi S. Tam, *Distant Vistas: Exploring the Historic Neighborhoods of Mar Vista* (Mar Vista, CA: Mar Vista Historical Society, n.d.).

Court Cases

Los Angeles, California, probate case file no. 144004, Harrison Post INCOMPETENT (1934–1949).
Mangam v. Estate of Clark.

Documents

Barbieri and Price catalog (Los Angeles: Ward Ritchie Press, 1934).

Jake Zeitlin, transcript of interview conducted by Joel Gardner, vol. 1 (Oral History Program, University of California, Los Angeles, 1980).

17. ESCAPE

Articles

"Nazi Songs Supplant Santa Claus," *Los Angeles Times*, December 23, 1937.

"Ex-Internee Says Kin Took $500,000," *Courier-Journal* (Louisville, KY), June 9, 1946.

"Rumania to Expel Jews," *The Oakland Tribune*, December 31, 1937.

Documents

Los Angeles, California, probate case file no. 144004, Harrison Post INCOMPETENT (1934–1949).

PART FOUR, 1938–1945

18. HELLESYLT

Articles

"The Destruction of the Norwegian Jews," *Holocaust Education and Archive Research Team*, www.holocaustresearchproject.org/nazioccupation/norwayjews.html.

Books

Samuel Abrahamsen, "The Holocaust in Norway," *Contemporary Views on the Holocaust*, ed. Randolph L. Braham (Boston: Kluwer-Nijhoff, 1983).

Knut Frøysa, *Unge Sabotørar*, trans. Richard Daly (Hellesylt, Norway: Trygg Trykk, 2015).

Trond Risro Nilssen and Jon Reitan, *Legacies of the Nazi Camps in Norway: Falstad 1941–49* (Münster, Germany: LIT Verlag, 2020).

Documents

Harrison Post, journals, 1941–1946.

Interviews

Svein Bjørdal, Aase-Turid Husøy, Kåre Stadheim, Knut Stadheim, and Roger Tryggestad.

19. MEXICO CITY

Articles

"Two Danish East Asiatic Liners Due," *Los Angeles Times*, November 26, 1938.
"Residence to Mean $38,000 Investment," *Los Angeles Times*, March 24, 1940.
"Fun in Mexico," *Life*, February 28, 1944.
Robert Bitto, "Hilde Krüger, Nazi Spy in Mexico," *Mexico Unexplained*, mexicounexplained.com, August 29, 2016, http://mexicounexplained.com/hilde-kruger-nazi-spy-mexico/.

Books

Juan Alberto Cedillo, *Hilda Krüger: Vida y obra de una espía nazi en México* (New York: Penguin Random House Grupo Editorial, 2016).

Documents

Home of Mr. and Mrs. Charles Crooks, by Cliff May, photo brochure, Architecture and Design Collection, Art, Design & Architecture Museum, University of California, Santa Barbara.
"Charles P. Crooks," US Department of State case no. F-2018-02566, Office of Information Programs and Services.

20. TRONDHEIM

Books

Kaare Viken, *Mer enn 1000 dager: Blant fanger og voktere i Vollan kretsfengsel 1942–45* [More Than 1,000 Days: Among Prisoners and Guards in Vollan Circuit Prison 1942–45] (Oslo: J. W. Cappelens Forlag, 1984). Translated by Richard Daly.

Court Cases

Case No. 36, Trial of Gerhard Friedrich Ernst Flesch, SS OB Sturmbannführer Oberregierungsrat, Frostating Court of Appeal (November–December 1946) and Supreme Court of Norway (February 1948).

21. GRINI

Articles

"Lawyer Tells How S.F. Man Lost Fortune," *San Francisco Examiner*, May 27, 1946.

"The Destruction of the Norwegian Jews," *Holocaust Education and Archive Research Team*.

Books

Odd Nansen, *From Day to Day: One Man's Diary of Survival in Nazi Concentration Camps*, ed. Timothy J. Boyce and trans. Katherine John (Nashville: Vanderbilt University Press, 2016).

Interviews

Rolf Olaf Haavik.

22. LAUFEN

Articles

"Reminiscences by George Lukes and Others of Life in the POW Camp Where Crowder Was Interned, with Mike Babich and Andrew Rybar, Laufen and Tittmoning, 2007," published on Allardyce Barnett Publishers website, abarnet/crowderlukes.htm.

"American Internees to Be Repatriated," *Poughkeepsie (NY) Journal*, February 25, 1944.

Books

Roger Harris, *Islanders Deported* (Ilford, Essex, UK: Channel Islands Specialists' Society, 1979).

Ambrose Sherwill, *A Fair and Honest Book* (Lulu.com, 2006).

Documents

Harrison Post, certificate of conditional baptism, Laufen, Upper Bavaria, Germany, July 1, 1943.

23. THE NORTHERN LIGHTS

Articles

Olav Tvergrov, "The Vision of the Union Hotel and Norangsdalen," *Møre Nytt*, June 4, 1991, translated by Kåre Stadheim.

Books

Frøysa, *Unge Sabotørar.*

Documents

Harrison Post, journals, 1941–1946.

Interviews

Svein Bjørdal, Aase-Turid Husøy, Kåre Stadheim, and Knut Stadheim.

Websites

Hotel Union Øye, www.unionoye.no/en.

PART FIVE, 1945–1946

24. THE ALIEN

Articles

"Inquiry Faced by Countess," *Los Angeles Times*, January 18, 1939.

Books

Emmet Fox, *Power through Constructive Thinking* (New York: Harper and Brothers, 1932).

Documents

"Dorothy di Frasso," Federal Bureau of Investigation case file.
Mary Pickford, letter to Harrison Post, December 3, 1945.
Harrison Post, journals, 1941–1946.

Interviews

Donna Wilson Long.

25. LAKE STREET

Articles

"Theodore Starrett Dies, Ill Four Weeks," *New York Sun*, October 10, 1917.
Nora Leishman, "The City of Paris," *Found SF*, www.foundsf.org/index.php?title=The_City_of_Paris.

Documents

Harrison Post, journals, 1941–1946.
Harrison Post, letter (n.d.).

26. THE EMPEROR'S PALACE

Articles

"Executives Find 'B' School Program Stiff Grind," *Harvard Crimson*, April 22, 1954.

Documents

"Charles P. Crooks," US Department of State case no. F-2018-02566, Office of Information Programs and Services.
Harrison Post, journals, 1941–1946.

27. "SCHÖNER GIGOLO, ARMER GIGOLO"

Articles

"Two Asserted Swindlers Sought $500,000 in Case," *Los Angeles Times*, June 4, 1946.
"Says His $500,000 Was Spent," *The New York Times*, June 9, 1946.
"Brother-in-Law Calls Post Complaint a Smear," *Los Angeles Times*, June 9, 1946.
"Post Refuses to Settle Suit," *San Francisco Examiner*, June 11, 1946.
Kevin Clarke, "Zwei Cowboys im 3/4-Takt: Emmerich Kálmáns Arizona Lady, oder wie die Wiener Operette in den Wilden Westen kam," *Operetta Research Center*, November 30, 2014, http://operetta-research-center

.org/zwei-cowboys-im-34-takt-emmerich-kalmans-arizona-lady-oder-wie-die-wiener-operette-den-wilden-westen-kam/.

Documents

Harrison Post, journals, 1941–1946.

28. LEGACY

Articles

"Fight Resumed over Estate," *Los Angeles Times*, April 9, 1948.
"Long Battle over Post Estate Ends," *Los Angeles Times*, April 20, 1949.
Mark Swed, "Salonen-Gehry Axis," *Los Angeles Times*, August 31, 2003.
"Clark Heir Weds Secretly," *Los Angeles Times*, March 13, 1937.

Court Cases

Los Angeles, California, probate case file no. 144004, Harrison Post INCOMPETENT (1934–1949).
San Francisco, California, probate case file no. 105029, Harrison Post (1949).
Starrett v. Crooks, petition for authority to compromise claims on estate, case file no. 374933 (1948–49).

Documents

Harrison Post, journals, 1941–1946.
Madeleine Post Starrett, journal, 1946.

Interviews

Stephen Gruse.

Television

Keeping Up with the Kardashians, season 7, episode 14. "Tales from the Kardashian Krypt," aired August 19, 2012.

29. THE PICTURE OF HARRISON POST

Interviews

Anne Pernille Gausdal and Kåre Stadheim.

SELECTED BIBLIOGRAPHY

BOOKS

Adler, Stella. *Stella Adler on America's Master Playwrights.* Edited by Barry Paris. New York: Alfred A. Knopf, 2012.

Ankerich, Michael. *Dangerous Curves Atop Hollywood Heels: The Lives, Careers, and Misfortunes of 14 Hard-Luck Girls of the Silent Screen.* Albany, GA: BearManor Media, 2015.

Astle, John. *Only in Butte: Stories off the Hill.* Butte, MT: Holt, 2004.

Baum, Vicki. *It Was All Quite Different: The Memoirs of Vicki Baum.* New York: Funk & Wagnalls, 1964.

Beauchamp, Cari. *Without Lying Down: Frances Marion and the Powerful Women of Early Hollywood.* Berkeley and Los Angeles: University of California Press, 1997.

Benét, Stephen Vincent. *The Beginning of Wisdom.* New York: Henry Holt, 1921.

Berlioz, Hector, and Richard Strauss. *Treatise on Instrumentation.* New York: Dover, 1991.

Bolgen, Kaare. *The Long Norwegian Night: A WWII Resistance Fighter's Life in Nazi Camps.* North Adams, MA: Fern Hill Press, 2013.

Brooks, Louise. *Lulu in Hollywood.* New York: Knopf, 1982.

Brownlow, Kevin. *The Parade's Gone By.* New York: Knopf, 1968.

Buntin, John. *L.A. Noir: The Struggle for the Soul of America's Most Seductive City.* New York: Three Rivers Press, 2009.

Burg, William. *Sacramento's K Street: Where Our City Was Born.* Charleston, SC: The History Press, July 2012.

Burk, Margaret Tante. *Are the Stars Out Tonight? The Story of the Famous Ambassador and Cocoanut Grove.* Los Angeles: Round Table West, 1980.

Cantwell, Robert. *The Real McCoy: The Life and Times of Norman Selby.* Princeton, NJ: Auerbach Publishers, 1971.

Cartwright, Gary. *Galveston, A History of the Island.* New York: Atheneum, 1991.

Chandler, Raymond. *The Big Sleep.* New York: Vintage, 1992.

Channing, Edward. *A Short History of the United States for School Use.* London: Macmillan, 1908.

Christie's. *Magnificent Jewels.* Christie's New York, April 17, 2012. Auction catalog.

———. *An American Dynasty: The Clark Family Treasures*. Christie's New York, June 18, 2014. Auction catalog.

Constructive Californians: Men of Outstanding Ability Who Have Added Greatly to the Golden State's Prestige. Edited by Sam T. Clover. Los Angeles: Saturday Night, 1926.

Conway, William E., and Robert Stevenson. *William Andrews Clark, Jr.: His Cultural Legacy*. Los Angeles: William Andrews Clark Memorial Library, University of California, Los Angeles, 1985.

Davis, Mike. *City of Quartz: Excavating the Future in Los Angeles*. New York: Verso, 2006.

Dedman, Bill, and Paul Clark Newell Jr. *Empty Mansions: The Mysterious Life of Huguette Clark and the Spending of a Great American Fortune*. New York: Ballantine, 2013.

Dickinson, Donald. *Dictionary of American Book Collectors*. Westport, CT: Greenwood Press, 1986.

Dynes, Wayne R., ed. *Encyclopedia of Homosexuality*. New York: Garland Press, 1990.

Ellmann, Richard. *Oscar Wilde*. New York: Knopf, 1988.

Fogelson, Robert. *The Fragmented Metropolis: Los Angeles, 1850–1930*. Berkeley: University of California Press, 1993.

Fox, Emmet. *Power through Constructive Thinking*. New York: Harper and Brothers, 1932.

Friedman, David F. *Wilde in America: Oscar Wilde and the Invention of Modern Celebrity*. New York: W. W. Norton, 2014.

Frøysa, Knut. *Unge Sabotørar* [Young Saboteurs]. Hellesylt, Norway: Trygg Trykk, 2015. Translated by Richard Daly.

Glasscock, C. B. *The War of the Copper Kings: Builders of Butte and Wolves of Wall Street*. Indianapolis: Bobbs-Merrill, 1935.

Gordon, Meryl. *The Phantom of Fifth Avenue: The Mysterious Life and Scandalous Death of Heiress Huguette Clark*. New York: Grand Central Publishing, 2014.

Hall, Lewis. *The William A. Clark Collection: Treasures of a Copper King*. Billings, MT: Yellowstone Arts Center, 1989.

Harlan, Robert. *John Henry Nash: The Biography of a Career*. Berkeley: University of California Press, 1970.

Harris, Roger. *Islanders Deported*. Ilford, Essex, UK: Channel Islands Specialists' Society, 1979.

Heyworth, Peter. *Otto Klemperer: His Life and Times*. New York: Cambridge University Press, 1983.

Hiney, Tom. *Raymond Chandler: A Biography*. New York: Grove Press, 1999.

Holbrook, Stewart H. *The Age of the Moguls*. Garden City, New York: Doubleday & Company, 1953.

Kelly, Marjorie. *The Divine Right of Capital: Dethroning the Corporate Aristocracy*. San Francisco: Berrett-Koehler, 2001.

Kuretz, Gary F. *Sir Robert E. Cowan and the Genesis of the UCLA Library Californiana Collection*. Los Angeles: UCLA Library, 2012.

Lambert, Gavin. *Nazimova: A Biography*. New York: Knopf, 1997.

Leider, Emily. *Dark Lover: The Life and Death of Valentino*. New York: Farrar, Straus and Giroux, 2003.

Malone, Michael P. *The Battle for Butte: Mining and Politics on the Northern Frontier, 1864–1906*. Helena, MT: Montana Historical Society Press, 1981.

Mangam, William D. *The Clarks: An American Phenomenon*. New York: Silver Bow Press, 1941.

Mann, William J. *Behind the Screen: How Gays and Lesbians Shaped Hollywood, 1910–1969*. New York: Viking, 2001.

———. *Wisecracker: The Life and Times of William Haines, Hollywood's First Openly Gay Star*. New York: Viking, 1998.

Marcus, Kenneth H. *Musical Metropolis: Los Angeles and the Creation of a Music Culture, 1880–1940*. New York: Palgrave Macmillan, 2004.

Marion, Frances. *Off with Their Heads: A Serio-comic Tale of Hollywood*. New York: Macmillan, 1972.

McComb, David G. *Galveston: A History*. Austin, TX: University of Texas Press, 1986.

McGroarty, John Steven. *Los Angeles from the Mountains to the Sea: With Selected Biography of Actors and Witnesses to the Period of Growth and Achievement*, vol. 2. Chicago: American Historical Society, 1921.

McWilliams, Carey. *Southern California: An Island on the Land*. Salt Lake City: Peregrine Books, 1973.

Miller, Patsy Ruth. *My Hollywood: When Both of Us Were Young*. Duncan, OH: BearManor Media, 2012.

Munn, Michael. *The Hollywood Connection: The True Story of Organized Crime in Hollywood*. London: Robson Books, 1993.

Nansen, Odd. *From Day to Day: One Man's Diary of Survival in Nazi Concentration Camps*. Edited by Timothy J. Boyce and translated by Katherine John. Nashville: Vanderbilt University Press, 2016.

Nilssen, Trond Risro, and Jon Reitan. *Legacies of the Nazi Camps in Norway: Falstad 1941–49*. Münster, Germany: LIT Verlag, 2020.

O'Day, Edward. *John Henry Nash: The Aldus of San Francisco*. San Francisco: San Francisco Bay Cities Club of Printing House Craftsmen, 1928.

Paramananda, Swami. *Book of Daily Thoughts and Prayers*. La Crescenta, CA: Ananda-Ashrama, 1926.

Rayner, Richard. *The Associates: Four Capitalists Who Created California*. New York: W. W. Norton, 2007.

———. *A Bright and Guilty Place: Murder, Corruption, and L.A.'s Scandalous Coming of Age*. New York: Anchor, 2010.

Ross, Alex. *The Rest Is Noise: Listening to the Twentieth Century*. New York: Farrar, Straus and Giroux, 2007.

Scott, Paula A. *Santa Monica: A History on the Edge*. Mount Pleasant, SC: Arcadia, October 2004.
Sherwill, Ambrose. *A Fair and Honest Book*. Lulu.com, 2006.
Sitton, Tom, and William Deverell, eds. *Metropolis in the Making: Los Angeles in the 1920s*. Berkeley: University of California Press, 2001.
Smith, Caroline Estes. *The Philharmonic Orchestra of Los Angeles: The First Decade, 1919–1929*. Los Angeles: Press of United Printing Company, 1930.
Smith, Catherine Parsons. *Making Music in Los Angeles: Transforming the Popular*. Berkeley: University of California Press, 2007.
St. Johns, Adela Rogers. *The Honeycomb*. New York: Doubleday, 1969.
Starr, Kevin. *Americans and the California Dream, 1850–1915*. New York: Oxford University Press, 1973.
———. *California: A History*. New York: Modern Library, 2006.
———. *Material Dreams: Southern California Through the 1920s*. New York: Oxford University Press, 1990.
———. *The Rise of Los Angeles as an American Bibliographical Center*. Sacramento: California State Library Foundation, 1989.
Steinbeck, John. *The Moon Is Down*. New York: Penguin, 1995.
Tellier, André. *Twilight Men: The True Story of a Homosexual*. New York: Lion Books, 1950.
Trope, Michael Lance. *Once Upon a Time in Los Angeles: The Trials of Earl Rogers*. Spokane, WA: Arthur H. Clark, 2001.
Twain, Mark. *Autobiography of Mark Twain*, vol. 2. Berkeley: University of California Press, 2013.
Tygiel, Jules. *The Great Los Angeles Swindle: Oil, Stocks, and Scandal During the Roaring Twenties*. Berkeley: University of California Press, 1996.
Ullman, Sharon. *Sex Seen: The Emergence of Modern Sexuality in America*. Berkeley: University of California Press, 1997.
Viertel, Salka. *The Kindness of Strangers*. New York: Holt, 1969.
Viken, Kaare. *Mer enn 1000 dager: Blant fanger og voktere i Vollan kretsfengsel 1942–45* [More Than 1,000 Days: Among Prisoners and Guards in Vollan Circuit Prison 1942–45]. Oslo: J.W. Cappelens Forlag, 1984. Translated by Richard Daly.
Wallace, David. *Exiles in Hollywood*. Pompton Plains, NJ: Limelight, 2006.
Ward, Elizabeth, and Alain Silver. *Raymond Chandler's Los Angeles*. Woodstock, NY: Overlook Press, 1987.
Watters, Sam. *Houses of Los Angeles, 1920–1935*. New York: Acanthus Press, 2007.
Wells, Webster. *A Short Course in Higher Algebra: For Academies, High Schools, and Colleges*. Boston: Leach, Shewell and Sanborn, 1889.
Wilde, Oscar. *The Ballad of Reading Gaol and Other Poems*. London: Penguin, 2010.
———. *Decorative Art in America: A Lecture*. New York: Brentano's, 1906.
———. *The Picture of Dorian Gray*. New York: Oxford University Press, 2008.

Wolf, Edwin. *Rosenbach: A Biography*. Cleveland: World, 1960.
Writers Project of Montana. *Copper Camp: The Lusty Story of Butte, Montana, the Richest Hill on Earth*. Montana State Department of Agriculture, Labor and Industry, 1943.
Young, Betty Lou. *Pacific Palisades: Where the Mountains Meet the Sea*. Santa Monica, CA: Casa Vieja Press, 2001.
———. *Rustic Canyon and the Story of the Uplifters*. Santa Monica, CA: Casa Vieja Press, 1975.
———. *Santa Monica Canyon: A Walk Through History*. Santa Monica, CA: Casa Vieja Press, 1997.
Young, Earle B. *Galveston and the Great West*. College Station: Texas A&M University Press, 1997.

WEBSITES

Adams Boulevard, adamsboulevardlosangeles.blogspot.com.
Influenza Encyclopedia, influenzaarchive.org.
LA as Subject, laassubject.org.
Lost LA, KCET, kcet.org/shows/lost-la.
Martin Turnbull, martinturnbull.com.
Oscar Wilde in America, oscarwildeinamerica.org.
The Portal to Texas History, texashistory.unt.edu.
Water and Power Associates, waterandpower.org.

ILLUSTRATION CREDITS

Pages 1, 4, 79, 92, 98: Liz Brown
Page 19: University of Southern California, on behalf of USC Libraries Special Collections
Pages 21, 180, 181, 243, 280, 286, 291: Susanna W. Lombardi
Pages 35, 58, 96, 103, 115, 137, 190: William Andrews Clark Memorial Library, University of California, Los Angeles
Pages 185, 195, 345, 346: Stephen Gruse, George Palé Archive
Page 217: Art, Design & Architecture Museum, University of California, Santa Barbara
Pages 241, 245, 247: Aase-Turid Husøy
Pages 251, 289: Arne Inge Tryggestad
Page 350: Hellesylt Community Center, Kyrkjelydhus